HSK核心词汇天天学
ONE HOUR PER DAY TO A POWERFUL HSK VOCABULARY

上册
VOLUME I

刘东青 编著

First Edition   2009

ISBN 978-7-80200-594-5
Copyright 2009 by Sinolingua
Published by Sinolingua
24 Baiwanzhuang Road, Beijing 100037, China
Tel: (86) 10-68320585
Fax: (86) 10-68326333
E-mail: hyjx@sinolingua.com.cn
Printed by Beijing Foreign Languages Printing House

Printed in the People's Republic of China

致学习者

本套书是为海外HSK考生及同等水平的学生编写的词汇学习用书。

通过使用本书，学生可以在一年内系统掌握3000个核心词汇。通过书中的用法示例和丰富习题，可以全面提高汉语词汇的运用能力和HSK考试的应试能力。本书有如下特点：

系统的学习计划——本书安排了为期一年的学习内容：每天学习12个词汇、5天的词汇学习加"周练习"构成1周的学习内容；每个月包括4周，每册书包括4个月，3册书共一年的学习内容，希望能帮助学习者在一年之内掌握这3000个词汇及示例、习题等拓展内容，达到HSK中级以上的要求。

合理的内容编排——每天学习的词汇由易到难、有难有易。每天的学习内容都包括一定比例的甲级词、乙级词、丙级词和丁级词，随着学习的深入，甲级词和乙级词会越来越少，丙级词和丁级词会越来越多。除词汇的常规项目外，本书还归纳了一些词汇的专项内容，如量词、关联词、尾词等，并配有相应的练习。

多样的学习板块——每天的学习项目包括词语、读音、词义、该词的同义词或反义词、常用搭配、用法示例、词义辨析以及多种形式的练习。尽管每个词的内容都十分全面，但经过作者的巧妙编排和多样的学习板块，学生能在1小时内轻松掌握1天的全部学习内容。

经典的语言材料——掌握词汇重在掌握其用法。本书提供了丰富、经典的例句和固定搭配，注重体现词汇的用法和HSK考试的重点和难点。

详细的英文注释——在词义、常用搭配、用法示例、词义辨析等板块均有详细的英语注释，以确保大家能够准确理解。

To the Reader

This series of textbooks contains a list of HSK words for foreign students to study and learn in preparation for the HSK.

Through the use of these textbooks, students should be able to master 3,000 words within one year. These textbooks contain many examples and exercises, which will improve students' Chinese, and ability to complete the HSK successfully.

These books have the following features:

Systematic learning program — The one-year study plan consists of three textbooks, with each book containing four months worth of study. A month of study is made up of four weeks, and each week is composed of five days of studying 12 words a day, with added 'weekly practice' sessions. This schedule will help students master the 3,000 words within one year, and will also allow them to fulfill the requirements for the intermediate level of HSK and above.

Methodical arrangement of content — The words to be studied daily range from the simple to the complex, and become more difficult as study progresses. Different levels of HSK words (e.g. A-level words, B-level, C-level, D-level) are included in the study. As students move forward, A-level and B-level words will appear less as they are replaced with more C-level and D-level ones. As well as this efficient method of studying vocabulary, these books also have added classifications and exercises for measure words, conjunctions and suffixes.

Diversity of study materials — Each daily study plan includes words and expressions, pronunciation, word definitions, synonyms and antonyms, commonly used collocations, examples of usage, as well as exercises. Despite the comprehensive coverage of each word, students can easily complete a whole day's content within one hour, due to the author's ingenious arrangement of the diverse study materials.

Typical language materials — This textbook series includes rich and illustrative sentences and allocations, and pays great attention to the usage of words, in order to help the students to learn the words and their practical applications. It also details the key or difficult points of the HSK test.

Detailed English annotations — Detailed annotations in English are given to multiple word definitions, collocations, and examples of usage, to ensure that students will understand the concise and correct meanings and usages.

1月 第1周的学习内容

星期一

ānpái
安排　（甲）动/名
① arrange　② arrangement

常用搭配
安排工作 assign work
会议的安排 the arrangement for the meeting

用法示例
那件事已提前安排好了。
It had been arranged beforehand.
我已经安排了一个职员到机场接你。
I have arranged for one of my staff members to meet you at the airport.
我希望这些安排会使你满意。
I hope the arrangements meet with your approval.

ānjìng
安静　反 吵闹 chǎonào　（甲）形
quiet; peaceful

常用搭配
保持安静 keep quiet　安静地看书 read a book quietly

用法示例
请让我安静地工作。
Please let me do my work in peace.
孩子们在学校上学时,家里很安静。
It's quiet at home when the children are at school.

zhōngyào
中药　（乙）名
traditional Chinese medicine

常用搭配
一副中药 a dose of traditional Chinese medicine
中药的味道 the taste of traditional Chinese medicine

用法示例
他生病的时候服用了中药。
He had traditional Chinese medicine when he was ill.
我觉得中药的味道太难闻了。
I think traditional Chinese medicine smells very bad.

xīcān
西餐　（乙）名
Western-style food

常用搭配
西餐厅 a Western restaurant

用法示例
我喜欢西餐。
I like Western food.
那是一家很有名的西餐厅。
It is a very famous Western restaurant.

fàngqì
放弃　（乙）动
abandon; give up

常用搭配
放弃机会 give up the chance　主动放弃 give up willingly
不愿放弃 reluctant to give up

用法示例
试了几次后,他们决定放弃。
After a few tries they decided to give up.
全都是因为他,我们才放弃这个计划的。
It was all because of him that we gave up the plan.

fàngxīn
放心　（乙）动
set one's mind at rest; to be at ease

常用搭配
请你放心 set your mind at rest
放心地离开 leave without worry
放心不下 unable to set one's heart at ease

用法示例
警察让她放心,她的孩子很安全。
The police reassured her of her child's safety.
请您放心,还款是有保障的。
Please rest assured that repayment is ensured.

zuòpǐn
作品　（乙）名
works (of art)

常用搭配
文学作品 literary works
一部优秀的作品 a piece of excellent work

用法示例
那部作品缺乏创造性。
The work lacks originality.
这是独一无二的艺术作品。
It's a unique work of art.

zuòwén
作文　（乙）名
composition

常用搭配
写作文 to write a composition
一篇作文 a composition

用法示例

每个学生必须每星期交一篇作文。
Each student has to hand in a composition a week.
他喜欢在作文中引用谚语。
He likes to quote proverbs in his compositions.

gǎnxiǎng
感想　　　　　　　　　　　　（乙）名
afterthought; impressions

常用搭配
交流感想 exchange reflections

用法示例
请你谈谈对这件事的感想。
Please tell us your thoughts on the matter.
他听到那个消息后有什么感想？
What was his reaction when he heard the news?

gǎnqíng
感情　　　◎ 情感　　　　　　（乙）名
emotion; feeling

常用搭配
感情丰富 rich with emotion
对……很有感情 cherish a deep affection for…

用法示例
她伤害了我的感情。
She hurt my feelings.
人们常说女人比男人更富于感情。
Women are often said to be more emotional than men.
他只是在玩弄她的感情。
He's just trifling with her affections.

ānzhì
安置　　　◎ 安顿　　　　　　（丁）动
find a place for; help settle down

常用搭配
移民安置 immigrant allocation

用法示例
把伤员安置在我家。
The wounded were given beds in my home.
政府正在努力安置这些难民。
The government is trying hard to house these refugees.
移民的住处已经安置好了。
The problem of lodging the immigrants has been settled.

ānzhuāng
安装　　　反 拆卸　　　　　　（丙）动
install

常用搭配
安装电话 install a telephone　　安装设备 install equipment

用法示例
她自己安装了空调。
She installed the air-conditioner by herself.
工人们正在安装供暖设备。
Workers are installing a heating system.

 词义辨析

安排、安置

　　两个词都是动词，都有妥善处理或布置的意思，"安排"可以用于人，也可以用于事，如"安排某事"或"安排某人做某事"。"安置"则多用于为别人安排工作或住处。"安排"还是名词，表示事先做好的计划，如：住宿安排，工作安排。

　　These two words, as verbs, both have the meaning of "to arrange". 安排 is often used for somebody or something, for example: "to arrange something" or "arrange for somebody to do something"; 安置 is mainly used for helping somebody arrange work, or a place to stay. 安排 is also a noun, meaning "a plan that is made in advance". For example: accommodation arrangements; arrangements for work.

练习

练习一、根据拼音写汉字，根据汉字写拼音

zuò（　）　fàng（　）　gǎn（　）　（cān　）zhì（　）
（　）品　（　）弃　（　）想　西（　）　安（　）

练习二、搭配连线

(1) 安置　　　　　　A. 作品
(2) 安装　　　　　　B. 机会
(3) 文学　　　　　　C. 安排
(4) 放弃　　　　　　D. 空调
(5) 工作　　　　　　E. 难民

练习三、从今天学习的生词中选择合适的词填空

1. 我们在上听力课，请你保持 _____ 。
2. 今天要开会讨论明年的工作 _____ 。
3. _____ 吧！你孩子的病很快就会好的。
4. 我刚买了一台电脑，可是我不会 _____ 软件，所以现在还不能用。
5. 虽然我已经毕业两年了，可我仍然对学校很有 _____ 。
6. 看了今天的新闻以后，你有什么 _____ ？
7. 为了提高我们的写作水平，老师每星期让我们写一篇 _____ 。
8. 因为要留在家里照顾孩子，她只好 _____ 了去国外学习的机会。
9. 下个星期，我们就要学习莎士比亚的 _____ 了。
10. 我来中国以后，请中医看过病，也吃过 _____ 。

答案

练习一：
略

练习二：
(1) E　　(2) D　　(3) A　　(4) B　　(5) C

练习三：
1. 安静　　2. 安排　　3. 放心　　4. 安装　　5. 感情
6. 感想　　7. 作文　　8. 放弃　　9. 作品　　10. 中药

---

yùndòng
运动　　　　　反 jìngzhǐ 静止　　（甲）动/名

① to exercise　② movement; sports

常用搭配
田径运动 track and field exercises
民族解放运动 the movement for national liberation

用法示例
足球和跑步是我喜欢的体育运动。
Football and running are my favorite sports.
你应当多运动以保持精力充沛。
You should exercise more so as to keep energetic.
工会运动旨在争取更高的工资和更好的工作条件。
The Trade Union Movement works to obtain higher wages and better conditions.

fángjiān
房间　　　　　　　　　　　　　　（甲）名
room

常用搭配
我的房间 my room　　打扫房间 clean a room

用法示例
我住在左边第一个房间。
I stayed in the first room on the left.
她的房间十分整洁。
Her room is very tidy and clean.

láodòng　　　　　xiūxi
劳动　　　　　反 休息　　　　　　（甲）动
labor; work

常用搭配
劳动人民 working people　　劳动节 Labor Day
体力劳动 manual labor

用法示例
农民整年在农场里劳动。
The farmer works on his farm all year round.
多年艰苦的劳动使他丧失了健康。
His years of hard work took a toll on his health.

cáng
藏　　　　　　　　　　　　　　　（乙）动
store; hide away; conceal

常用搭配
偷偷地藏 to hide secretly　　藏粮食 to strore grains
藏起来 to hide away

用法示例
我把打碎的盘子藏在餐桌后面了。
I hid the broken plate behind the table.

你把钱藏哪儿了？
Where did you hide the money?
狐狸尾巴是藏不住的。
A fox cannot hide its tail.

duǒ
躲 (乙)动
avoid; hide

常用搭配
躲汽车 watch out for the cars

用法示例
我们最好在这里躲一躲，等雨停了再走。
We had better take shelter here until the rain stops.
不要躲在门后，那不安全。
Don't hide behind the door, it's not safe.
该潜艇潜入水下以躲避敌舰。
The submarine submerged to avoid enemy ships.

jiàoxué
教学 (乙)名
teaching

常用搭配
教学材料 teaching materials　教学方法 teaching methods
语言教学 language teaching

用法示例
大学的任务是教学和科研。
The mission of a university is teaching and research.
他具有丰富的教学经验。
He has rich experience in teaching.
该学院采用新的外语教学法。
New methods of teaching foreign languages have been adopted by this institute.

jiàoxun
教训 (乙)动/名
(teach someone or learn a) lesson

常用搭配
教训某人 give sb. a lesson
吸取教训 draw up a lesson

用法示例
车祸给了他一个教训，使他不再开快车。
His car accident has been a lesson to him to stop driving too fast.
这样的宝贵教训应该铭记在心。
Such a lesson should be treasured in our memories.
这对我是个教训。
It was a lesson to me.
我再也不做那种事了，我已有了教训！
I'll never do that again; I've learned my lesson!

gǎigé
改革 (乙)动/名
reform

常用搭配
学校制度的改革 reforms in the school system
改革者(家) reformer

用法示例
他们要求对税收制度进行改革。
They called for a reform of our tax system.
改革开放的政策给我们带来了富裕的生活。
The policy of reform and opening up has brought us a more comfortable life.
他们强烈要求改革。
They clamored for reform.

gǎijìn　　　　　　　gǎishàn
改进　　⊜改善 (乙)动/名
① improve ② improvement

常用搭配
改进方法 improve the method　得到改进 be improved

用法示例
道德标准是否有所改进？
Have standards of morality improved?
近来各方面都有所改进。
There's been an overall improvement recently.

fángzi　　　　　　　fángwū
房子　　⊜房屋 (乙)名
house

常用搭配
买房子 purchase a house　租房子 rent a house

用法示例
他们正计划建一所新房子。
They are planning to build a new house.
他们正在为过新年装饰房子。
They are decorating the house for the New Year.

zhèngjiàn
证件 (丙)名
certificate

常用搭配
查验证件 check one's papers
证件齐全 complete certificates

用法示例
移民局的官员要求我出示证件。
Immigration officials asked to see my papers.
请你出示证件。
Please show us your papers.
警察查验了他的证件。
Police examined his credentials.
护照是外国人的重要证件。
A passport is a very important document for a foreigner to have.

zhèngjù
证据 (丙)名
proof; evidence

常用搭配
寻找证据 search for evidence
令人信服的证据 convincing evidence
提供……的证据 give proof of…

用法示例
没有充分的证据能证明他有罪。
There wasn't enough evidence to prove his guilt.
警察有证据证明,凶手是个女人。
The police have evidence that the killer was a woman.
我找不到证据来支持你的解释。
I found no evidence to support your theory.

 词义辨析

躲、藏

　　1、都是动词,不跟宾语时,两个词的意思和用法一样。"躲"可以重复使用,"藏"一般不能。

　　These two words, as verbs, have the same meaning and usage when not followed by objects. 躲 can be used in a repeated form, but 藏 usually can not.

　　2、当两个词后面跟宾语时,"躲"表示避开对象,不让对象看到自己;"藏"表示把对象掩盖起来,不让别人看到这个对象。

　　When followed by objects, 躲 means to keep away from the object, or let the object not find the subject; 藏 means to hide the object and let others not find it.

 练习

练习一、根据拼音写汉字,根据汉字写拼音

yùn（　　）（　　）jù　　jiāo（　　）（　　）gé　fáng（　　）
（　　）动　　证（　　）（　　）训　　改（　　）（　　）子

练习二、搭配连线

(1) 体力　　　　　　　A. 教训
(2) 体育　　　　　　　B. 劳动
(3) 吸取　　　　　　　C. 开放
(4) 改革　　　　　　　D. 方法
(5) 教学　　　　　　　E. 运动

练习三、从今天学习的生词中选择合适的词填空

1. 他家离公司比较远,所以他想在公司附近租_____。
2. 他说目前的教育制度必须彻底_____,否则大学的教育水平就不会提高。
3. 游泳是一项对身体特别有益的_____。
4. 律师向法官出示了她不在现场的_____。
5. 她已经在酒店预定了_____。
6. 老人喜欢_____,六十多岁的时候还经常在农场里干活。
7. 到国外旅行的时候,一定要带好各种_____。
8. 这位老师已有三十年的_____经验了。
9. 他家的花园总被人破坏,他决心要抓住这个人,并狠狠地_____他一顿。
10. 房子的主人突然回来了,小偷马上_____到了窗帘的后边。

答案

练习一：
略

练习二：
(1) B　　(2)E　　(3)A　　(4)C　　(5)D

练习三：
1. 房子　　2. 改革　　3. 运动　　4. 证据　　5. 房间
6. 劳动　　7. 证件　　8. 教学　　9. 教训　　10. 躲

星期三

juéde
觉得 （甲）动
think; feel

常用搭配
觉得冷 feel cold　　觉得不舒服 feel uncomfortable

用法示例
实际上，我觉得他的决定并不明智。
In reality, I don't think his decision is wise.
辛苦工作了四个小时后，他觉得非常饿。
He felt very hungry after four-hours' hard work.
你觉得他怎么样？
What do you think of him?

zhèngzhì
政治 （甲）名
politics

常用搭配
政治压力 political pressure
政治经济学 political economy
办公室政治 office politics

用法示例
我对政治从来不感兴趣。
Politics have never interested me.
他从事政治活动多年。
He was engaged in politics for many years.

zhèngfǔ
政府 （甲）名
government

常用搭配
地方政府 local government　　政府部门 governmental sector

用法示例
政府正打算提高税金。
The Government is planning new tax increases.
为人民服务是政府的职责。
It is the duty of the government to serve the people.

gǎnjué　　　　　　　gǎnshòu
感觉 　同 感受 （乙）动/名
① feel; sense ② perception

常用搭配
感觉到心跳 feel one's heart beat　　感觉不好 not feel well
疲劳的感觉 a sense of fatigue

用法示例
我感觉好像以前来过这里。
It feels like I've been here before.
这个房间给人一种非常温暖舒适的感觉。
The room has a nice, cosy feel.

马感觉到了危险，停了下来。
The horse sensed danger and stopped.

shēngqì
生气 （乙）动
be offended; get angry

常用搭配
因……而生气 get angry at …
生她的气 be angry with her

用法示例
他在生气，所以我害怕。
He was angry, wherefore I was afraid.
我们不同意他的观点，他生气了。
He was offended that we didn't agree with him.
别为这些小事生气。
Don't get angry over such trivial matters.

chángqī　　　　　　　duǎnqī
长期 　反 短期 （乙）名
① long term ② for a long time

常用搭配
长期投资 a long-term investment
长期的研究 long-term research

用法示例
我们希望长期获利。
We hope to make great profits in the long term.
他长期以来一直在努力解决这个问题。
He has been grappling with the problem for a long time.
为长期发展而牺牲短期利润是公司的方针。
It's the company's policy to sacrifice short-term profits for the sake of long-term growth.

chángtú　　　　　　　duǎntú
长途 　反 短途 （乙）名/形
① long distance ② distant

常用搭配
长途电话 a long-distance call　　长途旅行 long distance trip

用法示例
她乘船在海上长途旅行
She went on a long sea voyage.
长途汽车一小时开一班。
The long-distance bus runs hourly.

shìyè
事业 （乙）名
career; cause

常用搭配
干一番事业 make a career　　公共事业 public utility

用法示例
该协会致力于推动世界和平事业。
The society was dedicated to furthering the cause of world peace.
他是个事业心很强的人。
He is a man of great enterprise.

他已经登上了事业的顶峰。
He has reached the pinnacle of his career.

失业 shīyè　⊜下岗 xiàgǎng　（乙）动

① unemployment ② out of employ

常用搭配
失业率 rate of unemployment
失业保险 unemployment insurance

用法示例
因为失业严重，求职竞争十分激烈。
Because there is so much unemployment, the competition for jobs is fierce.
他有资格领取失业救济金吗？
Is he entitled to unemployment benefits?

约会 yuēhuì　（乙）名

appointment; engagement

常用搭配
有个约会 have an appointment
与某人约会 make an appointment with sb.

用法示例
他的秘书处理他的一切约会。
His secretary took care of all his appointments.
我下周有几个约会。
I have several engagements for next week.
他穿着整洁的制服去约会。
He wore an immaculate suit for the date.

东部 dōngbù　（乙）名

the east; the eastern part

常用搭配
亚洲东部 the east of Asia

用法示例
我出生于东部，但现在住在洛杉矶。
I was born in the east, but now live in Los Angeles.
他住在东部海岸地区。
He lives on the east coast.
日本在亚洲的东部。
Japan is in East Asia.

西部 xībù　（乙）名

the western part

常用搭配
中国西部 the west of China
西部牛仔 Western cowboys

用法示例
我住在这座城市的西部。
I live in the west side of the city.
他在一部西部电影中扮演一名牛仔。
He acted as a cowboy in a western movie.

政党 zhèngdǎng　（丙）名

a political party

常用搭配
解散政党 disband a party

用法示例
中国共产党是中国最大的政党。
The Chinese Communist Party is the biggest party in China.
你知道这个政党的宗旨吗？
Do you know the tenets of this party?

词义辨析

觉得、感觉

1、两个词都是动词，都有通过身体的感官感知或认为的意思，但"觉得"的口语色彩更浓，比如：觉得/感觉累，觉得/感觉不公平。

These two words act as verbs, both have the meaning of "to feel" and "to think", but 觉得 is more colloquial, e.g. to feel tired, to think it is unfair.

2、"感觉"还是名词，如：饥饿的感觉，回家的感觉真好！"觉得"不能用作名词。

感觉 also acts as a noun. For example: A sense of hunger. It feels good to be home. 觉得 can not be used as a noun.

练习一、根据拼音写汉字，根据汉字写拼音
gǎn（　）cháng（　）shī（　）zhèng（　）yuē（　）
（　）觉　（　）期　（　）业　（　）府　（　）会

练习二、搭配连线
(1) 长期　　　　　　　A. 保险
(2) 长途　　　　　　　B. 事业
(3) 失业　　　　　　　C. 牛仔
(4) 公共　　　　　　　D. 旅行
(5) 西部　　　　　　　E. 投资

练习三、从今天学习的生词中选择合适的词填空
1. 我 _____ 那件红色的衣服特别适合她。
2. 由于 _____ 从事繁重的体力劳动，他退休以后身体很不好。
3. 刚到北京时，玛丽很想家，天天给妈妈打国际 _____ 电话。
4. 总统在年轻的时候就对 _____ 和法律特别感兴趣。
5. _____ 正在努力解决失业问题，以确保社会稳定。
6. 邻居认为她不是一个好女孩，因为他们发现她同时和几个男孩子 _____。
7. 听说他 _____ 了，朋友们都在帮助他找新工作。
8. 这条地铁从城市的东部一直通到 _____。
9. 为了取得 _____ 的成功，他每天都忙于工作和应酬。
10. 我有一种奇怪的 _____，好像总有人在跟着我。

答案
练习一：
略
练习二：
(1) E　　(2) D　　(3) A　　(4) B　　(5) C
练习三：
1. 觉得　2. 长期　3. 长途　4. 政治　5. 政府
6. 约会　7. 失业　8. 西部　9. 事业　10. 感觉

---

jìxù
继续　≈ 停止　（甲）动
continue; go on

常用搭配
继续工作 continue one's work　继续讨论 go on discussing
继续调查 go on the investigations

用法示例
继续这种无聊的争辩是没用的。
It's useless to continue such a pointtess argument.
这个班最少要有六个学生才可以继续办下去。
The class needs a minimum of six pupils to continue.
继续干你的工作吧。
Go on with your work.

jiānchí
坚持　（甲）动
persist; insist on

常用搭配
坚持他的主张 maintain his opinion
坚持到底 stick to it until the end
努力坚持 persevere in an effort

用法示例
他在假期坚持学习汉语。
He persisted studying Chinese during the holidays.
我坚持要求他和我们一起来。
I insisted on his coming with us.
我知道如果我坚持下去就会成功。
I knew if I kept at it I would succeed.

zhǔnbèi
准备　= 预备　（甲）动/名
① be ready; prepare　② preparation

常用搭配
事前准备 prepare in advance
为……做准备 prepare for

用法示例
他正在准备明天会议的讲话。
He is preparing his speech for tomorrow's meeting.
他们为穷人准备了米、面和汤。
They prepared rice, wheat, and soup for the poor.
他考试前没做任何准备，所以不及格。
He didn't do any preparation for this exam, so he failed.

huāyuán
花园　（乙）名
garden

常用搭配
美丽的花园 a beautiful garden　　大花园 a big garden

用法示例

我们在花园里种了许多蔬菜。
We've grown many vegetables in our garden.
上午,她经常在花园里干活。
In the morning she often works in the garden.
我宁愿在花园里锄草,也不愿在运动场上跑来跑去。
I would rather rake the garden than run about on the playground.

zuòmèng
做梦　　(乙)动
① dream ② have a dream

常用搭配

做恶梦 have a bad dream　　做美梦 have a sweet dream

用法示例

她说她从来不做梦。
She claims she never dreams.
是真的还是我在做梦?
Was it real, or did I dream it?
我从没答应过把汽车借给你,你是在做梦吧!
I never promised to lend you my car. You must be dreaming!

bàngōng
办公　　(乙)动
① handle official business ② work (usually in an office)

常用搭配

办公室 office　　办公楼 office building

用法示例

圣诞节期间不办公。
The office is closed over Christmas.
我们公司购买了新的办公家具。
Our company bought some new office furniture.

shèjì
设计　　(乙)动/名
design; plan

常用搭配

设计一件服装 design a dress　　封面设计 cover design
最新设计 latest design

用法示例

他为我们设计了一所很漂亮的房子。
He designed us a beautiful house.
她是工业设计师。
She is an industrial designer.
她的设计十分新颖。
Her designs have great originality.

shèbèi　　　　　　　　　　shèshī
设备　　同 设施　　(乙)名
equipment; facilities; installations

常用搭配

实验室设备 laboratory equipment
视听设备 audio-visual equipment
电子设备 electronic equipment

用法示例

我们应该更好地利用这些设备。
We should make better use of this equipment.
我们学校得到了一些新设备。
Our school has been given some new equipment.

gānzào　　　　　　　　　shīrùn
干燥　　反 湿润　　(乙)形
dry; arid

常用搭配

干燥的空气 the dry air
皮肤干燥 dry skin

用法示例

在天气干燥时把点燃的香烟扔进树林可能会引起火灾。
A cigarette thrown into the woods in dry weather may start a fire.
因空气干燥皮子都皱了。
The dry air shrivels the leather.
干燥很多天之后,人人都希望下雨。
After many dry days, everyone hopes for rain.

yònggōng
用功　　(乙)形
diligent; industrious (in one's studies)

常用搭配

用功的学生 a diligent student

用法示例

他学习用功。
He is diligent in his studies.
我得用功,免得考试不及格。
I must study hard, so that I won't fail the examinations.
他和约翰一样用功。
He studies as hard as John.

liúchuán
流传　　(丙)动
spread; circulate

常用搭配

口头流传的故事 a story passed on by oral tradition

用法示例

这消息广为流传。
The news spread from mouth to mouth.
谣言很快就流传开了。
The rumor circulated rapidly.
他的故事在村子里流传开了。
His story spread through the village.

shīrùn
湿润　　(丙)形
moist; humid

常用搭配

湿润的空气 humid air
湿润的土壤 moist soil

用法示例

她的眼睛湿润了。
Her eyes moistened slightly.
湿润的风从南方吹来。
A humid wind blew from the south.

词义辨析

继续、坚持

1、两个动词都有保持同样状态、不中断的意思，但"继续"通常表示客观地不间断，或中断后再进行；"坚持"强调主观努力或毅力，尽管有困难或障碍也要坚决维护、维持某个想法、状态或事业等。

The two verbs mean "to continue", but 继续 means to keep on continuing objectively, or go on after an interruption; 坚持 implies subjective will, or power, and means to hold firmly and steadfastly to an opinion, a state, or an undertaking despite obstacles, warnings, or setbacks.

2、"坚持"可以带结果补语，而"继续"不可以，如：坚持到最后，坚持到胜利。

坚持 can take a complement of result, while 继续 can not, e.g. stick to the end, stick to it until victory.

练习

练习一、根据拼音写汉字，根据汉字写拼音

shī（　） liú（　） shè（　） （　）chí （　）xù

（　）润 （　）传 （　）备 坚（　） 继（　）

练习二、搭配连线

(1) 用功　　　　　　A. 设备
(2) 办公　　　　　　B. 干燥
(3) 皮肤　　　　　　C. 学习
(4) 电子　　　　　　D. 到底
(5) 坚持　　　　　　E. 家具

练习三、从今天学习的生词中选择合适的词填空

1. 明天我不想去踢球了，我得为下星期的考试做_____。
2. 她感到压力很大，晚上不是失眠就是_____。
3. 沙漠地带的气候十分_____。
4. 她学习很_____，汉语水平提高得很快。
5. 雨后的空气清新而_____。
6. 银行中午休息两个小时，下午两点才_____。
7. 她是著名模特，也是服装_____师。
8. 我们工厂引进了先进的生产_____。
9. 昨天我没做完作业，今天还得_____做。
10. 他_____每天读课文，三个月以后，他的发音有了很大的进步。

答案

练习一：
略

练习二：
(1) C　　(2)E　　(3)B　　(4)A　　(5)D

练习三：
1. 准备　2. 做梦　3. 干燥　4. 用功　5. 湿润
6. 办公　7. 设计　8. 设备　9. 继续　10. 坚持

星期五

zúqiú
足球 (甲)名
football; soccer

常用搭配
足球队 football team　足球比赛 football match
踢足球 play football

用法示例
他特别喜欢踢足球。
He likes playing football very much.
我们队在足球赛中获胜了。
Our team has won the football match.
这位足球运动员遭到了教练的批评。
The football player was criticized by the coach.

yùxí
预习 (甲)动
(of students) prepare lessons before class

常用搭配
预习课文 preview the text
充分预习 to fully preview

用法示例
你们最好自己预习生词。
You'd better prepare the new words by yourselves.
周末他预习新课,并复习以前学过的内容。
He previews new lessons, and reviews what he has studied on the weekends.

gǎnkuài　　　　　　　**gǎnmáng**
赶快 同 赶忙 (乙)副
at once; quickly

常用搭配
赶快来 to come at once　赶快写 to write quickly

用法示例
赶快！要是你不快点儿,我们就要迟到了。
Hurry up! We'll be late if you don't get a move on.
赶快开开门！
Quickly, open the door!
赶快过来一下儿！
Come here quickly!

bàodào
报到 (乙)动
check in; register

常用搭配
报到上班 report for duty

用法示例
我上午在处理学生报到的事。
I spent the morning registering students.

有人通知他到司令部去报到。
He was told to report to headquarters.
她得在九月前去那所大学报到。
She has to register in college before September.

dǎtīng
打听 (乙)动
inquire about; ask about

常用搭配
向某人打听一件事 ask sb. about something
打听价格 inquire about prices

用法示例
我建议你打听一下这项工作。
I recommend that you inquire about the job.
我不愿让他们打听我的私事。
I don't want them prying into my affairs.

bàodào　　**bàodǎo**
报道／报导 (乙)动／名
① report (news) ② news

常用搭配
报道(报导)……的情况
report the situation of…
新闻报道(报导) news report
一篇关于……的报道(报导) a report about

用法示例
报纸的报道(报导)在头版。
The newspaper report was on the front page.
他对事件的报道(报导),其全部细节都是准确的。
His report of the event was accurate in every detail.
两名记者报道(报导)了这则新闻。
Two reporters covered the news story.

gǎishàn　　　　　　　**èhuà**
改善 反 恶化 (乙)动
make better; improve

常用搭配
改善生活条件 improve one's situation in life
得到改善 be improved

用法示例
人民的生活水平明显改善了。
There has been a perceptible improvement in peoples standard of living.
他们之间的关系正在改善。
The relationship between them is improving.
我们将改善工人的工作环境。
We will improve the working environment of the workers.

xīfāng
西方 (乙)名
① the west ② Western countries

常用搭配
脸朝西方 face the west

【用法示例】
西方各国对这个国家实行了严厉制裁。
Western nations imposed tough sanctions on the country.
希腊人影响了西方人的思维方式。
It was the Greeks who shaped the thinking of Westerners.
美国是一个西方国家。
America is a western country.

dōngfāng
东方　　　　　反 西方　　　　　（乙）名
① the east ② Eastern countries
【常用搭配】
东方人 easterner
【用法示例】
中国是一个有着悠久历史的东方国家。
China is an Eastern country with a long history.
他专门研究东方史。
He specializes in Asian history.
直到太阳从东方升起,我们才出发。
We did not start until the sun rose in the east.

yònglì
用力　　　　　同 使劲　　　　　（乙）动
exert oneself (physically); put forth one's strength
【常用搭配】
用力推 give a hard push
别用力 don't exert strength
【用法示例】
我用力把螺丝往木头上拧。
I've put the screw in the wood as tightly as I can.
别用力关门。
Do not close the door loudly.
他用力转动轮子,但没成功。
He strained to turn the wheel, but failed.

gǎnmáng
赶忙　　　　　　　　　　　　　（丙）副
① hurriedly ② hasten
【常用搭配】
赶忙离开 left hurriedly　　赶忙停下来 stop hurriedly
【用法示例】
她赶忙将好消息告诉了她母亲。
She made haste to tell her mother the good news.
我走进他的房间时,他赶忙把一包东西藏到书桌里了。
He hurriedly hid a large parcel under his desk when I went into his study.

gǎibiān
改编　　　　　　　　　　　　　（丙）动
adapt
【常用搭配】
把小说改编成电视剧
adapt a novel into a play

【用法示例】
这部电影是由小说改编的。
The movie was adapted from a novel.
这是为儿童改编的莎士比亚的戏剧。
This is an adaptation for children of a play by Shakespeare.

 词义辨析

赶快、赶忙
　　两个词都表示加速行动,如:我挂上电话,赶忙/赶快回家了。但"赶快"多用于祈使句,而"赶忙"多用于已发生的事,如:①赶快来！②他赶忙说。
　　Both 赶快 and 赶忙 mean "hurry up" or "quickly", e.g. I hung up and went home hurriedly. 赶快 is often used in imperative sentences, and 赶忙 is often applied to things which have already happened, e.g. ① Come here quickly! ② He said quickly.

 练习

练习一、根据拼音写汉字,根据汉字写拼音
bào（　）yù（　）dǎ（　）（　）máng（　）biān
（　）导　（　）习　（　）听　赶（　）　改（　）

练习二、搭配连线
(1) 足球　　　　　　A. 剧本
(2) 改编　　　　　　B. 比赛
(3) 改善　　　　　　C. 课文
(4) 新闻　　　　　　D. 关系
(5) 预习　　　　　　E. 报道

练习三、从今天学习的生词中选择合适的词填空
1. 那家公司决定录用我了,让我下星期一去_____。
2. 在老师讲新课以前,她总是先_____一下。
3. _____起床,我们的闹钟坏了,现在已经快上课了。
4. 我不喜欢我的邻居,她总_____我的私事。
5. 早晨,太阳从_____升起。
6. 记者详细_____了办理这个案件的全过程。
7. 为了_____小区的环境,他们种了很多花和树。
8. 这部电影是根据鲁迅的小说_____的。
9. 听说孩子病了,他下了班就_____回家了。
10. 我个子不高,不善于打篮球,更喜欢踢_____,而且踢得很不错。

12

 答案

练习一：
略
练习二：
(1) B (2)A (3)D (4)E (5)C
练习三：
1. 报到 2. 预习 3. 赶快 4. 打听 5. 东方
6. 报道／报导 7. 改善 8. 改编
9. 赶快／赶忙 10. 足球

第1月,第1周的练习

练习一、根据词语给加点的字注音
1.（ ） 2.（ ） 3.（ ） 4.（ ） 5.（ ）
教训 设备 改编 安置 干燥

练习二、根据拼音填写词语
　　　shī　　　shì　　　zhèng　　zhèng　　　qì
1.（　）润 2.（　）业 3.（　）党 4.（　）件 5. 放（　）

练习三、辨析并选择合适的词填空
1. 根据会议的（　），下午将进行自由讨论。（安排、安置）
2. 地震发生后，首先要考虑如何（　）这些无家可归的市民。（安排、安置）
3. 他把枪（　）在了帽子里，但还是被警察发现了。（躲、藏）
4. 我觉得她是故意（　）着我，不愿意跟我见面。（躲、藏）
5. 我有一种奇怪的（　），好像以前来过这里。（觉得、感觉）
6. 我（　）蓝色比较适合你，你买这件蓝的吧。（觉得、感觉）
7. 该下班了，咱们明天再（　）修改这个报告吧。（继续、坚持）
8. 她虽然是长跑比赛的最后一名，但她（　）跑完了全程。（继续、坚持）
9. 她妈妈来电话，说家里发生了大事，让她（　）回国。（赶快、赶忙）
10. 听到街上有人喊"救命"，我就（　）跑了出去，看看发生了什么事。（赶快、赶忙）

练习四、选词填空
教学　教训　放心　放弃　长途
长期　改进　改革　设计　设备
1. 他不该（　）这次机会，如果再坚持一下，他也许就成功了。
2. 她是著名的服装（　）师，很多明星都购买她（　）的礼服。
3. 从北京到天津，可以坐火车，也可以乘坐（　）汽车。
4. 医院购买了一批先进的医疗（　）。
5. 孩子放学后没有回家，妈妈很不（　）。
6. 人们对中学教育不满意，要求彻底（　）现在的教育制度。
7. 这次失败给了他一个（　），从那以后，他再也不马马虎虎了。
8. 为了让人民满意，政府部门正在（　）工作作风。
9. 在未来的10年到20年间，我们希望能跟这家公司（　）合作。
10. 这个学校的（　）水平很高，相信你在这里学习会进步得很快。

练习五、写出下列词语的同义词
1. 改进（　） 2. 安置（　）
3. 失业（　） 4. 赶快（　）
5. 设备（　）

练习六、写出下列词语的反义词
1. 安静（　） 2. 干燥（　）
3. 安装（　） 4. 长期（　）
5. 运动（　）

 答案

练习一：
1. xùn 2. bèi 3. biān 4. zhì 5. zào
练习二：
1. 湿 2. 事 3. 政 4. 证 5. 弃
练习三：
1. 安排 2. 安置 3. 藏 4. 躲 5. 感觉
6. 觉得 7. 继续 8. 坚持 9. 赶快 10. 赶忙
练习四：
1. 放弃 2. 设计 3. 长途 4. 设备 5. 放心
6. 改革 7. 教训 8. 改进 9. 长期 10. 教学
练习五：
1. 改善 2. 安顿 3. 下岗 4. 赶忙 5. 设施
练习六：
1. 吵闹 2. 湿润 3. 拆卸 4. 短期 5. 静止

1月 第2周的学习内容

星期一

kǎoshì　　　　　cèshì
考试　　◎测试　　　　　（甲）名/动
① examination ② examine
常用搭配
通过考试 pass the exam
化学考试 Chemistry exam
期中考试 mid-term examination
入学考试 entrance examination
用法示例
他们正在准备考试。
They were preparing for the exam.
张雅,考试的情况怎么样?
How was the examination Zhang Ya?
我们什么时候可以收到考试结果?
When shall we receive the examination results?

zhòngyào
重要　　　　　　　　　　（甲）形
important
常用搭配
重要的决定 important decisions
重要的事 something important
重要的人物 very important person
用法示例
那是他一生中最重要的时刻。
It was a supreme moment in his life.
把交通安全常识教给孩子们是非常重要的。
It's very important to teach children about road safety.

zhǔyào　　　　　cìyào
主要　　⊘次要　　　　　（甲）形
main; principal
常用搭配
主要问题 main problem　主要目标 main objectives
主要矛盾 principal contradiction
用法示例
这是进城的主要道路。
This is the main road into town.
这个地区发生疾病的主要原因是水不清洁。
A major cause of the disease in this area is unclean water.
大多数美国人的汽车主要是用来上下班。
Most Americans use their cars mainly for travelling to and from work.

kǎo
考　　　　　　　　　　　（乙）动
test; examine
常用搭配
考大学 take a college entrance examination
考某人的物理 examine sb. in physics
用法示例
这次我没考好。
This examination did not go well.
老师要考咱们的英语了。
The teacher will give us an English test.

zuòwéi
作为　　　　　　　　　　（乙）动/介
regard as; as
常用搭配
作为老师 as a teacher
作为生日礼物 as a birthday gift
用法示例
他选择了教育作为终生的事业。
He chose education to be his lifelong career.
我以前把他作为朋友。
I used to look on him as a friend.
作为艺术品,这是十分拙劣的。
As a work of art it is very poor.

zuòyòng　　　　　gōngnéng
作用　　◎功能　　　　　（乙）名/动
① function; effect ② play a role
常用搭配
副作用 side-effect
起重大作用 perform an important function
用法示例
互联网在现代生活中发挥着非常重要的作用。
The internet plays a very important role in modern life.
教师在学习中的关键作用是不该忽视的。
The key role of the teacher in the learning process should not be neglected.

guīmó
规模　　　　　　　　　　（乙）名
scope; scale
常用搭配
小规模的调查 an investigation of small scope
学校的规模 the size of a school

【用法示例】
董事会决定大规模生产这种汽车。
The board of directors made the decision to produce the car on a larger scale.
他们正在大规模地备战。
They are preparing for war on a large scale.
九年来,这家公司的规模扩大了一倍。
The company doubled its size in nine years.

gōnggòng
公共　　　🛇 sīyǒu 私有　　　(乙)形
public; common (use)
【常用搭配】
在公共场所 in public places
公共秩序 public order
【用法示例】
不吸烟的人往往不赞成在公共场合吸烟。
Non-smokers often disapprove of smoking in public.
维护公共秩序是警察的职责。
It's the duty of the police to preserve the public order.

shǒugōng
手工　　　(乙)名
handcraft; handwork; manual
【常用搭配】
手工课 manual training
手工技术 manual skill
手工艺术品 handicraft
【用法示例】
机器生产已经代替了手工劳作。
Machine work has replaced manual labor.
采用这种新方法就无需再用手工检验产品了。
This new process has eliminated the need to check the products by hand.

lǒngzhào
笼罩　　　(丙)动
shroud; hover over
【常用搭配】
在……的笼罩下 under a shroud of
【用法示例】
大雾笼罩着城市。
The fog was a shroud over the city
整座监狱笼罩在黑暗之中。
The whole jail was shrouded in darkness.
经济衰退的威胁笼罩着世界。
The threat of an economic depression hangs over the world.

jiàodǎo
教导　　　(丙)名/动
① instruction ② teach
【常用搭配】
教导有方 skillful in teaching

【用法示例】
他教导年轻人自力更生。
He teaches young people to be self-reliant.
他在老师的教导下取得了进步。
He made progress under his teacher's tutelage.

cìyào
次要　　　(丙)形
subordinate; minor
【常用搭配】
处于次要地位 in a subordinate position
【用法示例】
她在剧中扮演了一个次要的角色。
She played a minor role in the play.
与健康相比,我认为,工作是次要的。
Compared with health, work I think is of minor importance.

词义辨析

考试、考

1、"考试"是名词,也是动词,但在句子中主要用作名词;"考"只是动词,不能用做名词,如①化学考试,期中考试;②考托福,考数学。

考试 is a noun or a verb, but it mainly serves as a noun. 考 is a verb, it can not serve as a noun, e.g. ① Chemistry exam, mid-term examination; ② take part in TOEFL, to have a math test.

2、作为动词,"考"口语色彩更浓,后可带宾语,"考试"不可以;"考"可以重叠使用,"考试"不可以,如①这次考试没考好;②我考考你,你认识这个字吗?

As verbs, 考 is more colloquial, and can be followed by an object; 考试 can not. 考 can be used in a repeated form, but 考试 can not. E.g. ① I didn't perform well in this examination. ② Let me test you, do you know this Chinese character?

 **练习**

练习一、根据拼音写汉字，根据汉字写拼音
lǒng（　）　guī（　）　kǎo（　）　yào　zuò（　）
（　）罩　（　）模　（　）试　重（　）（　）为

练习二、搭配连线
(1) 手工　　　　　　A. 秩序
(2) 扩大　　　　　　B. 考试
(3) 入学　　　　　　C. 矛盾
(4) 主要　　　　　　D. 劳作
(5) 公共　　　　　　E. 规模

练习三、从今天学习的生词中选择合适的词填空
1. 在母亲的_____下，三个孩子都懂礼貌，有文化。
2. 生产大楼失火了，要先抢救楼里的工人，设备是_____的。
3. 这些工艺品都是_____制作的，所以价格比较贵。
4. 经过几年的发展，学校的_____已经从400名学生增加到了现在的1200名学生。
5. 请你介绍一下这本书的_____内容。
6. 她以优异的成绩通过了入学_____。
7. 这个决定将对公司的发展起到非常_____的作用。
8. _____孩子的父母，你们应该照顾好他们。
9. 安眠药很快起了_____，现在他安静地睡着了。
10. 这些健身器材是_____设施，谁都可以使用，但不能破坏。

答案

练习一：
略
练习二：
(1) D　(2)E　(3)B　(4)C　(5)A
练习三：
1. 教导　2. 次要　3. 手工　4. 规模　5. 主要
6. 考试　7. 重要　8. 作为　9. 作用　10. 公共

xǐhuan
喜欢　　　　　　　　　　　　（甲）动
like; be fond of
▶常用搭配
喜欢唱歌 to like singing　喜欢京剧 enjoy Beijing Opera
喜欢孩子 to like a child
▶用法示例
他喜欢游泳。
He likes swimming.
我不喜欢洋葱的味道。
I don't like the taste of onion.
我喜欢书架上所有的书，但这本是我最喜欢的。
I like all the books on the shelf, but this one is my favorite.

jiù
旧　　　　　　　　　　　　　（甲）形
old (opposite of new)
▶常用搭配
旧家具 old furniture　一本旧书 an old book
旧鞋子 old shoes
▶用法示例
这台旧收音机恐怕不能修了。
I'm afraid this old radio is beyond repair.
你应该扔掉这辆旧自行车，买一辆新的。
You ought to scrap that old bike and buy a new one.

xīn
新　　　　　　　　　　　　　（甲）形
① new ② newly
▶常用搭配
一辆新车 a new car　新衣服 new clothes
一对新婚夫妇 a newly-married couple
▶用法示例
你跟你的新上司相处得怎么样？
How are you doing with your new boss?
这个轮胎已经磨平了，你应该换个新的。
There is no tread on that tire, you should put on a new one.
他们的公司就在一座新建的楼里。
Their company is in a newly constructed building.

àihào　　　　　　　　　　shìhào
爱好　　　　　　　圓嗜好　（乙）动／名
① like ② hobby; interest
▶常用搭配
爱好钓鱼 to like fishing　业余爱好 hobbies
▶用法示例
她爱好艺术。
She's keen on art.

你有什么爱好?
Do you have any hobbies?
我的业余爱好之一是画画。
One of my hobbies is painting.

爱情 àiqíng (乙)名
love
常用搭配
爱情故事 love story　对……产生爱情 fall in love (with)
用法示例
这枚戒指是他们爱情的象征,对她很重要。
The ring was important to her as an emblem of their love.
[谚] 爱情是盲目的
Love is blind.

新鲜 xīnxiān ❻陈旧 (乙)形
fresh (experience, food, etc.)
常用搭配
新鲜的蔬菜 fresh vegetables　新鲜事 novelty
用法示例
新鲜空气和运动有益于健康。
Fresh air and exercise are good for one's health.
这条鱼不新鲜,已经发臭了!
This fish isn't fresh; it smells!
在 1900 年,汽车是新鲜事物。
Cars were a novelty in 1900.

高大 gāodà ❻矮小 (乙)形
tall; lofty
常用搭配
高大的树 tall tree　高大的建筑 tall building
用法示例
河岸上生长着高大的棕树。
Growing along the river are tall palm trees.
她是一个身材高大的女人。
She is a tall woman.
那个城市有很多高大的烟囱。
There are a lot of tall chimneys in that city.

实验 shíyàn (乙)动/名
① to experiment ② experiments
常用搭配
科学实验 scientific experiment
实验室 laboratory
进行实验 to conduct an experiment
用法示例
我们正在做化学实验。
We are doing a chemical experiment.
这项技术还处于实验阶段。
The technique is still in the experimental stage.

试验 shìyàn (乙)动/名
① test ② experiment
常用搭配
试验新产品 test a new product
成功的试验 a successful test
用法示例
这种装置经过了广泛的试验。
The device had undergone extensive testing.
有些科学家用动物做试验。
Some scientists experiment on animals.

产物 chǎnwù (丙)名
product; result
常用搭配
新时代的产物 products of new era
用法示例
原子弹是 20 世纪物理学的产物。
The atom bomb is the offspring of the 20th century physics.
电脑病毒是电脑时代的产物。
Computer viruses are a product of the computer age.

产值 chǎnzhí (丙)名
production value; output value
常用搭配
总产值 total value of output　年产值 annual output value
用法示例
去年钢的年产值是两千万美元。
The annual output value of steel last year was $20 million.
工业总产值迅速提高。
The total value of industrial output increased rapidly.

高等 gāoděng ❻高级 (丙)形
higher; advanced
常用搭配
高等教育 higher education　高等代数 advanced algebra
用法示例
这是一道高等数学的难题。
It is a problem of advanced mathematics.
她在高等法院作秘书。
She works in the high court as a secretary.

 词义辨析

喜欢、爱好

1、两个词都是动词,都有乐于做某事的意思,如,他喜欢/爱好打篮球。"爱好"还是名词,如:我的业余爱好是下棋。而"喜欢"不能用作名词。

As verbs, both have the meaning of "to like", and can be applied as "like doing something", e.g. He likes playing basketball. 爱好 is also a noun, for example: My hobby is playing chess. 喜欢 can not be used as a noun.

2、"喜欢"一般用于具体事物或人,如:我们都喜欢那位老师。他喜欢这辆汽车。"爱好"一般表示对某事物有浓厚的兴趣或用于抽象的事物,如爱好和平,爱好艺术等;"爱好"不能用于人。

喜欢 is often applied to concrete things, or to somebody, e.g. We all like that teacher. He likes the car; 爱好 means "a great interest in (doing) something", and it is often applied to abstract things such as art, or peace. 爱好 can not be followed by persons.

练习一、根据拼音写汉字,根据汉字写拼音
chǎn（　）　shí（　）　ài（　）　（　）xiān　（　）děng
（　）值　　（　）验　　（　）好　　新（　）　　高（　）

练习二、搭配连线
(1) 新鲜　　　　　　A. 设备
(2) 提高　　　　　　B. 爱好
(3) 实验　　　　　　C. 教育
(4) 业余　　　　　　D. 空气
(5) 高等　　　　　　E. 产值

练习三、从今天学习的生词中选择合适的词填空
1. 道路两旁建起了很多 _____ 的建筑物。
2. 我从来不吃洋葱,因为我不 _____ 它的味道。
3. 他一到周末就在家里看电视,没有别的业余 _____。
4. 小伙子送来了一束象征着 _____ 的玫瑰花。
5. 教授正在指导学生做一个有趣的化学 _____。
6. 这台冰箱经常出毛病,我们得买一台 _____ 的了。
7. 他喜欢在早晨运动,因为早晨的空气特别 _____。
8. 我觉得在大学最难的课是 _____ 数学。
9. 去年中国国民生产 _____（GDP）增长了10%。
10. 这辆自行车是我十年前买的,现在虽然 _____ 了,但是非常好骑。

练习一:
略
练习二:
(1) D　　(2) E　　(3) A　　(4) B　　(5) C
练习三:
1. 高大　2. 喜欢　3. 爱好　4. 爱情　5. 实验
6. 新　　7. 新鲜　8. 高等　9. 总值　10. 旧

---

gǎnxiè
感谢 （甲）动/名
① thank ② gratitude

常用搭配
表示感谢 express thanks
感谢信 a grateful letter

用法示例
感谢你所做的一切。
Thank you for everything.
我们衷心感谢你。
Our grateful thanks go out to you.
我想借此机会对各位表示感谢。
I'd like to take this opportunity to thank everyone.

jīngguò　　　　　　　　　　lùguò
经过　　　　⊜ 路过　　　（甲）动/名
① to pass; through ② course

常用搭配
经过邮局 pass a post office
经过努力工作 through hard work
经过调查 through investigation

用法示例
我去图书馆得经过那家商店。
I have to pass the store on my way to the library.
经过几次失败,他终于通过了考试。
After some unsuccessful attempts, he has finally passed the exam.
跟我详细说说事故发生的经过。
Give me all the details of the accident.

gǎndào
感到　　⊜ 觉得　　（甲）动
feel; sense

常用搭配
对……感到满足(失望)
be satisfied (disappointed) with...
感到恶心 feel sick　　感到伤心 feel sad

用法示例
发现她也在那里,我感到很吃惊。
I was amazed to find her there too.
他的成就让他的父亲感到欣慰。
His achievement gratified his father.
看到我的家人都安全,我感到很庆幸。
It was a blessing to find that my family was all safe.

gǎnjī　　　　　　　zéguài
感激　　⊗ 责怪　　（乙）动
appreciate; be grateful

【常用搭配】
出于感激 out of gratitude
表达感激之情 express one's gratitude
【用法示例】
确实非常感激您！
Thank you very much indeed!
我真的很感激你的帮助。
I really appreciate your help.
为此你应该感激他。
You should be thankful to him for it.

bàogào
报告 （乙）动/名
① make known ② report
【常用搭配】
向……报告 report to sb　写报告 write a report
调查报告 report of a survey　事故报告 accident report
【用法示例】
我将向总部报告这些情况。
I will report the conditions to headquarters.
他正在看一篇关于道路状况的报告。
He is reading a report on the state of the roads.
报告披露他曾坐过牢。
The report disclosed that he had served time in prison.

bàomíng
报名 （乙）动
enter one's name; apply; sign up
【常用搭配】
报上名了 be enrolled
报名参军 sign up for military service
报名学习……课程 sign up for a course
【用法示例】
我已报名修一门文学课程。
I've signed up to take a literature course.
他已报名参加空军。
He signed up with the Air Force.
我已报名参加跳高比赛。
I've entered for the high jump.

dìdiǎn
地点 （乙）名
location; place; site
【常用搭配】
集合地点 assembling place　见面的地点 a place to meet
【用法示例】
他提前到达了会面地点。
He arrived at the meeting place beforehand.
咱们定好下次会议的时间和地点吧。
Let's arrange a time and place for our next meeting.
我这篇小说中所有的地点和人物都是虚构的。
All the places and characters in my novel are entirely fictitious.

gāodù
高度 （乙）名/形
① height ② high degree ③ highly
【常用搭配】
房间的高度 the height of a room
受到高度赞扬 be highly praised
【用法示例】
客机在两万米的高度飞行。
The airplane flew at an altitude of 20 km.
在这样的高度，雪永不融化。
At these altitudes snow never melts.
她的教学工作受到高度评价。
Her teaching was highly commended.

gǎndòng
感动 （乙）动
① moving ② to move (sb)
【常用搭配】
深受感动 be moved deeply
令人感动的话语 words that have the power to move
【用法示例】
我很受感动。
I was moved. (I was touched.)
我们都被他的爱国精神深深感动了。
We are all deeply moved by his patriotism.
她的热心感动了大家。
Her fervor moved all of us.

guīju
规矩 （丙）名/形
① rule; custom ② well-behaved
【常用搭配】
定一条规矩 make a rule　违反规矩 break rules
【用法示例】
妈妈叮嘱孩子要守规矩。
The mother bade the child behave himself.
他总是按规矩办事。
He always works by the rules.
放规矩些！
Behave yourself!

zhèngzhuàng
症状 （丙）名
symptom
【常用搭配】
临床症状 clinical symptom
中毒的症状 poisoning symptom
【用法示例】
这种病的症状是发烧和恶心。
The symptoms of this disease are fever and nausea.
医生研究病人的症状后，做出诊断。
The doctor made his diagnosis after studying the patient's symptoms.

高峰 gāofēng ⊛ 低谷 dīgǔ （丙）名

summit; peak

常用搭配
高峰会谈 summit talks
交通的高峰时间 peak traffic hours

用法示例
早晨九点是高峰时刻。
Traffic reaches a peak at 9:00 in the morning.
玩具销售额在圣诞节前夕达到最高峰。
Toy sales peaked just before Christmas.

感谢、感激

1、两个词都是动词，都有"be grateful"的意思，都可以做"表示"的宾语，都可以带宾语。如：①对他们表示感谢/感激。②我非常感谢/感激我的老师。

As verbs, both have the meaning of "be grateful", both can be the object of 表示, and both can be followed by objects. For example: Our grateful thanks are given to them. I really appreciate my teacher.

2、"感激"的感情比"感谢"更深刻，"感激"表达得比较含蓄、内在，通常可以带程度补语，如：感激得不知说什么好。而"感谢"比较外在，对通常的帮助或好意常用"感谢"。

The feeling of 感激 is more profound than 感谢, and 感激 is more implicit, and is often followed by a complement of degree. For example: I feel so grateful that I cannot express my gratitude with words. 感谢 is more overt, and applied to any usual kindness or help.

练习一、根据拼音写汉字，根据汉字写拼音

gǎn（　） bào（　） dì（　） （　）ju（　）zhuàng
（　）激   （　）告   （　）点   规（　） 症（　）

练习二、搭配连线
(1) 调查　　　　　A. 参军
(2) 集合　　　　　B. 伤心
(3) 报名　　　　　C. 报告
(4) 表示　　　　　D. 地点
(5) 感到　　　　　E. 感谢

练习三、从今天学习的生词中选择合适的词填空
1. _____ 三个月的学习,他已经有了很大进步。
2. 我们学校要举办太极拳学习班,我想 _____ 参加。
3. 他向总经理 _____ 了出国考察的情况。
4. 他肚子疼,头晕,还发烧,医生说这是中毒的 _____ 。
5. 这部电影非常感人,很多观众都 _____ 得落泪了。
6. 我们宿舍有个 _____ ——谁起得最晚,谁收拾房间。
7. 一想到女儿的病,她就 _____ 很难过。
8. 我要 _____ 所有关心和帮助过我的人。
9. 我们设计的施工方案受到了专家的 _____ 赞扬。
10. 他只告诉我聚会的时间,却没说 _____ ,我去哪儿参加呢?

练习一：
略

练习二：
(1) C　　(2)D　　(3)A　　(4)E　　(5)B

练习三：
1. 经过　　2. 报名　　3. 报告　　4. 症状　　5. 感动
6. 规矩　　7. 感到　　8. 感谢　　9. 高度　　10. 地点

jìnxíng
进行 (甲)动
be in progress; proceed

常用搭配
进行研究 conduct research
进行调查 carry out investigations

用法示例
工作正按计划进行。
The work is proceeding according to plan.
事情进行得怎么样?
How are things going?
表演正好进行到一半时停电了。
The light went out right in the middle of the performance.

zàijiàn
再见 (甲)动
① bye-bye ② goodbye

常用搭配
李老师,再见! Good-bye, Mr. Li!

用法示例
我得走了,再见!
I must go now, good-bye!
再见了,很高兴见到你。
Good-bye. Nice seeing you!
再见,旅途愉快。
Good-bye, and have a good journey.

jiàoyù
教育 (甲)动/名
① educate ② education

常用搭配
高等教育 advanced education
职业教育 vocational education
教育软件 educational software

用法示例
她受过良好的教育。
She has had a good education.
教育能开发人的潜能。
Education develops potential abilities.
老师的职责就是教育学生。
A teachers' duty is to educate students.

gǎizhèng
改正 (乙)动
to correct; amend

常用搭配
改正错误 to correct mistakes
改正缺点 to fix shortcomings

用法示例
请改正账单上的错误。
Please rectify the mistake in the bill.
他在信上改正了几个错误。
He made several corrections to the letter.
拼写错误已经得到了改正。
The spelling mistakes have been corrected.

jiūzhèng
纠正 (乙)动
to correct; to make right

常用搭配
纠正(他的)错误 to rectify (his) a fault

用法示例
你发音的毛病是可以纠正的。
Your faults of pronunciation can be remedied.
我们必须纠正社会上的不正之风。
We must rectify the corrupt practices in society.
他以为我是日本人,但我马上纠正了他。
He thought I was Japanese but I soon put him right.

fàngdà
放大 反 缩小 (乙)动
enlarge; magnify

常用搭配
放大照片 to enlarge a photo
放大镜 the magnifying glass

用法示例
这台显微镜将物体放大了100倍。
The microscope can magnify the object 100 times.
我打算放大这张照片。
I planned to enlarge this photograph.
警方把失踪姑娘的照片放大了。
The police had the photograph of the missing girl enlarged.

jiēchù
接触 (乙)动
contact; be in touch with

常用搭配
与他们保持接触。Keep in touch with them.

用法示例
他在大学里接触到了新思想。
He met with new ideas at college.
接触不良有时会造成断电。
A poor contact causes power to fail occasionally.
孩子们跟病人有过接触吗?
Have the children been in contact with the patient?

jiēdài
接待 同 招待 (乙)动
① receive (a visit) ② entertain

常用搭配
接待处 the reception desk
接待客人 to receive guests

【用法示例】
在接待处等我吧。
Wait for me at reception.
罗马每年要接待几百万名游客。
Rome welcomes millions of visitors each year.
他们很冷淡地接待了我。
They gave me a cool reception.

教材 jiàocái ◎ 课本 kèběn （乙）名
teaching material; textbook
【常用搭配】
一套教材 a series of textbooks
编写教材 compile teaching materials
【用法示例】
这所学校深受缺乏教材之苦。
The school labors under the disadvantage of not having enough textbooks.
李教授正在编写教材。
Professor Li is compiling a textbook.

放松 fàngsōng （丙）动
loosen; relax
【常用搭配】
放松一下 have a relaxing   放松警惕 relax vigilance
【用法示例】
让你的肌肉慢慢放松。
Let your muscles relax slowly.
别为这事担心,放松些。
Don't worry about it, just try to relax.
警惕性是一刻也不能放松的。
You cannot afford to relax your vigilance for a moment.

打破 dǎpò ⊚ 维持 wéichí （丙）动
break; smash
【常用搭配】
打破花瓶 smash the vase
打破僵局 break the ice
【用法示例】
你知道是谁打破了窗户吗?
Do you know who broke the window?
她想要打破世界纪录。
She is attempting to break the world record.
我们做些较小的让步,就可能会打破僵局。
We are making minor concessions, which might act as ice breakers.

手势 shǒushì （丙）名
gesture; gesticulation
【常用搭配】
做手势 makes gestures

用手势沟通 communicate through gestures
【用法示例】
演讲者常做手势来强调他所说的话。
A speaker often gesticulates to emphasize something he is saying.
他做手势要学生安静。
He gestured for the students to be quiet.

 词义辨析

改正、纠正
　　两个动词都是"使正确"的意思,"改正"用得更普遍一些,通常用于自己的错误,"纠正"则通常用于别人的错误,如:你应该先改正自己的毛病,再去纠正别人的错误。
　　The two verbs mean "to correct", 改正 is used more often than 纠正. 改正 is often applied to oneself; 纠正 is often applied to others. For example: You should correct your own faults before you try to correct others'.

 练习

练习一、根据拼音写汉字，根据汉字写拼音

dǎ（　） jiū（　） jiē（　） （　）sōng （　）shì
（　）破 （　）正 （　）触 放（　） 手（　）

练习二、搭配连线

(1) 放松　　　　　　A. 纪录
(2) 打破　　　　　　B. 缺点
(3) 改正　　　　　　C. 警惕
(4) 纠正　　　　　　D. 客人
(5) 接待　　　　　　E. 发音

练习三、从今天学习的生词中选择合适的词填空

1. 她对我做 _____，让我小声说话，因为孩子在睡觉呢。
2. 我们打算考完试去海边 _____ 两天。
3. 通过几次 _____，我发现那个古怪的老人其实很善良。
4. 他是导游，每周都要 _____ 两批来这里观光的客人。
5. 对于初学汉语的人来说，好的老师和好的 _____ 都很重要。
6. 大家都认为这张照片很漂亮，只是太小了，所以他就 _____ 了一张，挂在了墙上。
7. 我的车翻到了河里，幸好，我 _____ 了车窗玻璃，从里边爬了出来。
8. 老师耐心地 _____ 我的发音错误。
9. 政府正在 _____ 教育改革。
10. 从小，父母就 _____ 我对人要有礼貌。

答案

练习一：
略

练习二：
(1) C　　(2)A　　(3)B　　(4)E　　(5)D

练习三：
1. 手势　 2. 放松　 3. 接触　 4. 接待　 5. 教材
6. 放大　 7. 打破　 8. 纠正　 9. 进行　 10. 教育

 星期五

hǎoxiàng
好像 （甲）动

① as if ② seem like

常用搭配

他好像病了。He seemed to be ill.
好像要下雨。It looks like rain.

用法示例

她当时看起来好像什么事都没发生似的。
She looks as if nothing had happened to her.
他好像是个永远年轻的小伙子。
He seems to be an eternal child.
他的宠物猫死了，他好像很伤心。
When his pet cat died, he seemed very sad.

xiàng
像 （甲）动/介

① as if ② alike

常用搭配

像我这样做。Do as I do.
我像爸爸。I am like my father.

用法示例

你不像会发脾气的人。
It's not like you to take offense.
我希望能像她那样唱歌。
I wish I could sing like her.
他们俩像极了。
They are like two peas in a pod.

zhùyì
注意 （甲）动

① (pay) attention (to) ② notice ③ Look out!

常用搭配

请注意！Attention please!
引起注意 attract attention

用法示例

注意，汽车过来了。
Look out, there's a car coming.
请大家注意一下。
May I have your attention please?
我没注意到这个细节。
The detail escaped my notice.

zhǔyi
主意 （甲）名

idea

常用搭配

有个主意 have an idea　　好主意 good idea
改主意 change one's mind

用法示例
那听上去是个好主意。
That sounds like a good idea.
我已经改主意了。
I've changed my mind.
在户外聚会是我的主意。
It's my idea to hold the party outside of the house.

wánquán
完全　◎彻底　（甲）形
① complete ② completely; entirely

常用搭配
完全信任 absolute trust
完全独立 absolute independence
完全同意 entirely agree

用法示例
你完全误解了我的意思。
You mistook my meaning entirely.
这完全是我的错。
It's my fault entirely.
他说的完全正确。
What he said is completely right.

wánzhěng
完整　◎残缺　（乙）形
whole; full

常用搭配
完整的叙述 a full account
完整的故事 a complete story
领土完整 territorial integrity

用法示例
这只古代的碗保存得十分完整。
The ancient bowl remained intact.
那座古老的庙宇还在，但是不完整了。
The ancient temple is still there, but it is not intact.

dǎrǎo
打扰　◎干扰　（乙）动
disturb

常用搭配
请勿打扰 Do not disturb.

用法示例
我工作时，请不要打扰我。
Please don't disturb me while I'm working.
对不起，打扰一下。
I'm sorry to bother you.
他老是打扰我。
He's constantly disturbing me.

bànshì
办事　（乙）动
① handle affairs ② to work

常用搭配
帮某人办事 help sb to do sth

用法示例
双方都应按协议条款办事。
Both sides should act according to the provisions of the agreement.
我要出去办一件重要的事。
I am going out to take care of an important matter.

shǒuduàn
手段　（乙）名
method; means

常用搭配
军事手段 military means　违法的手段 illegal means
不择手段地 by fair means or foul

用法示例
无线电和电视是重要的通信手段。
Radio and television are both important means of communication.
他仅把结婚当作达到目的的手段，他只是想要妻子的财产。
He regarded his marriage merely as a means to an end: he just wanted his wife's wealth.
我宁可贫穷，也不愿用不正当手段赚钱。
I would rather remain poor than make money by dishonest means.

shǒuxù
手续　（乙）名
procedure; formalities

常用搭配
入境手续 immigration procedure
报关手续 customs formalities　出口手续 export procedures

用法示例
在银行开账户要办什么手续？
What's the procedure for opening a bank account?
必须办妥某些手续才能移民。
Certain formalities have to be completed before one can emigrate.
向公司索取退款的手续很繁琐。
Obtaining a refund from the company is a complicated procedure.

fàngyìng
放映　（丙）动
show (a movie)

常用搭配
放映电影 show a film

用法示例
昨天晚上学校放映了一部西部影片。
Yesterday evening the school showed a cowboy film.
这部电影已在电影院及电视上放映过了。
The film has been screened in the cinema, and on TV.

fángshǒu
防守　◎进攻　（丙）动
defend; protect (against)

📌 **常用搭配**
防守阵地 defend one's position

📌 **用法示例**
他们有三个队员防守球门。
They had three players defending the goal.
他善于防守，而我善于进攻。
He's good at defending; and I am good at attacking.

bànlǐ
办理 （丙）动
handle; transact

📌 **常用搭配**
办理登机手续 check in for a flight
办理手续 go through procedures

📌 **用法示例**
他们对办理的每项业务收取一定的费用。
They charge a fixed rate for each transaction.
我们正在办理申请签证的手续。
We are going through the procedures of applying for visas.

好像、像

1、"好像"和"像"都是动词，都可以用来推测或对比，表示"和……相像"或"似乎是"的意思；都可以与"似的"、"一样"连用，如：①他像/好像猫一样地爬上了树。②我像/好像是感冒了。

Both 好像 and 像 are verbs, meaning "to be alike" and "to seem to be", and are applied to conjectures or comparisons based on such similarities; they can collocate with 似的 and 一样. E.g. ① He climbed the tree like a cat. ② I feel like I'm catching a cold.

2、"好像"多用于推测，"像"多用于类比。比如：你好像反对这个计划。他们像是亲兄弟。"像"还有"比如""诸如""例如"的意思。比如：我认识他们，像老张、老王，都是老朋友了。

好像 is more often used to express conjecture; 像 is more often used to comparisons based on similarities. For example: It seems you object to the plan. They look like two siblings. 像 has another meaning of "for example" or "such as". For instance: I know some of them, such as Lao Zhang, Lao Wang, who are my old friends.

练习一、根据拼音写汉字，根据汉字写拼音
shǒu（　）wán（　）bàn（　）（　）shǒu（　）rǎo
（　）续　（　）整　（　）理　防（　）　打（　）

练习二、搭配连线
(1) 完全　　　　A. 安全
(2) 放映　　　　B. 主意
(3) 注意　　　　C. 同意
(4) 改变　　　　D. 手续
(5) 入境　　　　E. 电影

练习三、从今天学习的生词中选择合适的词填空
1. 她和姐姐是双胞胎，两个人长得特别_____。
2. 老师在讲课前，先给我们_____了一段介绍中国历史的纪录片。
3. 妈妈怕我们_____爸爸写作，就让我们去姥姥家过暑假了。
4. 你们不要着急，我们得按照法律程序_____。
5. 我认为你说得很对，我_____同意你的看法。
6. 比赛的时候，一部分球员负责_____，另一部分球员负责进攻。
7. 我们得提前到机场_____登机手续。
8. 他使用各种_____对付他的竞争对手，但最后还是失败了。
9. 他们想定居在加拿大，最近正在办理移民_____。
10. 他_____不知道自己得了很严重的病。

答案

练习一：
略

练习二：
(1) C　(2)E　(3)A　(4)B　(5)D

练习三：
1. 像　2. 放映　3. 打扰　4. 办事　5. 完全
6. 防守　7. 办理　8. 手段　9. 手续　10. 好像

第1月,第2周的练习

练习一、根据词语给加点的字注音
1.(　) 2.(　) 3.(　) 4.(　) 5.(　)
爱好　笼罩　规矩　接触　主意

练习二、根据拼音填写词语
　　shǒu　　shǒu　　shì　　shí　　shì
1.防(　) 2.(　)势 3.考(　) 4.(　)验 5.办(　)

练习三、辨析并选择合适的词填空
1. 他想明年参加汉语水平(　)。(考试、考)
2. 我妹妹想(　)北京大学。(考试、考)
3. 他的(　)是打篮球,一放学他就去操场打球。(喜欢、爱好)
4. 她(　)蓝色,她有很多蓝色的衣服。(喜欢、爱好)
5. 你们在我最困难的时候帮助了我,真不知道该如何表达我的(　)之情。(感谢、感激)
6. 新郎和新娘举起酒杯,向所有参加他们婚礼的来宾表示(　)。(感谢、感激)
7. 太极拳老师耐心地(　)学生的动作。(改正、纠正)
8. 我又检查了一遍试卷,(　)了两个错误。(改正、纠正)
9. 她走路的样子真(　)她妈妈。(好像、像)
10. 听到这个消息,她什么话也没说,(　)对此不太感兴趣。(好像、像)

练习四、选词填空
重要　主要　高等　高度　放大
放松　手续　手段　感到　感动
1. 这本书(　)介绍了中国改革开放以后的情况。
2. 中国的(　)教育发展得很快,越来越多的年轻人有机会上大学了。
3. 很多人在观看这部电影的时候都(　)得落泪了。
4. 最近太累了,这个周末我要好好(　)一下。
5. 这是一次非常(　)的会议,所有领导都必须参加。
6. 字太小了,看不清,能把它(　)3倍吗?
7. 听说公司要派我去中国学习汉语,我(　)特别幸运。
8. 在国外旅游时千万要看好自己的护照,如果丢了,补办的(　)很麻烦。
9. 在进行射击比赛的时候,运动员的注意力要(　)集中。
10. 恐怖分子可能使用各种(　)对我们进行干扰,所以一定不能放松警惕。

练习五、写出下列词语的同义词
1. 感到(　)　　2. 考试(　)
3. 完全(　)　　4. 接待(　)
5. 爱好(　)

练习六、写出下列词语的反义词
1. 新鲜(　)　　2. 高大(　)
3. 放大(　)　　4. 完整(　)
5. 主要(　)

 **答案**

练习一:
1. hào　2. zhào　3. ju　4. chù　5. zhǔ

练习二:
1. 守　2. 手　3. 试　4. 实　5. 事

练习三:
1. 考试　2. 考　3. 爱好　4. 喜欢　5. 感激
6. 感谢　7. 纠正　8. 改正　9. 像　10. 好像

练习四:
1. 主要　2. 高等　3. 感动　4. 放松　5. 重要
6. 放大　7. 感到　8. 手续　9. 高度　10. 手段

练习五:
1. 觉得　2. 测验　3. 彻底　4. 招待　5. 嗜好

练习六:
1. 陈旧　2. 矮小　3. 缩小　4. 残缺　5. 次要

1月 第3周的学习内容

星期一

pángbiān
旁边　　　　　　　　　　　　　（甲）名
① lateral ② side
【常用搭配】
站在门旁边 stand by the door
【用法示例】
我坐在他旁边。
I sat by his side.
中国银行就在邮局的旁边。
The Bank of China stands next to the post office.

jǐnzhāng　　　　　fàngsōng
紧张　　　反 放松　　　　　　　（甲）形
nervous; tense; intense
【常用搭配】
别紧张！Don't be nervous!
紧张的学习生活 intense study of life
【用法示例】
他看上去很紧张。
He looks nervous.
他一紧张就结巴。
He stammers when he feels nervous.
外科医生问他是否感到紧张。
The surgeon asked him if he felt nervous.

shīqù　　　　　huòdé
失去　　　反 获得　　　　　　　（甲）动
lose; to be bereaved of
【常用搭配】
失去工作 lose one's job
与某人失去联系 lose touch with sb
失去生命 lose one's life
【用法示例】
那一击打得他失去了知觉。
The blow caused him to lose consciousness.
我对那事已失去兴趣了。
I've lost interest in that subject.
他失去理智了。
He has lost his mind.

shīwàng
失望　　　　　　　　　　　　　（乙）形/动
① disappointed ② to despair
【常用搭配】
令人失望的结果 a disappointing result
我很失望。I'm disappointed.
【用法示例】
我们对我们的新老师很失望。
We are disappointed in our new teacher.
我父亲不同意给我买新自行车，我很失望。
To my disappointment, my father didn't agree to buy me a new bike.
结果使他很失望。
The result disappointed him.

dòngwù
动物　　　　　　　　　　　　　（乙）名
animal
【常用搭配】
冷血动物 cold-blooded animal　保护动物 protected species
动物园 zoo
【用法示例】
他在家中养了一些小动物。
He keeps some small animals in his home.
狮子是凶猛的动物。
As lion is a fierce animal.

àn
按　　　　　　　　　　　　　　（乙）动/介
① to press ② according to; in the light of
【常用搭配】
按门铃 press a doorbell　按理 according to reason
按规定 according to regulations
【用法示例】
按这个按钮开动引擎。
Press this button to start the engine.
工作正按计划进行。
The work is proceeding according to plan.
图书馆里的藏书是按科目分类的。
The books in the library were distributed according to subject.

ànzhào　　　　　yīzhào
按照　　　同 依照　　　　　　　（乙）介
according to; in accordance with
【常用搭配】
按照惯例 according to practice
按照法律 according to law
【用法示例】
我按照老板的指示售出了这所房子。
I sold the house in accordance with the boss' orders.

在词典中,词是按照字母拼写顺序排列的。
In dictionaries, words are listed according to their orthography.

ànshí
按时　　　　　　　　　　　　　(乙)副
on schedule; on time

常用搭配
按时回家 return home on time
按时完成工作 finish the work on schedule

用法示例
我们将按时开船。
We will sail on schedule.
老板吩咐工作必须按时完成。
The boss ordered that the work be done on time.
她总是按时上课。
She is always punctual for class.

fángzhǐ
防止　　　　　　　　　　　　　(乙)动
prevent

常用搭配
防止火灾 prevent a fire
防止污染 prevent pollution

用法示例
防止犯罪是警察的职责。
It is the job of the police to prevent crime.
我们该如何防止这种疾病蔓延呢?
How can we prevent the disease from spreading?
这些规章制度旨在防止发生事故。
These regulations are intended to prevent accidents.

jǐnjí　　　　　jǐnpò
紧急　　　◎紧迫　　　　　　　(丙)形
① urgent ② exigency

常用搭配
紧急出口 emergency exits
紧急状态 state of emergency
紧急任务 an urgent job

用法示例
出现紧急情况时,请给警察打电话。
In an emergency, telephone the police.
人们被召集到这里举行紧急会议。
People convened here for an emergency meeting.
这是一件十分紧急的事情。
This is a matter of great urgency.

fángzhì
防治　　　　　　　　　　　　　(丙)动
prevent and cure

常用搭配
防治污染 pollution prevention
防治传染病 prevent and cure infectious diseases

用法示例
政府拨款两百万元用于防治水灾。
The government appropriated two million yuan for flood control.
科学家们说,他们在防治癌症方面开始有所突破。
Scientists say they are beginning to make break throughs in the fight against cancer.

jǐnqiào
紧俏　　　　　　　　　　　　　(丙)形
(merchandise) in high demand

常用搭配
紧俏商品 scarce commodity

用法示例
把紧俏商品留给肯出大价钱的主顾们。
Keep the rare items for the customers who will pay the best prices for them.
这种水果在市场上很紧俏。
This kind of fruit is hard to get in the market.

词义辨析

按、按照、依照

1、三个介词都表示以某一事物作为言论行为的根据,有时可以互换。如:按(按照/依照)经理的指示,这事应该这样办。

These three prepositions mean "to take something as evidence or a basis", and are sometimes interchangeable. E.g. According to the managers instructions, it should be handled in this way.

2、其中"按",可以与单音节词搭配,如按日计算,按人分配,"按照"和"依照"不可以。与"按照"相比,"依照"更强调根据性,更为正式和书面化,涉及法律的句子一般用"依照"。如:这件事必须依照法律规定予以解决。

按 can be used with monosyllabic words, e.g. daily count(按日计算), distributed according to the number of people (按人分配), but 按照 and 依照 can not. Compared with 按照, 依照 stresses that an action is not groundless, and the statement is more formal and literary, it is often used in sentences relating to law. e.g. This matter should be resolved according to the law.

3、"按"还是动词,表示用手压,如按按钮。

按 is also a verb, means "to press with the hand", e.g. to press a button

 **练习**

练习一、根据拼音写汉字,根据汉字写拼音
jǐn (　) àn (　) fáng (　)(　) wàng páng (　)
(　)俏 (　)照 (　)治 失(　) (　)边

练习二、搭配连线
(1) 防治　　　　　A. 法律
(2) 失去　　　　　B. 失望
(3) 按照　　　　　C. 回家
(4) 感到　　　　　D. 生命
(5) 按时　　　　　E. 污染

练习三、从今天学习的生词中选择合适的词填空
1. 第一次在这么多人面前演讲,我感到很 _____。
2. 为了 _____ 水源被污染,政府采取了紧急措施。
3. 爸爸工作特别忙,很少 _____ 回家。
4. 这种产品的需求量很大,在市场上很 _____。
5. _____ 传统习俗,中秋节的时候,一家人要聚在一起吃月饼。
6. 他在学校很优秀,对人也十分友善,几乎从来没有让他的父母 _____ 过。
7. 对于这位孤独的老人来说,生活好像已经 _____ 了乐趣。
8. 这个医疗小组一直致力于 _____ 肺癌的研究工作。
9. 我刚到家就接到公司的电话,说有 _____ 的事情,让我马上回去。
10. 这是我们全家的照片,奶奶抱着妹妹,我站在他们的 _____。

答案

练习一:
略

练习二:
(1) E　　(2) D　　(3) A　　(4) B　　(5) C

练习三:
1. 紧张　　2. 防止　　3. 按时　　4. 紧俏　　5. 按照
6. 失望　　7. 失去　　8. 防治　　9. 紧急　　10. 旁边

 星期二

fùjìn
附近　　🔄 yáoyuǎn 遥远　　(甲)名
nearby

常用搭配
附近的警察局 a nearby police station
他住在附近。He lives nearby.

用法示例
教堂在学校附近。
The church is close to the school.
他通常在附近的超市购物。
He usually shops at the nearby supermarket.
我把钥匙掉在这附近了。
I dropped my key somewhere around here.

yǐqián　　　　yǐhòu
以前　　🔄 以后　　(甲)名
before; formerly

常用搭配
两年以前 two years ago
九点以前 before nine o'clock
天黑以前 before dark　很久以前 long ago

用法示例
我以前从来没有见过他。
I have never met him before.
法官否决了以前的判决。
The judge overruled the previous decision.
这与你以前说的恰恰相反。
It's a flat contradiction of what you said before.

cóngqián
从前　　(甲)名
① long ago ② at an earlier time

常用搭配
从前的事 things in the past

用法示例
从前,有一位美丽的公主。
Once upon a time, there lived a beautiful princess.
从前,在一个小村庄里住着一位老人。
Long ago, there was an old man living in a small village.
我从前没有见过他。
I hadn't seen him previously.

zuòjiā
作家　　(乙)名
author; writer

常用搭配
著名作家 famous writer
剧作家 playwriter

用法示例
谁是你最喜欢的作家?
Who is your favorite writer?
莎士比亚是一位伟大的作家。
Shakespeare is a great writer.

zuòzhě
作者 (乙) 名
writer
常用搭配
报告的作者 the writer of a report
文章的作者 the writer of an article
用法示例
这篇短文的作者是一个年轻人。
The writer of the passage is a young man.
演完戏之后，他们要求与作者见面。
After the play they called for the author to show himself.
这本书未经作者许可就被翻译成了英文。
The book was translated into English without permission from the author.

dìdài
地带 (乙) 名
zone
常用搭配
危险地带 a danger zone   森林地带 forest regions
用法示例
有些植物生长在沙漠地带。
Some plants grow in desert regions.
沿海地带的商业发展得很快。
Commerce develops rapidly in coastal areas.

jiàoshòu
教授 (乙) 名
professor
常用搭配
副教授 associate professor
名誉教授 honorary professor
用法示例
这所大学有许多外国教授。
There are many foreign professors in this university.
李教授现在是师范大学的系主任。
Professor Li is the head of the department at Normal University now.

jiàoshī   lǎoshī
教师 ⓝ 老师 (乙) 名
teacher
常用搭配
小学教师 elementary teacher
英语教师 English teacher
用法示例
她是一个有责任心的教师。
She is a conscientious teacher.

我母亲是一位语文教师。
My mother is a language teacher.
玛丽胜任教师的工作吗?
Is Mary a competent teacher?

dìqū
地区 (乙) 名
region; area
常用搭配
干旱地区 dry region   热带地区 tropical region
用法示例
仙人掌生长在干旱地区。
Cacti live in dry regions.
北极地区的人很少。
There are few people in the Arctic regions.
我们准备在这个地区建一所学校。
We are going to build a school in this area.

liúyù
流域 (丙) 名
river basin; drainage area
常用搭配
黄河流域 the Yellow River basin
用法示例
这就是著名的长江流域。
This is the famous Yangtse River basin.
他在密西西比河流域拥有一个大农场。
He has a large farm in the Mississippi Valley.

liúxíng   shèngxíng
流行   ⓝ 盛行 (丙) 动/形
popular; fashionable
常用搭配
流行歌曲 popular songs
用法示例
你喜欢流行音乐吗?
Do you like popular music?
这项运动在我们国家很流行。
This sport is very popular in our country.

jiàoliàn
教练 (丙) 名
coach
常用搭配
足球教练 football coach
用法示例
教练让李林上场,换下了王刚。
The coach substituted Li Lin for Wang Gang.
他是我们的篮球主教练。
He is our chief basketball coach.

 词义辨析

从前、以前

1、"从前"和"以前"都是时间名词,都可以表示"过去的时候"。比如,我以前/从前去过长城。

从前 and 以前 are time nouns, and both can indicate "at an earlier time". e.g. I have been to the Great Wall before.

2、"以前"可以用在动词或时间名词后,"从前"不可以。"从前"听起来往往比"以前"更久远,常用于讲传说故事。比如:他离开家以前,一年以前。从前,有个国王……

以前 can be used after a verb or a time noun, 从前 can not. 从前 refers to a longer time ago than 以前, so 从前 is often used in story telling. For example: Before he left home…, one year ago. Long long ago, there was a king…

 练习

练习一、根据拼音写汉字,根据汉字写拼音

zuò(　) liú(　) jiào(　) (　)jìn (　)dài
(　)者 (　)域 (　)授 附(　) 地(　)

练习二、搭配连线

(1) 著名　　　　A. 教练
(2) 学校　　　　B. 作家
(3) 英语　　　　C. 附近
(4) 篮球　　　　D. 歌曲
(5) 流行　　　　E. 教师

练习三、从今天学习的生词中选择合适的词填空

1. 他以前是著名的篮球运动员,现在是我们大学篮球队的_____。
2. 这位年轻的科学家是北京大学的副_____。
3. 妈妈要求她在晚上十一点_____回家。
4. 这位_____非常有名,他的作品也很受欢迎。
5. 体育馆就在我家_____,走路5分钟就到了。
6. 他现在的女朋友是一位中学物理_____。
7. 我喜欢古典音乐,很少听_____歌曲。
8. 这是一种热带_____的植物。
9. 爷爷最近喜欢谈_____的事,他小时候是在农村长大的。
10. 我想认识一下这部小说的_____,听说是一位很有才华的年轻人。

答案

练习一:
略

练习二:
(1) B　　(2)C　　(3)E　　(4)A　　(5)D

练习三:
1. 教练　2. 教授　3. 以前　4. 作家　5. 附近
6. 教师　7. 流行　8. 地区　9. 从前　10. 作者

星期三

dǎsuàn
打算 (甲)动/名
① intend; plan ② intention

常用搭配
你打算怎么做？How are you going to do it?
你有什么打算？What is your intention?

用法示例
今晚我打算早些睡觉。
I mean to go to bed earlier tonight.
今天我打算读完这本书。
Today I intend to finish reading this book.
他们目前没有结婚的打算。
At present they have no intention of getting married.

jìhuà
计划 (甲)动/名
plan; project

常用搭配
制订计划 draw up a plan 五年计划 a five-year plan
商业计划 a business program

用法示例
他们计划劫持一架飞机。
They planned to hijack a plane.
你同意我的计划吗？
Do you agree with my plan?
我开始实施我的计划了。
I began to carry out my plan.

zhōuwéi
周围 ◎ 四周 sìzhōu (甲)名
① surrounding ② around

常用搭配
向周围看 look around
学校周围的环境 school surroundings

用法示例
这座房子周围的环境很优美。
The house is localed in very beautiful surroundings.
周围的农田渐渐变成了住宅区。
Gradually the surrounding farmland was turned into residential areas.
我们聚集在篝火周围唱歌。
We gathered round the fire and sang songs.

duìmiàn
对面 (乙)名
opposite

常用搭配
对面的房子 the houses opposite
在教堂对面 opposite the church

用法示例
银行在超市对面。
The bank is opposite the supermarket.
他们在桌子两边面对面坐着。
They sat opposite each other at the table.
把画挂在窗户对面的墙上。
Hang the picture on the wall opposite the window.

gàikuò
概括 (乙)动/形
① summarize ② brief

常用搭配
概括要点 summarize the main points
概括地讲 in brief

用法示例
请用几句话概括一下你的观点。
Please summarize your views in a few words.
邮递员的工作,概括地说就是"送信"。
The mailman's job can be summed up in the phrase "Delivers the mail."

gàiniàn
概念 (乙)名
conception; concept

常用搭配
时空概念 space-time concept
抽象概念 abstract concept
清晰的概念 a clear conception

用法示例
这个概念是她的理论的核心。
This concept is central to her theory.
掌握无限空间的概念是很难的。
It is difficult to grasp the concept of infinite space.
这两个概念之间有什么联系？
What is the connection between the two ideas?

xuānbù
宣布 (乙)动
announce; declare

常用搭配
宣布停火 announce a cease-fire
宣布某人无罪 declare sb. (to be) innocent

用法示例
他宣布竞选州长。
He announced his campaign to run for governor.
我现在宣布会议开幕。
I now declare this meeting open.
总统宣布将发行新货币。
The president announced that a new currency would be issued.

xuānchuán
宣传 (乙)动/名
① publicize ② publicity

常用搭配
宣传新书 publicize a new book
宣传员 publicist
宣传部门 publicily section

用法示例
那出戏剧纯属政治宣传。
The play is a sheer political propaganda.
反对吸烟的宣传很多，许多人因此戒了烟。
There has been so much publicity given to the anti smoking campaigus that many people have given it up.
她的新书得到了广泛宣传。
Her new book has attracted a lot of publicity.

wàimiàn
外面　　　　　lǐmiàn 反里面　　（乙）名
outside

常用搭配
在外面吃饭 eat out　　学校外面 outside the school

用法示例
我写信时，孩子们在外面玩儿。
While I was writing a letter, the children were playing outside.
您请进，但您的宠物得留在外面。
You may come in, but your pet has to stay outside.
这盒子外面是红的，里面是绿的。
The box was red on the outside and green on the inside.

xìnxī
信息　　　　　xiāoxi 消息　　（丙）名
news; information

常用搭配
信息时代 the information age　　收集信息 collect information
信息产业 information industry

用法示例
他的信息不准确。
His information is inaccurate.
你读过有关信息革命的那篇文章吗？
Have you read the article on the information revolution?
信息技术的发展是二十世纪技术上的最大进步。
The development of information technology has been the greatest technological advance of the 20th century.

chángyuǎn
长远　　　　　　　　　　（丙）形
long-term; long-range

常用搭配
长远规划 long-term plan　　从长远看 in the long run

用法示例
短期内我们会赔钱，但从长远看，利润将会是丰厚的。
In the short term we will lose money, but in the long term our profits will be very large.
从长远看，物价肯定要涨。
Prices in the long run are bound to rise.

chángjiǔ
长久　　　　　duǎnzàn 反短暂　　（丙）形
① (for a) long time ② permanent

常用搭配
长久的和平 a lasting peace

用法示例
烟味会长久地附着在衣服上。
The smell of smoke clung to my clothes for a long time.
长久以来，我一直想见到她。
I have been hoping to see her for a long time.
我认为他们的婚姻不会长久。
I don't think their marriage will last very long.

词义辨析

打算、计划

　　1、"打算"和"计划"都是动词和名词，意思是对将要做的事情的安排或想法，如：在新的一年里，你有什么计划／打算？我打算／计划买一辆汽车。

　　打算 and 计划 are both verbs and nouns, and both mean "to plan" (verb) or "plan" (noun). E.g. What's your plan for the new year? I plan to buy a car.

　　2、"打算"比较随便，不太正式，多用于生活中的小事；"计划"更郑重、更正式，多用于政府、组织等。如：晚上打算吃什么？政府计划建一座桥。制定一个长期的发展计划。

　　打算 is more colloquial and casual, and is often used for the small events of our daily life; 计划 is more formal and serious, and is often used in official business in governments or organizations. For example: What would you like to eat for supper? The government plans to build a bridge. To develop a long-term project.

 练习

练习一、根据拼音写汉字，根据汉字写拼音
gài（　）zhōu（　）xuān（　）（　）xī（　）miàn
（　）括　（　）围　（　）布　信（　）　对（　）

练习二、搭配连线
(1) 邮局　　　　　　　A. 信息
(2) 抽象　　　　　　　B. 要点
(3) 概括　　　　　　　C. 对面
(4) 收集　　　　　　　D. 计划
(5) 制订　　　　　　　E. 概念

练习三、从今天学习的生词中选择合适的词填空
1. 明天就要举行新年联欢会了，你_____表演什么节目？
2. 在禁烟日这一天，很多电视节目都在_____不吸烟的好处。
3. 我正要出去的时候，发现有个人站在我家大门_____。
4. 政府正在实施教育发展和改革的五年_____。
5. 从_____看，保护环境对我们子孙后代的影响是非常重大的。
6. 通过计算机网络，我们可以查找很多有用的_____。
7. 银行_____从明年1月1日起提高存款利率。
8. 最后，老师_____了这节课的重点内容。
9. 我看见他在餐厅吃饭，坐在他_____的姑娘就是他的女朋友。
10. 室内污染会对人们的身体健康造成_____的危害。

 答案

练习一：
略
练习二：
(1) C　　(2)E　　(3)B　　(4)A　　(5)D
练习三：
1. 打算　　2. 宣传　　3. 外面　　4. 计划　　5. 长远
6. 信息　　7. 宣布　　8. 概括　　9. 对面　　10. 长久

 星期四

yuánlái
原来　　　　　yǐqián
　　　　　　同 **以前**　　　　　（甲）形
① original ② in fact

常用搭配
原来的计划 original plan

用法示例
这房子原来的主人不是他。
He is not the original owner of the house.
我以为她是学生，原来她是我们的新老师。
I thought she was a student. In fact, she is our new teacher.

zhīdao
知道　　　　　　　　　　　　（甲）动
be aware of; know

常用搭配
知道事实 know the facts
谁知道！（天知道！）Heaven knows!
知道问题的答案 know the solution to the problem

用法示例
我不知道发生了什么事。
I don't know what happened.
我不是猜的，我确实知道。
I'm not guessing; I really know.
我知道那是真的。
I know that is true.

zhōngjiān　　　　　liǎngbiān
中间　　　反 **两边**　　　　（甲）名
middle; intermediate

常用搭配
两山中间 between two mountains
在孩子们中间 amongst the children

用法示例
请站在屋子中间。
Please stand in the middle of the room.
在这两个镇的中间有一条河。
There is a river between these two towns.

běnlái
本来　　　　　　　　　　　　（乙）形
① essentially; originally ② of course

常用搭配
本来面目 real (unmasked) character

用法示例
他本来不必买这样一所大房子。
Of course he need not buy such a big house.
这件事本来就该这么办。
Of course the matter should have been handled in this way.

生活本来就是丰富多彩的。
It goes without saying that life is rich in color.

zhèngmíng
证明 (乙) 名/动
① certificate ② prove

常用搭配
出生证明 a certificate of birth
兹证明…… I hereby certify that...

用法示例
我可以证明她是诚实的。
I can certify to her honesty.
她证明了自己是当之无愧的冠军。
She proved herself a worthy champion.
你有什么证据证明这辆车是你的?
Have you got any proof that you own this car?

shēngmìng
生命 (乙) 名
life

常用搭配
冒生命危险 risk one's life　生命力 vitality

用法示例
动物和植物是有生命的。
Animals and plants have life.
写作是他的生命。
Writing is his life.
他牺牲了生命,把女儿从大火中救了出来。
He saved his daughter from the fire at the cost of his own life.

yōuměi
优美 (乙) 形
graceful; fine; elegant

常用搭配
优美的景色 a fine view
优美的乐曲 beautiful music

用法示例
这个芭蕾舞女演员的每一个动作都很优美。
All the ballerina's moves were graceful.
我们爬到山顶时,看到了优美的景色。
When we finally reached to top of the hill, we were met with a fine view.

yōuliáng zhuōliè
优良 反 拙劣 (乙) 形
fine; good

常用搭配
质量优良 fine quality　优良传统 good tradition

用法示例
我发现有些展品质量优良,设计美观。
I find some of the exhibits to be fine in quality, and beautiful in design.
两个队都表现了高超的技艺和优良的作风。
Both teams displayed first-rate technique, and a fine spirit.

她具有优良的品德。
She possesses good qualities.

yuánlǐ
原理 (丙) 名
principle

常用搭配
工作原理 principle of operation
经济学原理 the principles of economy

用法示例
该项装置是按照热力上升的原理运转的。
The system works on the principle that heat rises.
这两种医疗仪器的工作原理是一样的。
These two medical instruments work on the same principle.

guīhuà jìhuà
规划 同 计划 (丙) 名/动
① program ② plan

常用搭配
建设地铁的规划 a project to build a subway
五年规划 a five-year plan

用法示例
董事长用两个小时阐述了公司的规划。
The chairman expatiated for two hours on his plans for the company.
委员会正在制订建设新铁路的规划。
The committee is making a plan to build a new railway.

zhèngshí
证实 (丙) 动
confirm; attest

常用搭配
证实一则消息 confirm a piece of news

用法示例
证人证实了警察的陈述。
Witnesses corroborated the policeman's statement.
我们正在等待证实那则消息。
We are waiting for confirmation of the news.
我们的猜测已得到证实。
Our sneaking suspicions were confirmed.

shēnglǐ
生理 (丙) 名
physiology

常用搭配
生理机能 physiological function
生理反应 physiological reaction

用法示例
我在中学就学习过生理学。
We had studied physiology in middle school.
我们年老的时候头发会变白,这是正常的生理现象。
Our hair will turn white when we are old; it is a normal physiological phenomenon.

 ## 词义辨析

原来、本来

1、"原来"和"本来"都是形容词，都可以表示"起初"和"原有"的意思，如：我本来/原来想去上海参观，但是我现在改主意了。

Both 原来 and 本来 are adjectives, mean "former" and "original", e.g. I originally wanted to visit Shanghai, but now I have changed my mind.

2、"原来"用来表示发现了事情的真实情况或表示情况没有变化，也可以用于对比，往往作介宾结构的宾语。如：我以为她是大夫，原来她是护士。他还在原来的公司工作。他比原来胖多了。

原来 indicates that some fact has been found, or remains as usual. It can be used as a contrast, and is often used as the object of a preposition-object structure, for example: I thought she was the doctor; in fact, she was a nurse. He still works in the same firm. He is much fatter than he was.

3、"本来"可以表示按道理应该这样或早该这样的意思。如：你本来就不该迟到。

本来 indicates that something ought to have been so, e.g. Certainly, you shouldn't have been late.

 ## 练习

练习一、根据拼音写汉字，根据汉字写拼音

zhèng（　）yōu（　）guī（　）（　）lǐ　　zhī（　）
（　）实　　（　）良　　（　）划　　原（　）　　（　）道

练习二、搭配连线
(1) 风景　　　　　　　A. 生命
(2) 保护　　　　　　　B. 优良
(3) 质量　　　　　　　C. 优美
(4) 生理　　　　　　　D. 原理
(5) 工作　　　　　　　E. 现象

练习三、从今天学习的生词中选择合适的词填空

1. 你_____中国有多少个省吗？
2. 这是我们全家的照片，第一排左边的是我哥哥，右边的是我妹妹，我在他俩_____。
3. 我以为他听到这个消息会很吃惊，_____他早就知道了。
4. 中华民族有很多值得继承和发扬的_____传统。
5. 他们在会上讨论了公司未来发展的_____。
6. 事情发展的结果进一步_____了他当时的观点是对的。
7. 他病得很重，_____可能维持不了多长时间了。
8. 她_____的舞姿吸引了在场的每一位观众。
9. 在学习机器维修以前，你得先了解机器工作的_____。
10. 我_____打算学习一年汉语，现在觉得一年不够，还要延长一年。

答案

练习一：
略

练习二：
(1) C　　(2)A　　(3)B　　(4)E　　(5)D

练习三：
1. 知道　　2. 中间　　3. 原来　　4. 优良　　5. 规划
6. 证实　　7. 生命　　8. 优美　　9. 原理
10. 原来/本来

dǒng
懂 (甲)动
understand; know

常用搭配
懂道理 to have common sense
不懂礼貌 to be impolite

用法示例
我不懂这个词是什么意思。
I don't understand what the word means.
那个搬运工人听不懂我的话。
The porter could not understand me.
她懂法语。
She knows French.

biéde
别的 回其它 (甲)代
else; other

常用搭配
别的东西 anything else　别的路 another road

用法示例
你还要别的吗?
What else do you want?
今天没有别的事可做。
Nothing else remains to be done today.
这件衬衫太大了,我试件别的。
This shirt is too big; I'll try another.

wánchéng
完成 (甲)动
accomplish; complete

常用搭配
完成使命 accomplish a mission
完成任务 complete a task
完成作业 finish homework

用法示例
这个工作还没有完成。
The work is not yet complete.
拖了那么久,他终于完成了论文。
After much delay, he finished his paper at last.
什么时候才能完成这项工作?
When will the work be complete?

nuǎnhuo
暖和　　　liángkuài
　　　　　反 凉快 (甲)形
warm

常用搭配
天气很暖和。It's very warm.
感到暖和 to feel warm

用法示例
热饮料使他暖和起来了。
The hot drink warmed him.
到火旁边来暖和一下吧。
Come near the fire and warm yourself.
天气一天比一天暖和了。
It is getting warmer day by day.

shēngyi
生意　　　mǎimai
　　　　　同 买卖 (乙)名
business

常用搭配
做生意 do business
生意人 businessman

用法示例
这笔生意是无利可图的。
This business is unprofitable.
他们一起做过生意。
They've done some business together.
今年生意很糟糕。
Business has been bad this year.

shēngwù
生物 (乙)名
① living creature ② biological

常用搭配
海洋生物 marine animal
生物学 biology

用法示例
月球上没有生物。
There is no life on the moon.
这种生物生活在海洋深处。
This creature lives in the depths of the ocean.
李教授是中国著名的生物学家。
Professor Liu is a famous biologist in China.

cáiliào
材料 (乙)名
material

常用搭配
建筑材料 building materials

用法示例
这是一种防雨的材料。
This material is impervious to rainwater.
你可以把这些磁带当作听力材料。
You can use these tapes as listening materials.
他成批地购买原材料。
He buys the materials wholesale.

gǎizào
改造 (乙)动
change; convert

常用搭配
改造罪犯 to reform criminals

【用法示例】

那座楼房已改造成学校了。
That building has been converted into a school.
对罪犯的改造有了明显的效果。
The reformation of criminals has produced clear results.
他们把沙漠改造成了耕地。
They transformed a desert into farmland.

yuánliào
原料 （乙）名

【常用搭配】
工业原料 raw materials of industry

【用法示例】
这个工厂经常原料不足。
The factory is frequently lacking raw materials.
原料费用昂贵使得产品价格居高不下。
The high cost of raw materials is keeping prices up.

yuánzé
原则 （乙）名

principle

【常用搭配】
坚持原则 stick to one's principles
指导原则 governing principle
违背……原则 against the principle of

【用法示例】
他们原则上同意这个计划。
In principle they agree to the plan.
她把自己的原则体现在行动中。
She embodies her principles in her behavior.
勤俭节约的原则适用于各项事业。
The principles of diligence and frugality apply to all undertakings.

míngbai
明白  糊涂 （丙）形/动

① clear ② understand

【常用搭配】
我明白了。I've got it.

【用法示例】
我不明白她想说些什么。
I can not understand what she is trying to say.
我不明白他为什么放弃那个好机会。
I don't know why he gave up that chance.
他解释得很明白。
He explained it clearly.

gǎiliáng
改良 （丙）动

improve; to better

【常用搭配】
土壤改良 of soil quality   改良品种 improve breeds

【用法示例】
这还不够好,我要加以改良。
This is not good enough. I want to improve it.
他试图对传统的生产方式进行改良。
He tried to improve the traditional way of production.

词义辨析

懂、明白

1、"懂"和"明白"都可以表示知道的意思,比如:恐怕我不懂/明白你的意思。这篇文章很晦涩,我看不懂/明白。

懂 and 明白 mean "to understand", e.g. I am afraid I don't understand your meaning. The article is very obscure, I can not understand it.

2、"懂"可以表示掌握了某种技术等;"明白"不可以。"明白"还是形容词,表示清楚,容易理解;"懂"不能用作形容词。如：她懂日语。他解释得很明白。

懂 can indicate to master a skill; 明白 can not. 明白 is an adjective, meaning "clear", or "easy to understand"; 懂 can not be used as an adjective, For example: She can speak Japanese. He explained it clearly.

练习

练习一、根据拼音写汉字，根据汉字写拼音

gǎi（　）cái（　）shēng（　）nuǎn（　）（　）chéng
（　）造　（　）料　（　）意　　和　　完（　）

练习二、搭配连线
(1) 完成　　　　A. 暖和
(2) 天气　　　　B. 土壤
(3) 改良　　　　C. 材料
(4) 坚持　　　　D. 任务
(5) 建筑　　　　E. 原则

练习三、从今天学习的生词中选择合适的词填空

1. 为了提高大米的产量,科学家正在对水稻的品种进行_____。

2. 植物和动物都可以称作_____。

3. 春天来了,天气越来越_____了。

4. 他只喜欢画画,对_____都不感兴趣。

5. 这是一种防火_____,可以用来建房子。

6. 他们从当地购买_____,然后在工厂里加工成工艺品。

7. 按照平等互利的_____,我们合作开发新产品。

8. 他是一个精明的_____人,总能以很低的价格采购到优质的商品。

9. 小时候,每当我问姥姥一些问题时,她总是说:"等你长大了,就_____了"。

10. 他们提前 _____ 了今年的工作任务,现在他们很轻松。

答案

练习一:
略
练习二:
(1) D　　(2) A　　(3) B　　(4) E　　(5) C
练习三:
1. 改良　2. 生物　3. 暖和　4. 别的　5. 材料
6. 原料　7. 原则　8. 生意　9. 明白　10. 完成

第1月,第3周的练习

练习一、根据词语给加点的字注音
1.(　)　2.(　)　3.(　)　4.(　)　5.(　)
流域　　教授　　概括　　优美　　暖和

练习二、根据拼音填写词语
　　　jīn　　jǐn　　zhǐ　　zhì　　zhī
1. 附(　) 2.(　)张 3. 防(　) 4. 防(　) 5.(　)道

练习三、辨析并选择合适的词填空
1. 我的奖金是(　)件计算的,我每卖出一件家具,公司给我 200 元。(按、按照)
2. (　)市政府的规定,在地铁吸烟将被罚款 50 元。(按、按照)
3. 来北京(　),她已经学过两年汉语了。(从前、以前)
4. 科学家说,(　)这里的气候十分湿润,生活着十几种恐龙。(从前、以前)
5. 刚来这里留学的时候,我就制定了一个长期的学习(　)。(计划、打算)
6. 假期,我不(　)去旅游,我想上一个书法学习班。(计划、打算)
7. 他(　)的工作是钢琴教师,现在已经是著名歌手了。(原来、本来)
8. 你(　)就不该相信他,我早就警告过你。(原来、本来)
9. 汉语语法确实很难,很多中国人都讲不(　)。(懂、明白)
10. 其实他(　)法语,他知道你们在谈什么。(懂、明白)

练习四、选词填空
旁边　附近　周围　中间　对面
外面　原料　原来　原则　原理
1. 图书馆的两边是办公楼和教学楼,图书馆在这两个建筑(　)。
2. (　)风大,快进屋来吧。
3. 学校(　)的环境很好,附近有别的大学,还有一个很大的公园。

4. 她坐在我的(　),我们没说话,只是静静地看着对方的眼睛。
5. 这是我们全家的照片,爸爸妈妈抱着我和妹妹,姐姐站在(　)。
6. 邮局就在(　),不用打的,走路五分钟就到了。
7. 我以为那个女孩是他女朋友,(　)是他妹妹。
8. 这台机器是根据物理学的运动(　)设计的。
9. 生产这种产品的(　)是从国外进口的,所以成本比较高。
10. 在比赛时,裁判的行为体现了公平竞争的(　)。

练习五、写出下列词语的同义词
1. 紧急(　)　　2. 流行(　)
3. 信息(　)　　4. 生意(　)
5. 原来(　)

练习六、写出下列词语的反义词
1. 紧张(　)　　2. 长久(　)
3. 优良(　)　　4. 暖和(　)
5. 明白(　)

答案

练习一:
1. yù　2. jiào　3. gài　4. yōu　5. huo
练习二:
1. 近　2. 紧　3. 止　4. 治　5. 知
练习三:
1. 按　2. 按照　3. 以前　4. 从前　5. 计划
6. 打算　7. 原来　8. 本来　9. 明白　10. 懂
练习四:
1. 中间　2. 外面　3. 周围　4. 对面　5. 旁边
6. 附近　7. 原来　8. 原理　9. 原料　10. 原则
练习五:
1. 紧迫　2. 盛行　3. 消息　4. 买卖　5. 以前
练习六:
1. 放松　2. 短暂　3. 拙劣　4. 凉快　5. 糊涂

1月 第4周的学习内容

de (dé děi)
得 （甲）助／助动／动
① auxiliary, requires a complement ② have to ③ to obtain; to get
常用搭配
跑得快 run fast　起得早 get up early
děi 得想个办法。Something must be done about it.
dé 得奖 win the prize
用法示例
他弹钢琴弹得非常好。
He plays the piano very well.
我们得马上走了。
We've got to go straight away.
我得了一个不理想的成绩。
I got an unfavorable score.

dédào
得到 （甲）动
obtain; receive
常用搭配
得到权力 attain power　得到赏识 gain recognition
用法示例
他的所作所为使他的名声得到了改善。
What he did put him in better standing.
我不在乎我是否可以得到它。
I don't care whether I get it or not.
很遗憾，你没有得到那份工作。
I'm sorry that you didn't get the job.

shēngchǎn　　　　　　xiāofèi
生产　　反 **消费** （甲）动
manufacture; produce
常用搭配
生产力 productivity　生产粮食 produce grain
生产厂家 manufacturing plant
农业生产 agricultural production
用法示例
那家工厂生产轿车。
That factory produces cars.
军工厂是生产武器的工厂。
Weapons plants are factories that produce weapons.
生产者与消费者之间的利益冲突将永远存在。
The conflicting interests of producers and consumers will always exist.

gòuzào　　　　　　jiégòu
构造　　同 **结构** （乙）名
structure
常用搭配
人体构造 the structure of the human body
用法示例
今天我们学习了大脑的构造。
We learnt about the structure of the brain today.
他给学生讲解了地球的构造。
He explained the structure of the earth to his students.

lùxiàn
路线 （乙）名
route; official or prescribed policy
常用搭配
运输路线 transportation route　火车路线 a train line
党的路线 the party line
用法示例
我们在地图上画出了我们的旅游路线。
We traced our traveling route on the map.
那个邮递员负责这条投递路线。
That postman is in charge of this route.
她一贯奉行马克思主义路线。
She always takes a Marxist line.

gòuchéng
构成 （乙）动
constitute; compose
常用搭配
七天构成一个星期。7 days constitute a week
用法示例
人体组织是由细胞构成的。
Human tissue is made up of cells.
一年是由十二个月构成的。
Twelve months constitute one year.
英国是由英格兰、苏格兰和威尔士构成的。
England, Scotland and Wales make up the island of Great Britain.

xūxīn　　　　　　jiāoào
虚心　　反 **骄傲** （乙）形
modest; open-minded
常用搭配
虚心学习 learn with an open mind
虚心的人 modest person

【用法示例】
她非常虚心。
She is very modest.
虚心使人进步。
Modesty helps one to progress.
她对自己的成就很虚心。
She's very modest about her success.

zhēnduì
针对 (乙)动
direct towards; aim at
【常用搭配】
针对某人／某事 aim at sb/ sth
【用法示例】
我的评论不是针对你的。
My remarks were not aimed at you.
他的诗是针对敌人的。
His poems were directed at the enemy.

jiāo'ào
骄傲 (乙)形
① pride ② conceited
【常用搭配】
骄傲自大的人 an arrogant person
为……而骄傲 pride oneself on sth
【用法示例】
我的教学工作是我的快乐和骄傲。
My teaching is my pride and joy.
我骄傲我是中国人。
I'm proud I am Chinese.
知识使人谦虚，无知使人骄傲。
Knowledge makes one humble; ignorance makes one proud.

lùkǒu
路口 (丙)名
intersection (of roads)
【常用搭配】
铁路路口 railway crossing 十字路口 crossroad
【用法示例】
我们来到一个十字路口。
We came to a crossroad.
我想在十字路口下车，可司机不让。
I wanted to get off at the crossroad, but the driver refused to let me out.

zuòzhàn
作战 (丙)动
do battle; fight
【常用搭配】
与……作战 battle with… 作战基地 a base of operations
联合作战 combine operations
【用法示例】
这些战士在作战时打得很勇敢。
The soldiers fought bravely in the battle.

将军正在研究作战地图。
The general is studying the battle map.
他向将军汇报了作战计划。
He reported the plan of attack to the general.

qī
期 (乙)量
measure word, used for issue of a periodical
【常用搭配】
这本杂志的第三期 the third issue of the magazine
【用法示例】
最近一期的科学杂志报道了他的新发现。
The latest issue of Science reported his new discovery.
这种杂志每月出版两期。
Two issues of the magazine are published every month.

词义辨析

得、得到

1、作为动词都有获得的意思。但"得"还可以作助词，在动词后连接补语，也可以作助动词，表示需要，必须。如：他学得慢。得想个办法。

As verbs, both 得 and 得到 mean "to get", "to obtain" but 得 can also be an auxiliary, used after a verb which requires a complement, or an auxiliary verb, meaning "need" or "have to", e.g. He learns slowly. Something must be done about it.

2、动词"得"的宾语一般是分数、名次、病等，"不得"表示不允许。很多词都可以做"得到"的宾语，有时候有被动的含义。如：他得到了表扬。方法得到了改进。

Used as a verb, the object of 得 is often exam scores, a rank in a list of names, illness, etc. 不得 means "not permit", "shouldn't". A lot of words can be the object of 得 到, sometimes it indicates the use of a passive voice, e.g. He was praised. The method has been improved.

 **练习**

练习一、根据拼音写汉字，根据汉字写拼音
gòu（　）　xū（　）　jiāo（　）　（　）xiàn（　）duì
（　）造　（　）心　（　）傲　路（　）　针（　）

练习二、搭配连线
(1) 得到　　　　　　　A. 路口
(2) 十字　　　　　　　B. 学习
(3) 骄傲　　　　　　　C. 奖励
(4) 虚心　　　　　　　D. 厂家
(5) 生产　　　　　　　E. 自大

练习三、从今天学习的生词中选择合适的词填空
1. 你已经取得了很大的进步，但不要＿＿＿＿，还要继续努力。
2. 他告诉我过了十字＿＿＿＿，往前走100米有个邮局。
3. ＿＿＿＿目前存在的问题，他提出了两个建议。
4. 听说南方发洪水了，我们临时调整了旅游的＿＿＿＿。
5. 教授用模型和图片向学生展示心脏的＿＿＿＿。
6. 中国是玩具＿＿＿＿大国，每年向世界各国出口大量玩具。
7. 士兵们都已到达前线，正在准备与敌人＿＿＿＿。
8. 我们公司主要由四个大部门＿＿＿＿。
9. 她遇到不懂的问题就向别人＿＿＿＿请教，所以她进步得很快。
10. 她学习非常努力，成绩也很好，每年能＿＿＿＿奖学金。

答案

练习一： 略

练习二：
(1) C　(2) A　(3) E　(4) B　(5) D

练习三：
1. 骄傲　2. 路口　3. 针对　4. 路线　5. 构造
6. 生产　7. 作战　8. 构成　9. 虚心　10. 得到

 星期二

érqiě
而且　　　　　　　　　　　　（甲）连
① moreover ② and ③ not only ... but

常用搭配
机智而且勇敢 smart and brave
丑陋而且粗鲁 ugly and rude

用法示例
她不仅是一个成功的模特，而且是一位有名的演员。
She is not only a successful model, but also a famous actress.
她做了这件工作而且做得很好。
She did the work, and she did it well.
好的水果冬天难得见到，而且价格昂贵。
Good fruit is scarce in winter and is expensive.

máfan
麻烦　　　　　　　　　　　　（甲）动/形
① bother; trouble ② troublesome

常用搭配
不麻烦你了，多谢。Don't bother, thanks.
麻烦你…… I'll trouble you to…

用法示例
能麻烦您关一下窗吗？
May I trouble you to close the window?
修理这台机器很麻烦。
We had a lot of bother in repairing the machine.
养宠物很麻烦，真不值得。
Keeping pets is more trouble than it's worth.

bìngqiě
并且　　　　　　　　　　　　（乙）连
moreover; furthermore

常用搭配
应该并且必须守时 should, and must be punctual
讨论并通过了计划 discussed and decided on the plan.

用法示例
他被发现有罪，并且被定了罪。
He was found guilty and was convicted.
这只狗受了伤并且很快就死了。
The dog was hurt and soon died.
他与她结婚并且定居在伦敦。
He married her and took up residence in London.

chǎnpǐn
产品　　　　　　　　　　　　（乙）名
product

常用搭配
不合格产品 substandard products

石油产品 oil products   农产品 farm products

用法示例

这家公司出售塑料产品。
The company sells plastic products.
我们决定为我们的新产品做广告。
We decided to advertise our new product.

chǎnliàng
产量 (乙)名
output

常用搭配

日产量 daily output   总产量 gross output
钢的年产量 the annual output of steel

用法示例

该工厂的平均产量是每天20辆汽车。
The average output of the factory is 20 cars a day.
我们必须提高产量满足需求。
We must increase our output to meet demand.
产量已增加了两倍。
The output has tripled.

shēngdòng
生动 (乙)形
vivid

常用搭配

生动的描述 vivid description

用法示例

她向孩子们生动地讲述了那个传说。
She gave the children a vivid description of the tale.
这个地方使人回忆起许多生动的往事。
This place conjures up vivid memories.

shúxī   mòshēng
熟悉   反 陌生   (乙)动
to know well

常用搭配

对……熟悉 be familiar with sth   熟悉的面孔 familiar face

用法示例

这些学生对这本书很熟悉。
These students are familiar with this book.
这首歌听起来很熟悉。
This song sounds familiar.
你熟悉这种型号的汽车吗?
Are you familiar with this type of car?

shúliàn   shēngshū
熟练   反 生疏   (乙)形
skillful

常用搭配

熟练工人 skilled worker
一种熟练的技能 a practiced skill

用法示例

我能够熟练地操作计算机。
I am skilled in operating a computer.

她用筷子用得不太熟练。
She's not very skillful with her chopsticks.

ānwèi   quànwèi
安慰   同 劝慰   (乙)动/名
comfort

常用搭配

安慰她 comfort her
几句安慰的话 a few words of comfort

用法示例

她安慰这个生病的孩子。
She comforted the ill child.
她从她的儿女身上得到安慰。
She finds comfort in her children.
你是父母最大的安慰。
You are a great comfort to your parents.

shēngcún
生存 (丙)动
exist; survive

常用搭配

为生存而奋斗 a struggle for existence
在地球上生存 exist on earth

用法示例

没有空气人就不能生存。
Man cannot exist without air.
这个人病得很厉害,可是他生存了下来。
The man was very ill, but he survived.
污染对这一物种的继续生存造成了威胁。
Pollution poses a threat to the continued existence of this species.

zhèngshū
证书 (丙)名
certificate

常用搭配

毕业证书 graduate certificate
结婚证书 marriage certificate
专利证书 letter of patent

用法示例

她将参加剑桥初级证书考试。
She's going in for the Cambridge First Certificate.
去面试的时候,别忘了带上你的职业证书。
Don't forget to bring your vocational certificate when you go for an interview.
他已经取得了高级证书。
He has got the advanced certificate.

mén
门 (甲)名/量
① door ② measure word for cannons, subjects, etc.

常用搭配

关门 shut the door   敲门 knock at the door
大门 gate   一门语言 a language

一门大炮 a cannon

用法示例

请把门打开。
Open the door please.
大门太窄,汽车进不去。
The gate is too narrow for a car to enter through.
这是一门必修课。
This is a compulsory subject.

 词义辨析

而且、并且

　　两个词都是连词,表示补充或递进。但是,"而且"往往连接两个形容词,"并且"很少连接形容词;"不但"往往与"而且"连用,很少与"并且"连用。"并且"可以连接两个动词,表示两个动作同时或相继进行,"而且"没有这种用法。如:①小偷进入了我的房间并且偷走了我的手表。②她(不但)很漂亮而且很善良。

　　Both 而且 and 并且 are conjunctions in parts of speech, meaning "in addition" or "furthermore". But 而且 is usually used to connect two adjectives, while 并且 is seldom used in this way. 不但 is more often used together with 而且 than with 并且. 并且 is often used to connect two verbs or verb phrases, indicating "subsequently", while 而且 can not used in this way. For example: ① A thief broke into my room and walked off with my watch. ② She is not only beautiful, but also very kind.

 练习

练习一、根据拼音写汉字,根据汉字写拼音

má(　　)　(　　)cún　(　　)liàng　(　　)wèi　(　　)xī
(　　)烦　　生(　　)　产(　　)　安(　　)　熟(　　)

练习二、搭配连线

(1) 安慰　　　　　　A. 环境
(2) 塑料　　　　　　B. 产量
(3) 熟悉　　　　　　C. 证书
(4) 提高　　　　　　D. 产品
(5) 毕业　　　　　　E. 病人

练习三、从今天学习的生词中选择合适的词填空

1. 他的发明已经获得了专利_____。
2. 经过一段时间的学习和训练,他已经能_____地操作机器了。
3. 他故事讲得很_____,好像是他自己亲身经历过一样。
4. 他不但跑得快,_____跳得远。
5. 他找到了那家书店,_____买着了这本辞典。
6. 他们生产的电子_____很受欢迎。
7. 我们增加了两台生产设备,_____当然会提高。
8. 我刚来这里三天,对这座城市还不太_____。
9. 他们共学习五_____课程,每天要上六节课。
10. 她这次考试没考好,老师_____她说:"没关系,下次一定会考好的"。

 答案

练习一:
略

练习二:
(1) E　　(2)D　　(3)A　　(4)B　　(5)C

练习三:
1. 证书　2. 熟练　3. 生动　4. 而且　5. 并且
6. 产品　7. 产量　8. 熟悉　9. 门　10. 安慰

yǔyán
语言 （甲）名
language

常用搭配
官方语言 an official language　书面语言 written language

用法示例
不同国家的人说不同的语言。
People in different countries speak different languages.
他精通四门语言。
He has a good command of four languages.

hànyǔ
汉语　◎中文zhōngwén　（甲）名
Chinese language

常用搭配
说汉语 speak in Chinese　学汉语 learn Chinese

用法示例
我的母语是汉语。
My native language is Chinese.
我很少听他讲汉语。
I seldom hear him speak Chinese.

wàiyǔ
外语 （甲）名
foreign language

常用搭配
学习外语 study a foreign language
外语系 Foreign Languages Department

用法示例
掌握一门外语并不容易。
It's not easy to master a foreign language.
他毕业于一所知名的外语学院。
He graduated from a famous foreign language institute.
一般而言，女孩善于学习外语。
Generally speaking, girls are good at learning foreign languages.

dìwèi
地位 （乙）名
status; position

常用搭配
经济地位 economic status　国际地位 international status
有地位的人 a man of position

用法示例
贵族有很高的社会地位。
The aristocracy have a high status in society.
他对地位真是一点儿也不在乎。
He really doesn't care a bit about status.

他正在试图改善他在公司的地位。
He is trying to improve his position in the company.

shùnbiàn　　　tèyì
顺便　◎特意　（乙）副
① in passing ② conveniently

常用搭配
顺便问／说一下 by the way

用法示例
顺便问一下，他后来怎么样了？
By the way, what happened to him afterwards?
到伦敦时顺便来看我。
Drop in and see me when you're in London.
我现在该走了。顺便提一句，如果你要那本书，我下次带来。
I must go now. Incidentally, if you want that book I'll bring it next time.

xìnggé
性格 （乙）名
character

常用搭配
温和的性格 gentle character
性格演员 character actor

用法示例
我们的性格十分相似。
We are very similar in character.
他的性格坚强而温和。
His character is strong but gentle.
成功和财富改变了他的性格。
Success and wealth transformed his character.

shùnlì
顺利 （乙）形
① smooth ② without a hitch

常用搭配
工作顺利 work smoothly
顺利地完成了任务 complete the task successfully

用法示例
典礼进行得很顺利。
The ceremony went off without a hitch.
我们顺利地通过了考试。
We all passed the exam without difficulty.
在他的指导下，我们顺利地完成了工作。
Under his guidance, we finished the work without a problem.

dìzhǐ　　　dìdiǎn
地址　◎地点　（乙）名
address

常用搭配
通信地址 mailing address
学校的地址 the school's address

用法示例
请说出你的姓名和地址。
Please tell me your name and address.

让我记下你的地址和电话号码。
Let me take down your address and telephone number.
寄信前,他在信封上写上地址。
He addressed the envelope before mailing the letter.

地图 dìtú (乙) 名
map

常用搭配
中国地图 map of China
军事地图 military map

用法示例
地图上找不到这个地方。
The place cannot be found on the map.
图书馆里有城市地图、国家地图和世界地图。
In the library there are maps of cities, countries, and the world.

性能 xìngnéng (丙) 名
performance

常用搭配
性能实验 a performance test
使用性能 functional performance (engineering)

用法示例
新汽车的性能怎么样?
How is the new car performing?
你能为我们介绍一下这台机器的基本性能吗?
Can you introduce the basic functions of the machine for us?

个性 gèxìng ⊠ 共性 gòngxìng (丙) 名
personality; individuality

常用搭配
坚强的个性 a strong personality
有个性的人 a unique individual

用法示例
他是个性活跃的人。
He has a dynamic personality.
她很有个性。
She is quite a personality.
我们应该尊重个性。
We should respect peoples' individuality.

双 shuāng (甲) 量
① pair ② both

常用搭配
双人房间 a double room   双方 both sides
一双袜子 a pair of socks

用法示例
她吻了他的双颊。
She kissed him on both cheeks.

这双鞋很耐磨。
This pair of shoes is durable.
这只小动物有一双淡褐色的眼睛。
This small animal has a pair of hazel eyes.

 词义辨析

性格、个性

1、"性格"和"个性"都是名词,表示人格的特征。如:我喜欢他的性格/个性。

性格 and 个性 are nouns, meaning the features of one's character. For example: I like his character/personality.

2、但是,"性格"指一个人通常的思维、举止或反应的特征和方式;"个性"则更突出个人独特的品质。如:他的性格坚强而温和。她很有个性。

性格 indicates one's usual manner of thinking, behaving or reacting. 个性 indicates the distinctive qualities of a person. For example: His character is strong but gentle. She is quite a personality.

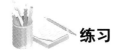 **练习**

练习一、根据拼音写汉字，根据汉字写拼音
shùn（　）dì（　）yǔ（　）（　）zhǐ（　）néng（　）
（　）便　（　）图　（　）言　地（　）　性（　）

练习二、搭配连线
(1) 性能　　　　　　　A. 地位
(2) 社会　　　　　　　B. 外语
(3) 学习　　　　　　　C. 良好
(4) 性格　　　　　　　D. 地址
(5) 通信　　　　　　　E. 坚强

练习三、从今天学习的生词中选择合适的词填空
1. 他_____地通过了公司的面试，下周就要上班了。
2. 我要去上海出差，_____去看看在那里工作的老同学。
3. 她的_____非常开朗，大家都喜欢和她一起共事。
4. 我想给他写信，可是他搬家了，我不知道他新的通信_____。
5. 这个大学的_____学院包括英语、法语和日语三个系。
6. 他今天买了两条裤子，一_____皮鞋。
7. 在教室的墙上，挂着一张中国_____。
8. 这个小男孩很有_____，他跟别人的想法总是不一样。
9. 以前，妇女在家中的_____很低，甚至不能跟男人在同一个桌子上吃饭。
10. 去年九月，我来北京学习_____，现在已经能跟中国人聊天了。

答案

练习一：
略

练习二：
(1) C　(2) A　(3) B　(4) E　(5) D

练习三：
1. 顺利　2. 顺便　3. 性格／个性　4. 地址
5. 外语　6. 双　7. 地图　8. 个性
9. 地位　10. 汉语

星期四

cānguān
参观　≡ 游览　　（甲）动
visit and observe
【常用搭配】
参观博物馆 visit a museum　　参观展览 see an exhibition
【用法示例】
我们去参观了这个小镇。
We went to look around the town.
那些外国人正在参观出土文物。
Those foreigners are visiting the excavations.

kàn
看　　（甲）动
see; watch
【常用搭配】
看一看 have a look　　看书 read books
看比赛 watch a game　　看病 see a doctor
【用法示例】
我们看电影去。
Let's watch a movie.
我只是随便看看。
I'm just having a look.
很久没有看到你了。
I haven't seen you for a long time.
看，他来了。
Look, he's coming.

kān
看　　（甲）动
look after; to guard
【常用搭配】
看孩子 babysit
看犯人 to guard a prisoner
【用法示例】
看着他，别让他逃掉了
Watch him, don't let him escape.
这条狗能看家。
The dog can guard the house.

zuòwèi
座位　　（乙）名
seat
【常用搭配】
这个座位有人吗？ Is this seat occupied?
预定座位 reserve seats
【用法示例】
他在最近的空座位上坐了下来。
He sat down on the nearest available seat.

他把座位让给了我。
He offered his seat to me.
这个会场有两千个座位。
The hall seats 2000.

chéngshì
城市　　　反 乡村　　　（甲）名
city

常用搭配
城市人口 the urban population　　大城市 big city

用法示例
伦敦是世界上最大的城市之一。
London is one of the largest cities in the world.
在这座陌生的城市里,她感到很寂寞。
She feels rather lonely in this strange town.

zhèngshì
正式　　　反 随便　　　（乙）形
official; formal

常用搭配
正式的场合 formal occasion
正式声明 official statement
正式批准 official permission

用法示例
在毕业典礼上,正式颁发了学位。
At graduation, the academic degrees were officially presented.
这家图书馆将在下周正式开放。
This library will be officially opened next week.
别忘了跟他要正式发票。
Don't forget to ask him for an official invoice.

xìngzhì
性质　　　（乙）名
nature; property

常用搭配
分子的性质 molecular properties
化学性质 chemical properties

用法示例
他一点也不了解我的工作性质。
He knows nothing of the nature of my work.
有的化学家研究物质的性质。
Some chemists study the properties of matter.

zhìliàng
质量　　　（乙）名
quality

常用搭配
工作质量 performance quality
高质量 high quality
教学质量 quality of teaching

用法示例
检查员检查产品的质量。
The inspector checks on the quality of the products.

这些货物的质量不好。
The goods are of poor quality.
这种新材料质量好,而且也不贵。
This new material is of high quality, and is not expensive either.

shùliàng
数量　　　（乙）名
quantity; amount

常用搭配
可观的数量 sizable quantity
产品的数量 quantity of products

用法示例
我重视质量胜过数量。
I value quality over quantity.
火车免费运送一定数量的行李。
The railroad will allow a certain amount of baggage to be carried for free.

shùzì
数字　　　同 数据　　　（乙）名
① digital ② number; figure

常用搭配
幸运数字 lucky number
数字代码 numeric code

用法示例
用文字和阿拉伯数字写出这个数。
Write the number in words and figures.
去年,这个数字上升到了72%。
This figure increased to 72 percent last year.

shùjù
数据　　　（丙）名
numeric data

常用搭配
测量数据 metrical data　　统计数据 statistical data

用法示例
你把那些数据存储到磁盘上了吗?
Have you stored the data on the disc?
为了收集数据我们发给他们一些调查表。
We gave them some questionnaires to use for collecting data.
从这些数据来看,我们的公司经营得不错。
According to these figures, our company is doing well.

lòumiàn
露面　　　（丙）动
appear (in public)

常用搭配
在电视节目中露面 appear on a TV program
公开露面 appear in public

用法示例
自从患病以来她第一次公开露面。
She was appearing in public for the first time since her illness.

这位老演员已十三年未在电影中露面了。
The old actor hadn't appeared in a film for thirteen years.
猫一露面,老鼠急忙钻进洞里。
The mouse scurried into its hole when the cat appeared.

声 shēng　　　　　　　　　　　　(甲) 名 / 量
① sound ② voice ③ a measure word for sounds

常用搭配

脚步声 the sound of footsteps　　爆炸声 an explosive sound
低声地说 say in a low voice　　说一声 give a word
喊一声 give a shout

用法示例

你听到雷声了吗?
Did you hear the thunder?
请大声讲话。
Speak loudly please.
他们听见了呼救声。
They heard a cry for help.
你要是需要帮助就叫我一声。
If you need any help, please call me.

参观、看

1、"参观"指实地观看,宾语一般是处所并且不是单音节词,如:参观长城、参观工厂。

参观 means "to visit", "to see on the spot". Its object is usually a place, the name of which can not be monosyllabic, e.g. to visit the Great Wall, to visit a factory.

2、"看"宾语可以是单音节词,可以是一个具体的东西或活动,除了表示观看,还有阅读、拜访、诊治、认为等意思,如:看电影,看比赛,看书,看病,看朋友,依我看。

The object of 看 can be monosyllabic, and can be a thing or an activity. Besides the meaning of "to look" or "to see", 看 means "to read", "to call on socially", "to diagnose", "to think", etc. For example: to watch a movie; to watch a match, to read a book, to see a doctor, to visit a friend, in my opinion.

练习一、根据拼音写汉字,根据汉字写拼音

shù (　) xìng (　) (　) shì (　) shì (　) miàn
(　)据　　(　)质　　城(　)　　正(　)　　露(　)

练习二、搭配连线

(1) 产品　　　　　　A. 数字
(2) 幸运　　　　　　B. 性质
(3) 统计　　　　　　C. 质量
(4) 正式　　　　　　D. 数据
(5) 化学　　　　　　E. 场合

练习三、从今天学习的生词中选择合适的词填空

1. 我在饭店预订了_____,我们去饭店吃晚饭吧。
2. 写私人信件可以很随意,但商业信函应该比较_____。
3. 上海是一座美丽的大_____,我非常喜欢在那儿工作。
4. 我需要这方面的统计_____,你能帮我查查吗?
5. 这种手机的_____非常好,我用了3年,从来没出过问题。
6. 很多中国人喜欢8,认为8是一个吉利的_____。
7. 我出去买奶粉的时候,你帮我_____一会儿孩子吧。
8. 我今天想住在朋友家了,不过我得先打电话,告诉妈妈一_____。
9. 今年学生的_____可能会增加一倍,所以我们要招聘新教师。
10. 周末老师带我们去_____了历史博物馆。

答案

练习一:
略
练习二:
(1) C　　(2)A　　(3)D　　(4)E　　(5)B
练习三:
1. 座位　2. 正式　3. 城市　4. 数据　5. 质量
6. 数字　7. 看　8. 声　9. 数量　10. 参观

星期五

bìxū
必须　　**búbì** 反 不必　　（甲）助动
must; have to

常用搭配
必须去 must go
必须离开 have to leave

用法示例
在英国,车辆必须靠左行驶。
In England traffic must keep to the left hand side of the road.
我们必须遵守诺言。
We must keep our word.
军人必须服从命令。
Soldiers must obey orders.

zhàogù
照顾　　同 照料　　（甲）动
take care of; look after

常用搭配
照顾伤员 care for the wounded
照顾孩子 take care of the children
照顾病人 look after the sick

用法示例
他这么大了,能照顾自己了。
He is old enough to look after himself.
当我不在的时候,你要照顾好你弟弟。
Take care of your brother while I am away.

shíjiàn
实践　　（甲）动/名
① put into practice ② practice

常用搭配
把理论运用于实践 apply theory to practice
社会实践 social practice
把……付诸实践 to practice something

用法示例
我们必须将计划付诸实践。
We must put our plans into practice.
我们的原则是理论与实践相结合。
It is our principle to combine theory with practice.
那计划不错,不过在实践中可行吗?
It's a good idea on paper, but will it work in practice?

zhàocháng
照常　　（乙）形
as usual

常用搭配
照常工作 work as usual

用法示例
一切照常进行,好像什么事也没有发生过。
Everything went on as though nothing had happened.
不论下不下雨,比赛照常举行。
Rain or shine, the game will be held as scheduled.
尽管早上起来头疼,我还是照常上班了。
Although I got up with a headache, I went to work as usual.

zhǎnkāi
展开　　（乙）动
① unfold ② carry out

常用搭配
展开地图 unfold a map　　展开双臂 unfold one's arms
展开讨论 carry out a discussion

用法示例
他展开报纸,看了起来。
He unfurled the newspaper and began to read.
随着影片的放映,故事情节展开了。
The story unfolds as the film goes on.
雄鹰展开了双翅。
The eagle spread its wings.

jiāxiāng
家乡　　**gùxiāng** 同 故乡　　（乙）名
hometown

常用搭配
回家乡 go back to one's hometown

用法示例
总有一天我会回到家乡。
I will go back to my hometown some day.
他的家乡只是一个普通的小镇。
His hometown is a small and insignificant town.
在我的家乡,七月是一年中最热的月份。
July is the hottest month of the year in my hometown.

chǎnshēng
产生　　（乙）动
① come into being ② bring about

常用搭配
产生影响 to produce an effect

用法示例
类似的原因往往产生类似的结果。
Similar causes tend to produce similar results.
舞台灯光产生了月夜景色的效果。
The stage lighting gives off the effect of a moonlit scene.

rénkǒu
人口　　（乙）名
population

常用搭配
人口总数 gross population
人口激增 population explosion

【用法示例】

这个国家的人口是多少？
What is the population of this country?
这个城市的人口密度非常高。
The population density of this city is very high.
我国每四年进行一次人口普查。
The census is taken once every four years in our country.

产地 chǎndì （丙）名
place of production; manufacturing location

【常用搭配】
水果的产地 the fruit producing area

【用法示例】
你得在合同上写明原料的产地。
You should write the manufacturing location of the raw materials into the contract.
你知道这种橘子的产地吗？
Do you know where this kind of orange is grown?

必需 bìxū  多余 duōyú （丙）动
necessary; indispensable

【常用搭配】
生活必需品 daily necessities

【用法示例】
空气是生命所必需的东西。
Air is indispensable to life.
衣服、食物和住所都是生活必需品。
Food, clothing and shelter are all necessities of life.
耐心加勤奋是成功所必需的。
Patience combined with diligence is necessary for success.

群 qún （乙）量
group; crowd

【常用搭配】
一群孩子 a group of children   一群蜜蜂 a swarm of bees

【用法示例】
我在人群中寻找她，但没看到。
I looked for her in the crowd but couldn't see her.
一群学生在学校旁边等着。
A group of students were waiting by the school.
一群人聚拢过来看发生了什么事。
A crowd gathered to see what had happened.

照耀 zhàoyào （丙）动
shine; illuminate

【用法示例】
太阳照耀着美丽的城市。
The sun shone brightly on the beautiful city.
太阳和煦地照耀着。
The sun shone kindly.

 词义辨析

必须、必需

1、"必须"是助动词，常用在动词前，表示一定要或只能的意思，比如：军人必须服从命令。
必须 is an auxiliary verb, often used before a verb, indicating "must", e.g. Soldiers must obey orders.

2、"必需"是动词，意思是一定需要，一定要具备。还有时做定语，表示不可缺少的。比如：食物是生命所必需的。
必需 is a verb, meaning "to be indispensable", or "must have something". It is sometimes used as an attributive, indicating "necessary", e.g. Food is essential for life.

练习

练习一、根据拼音写汉字，根据汉字写拼音
zhào（ ） bì（ ） zhǎn（ ）（ ） xiāng（ ） jiàn
（ ）顾　（ ）需　（ ）开　家（ ）　实（ ）

练习二、搭配连线
(1) 照顾   A. 影响
(2) 社会   B. 伤员
(3) 展开   C. 实践
(4) 产生   D. 数量
(5) 人口   E. 双臂

练习三、从今天学习的生词中选择合适的词填空
1. 纸和笔都是学习的_____用品。
2. 在夕阳的_____下，湖水变成了金黄色。
3. 他在工作_____中，积累了丰富的经验。
4. 这种花的原_____在非洲。
5. 我的_____在南方，我在那度过了童年和少年时光。
6. 老师要求我们_____在周五以前交作业。
7. 谢谢你，在我母亲生病的时候_____她。
8. 中国的银行和商店在周末也_____营业。
9. 他对京剧_____了浓厚的兴趣。
10. 中国的_____特别多，而且增长得很快，所以中国实行计划生育政策。

 答案

练习一：
略

练习二：
(1) B   (2)C   (3)E   (4)A   (5)D

练习三：
1. 必需　　2. 照耀　　3. 实践　　4. 产地　　5. 家乡
6. 必须　　7. 照顾　　8. 照常　　9. 产生　　10. 人口

第1月,第4周的练习

练习一、根据词语给加点的字注音
1.(　)　2.(　)　3.(　)　4.(　)　5.(　)
熟悉　　虚心　　安慰　　照耀　　顺便

练习二、根据拼音填写词语
　　zuò　　zuò　　shì　　shì　　jiāo
1.(　)谈　2.(　)战　3.城(　)4.正(　)5.(　)傲

练习三、辨析并选择合适的词填空
1. 来北京以后,我已经(　)过三次感冒了。(得、得到)
2. 为了(　)全部的遗产,他偷偷修改了遗嘱。(得、得到)
3. 老师来医院看望她,(　)给她带来了鲜花和水果。(而且、并且)
4. 这座建筑物不但十分美观,(　)非常安全。(而且、并且)
5. 这个作家有着独特的(　),有人很喜欢他,也有人很讨厌他。(性格、个性)
6. 尽管我们每个人的(　)都不同,但我们在一起合作得很愉快。(性格、个性)
7. 我们明天上午去博物馆(　),晚饭后再一起去(　)场电影。(参观、看)
8. 他发烧了,我得陪他去医院(　)病。(参观、看)
9. 老师要求我们明天(　)交作文,否则他就没时间帮我们修改了。(必须、必需)
10. 书、笔是学生的(　)品,可他上课时经常借我的。(必须、必需)

练习四、选词填空
照顾　　质量　　顺便　　熟悉　　构造
照常　　数量　　顺利　　熟练　　构成
1. 老师用一个模型为学生讲解地球的(　)。
2. 那个公司在亚洲的市场发展得很快,对我们公司的市场地位(　)了威胁。
3. 这个老工人能够(　)地操作生产线上的各种机器。
4. 我去南方度假的时候,请邻居帮我(　)宠物。
5. 你去寄包裹的时候,(　)帮我买几张明信片吧。
6. 我在这里生活了十年,对这儿的一切都十分(　)。
7. 由于准备充分,工作进行得很(　),提前一个星期就完成了任务。
8. 这个品牌的冰箱(　)特别好,我用了五年,从没出过毛病。
9. 这里的银行和商店在周末(　)营业,甚至在春节期间都不休息。
10. 圣诞节期间,邮局寄送包裹的(　)增加了两倍。

练习五、选择量词填空
声　　期　　门　　双　　群
1. 傍晚,牧民赶着一(　)羊回来了。
2. 你帮我跟老师说一(　),我今天去机场接朋友,不能上课了。
3. 这个学期,我们要学习四(　)课,分别是教程、口语、听力和阅读。
4. 他的论文发表在最近一(　)的《科学》杂志上。
5. 我的拖鞋坏了,得去商店买(　)新的。

练习六、写出下列词语的同义词
1. 构造(　)　　　　2. 数字(　)
3. 安慰(　)　　　　4. 照顾(　)
5. 参观(　)

练习七、写出下列词语的反义词
1. 虚心(　)　　　　2. 必须(　)
3. 必需(　)　　　　4. 熟悉(　)
5. 熟练(　)

 答案

练习一：
1. shú　　2. xū　　3. wèi　　4. yào　　5. biàn
练习二：
1. 座　　2. 作　　3. 市　　4. 式　　5. 骄
练习三：
1. 得　　2. 得到　　3. 并且　　4. 而且　　5. 个性
6. 性格　　7. 参观,看　8. 看　　9. 必须　　10. 必需
练习四：
1. 构造　　2. 构成　　3. 熟练　　4. 照顾　　5. 顺便
6. 熟悉　　7. 顺利　　8. 质量　　9. 照常　　10. 数量
练习五：
1. 群　　2. 声　　3. 门　　4. 期　　5. 双
练习六：
1. 结构　　2. 数据　　3. 劝慰　　4. 照料　　5. 游览
练习七：
1. 骄傲　　2. 不必　　3. 多余　　4. 陌生　　5. 生疏

2月 第1周的学习内容

星期一 Monday

hǎochù
好处 反 坏chù坏处 （甲）名
① benefit ② good

常用搭配
对某人有好处 do somebody good
从……中得到好处 benefit from...

用法示例
吸烟对你的身体没有好处。
Smoking is not good for your body.
这对你的健康有好处。
It will do your health good.
这项工程对每个人都大有好处。
This project will be of great benefit to everyone.

zhǎnlǎn
展览 （甲）名/动
① exhibit ② show; exhibition

常用搭配
美术展览 art exhibition　巡回展览 traveling exhibition
展览馆 exhibition hall

用法示例
许多人去看了鲜花展览。
Many people went to see the flower show.
她在我们学校展览她的画。
She exhibited her paintings at our school.
他的画正在展览会上展出。
His paintings are on display in the exhibition.

nèiróng
内容 （甲）名
content

常用搭配
报告的内容 the content of a report

用法示例
我喜欢他的写作风格，但是不喜欢他的内容。
I like the style of his writing, but I don't like the content.
她没看信，所以不知道信的内容。
She hadn't read the letter and so was unaware of its contents.
我已知道他们谈话的内容了。
I know what they talked about.

yōudiǎn　　**chángchù**
优点 同 长处 （乙）名
virtue; advantage

常用搭配
有耐心是他的优点。Patience is his virtue.

用法示例
你也许不喜欢他，不过他也有自己的优点。
You may not like him, but he has his merits.
温顺是他妻子的优点之一。
Docility is one of his wife's virtues.
他们因偏见而忽视了计划的优点。
Prejudice blinded them to the merits of the proposal.

zhǎnchū
展出 （乙）动
be on show; exhibit

常用搭配
展出文物 exhibit cultural artifacts

用法示例
下周将展出这些画。
These pictures will be on show next week.
博物馆展出了许多文物。
Many cultural artifacts were exhibited at the museum.
展出的服装都过时了。
The dresses on display are outdated.

zhàndòu
战斗 （乙）动/名
① battle ② fight ③ combat

常用搭配
战斗机 fighter plane　战斗英雄 a war hero
为……而战斗 fight for...

用法示例
他们在战斗中牺牲了。
They died in battle.
人们往往不得不为自由而战斗。
People often have to fight for their liberty.
他们为维护独立而战斗。
They were fighting in order to preserve their independence.

zhànzhēng　　**hépíng**
战争 反 和平 （乙）名
war

常用搭配
战争罪犯 a war criminal　核战争 nuclear war
卷入战争 drift into war
发动一场战争 unleash a war

【用法示例】
战争带来的必然结果就是生产力下降。
One inevitable outcome of a war is a fall in the production of goods.
现代战争中,战斗人员与非战斗人员都可能死亡。
In modern day wars it is possible that both soldiers and civilians will be killed.
正是这个事件导致了国内战争。
It was the event that led to the civil war.

quēdiǎn
缺点　　　　　回不足　　　　　　（乙）名
shortcoming; weakness
【常用搭配】
克服缺点 overcome one's shortcomings
【用法示例】
他最大的缺点是不守时。
Not being punctual is his greatest shortcoming.
我们都有些小缺点。
We all have our little weaknesses.
花钱太多是她的缺点。
Spending too much money is her weakness.

nèibù
内部　　　　　　　　　　　　　（乙）名
inside; internal; interior
【常用搭配】
房屋内部 the inside of the house
内部信息 internal information
【用法示例】
大楼内部装饰得富丽堂皇。
The interior of the building is magnificent and luxurious.
这些内部纠纷削弱了这个政党的力量。
These internal disputes have weakened the party's power.
地球内部是什么样子?
What is it like in the interior of the earth?

néngyuán
能源　　　　　　　　　　　　　（乙）名
energy sources; power sources
【常用搭配】
节省能源 conserve energy　　利用能源 use energy
消耗能源 consume energy
【用法示例】
太阳能是一种新型能源。
Solar energy is a new form of energy.
就石油能源而言,我们一定不能浪费。
As far as our oil is concerned, we cannot afford any wastage.

néngliàng
能量　　　　　　　　　　　　　（丙）名
energy
【常用搭配】
累积能量 accumulate energy　　转换能量 switch energy

【用法示例】
太阳是能量的最基本来源。
The sun is the ultimate source of energy.
碳水化合物给我们的身体提供热量和能量。
Carbohydrates provide our bodies with heat and energy.
太阳能电池能把阳光的能量转化为电能。
Solar cells can convert the energy from sunlight into electricity.

hòutuì
后退　　　　　　　　　　　　　（丙）动
recede; retreat
【常用搭配】
迫使敌人后退 force the enemy to retreat
向后退 draw back
【用法示例】
他们没前进,反而后退了。
Instead of pressing forward, they drew back.
人群向后退,让救护车可以开过去。
The crowd drew back so that the ambulance could pass.

词义辨析

好处、优点

　　"好处"表示对人或事物有利,经常用作"对……(没)有好处";"优点"表示人或事物好的方面。如果一个事物好的方面也是对人或事有利的方面,那么这时两个词都可以使用。比如:①这些药对你有好处。②他有很多优点。③这个计划的优点/好处是简单易行。

　　好　处 means "good for somebody or something", and is often used in the structure of "对……(没)有好处"; 优点 means "the good points or merits of something or somebody". If the merit of something is also good for somebody or something, we can use either of them. For example: ① This medicine will do you good. ② He has many merits. ③ The plan had the virtue of being easy to implement.

练习一、根据拼音写汉字，根据汉字写拼音

zhǎn (　) zhàn (　) néng (　)(　) tuì què (　)
(　)览　(　)斗　(　)源　后(　)　(　)点

练习二、搭配连线

(1) 战斗　　　　　A. 战争
(2) 国内　　　　　B. 英雄
(3) 克服　　　　　C. 能量
(4) 转化　　　　　D. 能源
(5) 节约　　　　　E. 缺点

练习三、从今天学习的生词中选择合适的词填空

1. 今年五月，中国美术馆举办了一次德国艺术_____。
2. 参加比赛的作文都在楼下_____。
3. _____对这个国家造成了巨大的损失，使该国经济倒退了20年。
4. 从外面看，这套房子很普通，但它的_____装修特别豪华。
5. 他最大的_____就是脾气好。
6. 经常锻炼对身体有_____。
7. 这场激烈的_____持续了近18小时。
8. 这个电视节目经常介绍一些节约_____的方法。
9. 每个人都有优点，也有_____。
10. 在学习上遇到困难时要迎难而上，不能害怕，更不能_____。

答案

练习一：
略

练习二：
(1) B　(2) A　(3) E　(4) C　(5) D

练习三：
1. 展览　2. 展出　3. 战争　4. 内部　5. 优点
6. 好处　7. 战斗　8. 能源　9. 缺点　10. 后退

dú
读　　　　　　　　　　　　　　　　（甲）动
read

常用搭配
读课文 read the text　　宣读 read out
朗读 read aloud

用法示例
你有什么可读的书吗？
Have you any books to read?
他既不会读也不会写。
He can neither read nor write.
我喜欢读科幻小说。
I like to read science fiction.

xuésheng
学生　　　　　　　　　　　　　　　（甲）名
student

常用搭配
学生会 student union　　留学生 foreign student
大学生 college student

用法示例
他是历史系的学生。
He is a student in the History Department.
我们班有15名学生。
There are 15 pupils in my class.
她对学生很有耐心。
She is very patient with her students.

tóngxué
同学　　　　　　　　　　　　　　　（甲）名
schoolmate

常用搭配
同班同学 classmate
大学同学 college classmates

用法示例
他们是我的同班同学。
They are my classmates.
他是我小学的同学。
He was my primary schoolmate.

gǔzhǎng
鼓掌　　　　　　　　　　　　　　　（乙）动
clap one's hands; applaud

常用搭配
热烈鼓掌 applaud warmly

用法示例
演出结束时，大家都热烈鼓掌。
Everyone applauded warmly when the play ended.

她讲完后，听众们鼓掌。
When she finished her speech, the audience applauded.
咱们为下一个表演者热烈鼓掌吧。
Let's give a good round of applause to the next performer.

shāngchǎng
商场 （乙）名
market
常用搭配
百货商场 department store　大商场 large store
用法示例
那家商场的镜子看上去很特别。
The mirror in that shop looks special.
为了消磨时间，我们逛了逛商场。
We looked round the shops to kill time.

shāngpǐn
商品 （乙）名
goods; commodity
常用搭配
高档商品 goods of quality　季节性商品 seasonal goods
用法示例
你们商店卖哪些商品？
What does your shop sell?
这个妇女先买了些小商品。
The woman first bought a few small articles.
你知道这种商品的商标吗？
Do you know the trade name of this product?

dǎzhàng
打仗 ◎战斗 （丙）
make war; fight
常用搭配
打过仗 have been in a war
用法示例
这两个国家打了十年仗了。
The two countries were at war for ten years.
那时正在打仗。
The war was upon them.
该国正准备打仗。
The country is preparing for war.

tóngqíng
同情 ◎怜悯 （乙）动
sympathize with; show sympathy for
常用搭配
引起同情 arouse one's sympathy
对……同情 have sympathy for…
用法示例
我同情那些无家可归的人。
I have sympathy with those homeless people.
他的痛苦引起了我们的同情。
His suffering aroused our sympathy.
我对盲人深感同情。
I feel sympathy for the blind.

niándài
年代 （乙）名
① a period in time ② a decade
常用搭配
在六十年代 in the sixties
用法示例
他出生在二十世纪八十年代。
He was born in 1980s.
我不能确切地说出那所房子的年代，但一定是很古老的。
I can't exactly guess which period that house is from, but it must be very old.

niánlíng　　niánjì
年龄 ◎年纪 （乙）名
age
常用搭配
法定年龄 legal age
用法示例
我妹妹和你年龄相仿。
My sister is around your age.
这个班男生的平均年龄是15岁。
The average age of the boys in this class is fifteen.
请登记你的姓名、年龄和住址。
Please fill in your name, age and address.

tóngméng　　liánméng
同盟 ◎联盟 （丙）名
ally; alliance
常用搭配
结成同盟 form an alliance　经济同盟 economic alliance
军事同盟 military alliance
用法示例
英国和法国结成同盟。
England formed an alliance with France.
美国和英国在这次战争中是同盟国。
America and England were allies in the war.

dǎjià
打架 （丙）动
fight
常用搭配
跟……打架 fight with…
用法示例
这些男孩儿为什么打架？
What are the boys fighting about?
我养了一只猫和一只狗，它们总是打架。
I have a dog and a cat, and they fight all the time.
他在学校总打架。
He was always fighting at school.

打击 dǎjī (丙)动

hit; beat; blow

常用搭配
打击敌人 beat the enemy
意外的打击 unexpected blow
无情的打击 merciless blow

用法示例
政府严厉打击了违法者。
The government cracked down on criminals.
母亲去世对她是个沉重的打击。
It was a great blow to her when her mother died.

学生、同学

1、"学生"和"同学"都可以表示在学校学习的人，比如这些学生/同学学习很努力。他们是我们班的学生/同学。

Both 学生 and 同学 mean students in a school, e.g. These students work hard. They are the students of our class.

2、"同学"还表示在同一个学校学习的关系，比如：我们是大学同学。"学生"表示的关系则是与老师的关系。比如：他们是李教授的学生。

同学 expresses a relationship between people in the same school or college, e.g. We were classmates in University. 学生 expresses a relationship between the student and the teacher, e.g. They are Professor Li's students.

练习一、根据拼音写汉字，根据汉字写拼音
(　)líng　shāng(　)(　)méng(　)zhǎng(　)zhàng
年(　)　(　)场　同(　)　鼓(　)　打(　)

练习二、搭配连线
(1) 同班　　　　　A. 商场
(2) 热烈　　　　　B. 同盟
(3) 百货　　　　　C. 同学
(4) 军事　　　　　D. 敌人
(5) 打击　　　　　E. 鼓掌

练习三、从今天学习的生词中选择合适的词填空
1. 为了保卫祖国，这些年轻的战士要到前线去_____。
2. 这个大学的老师有两千多名，_____超过了两万。
3. 父母那个_____的人思想都比较保守。
4. 我们学校附近就有一个大_____，我的一些衣服是从那儿买的。
5. 交往五年的男朋友提出要分手,她很受_____。
6. 小王结婚了，丈夫是她大学时的_____。
7. 妈妈不喜欢儿子们放假，因为三个男孩子在一起总_____。
8. 现在的孩子，_____很小，可是说出的话像大人。
9. 那个超市顾客很多，因为那儿_____丰富、价格合理、服务周到。
10. 打仗时，这个国家和邻国结成_____，共同对付敌人。

答案

练习一：
略

练习二：
(1) C　　(2)E　　(3)A　　(4)B　　(5)D

练习三：
1. 打仗　2. 学生　3. 年代　4. 商场　5. 打击
6. 同学　7. 打架　8. 年龄　9. 商品　10. 同盟

星期三

hūrán
忽然　≡ 突然　（甲）副
suddenly; all of a sudden

常用搭配
忽然停止 stop suddenly

用法示例
我一转身，忽然看见了她。
I turned around, and suddenly caught sight of her.
我忽然想起一个好主意。
A good idea suddenly occurred to me.
那男孩忽然哭了起来。
All of a sudden the boy began to cry.

tūrán
突然　（甲）形
sudden; unexpectedly

常用搭配
突然袭击 sudden strike
突然的消息 sudden news
突然的决定 a sudden decision

用法示例
他的突然去世使大家深感悲伤。
His sudden death upset everybody.
他们的突然到来打乱了我们的计划。
Their unexpected arrival threw our plans into confusion.
窗帘突然被拉开了，一道强光照了进来。
The curtains were suddenly opened and a bright light shone in.

shènglì
胜利　≡ 成功　（甲）名
victory; win

常用搭配
赢得胜利 win a victory

用法示例
他们在战斗中获得了胜利。
They won a victory in the battle.
建造这座纪念碑是为了纪念胜利。
The monument was built to commemorate the victory.
那天我们很高兴，我们的足球队获得了胜利。
It was a happy day when our football team won.

shēngrì
生日　≡ 诞辰　（甲）名
birthday

常用搭配
生日蛋糕 a birthday cake　　生日聚会 a birthday party
生日礼物 a birthday gift

用法示例
我祝你生日快乐。
I wish you a happy birthday.
这是给我的生日礼物。
This was given to me as a birthday present.

zhíyè
职业　（乙）名
occupation; profession

常用搭配
职业妇女 a career woman
职业画家 a professional painter
职业道德 professional ethics
以……为职业 make it a profession to do sth.

用法示例
我不知道什么职业适合我。
I don't know what profession would suit me.
对于职业足球运动员来说，受伤是职业本身具有的危险。
For professional footballers, injuries are an occupational hazard.
他从事什么职业？
What is his occupation?

rìchéng
日程　（乙）名
schedule; itinerary

常用搭配
旅游日程 tour itinerary　　工作日程 work schedule

用法示例
你明天的日程安排是什么？
What's your schedule for tomorrow?
他的日程一向排得很紧。
He always has a full schedule.
我们的下一项日程安排是开会。
The next thing on our schedule is to hold a meeting.

rìcháng
日常　（乙）形
daily; everyday

常用搭配
日常生活 daily life　　日常用品 daily necessities
日常工作 everyday routine

用法示例
在日常会话中，你也要注意礼貌。
You should be polite in everyday conversation as well.
那部书对古罗马人的日常生活描写得很生动。
This book gives readers a good picture of everyday life in ancient Rome.

rìqī
日期　（乙）名
date

常用搭配
出生日期 date of birth　　出厂日期 release date

交货日期 delivery date

用法示例

你们选定结婚日期了吗？
Have you fixed a date for the wedding?
别忘了在你的支票上写日期。
Don't forget to date your check.
会议日期从星期五提前到星期一了。
The date of the meeting was moved forward from Friday to Monday.

chénggōng
成功　　　　　　　　　　　　　（乙）动／形

① succeed ② successful

常用搭配

获得成功 achieve success
成功的试验 a successful experiment

用法示例

如果你努力，就会成功。
If you try hard, you will succeed.
失败是成功之母。
Failure is the mother of success.
宇航员成功地从月球返回到了地球。
The astronaut succeeded in returning from the moon to the earth.

chéngfèn
成分　　　　　　　　　　　　　　　（乙）名

component; element

常用搭配

营养成分 nourishing ingredients
矿物成分 mineral components

用法示例

分析这个句子的成分。
Break the sentence down into its essential components.
化学家能把一种药物的各种成分分解出来。
A chemist can decompose a medicine into its components.

chéngběn
成本　　　　　　　　　　　　　　　（丙）名

cost

常用搭配

生产成本 production costs
降低成本 reduce costs
成本价 cost price

用法示例

如果生产成本增加，则价格也要相应提高。
If production costs go up, prices will increase pro rata.
实际成本比我们预料的高得多。
The actual cost was much higher than we had expected.

zhíyuán
职员　　（丙）名

clerk; office worker

常用搭配

银行职员 bank clerk　小职员 a deputy

用法示例

王先生是法国航空公司的一名职员。
Mr. Wang workes for Air France.
有些职员要被解雇。
Some of our staff members are going to be dismissed.
我们难以招到素质好的职员。
We are having difficulties in recruiting well-qualified staff members.

gǔdòng
鼓动　　　　　　　　　　　　　　　（丙）动

agitate; arouse

常用搭配

鼓动罢工 agitate for a strike
进行宣传鼓动 encouraging propaganda and stirring up agitation

用法示例

他的讲话是有意鼓动群众。
His speech was calculated to stir up the crowd.
他热情洋溢的讲话鼓动了青年学生。
His fiery speech roused the young students.

词义辨析

忽然、突然

1、"突然"和"忽然"都可以用作状语，表示事情发生得迅速而且意外。比如：汽车突然／忽然停了。

Both 突然 and 忽然 can be used as an adverbial, meaning "suddenly", e.g. The car stopped suddenly.

2、"突然"是形容词，还可以用作定语、补语等，"忽然"不可以。如：突然的决定。听到这个消息，我感到很突然。

突然 can be an adjective, and used as an attributive or complement. 忽然 can not. For example: A sudden decision. I was surprised when I heard the news.

 练习

练习一、根据拼音写汉字，根据汉字写拼音
(　)rán　shèng(　)　zhí(　)　chéng(　)　gǔ(　)
忽(　)(　)利　(　)业　(　)分　(　)动

练习二、搭配连线
(1) 营养　　　　　　　　A. 道德
(2) 日程　　　　　　　　B. 成功
(3) 取得　　　　　　　　C. 成分
(4) 职业　　　　　　　　D. 袭击
(5) 突然　　　　　　　　E. 安排

练习三、从今天学习的生词中选择合适的词填空
1. 事情发生得很 _____，他一下子不知道该怎么办了。
2. 昨晚德国和土耳其的比赛，德国队最终取得了 _____。
3. 我弟弟最喜欢的 _____ 是律师。
4. 这件衣服的生产 _____ 其实很低，到商场里就卖得很贵。
5. 王芳是护士，她的 _____ 工作就是照顾病人。
6. 那个电影明星事业上很 _____，可是婚姻却不幸福。
7. 谈到这件事，她 _____ 伤心地哭了。
8. 研究发现，香烟里的尼古丁(nicotine) _____ 可致癌。
9. 这个公司在中国发展得很好，目前有一千多名 _____。
10. 秘书说，老板这个星期的 _____ 都安排满了。

 答案

练习一：
略

练习二：
(1) C　　(2)E　　(3)B　　(4)A　　(5)D

练习三：
1. 突然　　2. 胜利　　3. 职业　　4. 成本　　5. 日常
6. 成功　　7. 忽然/突然　　8. 成分　　9. 职员
10. 日程

 星期四

yīshēng
医生　　dàifu
　　　　　　⊜ 大夫　　(甲) 名

doctor; physician

常用搭配
请医生 send for a doctor　　牙科医生 dentist
外科医生 surgeon

用法示例
医生仔细检查了她的身体。
The doctor examined her carefully.
你应该去看医生。
You should see a doctor.
他正接受内科医生的治疗。
He is under the care of a physician.

yǐhòu
以后　　(甲) 名

later; after; in the future

常用搭配
三天以后 three days later
毕业以后 after graduation
在以后的岁月中 in the following years

用法示例
走了四个小时以后，我们开始感到累了。
After walking for four hours we began to feel tired.
离婚以后，孩子由父亲监护。
After their divorce, the father was awarded custody of their son.
到了这里一个月以后，学生们开始想家了。
The students began to feel homesick after they had been here for a month.

yīyuàn
医院　　(甲) 名

hospital

常用搭配
妇产医院 maternity hospital
儿童医院 children's hospital

用法示例
我父亲是一所大医院的医生。
My father is a doctor in a big hospital.
我昨天去医院看望朋友了。
Yesterday, I went to see a friend in the hospital.

jīnhòu
今后　　(乙) 名

henceforth; from now on

常用搭配
今后请准时。In the future, please be punctual.

【用法示例】
我发誓今后再也不对你说谎话了。
From now on I promise never to lie to you.
我今后会小心。
Henceforth I shall be careful.
今后任何违反秩序的行为都会受到严厉惩罚。
From now on, any violation of the regulations will be severely punished.
希望今后两国人民之间有更多的交往。
We hope that from now on there will be greater relations between our two peoples.

zhǐchū
指出 (乙)动
indicate; point out
【常用搭配】
明确指出 point out clearly
【用法示例】
请指出这句话中的错误。
Point out the mistake in this sentence, please.
必须明确指出,部长的言论有两点是错误的。
Just for the record, the minister's statement is wrong on two points.
我指出了那个方案的不足之处。
I pointed out the shortcomings of the scheme.

shōurù   zhīchū
收入   反 支出   (乙)名
income; earning
【常用搭配】
高收入 high income   月收入 monthly income
家庭收入 household income
【用法示例】
他只能靠微薄的收入来养家。
He had to support his family with his meager income.
低收入家庭需要政府帮助。
Low-income families need governmental help.
工资是我收入的主要来源。
My wages are the principal source of my income.

tuīguǎng
推广 (乙)动
popularize; generalize
【常用搭配】
推广一项新发明 promote a new invention
【用法示例】
我们决定推广这种教学方法。
We decided to spread this teaching method.
推广这种新方法不是件容易的工作。
Popularizing this new method is not an easy job.

tuīdòng   zǔài
推动   反 阻碍   (乙)动
push; promote

【常用搭配】
推动经济发展 promote the development of the economy
【用法示例】
该协会致力于推动世界和平事业。
The society was dedicated to furthering the cause of world peace.
这项活动旨在推动贸易的发展。
The aim of the activity is to promote the development of trade.

jìnzhǐ
禁止 (乙)动
prohibit; forbid
【常用搭配】
禁止停车 !No standing!
禁止拍照 !Cameras are forbidden!
【用法示例】
这里禁止吸烟。
Smoking is prohibited here.
法律禁止向18岁以下的人出售含酒精的饮料。
The law forbids the sale of alcohol to people under 18.
国会通过了一项法令,禁止捕杀珍稀动物。
Parliament has passed an Act forbidding the killing of rare animals.

yǔnxǔ   zhǔnxǔ
允许   同 准许   (乙)动
permit; allow
【常用搭配】
未经允许 without permission
请允许我(介绍) Allow me to (introduce)
【用法示例】
情况不允许有任何耽搁。
The situation does not allow for any delay.
每位旅客允许携带二十五公斤的行李。
Each passenger is allowed twenty-five kilograms of luggage.
如果情况允许,我们将在下周举行会议。
Circumstances permitting, we shall hold the meeting next week.

zhīchū
支出 (丁)动/名
① spend ② expenditure
【常用搭配】
行政支出 administrative expenditure
支出账目 expense account
【用法示例】
他把自己的所有支出都记在本子上。
He entered all his expenses in a notebook.
我的支出受到收入的限制。
My expenditure is restricted by my income.

zhǐdiǎn
指点 （丙）动

give advice (directions)

常用搭配
给予指点 give some instructions

用法示例
你最好跟你的老师谈一谈，也许他能给你指点指点。
You'd better talk about it with your teacher. Maybe he can give you some useful advice.
关于怎样处理这件事，她给了我一些有益的指点。
She gave me some useful hints on how to deal with the matter.

以后、今后

1、"今后"和"以后"都可以表示将来的时间，在日常生活中"以后"更常用，"今后"往往用作书面语言。如：今后/以后我会尽力做得更好。

Both 今后 and 以后 indicate a time in the future. In our daily life, 以后 is used more often, and 今后 is usually used in writing. For example: I will try to do better in the future.

2、"今后"指从今天（现在）之后，表示将来的时间；"以后"可以表示过去的一个时间之后。如：一年以后，结婚以后。

今后 means "from now on", indicating a time in the future; 以后 can indicate the time after a certain moment in the past, e.g. one year later, after marriage.

练习一、根据拼音写汉字，根据汉字写拼音

( )xǔ jìn( ) zhǐ( ) tuī( ) ( )yuàn
允( ) ( )止 ( )出 ( )广 医( )

练习二、搭配连线
(1) 指出   A. 支出
(2) 行政   B. 医院
(3) 儿童   C. 医生
(4) 内科   D. 吸烟
(5) 禁止   E. 错误

练习三、从今天学习的生词中选择合适的词填空

1. 两个月_____，他的病好了。
2. 在美国，牙医是_____很高的职业。
3. 为了节约能源，国家加大了新产品的研发和_____。
4. 我刚来中国，什么都不懂，请老师多_____。
5. 教室的墙上有几个字：_____吸烟。
6. 公司开会时，老板讲了_____五年的发展规划。
7. 这篇文章的优点很多，但现在我只_____不足之处。
8. 这个月的_____比原来计划的多，所以我不得不向朋友借钱。
9. 科学_____社会向前发展。
10. 妈妈每天只_____我吃一个冰激淋。

练习一：
略

练习二：
(1) E (2)A (3)B (4)C (5)D

练习三：
1. 以后   2. 收入   3. 推广   4. 指点   5. 禁止
6. 今后   7. 指出   8. 支出   9. 推动   10. 允许

星期五

yǒuyìsi
有意思 (甲)
interesting

常用搭配
一个有意思的想法 an interesting idea
一个有意思的故事 an interesting story

用法示例
将这两位作家加以比较是很有意思的。
It is interesting to compare the two writers.
我觉得那部电影没有意思。
I don't think that film is interesting.
这本书很有意思。
This book is very interesting.

zuòyè
作业 (甲)名
work; task; operation

常用搭配
留家庭作业 assign homework
作业本 workbook
流水作业 line production

用法示例
这个学生一到家就做作业。
This student does his homework as soon as he gets home.
今天晚上我们有很多作业要做。
We have a lot of homework to do tonight.

gùyì
故意   同 有意 (乙)形
intentional; deliberate; designed

常用搭配
故意谋杀 a deliberate murder
故意迟到 be late deliberately

用法示例
他故意把那个老人撞倒了。
He knocked the old man down on purpose.
他故意不到会。
He deliberately absented himself from the meeting.
你故意与我作对。
You have deliberately acted against me.

jìnkǒu
进口 (乙)动
import

常用搭配
进口税 import tax
从日本进口鱼 to import fish from Japan

用法示例
我们从澳大利亚进口小麦。
We imported wheat from Australia.
我们医院进口了一些外科器械。
Our hospital imported some surgical instruments.
政府已经对进口加以限制了。
The government has imposed a limitation on imports.

chūkǒu
出口 (乙)动/名
① export ② exit

常用搭配
紧急出口 emergency exit

用法示例
他对出口手续很熟悉。
He is familiar with the export procedures.
巴西出口咖啡。
Brazil exports coffee.
他们做进出口贸易。
They are engaged in the import and export trade.
剧院的出口在哪儿?
Where is the exit in the theater?

duǎnqī
短期 (乙)形
short-term

常用搭配
短期贷款 short-term loans
短期培训班 short course

用法示例
那是长期投资,不是短期的。
That is a long-term investment, not a short one.
他只是短期外出,最多一周。
He's only away for short periods of time, a week at the longest.
短期内我们会赔钱,但从长远看,利润将会是丰厚的。
In the short term we will lose money, but in the long term our profits will be very large.

bùxíng
不行 (乙)形
① be not allowed ② not be possible

常用搭配
就是不行! It just won't do!

用法示例
明天恐怕不行。
Tomorrow won't do, I'm afraid.
期待别人的帮助是不行的。
It is no good hoping for other's help.
他不行,他太年轻,不能干这个工作。
He can't. He is too young to do that job.

bùxìng
不幸   反 幸运 (乙)形
misfortune; unfortunate

常用搭配
遭遇不幸 suffer a misfortune
不幸的事故 unlucky accident

用法示例
真不幸,她在冰上摔倒了。
Unfortunately, she fell down on the ice.
我不幸错过了末班火车。
Unfortunately, I missed the last train.
他总是抱怨他的不幸。
He always moaned about his misfortunes.

业余 yèyú 反 专业 zhuānyè (乙)形
① spare time ② amateur

常用搭配
业余时间 spare time
业余爱好 hobby

用法示例
他不知道怎样安排业余时间。
He doesn't know what to do with his spare time.
你是专业的,我是业余的。
You are a professional, but I am an amateur.
他是一个业余画家。
He is an amateur painter.

推辞 tuīcí (丙)动
decline

常用搭配
别推辞了!Don't turn it down!

用法示例
他推辞说不能参加会议。
He excused himself from the meeting.
我觉得他适合这个职位,希望他不要推辞。
I think he is the right person for this position. I hope he won't turn it down.

有意 yǒuyì (丙)动
① intend; have a mind to ② intentionally

常用搭配
有意离开 intend to leave

用法示例
我决不会有意伤害你的感情。
I would never intentionally hurt your feelings.
我有意让你接管公司。
I intend for you to take over the business.

打扫 dǎsǎo 同 清扫 qīngsǎo (丙)动
sweep; clean

常用搭配
打扫房间 clean the room

用法示例
她把地板打扫得很干净。
She swept the floor clean.
学生们轮流打扫教室。
The students take turns to clean the classroom.
你打扫厨房了吗?
Have you cleaned the kitchen?

故意、有意
"故意"和"有意"都可以表示有意识地做事情;但"有意"还表示"有做某事的意愿"的意思,"故意"没有。如:①如果我伤害了你的感情,那完全不是故意/有意的。②他们有意与我们合作。

Both 故意 and 有意 mean "to do something deliberately", but 有意 has another meaning of "intend to do something"; 故意 hasn't. For example: ① If I've hurt your feelings, it was unintentional. ② They intend to cooperate with us.

练习一、根据拼音写汉字,根据汉字写拼音
( )cí zuò( ) ( )yì ( )xìng ( )qī
推( ) ( )业 故( ) 不( ) 短( )

练习二、搭配连线
(1) 家庭   A. 贷款
(2) 短期   B. 时间
(3) 遭遇   C. 厨房
(4) 打扫   D. 不幸
(5) 业余   E. 作业

练习三、从今天学习的生词中选择合适的词填空
1. 当年,我_____出国留学,可是我的父母不同意。
2. 超市里,从日本_____的大米卖得很贵,所以叫天价大米。
3. 这个孩子很_____,他的父母在战争中都去逝了。
4. 他不喜欢参加那个活动,找了个借口_____了。
5. 男朋友跟丽丽道歉说:"我不是_____的,请你原谅"!
6. 这个国家的经济危机非常严重,_____内不会有明显的改善。
7. 那部小说很_____,我看了三遍。
8. 成为歌星之前,她只是个_____歌手,没受过专业的训练。
9. 他不爱_____房间,所以他的房间很乱。
10. 中国_____到欧洲的服装在商场上价格很低。

 **答案**

练习一：
略
练习二：
(1) E　　(2) A　　(3) D　　(4) C　　(5) B
练习三：
1. 有意　2. 进口　3. 不幸　4. 推辞　5. 故意
6. 短期　7. 有意思　8. 业余　9. 打扫　10. 出口

第2月，第1周的练习

练习一、根据词语给加点的字注音
1.(　)　2.(　)　3.(　)　4.(　)　5.(　)
鼓掌　　成分　　允许　　推辞　　后退

练习二、根据拼音填写词语
　　　zhǐ　　　zhǐ　　　zhí　　　zhī　　　hū
1. 禁(　) 2.(　)点　3.(　)业　4.(　)出　5.(　)然

练习三、辨析并选择合适的词填空
1. 他最大的(　)是热情好客、乐于助人。（好处、优点）
2. 适量运动对身体健康有(　)。（好处、优点）
3. 我的爱人是我大学时的(　)。（学生、同学）
4. 老师在指导他的(　)写毕业论文。（学生、同学）
5. 这个问题出现得太(　)了，我一时不知道该怎么处理。（忽然、突然）
6. 他在上课的时候(　)倒在了地上，同学们赶快把他送到了医院。（忽然、突然）
7. 他打算毕业(　)去上海，在一家大公司工作。（以后、今后）
8. (　)十年，公司会着力开拓亚洲市场，使产品覆盖率达到50%。（以后、今后）
9. 她(　)参加这个比赛，但不知道怎么报名。（故意、有意）
10. 他知道老师今天一上课就要听写生词，所以他(　)迟到了二十分钟。（故意、有意）

练习四、选词填空
内部　　职员　　商场　　作业　　推广
内容　　职业　　商品　　业余　　推动

1. 他现在的(　)是会计，不过，他想找别的工作。
2. 他发现中国的小学生很累，因为他们几乎每天要做很多(　)。
3. 他在博物馆工作，他的(　)爱好是写作和听音乐。
4. 你们的公司规模大吗？一共有多少名(　)？
5. 银行正在进行(　)装修，两个月后完工。
6. 使用这种设备可以节约大量能源，政府正准备在全国范围内(　)。
7. 这个大型(　)出售各种各样的(　)。
8. 通过举办国际青年研讨会，可以(　)各国青年之间的交流和学习。
9. 她在(　)时间喜欢和朋友一起逛(　)。
10. 这种杂志的(　)特别吸引人，深受青年人的欢迎。

练习五、写出下列词语的同义词
1. 同情(　)　　2. 年龄(　)
3. 缺点(　)　　4. 故意(　)
5. 允许(　)

练习六、写出下列词语的反义词
1. 推动(　)　　2. 收入(　)
3. 胜利(　)　　4. 业余(　)
5. 好处(　)

 **答案**

练习一：
1. zhǎng　2. fèn　3. yǔn　4. cí　5. tuì
练习二：
1. 止　2. 指　3. 职　4. 支　5. 忽
练习三：
1. 优点　2. 好处　3. 同学　4. 学生　5. 突然
6. 忽然/突然　7. 以后　8. 今后　9. 有意
10. 故意
练习四：
1. 职业　2. 作业　3. 业余　4. 职员　5. 内部
6. 推广　7. 商场，商品　8. 推动
9. 业余，商场　10. 内容
练习五：
1. 怜悯　2. 年纪　3. 不足　4. 有意　5. 准许
练习六：
1. 阻碍　2. 支出　3. 失败　4. 专业　5. 坏处

2月 第2周的学习内容

星期一

hǎokàn
好看 （甲）形
① good-looking ② interesting

常用搭配
好看的花 beautiful flower

用法示例
那是一部老电影，但是很好看。
It's an old film, but it's very good.
这本书很好看。
The book is interesting.
她穿那条新裙子很好看。
She looks very pretty in that new skirt.

měilì
美丽 反 丑陋 （乙）形
beautiful

常用搭配
美丽的国家 beautiful country
美丽的草原 beautiful grasslands

用法示例
王子住在一座美丽的大城堡里。
The prince lived in a large and beautiful castle.
他爱上了那位美丽的姑娘。
He fell in love with that beautiful girl.
我喜欢家乡美丽的风景。
I like the beautiful scenery in my hometown.

piányi
便宜 反 昂贵 （甲）形
cheap; inexpensive

常用搭配
便宜货 cheap goods　　便宜的鞋 cheap shoes
占便宜 gain an unfair advantage

用法示例
自行车比小汽车便宜多了。
A bicycle is much cheaper than a car.
这家超市的面包是自制的，所以很便宜。
Bread is cheap in this supermarket because they bake it themselves.
这种汽车便宜。
This kind of car is inexpensive.

yóu
由 （乙）介
from; by

常用搭配
由……构成／组成 be composed of …

用法示例
许多疾病是由细菌引起的。
Many diseases are caused by bacteria.
由车站走到这里只有十分钟的路程。
It is no more than ten minutes' walk from the station.
水是由氢和氧组成的。
Water is composed of hydrogen and oxygen.

shāngliang
商量 同 商议 （乙）动
talk over; discuss; consult

常用搭配
与律师商量 consult with one's lawyer

用法示例
我有点私事要和你商量。
I have something personal to discuss with you.
我跟朋友商量一件事。
I consulted with a friend on a matter.
关于这件事，我必须跟委托人商量一下。
I must consult my principal on this matter.

zhànshì
战士 （乙）名
soldier

常用搭配
一名解放军战士 a soldier of the People's Liberation Army

用法示例
他的儿子是一名战士。
His son is a soldier.
他既是个战士，又是个诗人。
He is both a soldier and a poet.
这个战士非常勇敢。
The soldier is very brave.

tǒngzhì
统治 （乙）动
control; rule

常用搭配
统治国家 rule over a country
专制统治 despotic rule

用法示例
他统治了这个国家四十年。
He reigned over the country for forty years.

女王英明地统治着她的王国。
The queen ruled her kingdom wisely.
谁统治这个国家？
Who rules this country?

tōngxùn
通讯 （乙）名
communication

常用搭配
通讯系统 communication systems
通讯技术 communication technology
通讯设备 communications equipment
通讯卫星 communications satellites

用法示例
无线电通讯已消除了空间的阻隔。
Radio communication has reduced the distance between people.
一切通讯都因地震而中断了。
All lines of communication have been broken by the earthquake.
无线电和电视是重要的通信手段。
Radio and television are important means of communication.

biànlì / fāngbiàn
便利 ≈ 方便 （丙）形
convenient

常用搭配
便利店 convenience store
便利的位置 convenient locations

用法示例
我们买下这所房子是因为它很便利。
We bought this house for its convenience.
玛丽英语说得好，因为她有一个便利条件，她妈妈是英国人。
Mary speaks English well, because she has the advantage of her mother being English.

tōngxìn
通信 （丙）动
communicate by letter; correspond

常用搭配
与他通信 correspond with him
停止通信往来 end a correspondence

用法示例
我们定期通信。
We correspond regularly.
你一直和你父母通信吗？
Are you still writing to your parents?
我们已经通信多年了，可是我从未见过他本人。
We've corresponded for years but I've never actually met him.

cèliáng
测量 （丙）动
measure

常用搭配
测量长方形的面积
measure the area of a rectangle

用法示例
他测量了墙的高度。
He measured the height of the wall.
声波是根据其振幅来测量的。
Sound waves are measured by their amplitude.
我们测量了这辆车的耗油量。
We have measured the car's fuel consumption.

zhànyǒu
战友 （丙）名
comrade-in-arms; fellow soldier

常用搭配
老战友 old comrade-in-arms

用法示例
他们是战友。
They were comrades in arms.
我经常接到我们战友的来信。
I often hear from my fellow soldiers from the army.
见到老战友使我回想起自己在部队中的日子。
The sight of the old comrades carried me back to my days in the army.

词义辨析

好看、美丽

"好看"和"美丽"都表示漂亮，"好看"比较口语化，可以用来形容风景、人、书、电影等用眼睛能看到的具体的事物；"美丽"比较正式，一般用于书面语，可以用来形容抽象的事物。比如：①好看／美丽的姑娘。②西湖以好看／美丽的风景著称。③好看的电影。④美丽的心灵。

Both 好看 and 美丽 mean beautiful. 好看 is quite colloquial, and can be used to modify scenery, people, books, movies, and other things which are concrete, and that are limited to the visual sense. 美丽 is quite formal and literary, and can modify something abstract. For example: ① A beautiful girl. ② The West Lake is famous for its beautiful scenery. ③ An interesting movie, ④ beautiful soul.

练习一、根据拼音写汉字，根据汉字写拼音
(　)lì　tōng(　)　tǒng(　)　(　)yi　shāng(　)
便(　)　(　)讯　(　)治　便(　)　(　)量

练习二、搭配连线
(1) 好看的　　　　　A. 商品
(2) 美丽的　　　　　B. 草原
(3) 便利的　　　　　C. 战士
(4) 便宜的　　　　　D. 位置
(5) 勇敢的　　　　　E. 电影

练习三、从今天学习的生词中选择合适的词填空
1. 丽莎和她的姐姐生活在不同的国家,但她们一直_____,保持联系。
2. 杰克说他喜欢在中国生活,因为东西很_____,生活压力小。
3. 这个小_____死时还不到十九岁,但他在战场上表现得非常勇敢。
4. 情况我已经说了,怎么办_____他来决定。
5. 这部电影真_____,我还想再看一遍。
6. 我们俩曾经是_____,我们是同一年参军的。
7. 去山里探险,一定要带着_____设备,以便与外界联络。
8. 在这个地方租房子不错,买东西方便,交通也_____。
9. 桂林是个_____的地方,山美、水美、人更美。
10. 人们虽然不喜欢他的_____,但更不喜欢战争。

答案

练习一：
略

练习二：
(1) E　　(2) B　　(3) D　　(4) A　　(5) C

练习三：
1. 通信　2. 便宜　3. 战士　4. 由　5. 好看
6. 战友　7. 通讯　8. 便利　9. 美丽　10. 统治

比　bǐ　（甲）介
① than　② compare

常用搭配
与……比 compare with...
他比我高。He is taller than I am.

用法示例
这条街比那条街宽三倍。
This street is three times wider than that one.
迟到总比不到好。
Better late than never.
她无比美丽。
Her beauty is beyond compare.
走路比不上飞行。
Walking can't compare with flying.

以为　yǐwéi　同 认为 rènwéi　（甲）动
① presume　② think

常用搭配
我原以为…… I thought that…

用法示例
过去人们以为地球是扁的。
People used to believe that the earth was flat.
根据你的名字,我还以为你是外国人呢。
I presume from your name that you are a foreigner.
别那么幼稚,以为政客说的一切都是可信的。
Don't be so naive as to believe everything the politicians tell you.

似乎　sìhū　反 肯定 kěndìng　（乙）副
① seem　② as if

常用搭配
似乎明白 seem to understand
似乎认识 seem to know

用法示例
他似乎和往常一样忙碌。
He seems to be as busy as ever.
他似乎什么都懂。
It seems as if he knows everything.
问题似乎很复杂。
The problem seems very complicated.

仿佛　fǎngfú　（乙）动
① as though; as if　② be alike

68

常用搭配
仿佛在梦里 feel as if one is living in a dream
仿佛回到了故乡 feel as if one has returned to one's hometown

用法示例
他从我身边走过仿佛不认识我似的。
He passed me by as though he didn't know me.
连公牛仿佛也为这个醉汉感到遗憾。
Even the bull seemed to feel sorry for the drunk.
她看起来仿佛是冰做的。
It looked as if she were made of ice.

chūshì
出事　　　　　　　　　　（丙）动
have an accident; meet with a mishap

常用搭配
她出事了。She had an accident.

用法示例
他出事了,被一辆汽车撞倒了。
He's had an accident: he's been knocked down by a car.
不要这么干,否则你会出事的。
Do not rush or you may have an accident.
我们猜想他一定出事了。
We surmised that he must have had an accident.

tūchū　　　　　　āoxiàn
突出　　　反 凹陷　　　（乙）形/动
① prominent; outstanding ② highlight

常用搭配
突出的成就 outstanding achievement
突出的牙齿 prominent teeth
突出重点 highlight the main points

用法示例
那个女孩的表现在班里很突出。
That girl's performance in class is outstanding.
他身材高大,因此在人群中很突出。
His height makes him stand out in the crowd.
他的眉毛特别突出。
His eyebrows are very prominent.

tūjī
突击　　　　　　　　　　（乙）动
assault

常用搭配
突击队 an assault force　进行突击 do a rush job

用法示例
突击队要参加令人筋疲力尽的突击课程。
Commandos are put through an exhausting assault course.
他们计划对这个城市进行突击。
They planned to take the city by assault.

dēngjì
登记　　　　　　　　　　（乙）动
register; check in

常用搭配
登记入伍 sign up for the army
登记姓名 register one's name

用法示例
他把我们的名字登记下来了。
He registered our names.
她登记了孩子的出生日期。
She registered the birth date of her child.
在哪儿办理登记手续?
Where can I check in?

búduàn　　　　　　bùtíng
不断　　　同 不停　　　（乙）形
continuous; uninterrupted

常用搭配
连续不断的练习 continual practice
不断取得进展 make progress steadily

用法示例
大脑需要不断地供血。
The brain needs a continuous supply of blood.
语言在使用中不断地发展。
Languages develop through continuous usage.
整个早上都有人不断给办公室打电话。
The telephone has been continuously ringing in the office all morning.

zhīpèi
支配　　　　　　　　　　（丙）动
① arrange ② dominate

常用搭配
支配别人 dominate others
合理支配时间 arrange one's time properly

用法示例
你决不要受别人意见的支配。
You must not be governed by the opinions of others.
她想要支配别人,这引起了家庭纠纷。
Her desire to dominate the others caused trouble in the family.

zhànlüè
战略　　　　　　　　　　（丙）名
strategy

常用搭配
经营战略 business strategy　战略目的 strategic purpose

用法示例
这名军官善于学习战略与战术。
The officer is good at learning strategy and tactics.
我们作了一次战略性撤退,以便我们能保存实力再次进攻。
We made a strategic withdrawal, so that we could build up our forces for a renewed attack.

zhànchǎng
战场　　　　　　　　　　（丙）名
battleground; battlefield

常用搭配
上战场 go to the battlefield

用法示例
我们把伤员抬出了战场。
We carried the wounded off the battlefield.
这个战场被视为圣地以纪念战死在这里的战士。
This battlefield is dedicated to the memory of the soldiers who died here.
战场上到处都是尸骨。
The battlefield is covered with the bones of the dead.

 词义辨析

似乎、仿佛

1、"似乎"和"仿佛"都可以做状语，表示不十分确定的意思，"似乎"比"仿佛"更口语化。如：①我似乎/仿佛听到远处有说话声。②他工作不错，但似乎缺乏信心。

似乎 and 仿佛 can be used as adverbials, indicating "to seem to be", and 似乎 is more colloquial than 仿佛. For example: ① I seemed to hear a voice in the distance. ② He is good at his job, but he seems to lack confidence.

2、"仿佛"是动词，表示"和……相像"，有时候和"似的"连用；"似乎"是副词，没有这样的用法和意思。

仿佛 is a verb meaning "to be like". Sometimes it can be used in the structure "仿佛…似的"; 似乎 can not be used in this way.

 练习

练习一、根据拼音写汉字，根据汉字写拼音
( )jī tū( ) zhàn( ) ( )fú ( )hū
登( ) ( )击 ( )略 仿( ) 似( )

练习二、搭配连线
(1) 不断　　　　A. 姓名
(2) 经营　　　　B. 发展
(3) 支配　　　　C. 战略
(4) 登记　　　　D. 重点
(5) 突出　　　　E. 他人

练习三、从今天学习的生词中选择合适的词填空
1. 爸爸今天_____不高兴，一回家就进了书房，直到吃饭时才出来。
2. 别_____考试成绩好就行，用人单位更看重能力。
3. 毕业后很少说英语，很多都忘了，所以在出国之前，我得再_____一下。
4. 地震发生后，全国各地的救灾物资_____运送到灾区。
5. 对这个问题，我们不能大意，要从_____高度看这个问题。
6. 经理发现新来的这个员工工作能力很_____。
7. 我明明是第一次来这个城市，但我却觉得_____来过这里。
8. 妈妈让孩子自己_____这笔钱。
9. 刚打完仗，_____上有很多尸体。
10. 男人和女人，谁也不_____谁笨。

答案

练习一：
略

练习二：
(1) B (2)C (3)E (4)A (5)D

练习三：
1. 似乎 2. 以为 3. 突击 4. 不断 5. 战略
6. 突出 7. 仿佛 8. 支配 9. 战场 10. 比

星期三 Wednesday

gāoxìng
高兴 （甲）形/动
① glad; happy ② delight

常用搭配
高兴地大笑 to laugh with delight
高兴做某事 be happy to do sth.
高兴的样子 a joyful look

用法示例
你喜欢,我就高兴。
I'm glad you enjoyed it.
他总是高高兴兴的，即使在输了的时候也是如此。
He always looked cheerful, even in defeat.
想到能再次见到她,他就高兴起来了。
He was happy at the thought of seeing her again.

wéi
为 （甲）介
for; as

常用搭配
作为礼物 as a gift 视他为朋友 look on him as a friend

用法示例
炸弹把那座建筑夷为平地了。
The bombs razed the building to the ground.

wèi
为
for; (in order) to

常用搭配
为了生存 in order to survive
为安全起见。Just to be on the safe side.

用法示例
为学习汉语,汤姆来到了北京。
In order to learn Chinese, Tom came to Beijing.
我为女儿买了一本词典。
I bought a dictionary for my daughter.
妈妈正在为我们准备午餐。
My mother is preparing lunch for us.

sīxiǎng
思想 （甲）名
thought; idea

常用搭配
中心思想 the central tenet 思想家 a thinker

用法示例
他清楚地表达了自己的思想。
He formulated his thoughts clearly.
我们用词句来表达思想。
We express our thoughts by means of words.

电视已成为传播政治思想的重要媒介。
Television has become an important vehicle for spreading political ideas.

chēngzàn
称赞 （乙）动
praise; compliment

常用搭配
称赞她 praise her 由衷的称赞 sincere compliment

用法示例
他总是称赞他的女儿。
He always speaks well of his daughter.
人人都称赞这本书。
Everybody praised the book.
我们称赞他是个热心人。
We laud him as being a warmhearted man.

zànchéng
赞成 反反对 （乙）动
approve; agree with

常用搭配
赞成他的意见 endorse his opinions
用微笑表示赞成 showed approval by smiling

用法示例
她点头表示赞成。
She nodded her approval.
我父亲赞成我去国外学习。
My father approved my studying abroad.
主席赞成委员会的建议。
The chairman assented to the committee's proposals.

nánshòu
难受 反舒服 （乙）形
feel uncomfortable

常用搭配
感到难受 feel uncomfortable 心里难受 feel sorry

用法示例
我觉得难受极了。
I feel awful.
我可能感冒了,感到很难受。
Maybe I have a cold. I feel very uncomfortable.
她的不幸让我感到很难受。
Her wretchedness made him feel miserable.

sīrén
私人 （乙）形
private; personal

常用搭配
私人访问 private visit
私人秘书 private secretary
私人财产 private property

用法示例
这是私人土地,你不能通过。
This is private land, you can't walk across it.

总统正在对欧洲进行私人访问。
The president is paying a private visit to Europe.
私人小汽车能给人带来很大的便利。
A private car can bring great convenience to people.

避免 bìmiǎn 同 防止 fángzhǐ （乙）动
avoid

常用搭配
避免犯错误 avoid making mistakes
避免传染 avoid infection

用法示例
尽量避免危险。
Try to avoid danger.
死是不可避免的。
Death is inevitable.
为避免混淆,两队穿着不同颜色的衣服。
To avoid confusion, the teams wore different colors.

道德 dàodé （乙）名
① moral ② ethics

常用搭配
道德标准 moral standards
道德败坏 moral corruption
道德品质 moral trait

用法示例
她是个有道德的女性,人人都尊敬她。
She was such a virtuous woman that everybody respected her.
他的行为违背了道德准则。
His behavior transgressed morality.
我们对道德标准看法不一致。
We differ in our moral standards.

难民 nànmín （丁）名
refugee

常用搭配
难民营 refugee camp

用法示例
这些难民非常感激政府的救援。
These refugees are very grateful for the government's assistance.
他负责把食物分发给难民。
He is in charge of the dispensation of food to the refugees.
难民被暂时安置在一座旧军营里了。
The refugees are being lodged in an old army camp.

快乐 kuàilè （乙）形
happy; cheerful

常用搭配
生日快乐！Happy birthday!
快乐的家庭 a joyous family
快乐的童年 happy childhood

用法示例
财富并不一定带来快乐。
Money doesn't always bring happiness.
她是个快乐的小姑娘。
She is a happy girl.
我祝你健康快乐。
I wish you well and happy.

思索 sīsuǒ 同 思考 sīkǎo （丙）动
think deeply; think over

常用搭配
思索问题 ponder upon the problem
认真思索 think over carefully

用法示例
仔细思索之后再回答。
Think carefully before you answer.
那位哲学家在思索人类的前途。
The philosopher is thinking about the future of the human race.
秘书一夜没睡,反复思索着是离开还是留下。
The secretary lay awake all night pondering whether to leave or stay.

 **词义辨析**

高兴、快乐

1、"高兴"和"快乐"都可以用作形容词,意思是感到愉快。但"高兴"比较口语化,"快乐"比较正式,多用于书面语。如：他看上去很高兴/快乐。很高兴见到你。快乐的时光。

As adjectives, 高兴 and 快乐 mean to feel happy. But 高兴 is more colloquial, while 快乐 is formal and literary. For example: He looks happy. Glad to meet you! Happy time.

2、"快乐"有幸福的意思,往往用来表达祝福或形容长久的愉快的状态；"高兴"往往表示当时的心情是兴奋而愉快的,另外,"高兴"还是动词,表示喜欢、乐意的意思。如：快乐地生活,生日快乐,你不高兴去就甭去。

快乐 also implies happiness, and is often used to indicate a long lasting happy state, or good wishes; 高兴 often means "feel delight and excite ment at one moment or occasion", and is also a verb too, meaning "be willing to do", or "like to do". For example: Live happily. Happy birthday! You don't have to go there if you don't wish to.

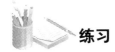 **练习**

练习一、根据拼音写汉字，根据汉字写拼音
( )mín sī ( ) bì ( ) ( )shòu ( )zàn
难( ) ( )索 ( )免 难( ) 称( )

练习二、搭配连线
(1) 表达　　　　　　A. 误会
(2) 避免　　　　　　B. 思想
(3) 私人　　　　　　C. 思索
(4) 认真　　　　　　D. 品质
(5) 道德　　　　　　E. 财产

练习三、从今天学习的生词中选择合适的词填空
1. 爸爸不_____儿子的这个计划。
2. 战争爆发后，很多_____无家可归。
3. 我的童年是在乡下度过的，那时候我很_____。
4. 那个年代的孩子，大多_____单纯。
5. 一般情况下，秘书不会拆看我的_____信件。
6. 弟弟听说暑假去海边，_____得跳了起来。
7. 邻居们都_____这个孩子勤奋、努力。
8. 昨天吃了辣的东西，胃有点儿_____。
9. 我一夜没睡，反复_____这个问题。
10. 做这份工作，一定要小心，_____出错。

 **答案**

练习一：
略
练习二：
(1) B　　(2)A　　(3)E　　(4)C　　(5)D
练习三：
1. 赞成　　2. 难民　　3. 快乐　　4. 思想　　5. 私人
6. 高兴　　7. 称赞　　8. 难受　　9. 思索　　10. 避免

yěxǔ
也许　　　　　　　　　　　　　　（甲）副
perhaps; maybe

常用搭配
他也许会来。Perhaps he will come.
也许要下雨。Maybe it'll rain.

用法示例
哦，也许是我错了。
Oh, maybe I was wrong.
也许这本书会对你的研究有用处。
Perhaps this book will be of some use to you in your studies.
也许他们需要我们的帮助。
Perhaps they are in need of our help.

kěnéng
可能　　　　　　　　　　　　（甲）助动／名
① possible; probable ② possibility; probability

常用搭配
可能的话 If possible
可能性 possibility
不可能…… There is no probability of ...

用法示例
我认为这可能是真的。
I think it may be true.
我会尽一切可能帮助你。
I'll do everything possible to help you.
只要有可能，他总是设法帮忙。
Wherever it is possible, he tries to help.
如果可能，她想跟我们走。
If possible, she wants to go with us.

zài
在　　　　　　　　　　　　　　（甲）介
in; at

常用搭配
在家 at home
在七十岁时 at 70 years of age
在海里游泳 swim in the sea
在 20 世纪 in the 20th century

用法示例
全镇沉浸在节日的气氛之中。
The whole town is in a festive mood.
在盒子里有一枝铅笔。
There is a pencil in the box.
我在十点钟之后很少出去。
I seldom go out after 10 o'clock.

73

水在摄氏零度结冰。
Water freezes at 0 degrees celsius.

投入 tóurù 圆 取出 qǔchū (乙) 动
① throw into ② invest ③ devote

常用搭配
投入调查 throw oneself into an investigation
投入大量资金 invest a large sum of money

用法示例
他把全部时间都投入在工作上了。
He devoted all his time to his job.
他们一到那儿就干劲十足地投入了工作。
They throw themselves into the work, as soon as they arrived.
他往投币孔投入了一枚硬币。
He put a coin into the slot.

要紧 yàojǐn (乙) 形
① important ② be critical

常用搭配
要紧的事 something urgent
不要紧。It doesn't matter.

用法示例
不要紧,别为它烦心了。
It's not important; don't worry about it.
现在我不能接见客人,因为我有一件要紧的事要办。
I can't see the visitors right now, I have an urgent matter to attend to.
你如果迟到也不要紧。
It doesn't matter if you are late.

供给 gōngjǐ 圆 供应 gòngyìng (乙) 动
provide; supply

常用搭配
由……供给 be supplied by…
保障供给 ensure the supply
燃油供给 fuel oil supply

用法示例
我将供给你所需要的一切。
I will furnish you with all you need.
他们为我们供给食物。
They provide us with food.
我们应该确保燃料供给不中断。
We must ensure the continuity of fuel supplies.

提供 tígōng (乙) 动
provide; offer

常用搭配
提供帮助 to offer help
提供服务 to provide a service

用法示例
这家公司将为运动员提供全套运动服装。
The company will provide the players with sports uniforms.
这家旅馆为旅客提供订票服务。
The hotel offers to reserve tickets for its guests.
碳水化合物给我们的身体提供能量。
Carbohydrates provide our bodies with energy.

必要 bìyào (乙) 形
necessary

常用搭配
如果必要的话…… if necessary …
必要条件 necessary condition

用法示例
没必要担忧。
There's no need to be concerned.
睡眠对健康是必要的。
Sleep is necessary for health.
你有必要去那里吗?
Is there any need for you to go there?

道歉 dàoqiàn 圆 致歉 zhìqiàn (乙) 动
apologize; make an apology

常用搭配
为某事向他道歉 apologize to him for sth
接受道歉 accept an apology

用法示例
我应向他道歉。
I owe him an apology.
他再三道歉。
He apologised profusely.
我因踩了她的脚而向她道歉。
I apologized to her for stepping on her foot.

透明 tòumíng (丙) 形
transparent; clearing

常用搭配
不透明玻璃 opaque glass

用法示例
这种玻璃是透明的。
The glass is transparent.
今天有雾,大气的透明度很低。
It's foggy. The visibility is low.

优越 yōuyuè (丙) 形
superior; advantageous

常用搭配
优越感 sense of superiority
优越的环境 advantageous circumstances

用法示例

她汉语说得好,因为她有一个优越条件,她妈妈在中国工作。
She speaks good Chinese, because she has the advantage of her mother working in china.

这台机器的性能比那台优越。
The performance of this machine is superior to that one.

优势 yōushì 反 劣势 lièshì (丙)名
superiority; advantage

常用搭配
取得优势地位 secure a position of advantage
集中优势兵力 concentrate superior forces
质量上占优势 superior in quality

用法示例
经过一个小时的比赛,他已取得了优势。
At the end of an hour's play the advantage lay with him.

或许对他们是坏事,但对我们正是优势。
Maybe it is bad to them, but it is just our advantage.

李奇比你占优势,因为他会讲德语。
Li Qi has an advantage over you since he can speak German.

词义辨析

也许、可能

1、"可能"和"也许"都可以表示猜测,意思是估计、大概。如:今天可能/也许会下雨。他也许/可能不能来了。

可能 and 也许 mean "probably, maybe", indicating "to guess", e.g. It seems to be raining. He probably can not come.

2、"可能"是名词,表示可能性,经常用作"有可能"、"尽可能";用作助动词的时候,"不"、"很"可以修饰"可能",如"不可能""很可能";"也许"没有这些用法。例如:①他有可能成为电影明星。②我们会尽可能地帮助他。③我不可能相信他。

可能 is a noun, meaning possibility, and is often used as "有可能" (it is possible …), "尽可能" (as … as possible). As an auxiliary verb, 可能 can be modified by "不"、"很", e.g. "不可能" (it is impossible), "很可能" (It is highly likely); these usages have nothing common with 也许. For example: ① It is possible for him to become a movie star. ② I will try my best to help him. ③ It is impossible for me to believe him.

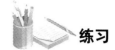

练习

练习一、根据拼音写汉字,根据汉字写拼音

yào (　) yōu (　) (　) jǐ (　) qiàn (　) míng
(　)紧 (　)越 供(　) 道(　) 透(　)

练习二、搭配连线

(1) 透明的　　　　A. 条件
(2) 要紧的　　　　B. 玻璃
(3) 优越的　　　　C. 事情
(4) 明显的　　　　D. 环境
(5) 必要的　　　　E. 优势

练习三、从今天学习的生词中选择合适的词填空

1. 去中国,没_____带这么多东西,很多东西都可以在那儿买。
2. 我学习的大学给学生_____多种免费服务。
3. 我没有认真复习,这次考试及格的_____性不大。
4.A: 安娜,你好点没？我陪你去医院吧？
　B: 不_____,我刚吃了药,好多了。
5. 他没来上课,我猜他_____生病了。
6. 需求量太大,_____跟不上。
7. 这个农民觉得大城市的人总有一种_____感。
8. 我们研发的新产品,现已_____生产。
9. 在联合国工作,她很有_____,因为她会说五种语言。
10. 水是_____的无色无味的液体。

练习一:
略

练习二:
(1) B　　(2)C　　(3)D　　(4)E　　(5)A

练习三:
1. 必要　　2. 提供　　3. 可能　　4. 要紧
5. 也许/可能　　6. 供给　　7. 优越
8. 投入　　9. 优势　　10. 透明

星期五

xiāoxi
消息 (甲)名
news; information

常用搭配
好消息 good news
一则消息 a piece of news
泄漏消息 news leak

用法示例
我好久没听到他的消息了。
I have had no news from him for a long time.
他的消息不准确。
His information is inaccurate.
这则消息使他们很吃惊。
The news greatly surprised them.

gēn
跟 (甲)介
① with ② and

常用搭配
跟……一起 together with ...
跟……有联系 connect with...
跟……谈话 talk with...

用法示例
他跟哥哥一样高。
He is as tall as his elder brother.
我能跟你谈一谈吗?
Can I have a word with you?
你想跟我去公园散步吗?
Do you feel like going for a walk in the park with me?

tōngguò
通过 (甲)动/介
① pass ② through; by

常用搭配
我通过了考试。I have passed the exam.
通过这种方法 by means of…

用法示例
众议院通过了这项议案。
The House of Representatives passed the bill.
小偷是通过这扇窗户进来的。
The thief got in through the window.
我通过职业介绍所找到了这份工作。
I got this job through an employment agency.

jiéshěng
节省 (乙)动
economize; spare

常用搭配
节省时间(精力、金钱) economize time (energy, money)

用法示例
冬天他们得节省燃料。
They have to skimp on fuel in winter.
我们的电费已经高得付不起了——得节省些了。
Our electricity bills are higher than we can afford—we must start to economize.
这项技术革新可以为我们节省大量的时间和劳动力。
This technical innovation will save us much time and labor.

jiéyuē　　　　　　　làngfèi
节约 反 浪费 (乙)动
① economize ② frugal

常用搭配
厉行节约 practice economy　　节约时间 save time

用法示例
节约等于增加收入。
Saving is earning.
厉行节约是美德。
To practice thrift is a virtue.
她说节约是解决危机的关键。
She said practising economy is the best means of solving the crisis.

làngfèi
浪费 (乙)动
waste; lavish; squander

常用搭配
浪费精力 dissipate efforts　　浪费的习惯 wasteful habits
浪费公款 waste public money

用法示例
别再浪费我的时间了!
Don't waste my time anymore.
浪费粮食是可耻的。
It is wicked to waste food.
把好的食物扔掉是浪费。
It is a waste to throw away good food.

yáncháng
延长 (乙)动
prolong; extend

常用搭配
延长寿命 prolong one's life　　延长线 an extension cord

用法示例
他申请延长签证有效期。
He asked for an extension of his visa.
校长把我们的假期延长了四天。
The headmaster extended our holiday by four days.
明年将要延长这条铁路。
The railway will be extended next year.

běnzhì
本质 (乙)名
essence; inbeing

常用搭配
本质上 in essence　　本质的区别 essential difference

用法示例
那两样东西在外表上相同,但在本质上不同。
The two things are the same in appearance but different in essence.
他本质上具有一种隐士的气质。
He is, in essence, a reclusive sort.
这两种经济体制的本质区别是什么?
What is the essential difference between these two economic systems?

běnlǐng
本领　　同 nénglì 能力　　(乙)名
ability; capability

常用搭配
自卫的能力 ability to defend oneself
提高本领 improve abilities

用法示例
她是怎样学到本领的?
How did she acquire her skill?
学生应提高为人民服务的本领。
Students should improve their abilities so as to serve the people.

tōngshùn
通顺　　同 tōngchàng 通畅　　(丙)形
clear and coherent; smooth

常用搭配
通顺的句子 fluent sentences

用法示例
学习了一年汉语之后,他现在已经能通顺地表达了。
Having learned Chinese for one year he can express himself clearly and coherently.
他写的不太通顺。
What he wrote is not very clear.

yáoyán
谣言 (丙)名
rumor

常用搭配
捏造谣言 fabricate a rumor　　传播谣言 spread rumors

用法示例
各种关于战争的谣言正四处流传。
All sorts of rumors about war are going around.
那条谣言毫无根据。
The rumor was without foundation.
他为谣言所困扰。
He was disturbed by the rumor.

suōduǎn
缩短　　延长　　(丙)动
shorten

常用搭配
缩短假期 shorten holidays
缩短学制 shorten the period of schooling

用法示例
老师让我把报告缩短为一页。
My teacher told me to shorten the report to one page.
总统不得不缩短他的访问时间。
The President had to curtail his visit.
据说抽烟会缩短寿命。
It's said that smoking will shorten one's life.

 词义辨析

节省、节约
　　"节约"和"节省"都是动词,都有避免浪费或减少耗费的意思。但"节省"一般用于具体的事,强调结果;"节约"比较正式,强调意义。如:节省了两个小时。勤俭节约。增产节约。这种新型设计能节约/节省燃料。
　　Both 节约 and 节省 are verbs, mean "to avoid waste, or reducing expenditure". 节省 is often applied to concrete things, and stresses the result of action; while 节约 is formal, and stresses significance. For example: to save two hours; be diligent and thrifty; to increase production and practice economy; the new model delivers fuel economy.

练习

练习一、根据拼音写汉字,根据汉字写拼音
(　)shùn　yáo(　)　(　)fèi　yán(　)　(　)duǎn
通(　)　(　)言　浪(　)　(　)长　缩(　)

练习二、搭配连线
(1) 提高　　　　　A. 消息
(2) 传播　　　　　B. 本领
(3) 延长　　　　　C. 时间
(4) 泄露　　　　　D. 寿命
(5) 节约　　　　　E. 谣言

练习三、从今天学习的生词中选择合适的词填空
1. 孩子已经有三天没_____了,这个母亲也急得三天没吃东西了。
2. 这件事情表面上看是这样,_____却正好相反。
3. 因为工作的关系,他不得不_____了度假的时间。
4. 老师把我作文中不_____的句子都改了。
5. 农民种地很辛苦,不要_____粮食。
6. 很多动物都有人类没有的特殊_____。

7. 他上大学时花钱很_____,因为他的钱都是自己打工赚的。
8. 前面在修路,车辆不能_____。
9. 由于论文没写完,杰克把签证又_____了半年。
10. 事实证明,老板和秘书的关系不是_____。

 **答案**

练习一:
略
练习二:
(1) B   (2)E   (3)D   (4)A   (5)C
练习三:
1. 消息   2. 本质   3. 缩短   4. 通顺   5. 浪费
6. 本领   7. 节省   8. 通过   9. 延长   10. 谣言

第2月,第2周的练习

练习一、根据词语给加点的字注音
1.( )   2.( )   3.( )   4.( )   5.( )
便宜   便利   难民   难受   测量

练习二、根据拼音填写词语
　　　sī　　　sī　　　bì　　　zhì　　　zhì
1.( )索 2.( )人 3.( )免 4.统( ) 5.本( )

练习三、辨析并选择合适的词填空
1. 尽管她的外表并不漂亮,但她有一颗( )的心灵。(好看、美丽)
2.《007》这部电影特别( ),我看了三遍,还想看。(好看、美丽)
3. 这里的风景美极了,( )仙境似的。(似乎、仿佛)
4. 她看着我,( )没明白我的意思。(似乎、仿佛)
5. 父母希望自己的孩子永远健康( )、无忧无虑。(高兴、快乐)
6. 他听到这个好消息时,( )得又唱又跳。(高兴、快乐)
7. 你告诉我发生了什么事,( )我能帮助你。(也许、可能)
8. 要是不参加考试,就不( )获得毕业证书。(也许、可能)
9. 她算了一下,这个月没逛街,比上个月( )了五百块钱。(节省、节约)
10. 尽管他现在很富有,但他仍然保持着勤俭( )的作风。(节省、节约)

练习四、选词填空
突出　　商量　　称赞　　优越　　延长
突击　　测量　　赞成　　优势　　谣言
1. 我刚刚接到电话,半小时后总部的专家组要来我们分公司进行( )检察。

2. 这个士兵因为坚强和勇敢而得到了领导的( )。
3. 在春节期间,商场( )了营业时间,晚上11:00才关门。
4. 医生正在为病人( )血压和体温。
5. 本地人在外地人面前总有一种( )感,其实他们不一定比外地人优秀。
6. 李老师高高的个子,站在一群小学生当中,显得特别( )。
7. 如果你会说两门外语,在找工作的时候你就会更有( )。
8. 我自己决定不了这件事,得跟主任( )一下。
9. 不要相信那些( ),总统根本没有受伤。
10. 我们不( )把公园改成停车场,因为这会破坏本地区的环境。

练习五、选择介词填空
由　　比　　为　　在　　跟
1. 他跑得( )我快多了,我不( )他比赛。
2. 他赢得了冠军,我真( )他感到高兴。
3. 不要( )一点小事就( )同学争吵。
4. 我还( )睡觉的时候,他就已经( )教室学习了。
5. 真没想到,这么多工作都是( )她一个人完成的。

练习六、写出下列词语的同义词
1. 商量( )   2. 避免( )
3. 道歉( )   4. 本领( )
5. 思索( )

练习七、写出下列词语的反义词
1. 美丽( )   2. 便宜( )
3. 赞成( )   4. 缩短( )
5. 节约( )

 **答案**

练习一:
1. pián   2. biàn   3. nàn   4. nán   5. liáng
练习二:
1. 思   2. 私   3. 避   4. 治   5. 质
练习三:
1. 美丽   2. 好看   3. 仿佛   4. 似乎   5. 快乐
6. 高兴   7. 也许   8. 可能   9. 节省   10. 节约
练习四:
1. 突击   2. 称赞   3. 延长   4. 测量   5. 优越
6. 突出   7. 优势   8. 商量   9. 谣言   10. 赞成
练习五:
1. 比,跟   2. 为   3. 为,跟   4. 在,在   5. 由
练习六:
1. 商议   2. 防止   3. 致歉   4. 能力   5. 思考
练习七:
1. 丑陋   2. 昂贵   3. 反对   4. 延长   5. 浪费

2月 第3周的学习内容

星期一

xūyào
需要 ⊜ 需求 xūqiú （甲）动/助动
① require ② need
常用搭配
我需要钱。I need money.
需要帮助 be in need of help
满足某人的需要 satisfy one's needs
用法示例
所有的植物都需要水和阳光。
All plants need water and light.
我的车需要修理。
My car needs fixing.
他需要帮忙吗？
Does he need any help?

tiáojiàn
条件 （甲）名
condition; qualification; term
常用搭配
天气条件 weather conditions
身体条件 physical qualifications
无条件地 unconditionally
受条件限制 impose conditions upon
用法示例
能力是成功的条件之一。
Having ability is one of the qualifications necessary for success in life.
和解的条件还算公平。
The terms of the settlement seem fair.
仍有许多人的生活条件是很艰苦的。
There are still many people whose living conditions are miserable.

gūjì
估计 ⊜ 估算 gūsuàn （乙）动
estimate; reckon
常用搭配
初步估计 preliminary estimate
估计成本 estimate the cost
用法示例
我估计她有35岁。
I estimate her age to be 35.

我对他的能力估计错了。
My estimation of his abilities was wrong.
我估计大约要100英镑。
I reckon it will cost about £100.

guānyú
关于 （乙）介
about; concerning; with regard to
常用搭配
关于某人 in sb.'s regard
关于那件事 concerning the matter
关于蛇的书 a book about snakes
用法示例
我们听过他的关于人际关系的讲座。
We have listened to his lecture on human relations.
电视正在播放一个关于艾滋病的节目。
There is a TV show about AIDS on right now.
关于这件事，你能给我一些建议吗？
Can you give me any suggestions on this matter?

gǔjì
古迹 （乙）名
historic place; historical sites
常用搭配
名胜古迹 places of interest
用法示例
他喜欢参观名胜古迹。
He likes to visit places of interest.
那是一处中国著名的古迹。
That is a very famous place of interest in China.
我们参观了一处明朝的古迹。
We visited a historical site of the Ming Dynasty.

biàntiáo
便条 （乙）名
informal note
常用搭配
留便条 leave a note   给某人写便条 write a note for sb
用法示例
我在他桌上留了张便条。
I left a note on his desk.
他把便条揉成团扔进火里了。
He screwed up the note and threw it on the fire.
请务必把这张便条交到可靠的人手里。
Please see that this note gets into the right hands.

píngcháng
平常 ⊜ 普通 pǔtōng （乙）名/形
① usually ② ordinary

常用搭配
跟平常一样 as usual   平常人 ordinary people
用法示例
今天是很平常的一天。
It was a very ordinary day today.
你平常几点起床？
What time do you usually get up?
在寒冷的国家雪是很平常的。
Snow is very common in cold countries.

píngděng
平等 (乙) 形 / 名
① equal ② equality
常用搭配
人人平等。All people are equal.
平等互利的原则
the principle of equality and mutual benefit
与……平等 be on a par (with)
用法示例
男性和女性是平等的。
Males and females are equal.
国家不论大小，一律平等。
All countries, big and small, should be equal.
这个国家的宪法体现了自由和平等的理想。
The country's constitution embodies the ideals of freedom and equality.

pāndēng
攀登 (丙) 动
climb; clamber
常用搭配
向山顶攀登 climb to the peak
用法示例
那小队攀登山的北坡。
The team climbed the north face of the mountain.
他跌下来也并未气馁，继续攀登。
He continued the climb, undaunted by his fall.

tiáoyuē xiéyì
条约 ⊜协议 (乙) 名
treaty; pact
常用搭配
和平条约 a peace treaty   友好条约 a treaty of friendship
退出条约 withdraw from a treaty
用法示例
根据条约，中国于1997年7月1日收回香港。
According to the treaty, China took back Hong Kong on July 1st, 1997.
政府已与他们签署了一项条约。
The Government has signed a treaty with them.

néng
能 (丙) 助动
be able to; can; be capable of

常用搭配
我能进来吗？Can I come in？
用法示例
别对我大声嚷嚷，我能听清楚。
Don't shout in my ears, I can hear you clearly.
明天我能来。
I shall be able to come tomorrow.
你能爬上那棵树吗？
Are you capable of climbing that tree?
每个沙发能坐两个人。
Each sofa will seat two persons.

huì
会 (甲) 助动 / 动
① will ② can ③ be able to
常用搭配
我会游泳。I can swim.
我会电脑。You can use a computer.
一切都会好的。Everything will be OK.
用法示例
你会弹钢琴吗？
Can you play the piano?
她会日语和英语。
She can speak Japanese as well as English.
你的状况会好起来的。
You will be better off.

词义辨析

会、能

1、"会"和"能"都是助动词，表示具备某种能力，但"会"表示通过学习、练习才掌握的知识和技能，有时，表示可能性。"会"还可以用作动词，如：她会法语。如果有困难，老师会帮助你的。阴天了，今晚会下雨。

Both 会 and 能 are auxiliary verbs, meaning "be able to do". But 会 indicates to master a skill or knowledge by learning and practicing; sometimes it means probability. 会 can be used as a verb, too. For example: She can speak French. If you have any trouble, the teacher will help you. It's cloudy, it will be raining tonight.

2、"能"表示有做某事的能力、条件，有时表示"被允许"。比如：他病了，不能工作了。这里不能游泳。

能 indicates to have the ability or qualification to do something, sometimes it also refers to being allowed, e.g. He is ill, and can not work. You are not allowed to swim here.

练习一、根据拼音写汉字，根据汉字写拼音

( )jì ( )jì ( )děng ( )děng xū ( )
古( ) 估( ) 平( ) 攀( ) ( )要

练习二、搭配连线

(1) 名胜　　　A. 成本
(2) 满足　　　B. 古迹
(3) 一律　　　C. 需要
(4) 估计　　　D. 条约
(5) 签署　　　E. 平等

练习三、从今天学习的生词中选择合适的词填空

1. 小王的家庭_____不太好，但她学习很努力。
2. 法律规定人人_____。
3. 我到宿舍的时候，同屋不在，她给我留了张_____，说她去超市了。
4. 情况与他_____的差不多。
5. 小强没来上课，老师给他妈妈打电话说："明天上午十点您_____到学校来一趟吗？"
6. 再等等吧，他答应我来，就一定_____来的。
7. 这个国家被迫签订了一些不平等_____。
8. 他_____坐公共汽车上班，只有周末才开车去郊游。
9. _____这件事，我们以后再谈。
10. 在北京我参观了很多名胜_____。

练习一：
略

练习二：
(1) B　(2) C　(3) E　(4) A　(5) D

练习三：
1. 条件　2. 平等　3. 便条　4. 估计　5. 能
6. 会　7. 条约　8. 平常　9. 关于　10. 古迹

星期二

gèng
更　　　　　　　　　　　　　　（甲）副
more

常用搭配
更好 better
更难 more difficult

用法示例
我认为他是更合适的人选。
I think he is the more suitable candidate.
他哥哥就很机灵，他比他哥哥更机灵。
His brother is quite clever, and he is even cleverer than his brother.
他的病比医生原来预料的更严重。
His illness was more serious than the doctor first thought.

jiǎnchá　　　　　　jiǎnyàn
检查　同 检验　　　　　　　（甲）动
check; inspect

常用搭配
体格检查 a medical examination
检查作业 check homework
质量检查 quality inspection

用法示例
他们检查了学院的工作。
They inspected the work of the institute.
她在医院里接受了全面检查。
She underwent a thorough examination at the hospital.
检查人员检查了我们产品的质量。
The inspector checks on the quality of our products.

wèile
为了　　　　　　　　　　　　（甲）介
① for ② in order to

常用搭配
为了生存 in order to survive
为了安全 for the sake of safety
为了某人的健康干杯 drink to one's health

用法示例
绝不要为了钱而做坏事。
Never do wrong for the sake of money.
为了下一场比赛这位冠军正在进行训练。
The champion is in training for his next fight.
为了赶火车，她匆匆做完了她的工作。
In order to catch the train, she rushed through her work.

gèngjiā
更加　　　　　　　　　　　　（乙）副
further; more

常用搭配
使国家更加富饶 make the country richer
比以前更加努力 work harder than before
用法示例
你要更加努力地工作。
Put more effort into your work.
你的鼓励使我对未来更加有信心了。
Your encouragement made me more confident of my future.
他比以前更加仔细了。
He is more careful than before.

接到 jiēdào 回 收到 （乙）动
receive
常用搭配
接到请帖 receive an invitation　接到命令 receive an order
用法示例
部队接到命令。
The troops received the order.
一接到通知，我们就出发了。
We set out as soon as we received the notice.

石油 shíyóu （乙）名
petroleum; mineral oil
常用搭配
石油公司 oil company　人造石油 artificial petroleum
石油市场 oil market
用法示例
石油的价格已经上涨了。
The price of oil has gone up.
这个国家盛产石油和煤。
The country is rich in oil and coal.
这个国家的财富来源于石油。
This country's wealth comes from its oil.

食物 shíwù 回 食品 （乙）名
food
常用搭配
食物中毒 food poisoning　食物短缺 food shortage
食物链 food chain
用法示例
你最喜欢的食物是什么？
What's your favorite food?
大米是我们的主要食物。
Rice is our staple food.
多吃油腻的食物对身体有害。
A surfeit of rich food is bad for you.

食品 shípǐn （乙）名
food; food product

常用搭配
膨化食品 popcorn-like food
食品卫生 food sanitation
副食品 subsidiary foodstuff
用法示例
她把食品发放给所有的孩子们。
She doled out the food to the children.
他把食品存放在碗橱里。
He stored food in his cupboard.
他不习惯吃方便食品。
He is not used to fast food.

街道 jiēdào 回 大街 （乙）名
street
常用搭配
狭窄的街道 narrow street
街道对面 opposite the street
穿过街道 through the streets
用法示例
他们穿过街道，进了商店。
They crossed the street and went into the shop.
整条街道的人们都反对这一新的停车条例。
The whole street protested the new parking regulations.
他住在街道的尽头。
He lives at the end of the street.

街坊 jiēfang （丁）名
neighbor; neighborhood
常用搭配
我们是街坊。We are neighbors.
用法示例
我的街坊就住在紧挨着我家的房子里。
My neighbor lives in the house next to mine.
她是个热心的街坊。
She is a warmhearted neighbor.

打交道 dǎjiāodào （丙）
associate with; make dealings with
常用搭配
跟他打交道 deal with him
用法示例
他很友好，很容易打交道。
He is very friendly and easy to deal with.
我讨厌与那些没有人情味的大公司打交道。
I hate dealing with large impersonal companies.
作为会计师，他习惯于同数字打交道。
Being an accountant, he is used to dealing with figures.

为止 wéizhǐ （丙）动
until

常用搭配
直到天亮为止 until dawn
直到会议结束为止 until the meeting was over

用法示例
他一遍又一遍地读,直到记住为止。
He read it again and again until he could remember it.
把黄油加热,直到变成褐色为止。
Heat the butter until it browns.
一直往前走,走到一座大楼为止。
Go straight ahead until you come to a large building.

词义辨析

更、更加

"更"和"更加"都用于比较,表示程度又深一层或进一步的意思。"更"使用得比较广泛,比较口语化;"更加"用来修饰双音节或多音节词语,多用于书面语。比如:①他看上去比以前更壮了。②他比他哥哥更加明智。

Both 更 and 更加 are used in comparisons to indicate a further degree, or a greater extent. 更 is used widely and more colloquially; while 更加 is quite literary, and often modifies poly-syllabic words, e.g. ① He looks stronger than before. ② He is more sensible than his brother.

练习

练习一、根据拼音写汉字,根据汉字写拼音
(　)chá　(　)yóu jiē(　)　(　)zhǐ　gèng(　)
检(　)　石(　)　(　)坊　为(　)　(　)加

练习二、搭配连线
(1) 体格　　　A. 中毒
(2) 食物　　　B. 食品
(3) 接到　　　C. 检查
(4) 速冻　　　D. 努力
(5) 更加　　　E. 通知

练习三、从今天学习的生词中选择合适的词填空
1. 常吃速冻_____对胃不好。
2. 她长得很漂亮,穿上这件新衣服以后就_____动人了。
3. 许多动物喜欢以青草作为_____。
4. 科学家在这一地区的地下发现了_____。
5. _____让孩子接受更好的教育,他们一家搬到了另一个城市。
6. 这个办法不错,但我觉得那个办法_____好。
7. 这个地方老堵车,政府决定拓宽_____。
8. 小王说她最快乐的一天是_____大学录取通知书的那一天。
9. 他们是_____,平时有什么事总是互相帮忙。
10. 到今天_____,离毕业只有30天了。

答案

练习一:
略

练习二:
(1) C　　(2)A　　(3)E　　(4)B　　(5)D

练习三:
1. 食品　2. 更加　3. 食物　4. 石油　5. 为了
6. 更　　7. 街道　8. 接到　9. 街坊　10. 为止

星期三

zēngjiā
增加　　　反 jiǎnshǎo 减少　　（甲）动
increase; raise

常用搭配
增加体重 increase one's weight
增加工资 increase one's wage
逐年增加 increase with years

用法示例
我的工资今年增加了。
My wages have increased this year.
他晚上去教书以增加收入。
He supplements his income by teaching in the evenings.
如果我们要增加教育经费就必须加税。
We must increase taxation if we are to spend more on education.

shuǐpíng
水平　　（甲）名
level

常用搭配
生活水平 living standard　　高水平 high-level
提高……的水平 to improve the level of...

用法示例
这所大学的教学水平很高。
This university has high standards of teaching.
我要努力提高自己的英语水平。
I will try my best to improve my English.
在地图上有水平的线和垂直的线。
On a map there are horizontal lines, and vertical lines.

jiémù
节目　　（甲）名
program

常用搭配
电视节目 TV program　　新闻节目 news program

用法示例
今天晚上有一个有意思的电视节目。
There is an interesting program on television tonight.
接收节目前,你应该先装天线。
You need to fix the television antenna before you can start receiving programs.
节目涉及流行音乐和京剧等题材。
The program deals with subjects such as pop music and Beijing Opera.

zēngzhǎng
增长　　反 jiàngdī 降低　　（乙）动
increase; grow

常用搭配
大幅度增长 substantial increase
随……而增长 increase with

用法示例
奶油厂的产量正在增长。
The output of the creamery is increasing.
智慧与机灵不同,前者可随着年龄增长。
Intelligence, unlike cleverness, may increase with age.
经济学家预言通货膨胀率将会增长。
The economists predict an increase in the rate of inflation.

lìqi
力气　　（乙）名
strength

常用搭配
他力气很大。He has great strength.

用法示例
我连移动双脚的力气都几乎没有了。
I have hardly enough strength left to move my feet.
在这项比赛中,技巧比力气更重要。
In this game, you need more skill than strength.
留点力气准备攀登吧。
Marshalt your strength for the climb.

chōngzú
充足　　反 kuīfá 匮乏　　（乙）形
sufficient; abundant

常用搭配
充足的食品 adequate food　　充足的空间 ample space
充足的供应 plentiful supply

用法示例
我们有充足的时间赶火车。
We have plenty of time to catch the train.
我们的身体需要充足的营养。
Our bodies need adequate nutrition.
营地有充足的食品供应。
The camp has a plentiful supply of food.

píngān
平安　　（乙）形
① safe and sound ② safely

常用搭配
平安归来 return safe and sound
平安到达 arrive safely

用法示例
他们已经平平安安地到这里了。
They have arrived here safe and sound.
告诉你母亲你已经平安到达学校了。
Tell your mother you have arrived at college without mishap.
知道你平安无事我就放心了。
It's a great relief to know you're safe.

fǎlǜ
法律　　　　　　　　　　　　　　（乙）名
law; statute

常用搭配
遵守法律 abide by the law　　违犯法律 break the law
当地的法律 the local laws

用法示例
她的儿子正在大学学习法律。
Her son is studying law at university.
这些法律仍然有效。
The laws are still in effect.
法律禁止向18岁以下的人出售香烟。
The law forbids the sale of cigarettes to people under 18.

dòngzuò
动作　　　　　　　　　　　　　　（乙）名
action; movement

常用搭配
舞蹈动作 movements of a dance
优雅的动作 graceful movement

用法示例
他是个优秀的运动员，他所有的动作都非常协调。
He is an excellent athlete; all his movements are perfectly coordinated.
她那流畅的动作让我们惊奇。
Her fluid movements surprised us.
她观察那个跳舞的人，想模仿她的动作。
She watched the dancer and tried to copy her movements.

jiénéng
节能　　　　　　　　　　　　　　（丁）形
① conserve energy ② energy-saving

常用搭配
节能技术 energy conservation technology

用法示例
他致力于开发节能产品。
He is engaged in developing energy-saving products.
节能事业在我们社会中越来越重要了。
The development of energy conservation is becoming more and more important in our society.

chōngshí　　　　　　kōngxū
充实　　　　反 空虚　　　　　　（丙）形／动
① substantial ② enrich

常用搭配
内容充实 substantial content

用法示例
购买新书使图书馆的库藏得到了充实。
The library was enriched by the new books.
艺术欣赏将会充实你的生活。
The appreciation of art will enrich your life.
好书可以使我们生活充实。
Good books can enrich our lives.

zēngjìn
增进　　　　　　　　　　　　　　（丙）动
promote

常用搭配
增进了解 promote understanding
增进团结 promote solidarity

用法示例
会议的目的是增进国际间的友谊。
The aim of the conference is to promote international friendship.
我们彼此之间要增进了解。
We should promote a better understanding of each other.

 词义辨析

增加、增长

　　"增加"和"增长"都表示变得更多或更大。"增加"使用得比较广泛，多表示数量的增加，多用于具体事物；"增长"多表示程度的提高和数量的增多，多用于抽象事物。如：①人口在不断增加／增长。②产量增长得很快。③你的工资将逐年增加。

　　增加 and 增长 are used to indicate "to become greater or larger". 增加 is used widely, it stresses an increase in quantity, and is often applied to something concrete. 增长 is mainly applied to something abstract, stressing the raise in degree and amount. For example: ① There was a steady increase in population. ② The output increased rapidly. ③ Your wages will increase over the years.

练习

练习一、根据拼音写汉字，根据汉字写拼音
zēng（　）chōng（　）（　）lǜ jié（　）（　）zuò
（　）长　　（　）足　　法（　）　（　）能　　动（　）

练习二、搭配连线
(1) 电视　　　　　　A. 工资
(2) 汉语　　　　　　B. 节目
(3) 增进　　　　　　C. 法律
(4) 增加　　　　　　D. 水平
(5) 遵守　　　　　　E. 了解

练习三、从今天学习的生词中选择合适的词填空
1. 我很喜欢学跳舞，可是 _____ 太难，我学不会。
2. 山下氧气很 _____，他没觉得难受，可是爬到山顶就有点受不了了。
3. 虽然每天工作累得要死，可是她觉得日子过得很 _____。
4. 为了节约用电，我们家都用 _____ 灯。
5. 妻子逛完商场，已经累得没有 _____ 走路了，只好打车回家。
6. 明年，这个家庭就要 _____ 一口人，变成三口之家了。
7. 三十年之内，这里的人口 _____ 了一倍。
8. 中国希望通过2008年奥运会，让世界了解中国，_____ 中国与世界各国人民的友谊。
9. 晚会上这个 _____ 最受欢迎。
10. 这个留学生在中国学习三年了，他的汉语 _____ 很高。

答案

练习一：
略

练习二：
(1) B　　(2)D　　(3)E　　(4)A　　(5)C

练习三：
1. 动作　　2. 充足　　3. 充实　　4. 节能　　5. 力气
6. 增加　　7. 增长　　8. 增进　　9. 节目　　10. 水平

有名 yǒumíng （甲）形
well-known; famous

常用搭配
有名的运动员 famous athlete

用法示例
那位音乐家非常有名。
That musician is very famous.
她年轻时是个有名的美人。
She was a famous beauty in her youth.
有名的比萨塔是斜的。
The famous tower of Pisa leans at an angle.

给 gěi （甲）动／介
① give ② for; to

常用搭配
给我尺子 Give me the ruler
给我打电话 telephone me
给我写信 write to me

用法示例
你能给我一些建议吗？
Can you give me some advice?
他给玛丽买了一个电吹风。
He bought an electric hair-drier for Mary.
请把字典递给我。
Please pass me the dictionary.

节日 jiérì （甲）名
festival

常用搭配
庆祝节日 celebrate a festival　　节日盛装 holiday splendor
节日的夜晚 festival night

用法示例
圣诞节是基督教的节日之一。
Christmas is one of the Christian festivals.
整个镇上充满了欢乐的节日气氛。
A happy festival atmosphere pervaded the whole town.
在重要的节日，人们把国旗悬挂在门外。
People hang national flags out on important holidays.

著名 zhùmíng （乙）形
famous; celebrated

常用搭配
因……著名 be famous for…
著名律师 a notable lawyer

用法示例
他是一位著名的艺术家。
He is a notable artist.
那位著名经济学家给我们做了一次演讲。
The famous economist gave us a speech.

gǔlǎo
古老 （乙）形
ancient

常用搭配
古老的建筑 an old building　　古老的雕像 archaic statue
古老的传说 an old legend

用法示例
在英格兰有许多古老的家宅。
There are many old estates in England.
小女孩对古老的传说很感兴趣。
The little girl is very interested in the old legend of the immortal creatures.
这些美丽的古老宫殿是我们民族遗产的一部分。
These beautiful old palaces are part of our national heritage.

tiānzhēn
天真 （乙）形
naive

常用搭配
天真的话 a naive remark　　天真的女孩 a naive girl

用法示例
他嘲弄她天真的态度。
He derides her naive attitude.
她总问一些天真的问题。
She always asks naive questions.
她有一些天真的想法。
She has some naive ideas.

dàliàng
大量　　反 少量(shǎoliàng) （乙）形
large quantity; many; a great deal

常用搭配
大量的产品 a great quantity of products
花大量的时间 spend a great deal of time

用法示例
暴风雨造成了大量的物质损失。
The storm caused a great deal of damage.
我们为这个项目付出了大量的时间和精力。
We've put a great deal of time and effort into this project.
我阅读了大量的参考书。
We read a large number of reference books.

dòngrén
动人　　同 感人(gǎnrén) （乙）形
moving; touching; affecting

常用搭配
动人的情景 a moving sight

美丽动人的童话 a beautiful and touching tale

用法示例
这部小说既幽默又动人。
The novel is humorous and moving.
这是一部动人的影片。
It is a moving film.
她的故事十分动人。
Her story is very touching.

dòngshēn
动身 （乙）动
start out; set forth

常用搭配
立即动身 start out at once

用法示例
我们将在黎明时动身。
We will leave at daybreak.
他即将动身。
He is about to start.
你打算动身去北京吗？
Are you going to leave for Beijing?

yòuzhì
幼稚　　反 成熟(chéngshú) （丙）形
childish; puerile

常用搭配
幼稚的行为 naive action
幼稚的话 naive remark
幼稚的观点 childish arguments

用法示例
他们嘲笑他的做法很幼稚。
They derided his efforts as childish.
他竟然幼稚得连这种谎言都相信。
He is so naive to believe such a lie.

dǎliang
打量　　同 端详(duānxiáng) （丙）动
scrutinize closely

常用搭配
上下打量他 look him up and down

用法示例
他一进来就上下打量我。
He looked me up and down when he entered.
我们初次见面时相互打量了一番。
We sized each other up at our first meeting.
我上下打量了她一番，决定拒绝她。
I looked her up and down and decided to refuse her.

jiézòu
节奏 （丁）名
rhythm; regular pattern

常用搭配
音乐的节奏 musical rhythm
节奏感 sense of rhythm

用法示例

我喜欢节奏快的音乐。
I like fast music.
他正试图用不同节奏演奏同一个曲子。
He is trying to play the same tune in a different rhythm.
说英语时，重音和节奏是很重要的。
Stress and rhythm are important when speaking English.

词义辨析

有名、著名
　　"有名"和"著名"都有广泛地为人所知的意思。"著名"一般用于褒义词，比较正式；"有名"可以用于褒义，也可以用于贬义，作定语时，后面往往跟"的"。例如：有名的/著名医生，著名钢琴家，有名的无赖。
　　Both 著名 and 有名 mean "well, or widely known". 著名 is quite formal and is often applied in a laudatory sense. 有名 can be used in a laudatory sense, or a derogatory sense. Serving as an attributive, 有名 is usually followed by 的. For example: a famous doctor, a famous pianist, a famous villain.

练习

练习一、根据拼音写汉字，根据汉字写拼音

zhù（　） yòu（　） dǎ（　） zòu（　） zhēn（　）
（　）名　（　）稚　（　）量　节（　）　天（　）

练习二、搭配连线
(1) 古老的　　　　　A. 货物
(2) 天真的　　　　　B. 传说
(3) 大量的　　　　　C. 想法
(4) 著名的　　　　　D. 情景
(5) 动人的　　　　　E. 演员

练习三、从今天学习的生词中选择合适的词填空
1. 她的歌声很 ＿＿＿＿＿＿。
2. 我们学校图书馆有 ＿＿＿＿＿＿ 的外文资料。
3. 这个人从头到脚 ＿＿＿＿＿＿ 了我一下，然后说："不好意思，认错人了"。
4. 大城市的生活 ＿＿＿＿＿＿ 很快。
5. 我只是说出了自己的真实想法，可是他说我思想 ＿＿＿＿＿＿。
6. 你到了家，别忘了 ＿＿＿＿＿＿ 我打个电话。
7. 我父母在北京住了一个月，明天就要 ＿＿＿＿＿＿ 回老家了。
8. 晚会上那个 ＿＿＿＿＿＿ 活泼的小男孩给所有客人留下了深刻的印象。
9. 这部电影由国际 ＿＿＿＿＿＿ 影星布拉德·皮特（William Bradley Pitt）主演。
10. 他在我们学校是 ＿＿＿＿＿＿ 的好学生，可是考到北京大学以后，发现自己并不突出。

答案

练习一：
略
练习二：
(1) B　　(2)C　　(3)A　　(4)E　　(5)D
练习三：
1. 动人　2. 大量　3. 打量　4. 节奏　5. 幼稚
6. 给　　7. 动身　8. 天真　9. 著名　10. 有名

星期五 Friday

shēngyīn
声音 圆 声响 （甲）名
sound; voice

常用搭配
嘶哑的声音 a hoarse voice 钢琴的声音 sound of a piano
开门的声音 sound of opening a door

用法示例
我听到远处有个微弱的声音。
I heard a faint sound in the distance.
声音是通过空气传播的。
Sound travels through the air.
你能听到鸟儿叫的声音吗?
Can you hear the birds singing?

yāoqiú
要求 （甲）动/名
① demand ② request

常用搭配
要求道歉 demand an apology
要求明确的答复 demand a clear answer
满足他的要求 to meet his needs

用法示例
警察局长要求严惩罪犯。
The chief of the police department demanded severe punishments for criminals.
他提出了一个合理的要求。
He made a reasonable demand.

fānyì
翻译 （甲）动/名
① translate; interpret ② interpreter; translation

常用搭配
为某人翻译 interpret for sb
逐字翻译 translate literally
电子翻译器 electronic interpreter

用法示例
你能把这句话翻译成英文吗?
Can you translate the sentence into English?
请你为我翻译一下好吗?
Would you please interpret for me?
我不太满意他对这个句子的翻译。
I'm not satisfied with his interpretation of this sentence.

yuányīn
原因 圆 缘故 （乙）名
reason

常用搭配
迟到的原因 the reason for being late
由于某种原因 for some reason

用法示例
大雨是洪水产生的原因。
The heavy rain was the cause of the flood.
由于各种原因,我不愿见他。
For various reasons I'd prefer not to meet him.
不知什么原因,她自杀了。
For some unknown reason, she committed suicide.

jiējí
阶级 （乙）名
class; rank

常用搭配
工人阶级 working-class 阶级斗争 class warfare

用法示例
这两个阶级之间有很深的仇恨。
There is great animosity between the two classes.
在履行职责的时候,他得会见各个阶级的人。
In the prosecution of his duties, he had to interview people of all classes.
现在社会上各阶级的区分不像过去那样明显了。
The divisions between the various classes of society are not so clearly defined as they used to be.

jiēduàn
阶段 （乙）名
stage; phase

常用搭配
试验阶段 experimental stage 初级阶段 incipient stage
适应阶段 adaptive phase

用法示例
目前我们公司的发展正处在过渡阶段。
Our company is in its developmental stages right now.
这个项目可以划分三个连续的阶段。
The project can be broken up into three successive phases.

fāng'àn
方案 （乙）名
plan; scheme

常用搭配
拟订方案 plot a scheme
可行的方案 a practical scheme

用法示例
他想出了一个活动方案。
He thought out a plan of activity.
他并不反对那项方案。
He did not oppose the scheme.
这个方案看来很可行。
The scheme seems to be quite practical.

fāngzhēn
方针 圆 原则 （乙）名
policy; guiding principle

89

【常用搭配】
教育方针 the educational policy
贷款方针 loan policy
【用法示例】
节俭的方针适用于一切事业。
The principle of frugality applies to all undertakings.
现在改变方针是不明智的。
It would be unwise to change tack now.

dòngshǒu
动手　　　　　　　　　　　　　　　　（乙）动
start to work; to touch
【常用搭配】
动手准备 start to prepare
【用法示例】
她立即动手处理难题。
She attacked the difficulties at once.
只能看，参观者请勿动手。
Please observe only! Visitors are not allowed to touch it.
准备好了吗？我们动手调查吧。
Are you ready？ Let's start the investigation.

tóngbāo
同胞　　　　　　　　　　　　　　　　（丙）名
① born of the same parents ② compatriots
【常用搭配】
香港同胞 Hong Kong compatriots
【用法示例】
我把他们都视为同胞。
I look upon them as my compatriots.
他和我是同胞，我俩都是苏格兰人。
He and I are compatriots, because both of us come from Scotland.

yuángù
缘故　　　　　　　　　　　　　　　　（丙）名
cause; reason
【常用搭配】
来晚的缘故 the reason for being late
因为金钱的缘故 for the sake of money
【用法示例】
她出于情感的缘故做了此事。
She did it for sentimental reasons.
因为健康的缘故，我戒烟了。
I stopped smoking for the sake of my health.
我总感觉到她因某种缘故而对我怀恨在心。
I always have the feeling that for some reason she bears a grudge against me.

tóngbàn　　　　　huǒbàn
同伴　　　　　◎伙伴　　　　　　　　（丙）名
companion
【常用搭配】
忠实的同伴 a faithful companion

【用法示例】
他是我在美国期间的唯一的中国同伴。
He was my only Chinese companion during my stay in the USA.
他和同伴失去了联系。
He was cut off from his peers.
她逐渐对同伴心怀不满。
She began to grow discontented with her companions.

原因、缘故
　　"原因"和"缘故"都表示某种行为、决定或事件的根源或动机。"原因"用于书面语和口语，经常指直接的、客观的因素。"缘故"比较口语化，往往指影响感情、情绪等方面的复杂因素，适用范围比较小。例如：①出于某种缘故，她对丈夫不满意。②大雨是洪水产生的原因。
　　原因 and 缘故 mean "the reason, the basis, or the motive for an action, a decision, or an event". 原因 can be applied to written and spoken language, usually indicating an immediate or external reason. 缘故 is quite colloquial, mainly indicating complicated reasons such as feelings or emotions, and thus has a narrow range of applications. For example: ① For some reason she is dissatisfied with her husband. ② The heavy rain was the cause of the flood.

练习一、根据拼音写汉字，根据汉字写拼音
shēng（　）（　）gù（　）àn　jiē（　）fān（　）
（　）音　缘（　）　方（　）　（　）级　（　）译

练习二、搭配连线
(1) 迟到的　　　　　　A. 方案
(2) 弹琴的　　　　　　B. 同伴
(3) 行动的　　　　　　C. 翻译
(4) 准确的　　　　　　D. 声音
(5) 忠实的　　　　　　E. 原因

练习三、从今天学习的生词中选择合适的词填空
1. 我们给灾区_____送去了很多食品。
2. 必须要在两个_____中选一个，要不没时间了。
3. 这个领导在发言中强调了我国的教育_____。
4. 报上说，达到中产_____的最低标准是年收入35万人民币。
5. 老师，对不起，孩子迟到是因为我的_____。
6. 照片中的这个小学生为救自己的_____而被河水冲走了。
7. 有话好好说，_____打人可不对。

8. 最近这一_____,我要抓紧时间写论文。
9. 现在应该做的是好好分析事故发生的_____,而不是推卸责任。
10. 她想好好学习汉语,将来做一名_____。

答案

练习一:
略
练习二:
(1) E　　(2)D　　(3)A　　(4)C　　(5)B
练习三:
1. 同胞　2. 方案　3. 方针　4. 阶级　5. 缘故
6. 同伴　7. 动手　8. 阶段　9. 原因　10. 翻译

第2月,第3周的练习

练习一、根据词语给加点的字注音
1.( )　2.( )　3.( )　4.( )　5.( )
需要　要求　攀登　幼稚　缘故

练习二、根据拼音填写词语
　　　gū　　　gǔ　　　jiē　　　jié　　　jiē
1.( )计　2.( )迹　3.( )坊　4.( )奏　5.( )段

练习三、辨析并选择合适的词填空
1. 他( )游泳,但是公园的管理人员说不( )在这个湖里游泳。(会、能)
2. 天气预报说今晚( )下雪,那我们明天就不( )去爬长城了。(会、能)
3. 我今天很早就到单位了,可我发现他( )早,他是第一个到单位的。(更、更加)
4. 祝愿我们的祖国( )繁荣、昌盛。(更、更加)
5. 大学生参加社会实践,既能积累经验,又能( )才干。(增加、增长)
6. 由于时间紧、任务重,我们向上级申请( )5名技术人员。(增加、增长)
7. 他的父亲是一位( )导演。(有名、著名)
8. 他是我们班( )的"马大哈",平常总是丢三落四的。(有名、著名)
9. 不知道是因为什么( ),他没有和妻子一起参加聚会。(原因、缘故)
10. 警方正在调查火灾的( )。(原因、缘故)

练习四、选词填空
动人　动手　街道　需要　充足
动身　接到　街坊　要求　充实

1. 我已经买好了火车票,下午就( )去广州。
2. 我们有( )的时间,不必这么急急忙忙的。
3. 春节的时候,( )两旁的商店都挂起了红色的灯笼。
4. 我刚上班就( )通知,让我下班前交市场调查报告。
5. 这是一个( )的爱情故事,我希望把它改编成电影。
6. 这段时间虽然又忙又累,但是我的收获也特别大,我感到很( )。
7. 学校( )学生周一穿校服上学。
8. 我们大家一起( )打扫教室,很快教室就变得干净明亮了。
9. 学完这本书大概( )四个月的时间。
10. 这两户人家一直住在这条胡同里,他们是老( )。

练习五、写出下列词语的同义词
1. 平常( )　　2. 同伴( )
3. 打量( )　　4. 方针( )
5. 接到( )

练习六、写出下列词语的反义词
1. 增加( )　　2. 增长( )
3. 大量( )　　4. 幼稚( )
5. 充实( )

答案

练习一:
1. yào　2. yāo　3. pān　4. zhì　5. yuán
练习二:
1. 估　2. 古　3. 街　4. 节　5. 阶
练习三:
1. 会,能　2. 会,能　3. 更　4. 更加　5. 增长
6. 增加　7. 著名　8. 有名　9. 缘故　10. 原因
练习四:
1. 动身　2. 充足　3. 街道　4. 接到　5. 动人
6. 充实　7. 要求　8. 动手　9. 需要　10. 街坊
练习五:
1. 普通　2. 伙伴　3. 端详　4. 原则　5. 收到
练习六:
1. 减少　2. 降低　3. 少量　4. 成熟　5. 空虚

2月 第4周的学习内容

guó
国 （甲）名
state; country

常用搭配
外国 foreign countries　　国旗 national flag
回国 return to one's country

用法示例
在中国,铁路是国有的。
In China, the railways are owned by the state.
他是居住在中国的美国侨民。
He is an American expatriate in China.

guójiā
国家 （甲）名
country; nation

常用搭配
国家公园 national park　　发达国家 developed country

用法示例
很多国家是反对战争的。
Many countries are opposed to war.
法国和瑞士是欧洲国家。
France and Switzerland are European countries.

tóu
头 （甲）名/量
① head ② measure word for cattle or garlic

常用搭配
头疼 headache　　头巾 headdress　　点头 nod
一头牛 one head of cattle　　一头蒜 a garlic bulb

用法示例
我走进她的办公室时,她连头都没抬。
When I entered her office, she didn't raise her head.
她点头表示同意我的意见。
She nodded to show that she agreed with me.
一头狮子从动物园里逃了出来。
A lion escaped from the zoo.
我在市场买了两头洋葱。
I bought two onions at the market.

zháojí　　　　jiāojí
着急 〓 焦急　　（甲）形
① worry ② feel anxious

常用搭配
别着急! Don't worry!　　我很着急。I was very worried.

用法示例
别着急,安心养病。
Just take care of yourself and don't worry about anything else.
你用不着那么着急。
You needn't have been so worried.
她的孩子咳得很厉害,这让她很着急。
Her child has a bad cough, and it worries her.

hūxī
呼吸 （乙）动
breathe

常用搭配
深呼吸 deep breath　　屏住呼吸 hold one's breath

用法示例
我们到外面去呼吸新鲜空气吧。
Let's go out for a breath of fresh air.
鱼通过鳃呼吸。
A fish breathes through its gills.
老人昨晚停止了呼吸。
The old man ceased breathing last night.

gùxiāng
故乡 （乙）名
hometown; native place

常用搭配
回到故乡 return to one's hometown
思念故乡 miss one's hometown
离开故乡 leave one's hometown

用法示例
我在故乡度过了童年。
I spent my early childhood in my hometown.
她对故乡念念不忘。
She clung to her memories of her home town.
我依恋故乡的一草一木。
I am attached to every tree and bush in my hometown.

yángé
严格 （乙）形/动
strict; rigorous

常用搭配
严格管制 strict control
对……严格 be strict with…
严格的标准 strict standards

用法示例
学校的纪律很严格。
Discipline at school is very strict.

老师对他的学生非常严格。
The teacher is very strict with his students.
医生严格限制我的饮食。
The doctor put me on a very strict diet.

zhàokāi
召开 (乙)动
call (a meeting)

常用搭配

召开会议 call a meeting

用法示例

今天不能召开会议了。
The meeting is unable to be held today.
我们得立即召开会议。
We should call a meeting at once.
日内瓦已成为世界领袖经常召开会议的地方。
Geneva has become the stage for many meetings of world leaders.

tíqián
提前 同 提早 (乙)动
① advance ② in advance ③ ahead of time

常用搭配

提前完成 complete ahead of schedule
提前通知 inform in advance
提前预订 book in advance

用法示例

他提前到达了会面的地点。
He arrived at the meeting place ahead of time.
她总是提前付房租。
She is always beforehand with the rent.
会议日期已经从星期五提前到星期一了。
The date of the meeting has been moved forward from Friday to Monday.

fùshù
复述 (乙)动
retell; repeat

常用搭配

复述课文 repeat the text
复述他的话 repeat what he said

用法示例

老师要求学生们复述他们刚读的故事。
The teacher asked the students to retell the story they just read.
他一字不差地复述了您说的话。
He repeated what you said word for word.
你能把这个问题复述一下吗?
Could you repeat the question?

tuīchí
推迟 反 提前 (丙)动
postpone; put off

常用搭配

推迟一个小时 be postponed for an hour
推迟装船日期 postpone the shipping date

用法示例

晚会推迟到8点举行。
The party was postponed until 8 o'clock.
今日能做完的事就不要推迟到明天。
Don't put off until tomorrow what can be done today.
我们把比赛从3月5日推迟到3月19日举行。
We postponed the match from March 5th to March 19th.

zhàojí
召集  遣散 (丙)动
call together

常用搭配

召集志愿者 gather volunteers
召集会议 call a meeting

用法示例

把学生召集到学校的礼堂里。
Gather the pupils together in the school hall.
他召集了所有的部队。
He mustered the troops.
人们被召集到这里举行紧急会议。
People were convened here for an emergency meeting.

词义辨析

国、国家

"国"和"国家"是都名词,但"国家"可以独立运用,"国"不能独立运用,而必须与名词、数次、代词或动词连用。如:美国;中、美两国;我国,世界各国;出国等。

Both 国 and 国家 are nouns. 国家 can be used independently, while 国 can not, it has to be used with other words, such as nouns, numerals, pronouns or verbs, e.g. America; the two countries—China and America; our country, all countries in the world; go abroad, etc.

**练习**

练习一、根据拼音写汉字，根据汉字写拼音
( )xī ( )xiāng zháo( ) tuī( ) zhào( )
呼( ) 故( ) ( )急 ( )迟 ( )集

练习二、搭配连线
(1) 严格　　　　　　A. 到达
(2) 呼吸　　　　　　B. 管理
(3) 提前　　　　　　C. 课文
(4) 召集　　　　　　D. 空气
(5) 复述　　　　　　E. 会议

练习三、从今天学习的生词中选择合适的词填空
1. 领导说事情紧急，现在就打电话_____大家开会。
2. 中国是一个发展中_____。
3. 五星红旗是中国的_____旗。
4. 这个德国小伙子和一个中国姑娘结婚了，所以他常说中国是自己的第二个_____。
5. 今天我坐朋友的车去上班，因此_____二十分钟就到公司了。
6. 足球赛因为下雨的缘故_____到明天下午举行了。
7. 2008年第29届奥运会在北京_____。
8. 孩子晚上没回家，妈妈很_____。
9. 孩子们的事让妈妈很_____疼。
10. 在她还很小的时候，父亲就对她要求很_____。

答案

练习一：
略
练习二：
(1) B　　(2)D　　(3)A　　(4)E　　(5)C
练习三：
1. 召集　2. 国家　3. 国　4. 故乡　5. 提前
6. 推迟　7. 召开　8. 着急　9. 头　10. 严格

---

xiànzài
现在　　　　　　　　　　　（甲）名
① now ② at present

常用搭配
现在的政府 present government
现在的领导 present leader
现在开始！ Start now！

用法示例
现在是十一点钟。
It's eleven o'clock now.
别哭，你现在已经是大男孩了。
Don't cry, you are a big boy now.
我们以前住在上海，但现在住在北京。
We used to live in Shanghai, but now we live in Beijing.

píqi　　　　　　　xìnggé
脾气　　≡ 性格　　（乙）名

temper

常用搭配
坏脾气 ill temper　　暴躁的脾气 a hot temper
发脾气 lose one's temper

用法示例
他发脾气了。
He lost his temper.
他努力控制自己的脾气。
He struggled to control his temper.
他脾气糟糕时让人无法忍受。
He is unbearable when he's in a bad temper.

gùshi
故事　　　　　　　　　　　（甲）名
story

常用搭配
讲故事 tell a story　　爱情故事 love story
童话故事 fairy tale

用法示例
她的故事使我很感动。
I was very moved by her story.
每天晚上妈妈给我们读一个故事！
Mother read us a story every night!
她知道许多有关培根的小故事。
She knows many anecdotes about Bacon.

chuàngzuò
创作　　　　　　　　　　（乙）动/名
① indite; write ② creation

常用搭配
创作一首诗 write a poem

创作艺术作品 create artistic works
创作才能 creative talent

用法示例
丰富的经历对他的艺术创作有好处。
Abundant experiences are good for his artistic development.
美丽的景色激发他创作出伟大的诗篇。
The beautiful scenery inspired him to write the greatest poetry.
在交响乐的创作方面，他堪称技艺大师。
He is the master craftsman of symphonic writing.

chuàngzào
创造　　　反 毁灭　　　（乙）动/名

① create ② creation

常用搭配
伟大的创造 great creation
创造性的工作 creative work
创造力 creativity

用法示例
这个运动员创造了新的世界纪录。
The athlete created a new world record.
这本书表明他是一个有创造力的作家。
This book shows that he is an ingenious author.
那作品缺乏创造性。
The work lacks originality.

dòngyuán
动员　　　同 发动　　　（乙）动

mobilize

常用搭配
动员群众 mobilize the masses
动员部队 mobilize the troops
动员令 mobilization orders

用法示例
学生们很快就动员起来了。
The students mobilized quickly.
我们的国家面临危险，我们必须把军队动员起来。
Our country is in danger; we must mobilize the army.

zìwǒ
自我　　　（乙）代

self

常用搭配
自我意识 self-awareness; ego
自我欣赏 self-appreciation
以自我为中心 self-centered

用法示例
随着年龄的增长，人们的自我认识也在不断增强。
One's sense of self increases as one gets older.
批评和自我批评对人的发展都很重要。
Self-criticism is just as important as criticism in terms of one's development.

píláo
疲劳　　　（乙）形

tired; weary

常用搭配
感到疲劳 to feel tired　　疲劳的司机 a weary driver

用法示例
人们疲劳时容易出差错。
People are prone to make mistakes when they are tired.
他很疲劳，很快就睡着了。
He was so tired that he quickly fell asleep.
紧张和疲劳常使人精神不集中。
Stress and tiredness often result in a lack of concentration.

shìgù
事故　　　（丙）名

accident

常用搭配
交通事故 traffic accident
事故的原因 the cause of an accident

用法示例
这场事故是人为过失造成的。
The accident was caused by human error.
这次事故造成了三人死亡。
The accident resulted in three people being killed.

dòngyáo
动摇　　　反 坚定　　　（丙）动

waver

常用搭配
动摇了信念 to waver in one's faith

用法示例
他的决心开始动摇了。
His resolve began to waver.
但这并没有使他们动摇或退缩。
However this did not make them waver or retreat.
他们毫不动摇地支持他。
They did not waver in their support for him.

zìshēn
自身　　　（丙）名

① self ② own

常用搭配
自身的过错 one's own fault

用法示例
这种汽车可以在自身长度范围内掉头。
This car can turn in a space of its own length.
他很自负，从来看不到自身的弱点。
He is so conceited that he never sees his own weaknesses.

tiáo
条　　　（甲）量

measure word for long, thin things or news (i.e. ribbon, river, etc.)

常用搭配
一条路 a road   两条领带 two neckties
一条手帕 a handkerchief

用法示例
今天早晨我从报纸上知道了这条消息。
I saw the news in the newspaper this morning.
修筑一条铁路要花费许多钱。
It takes a lot of money to build a railway.
山前有一条小河。
There is a river in front of the hill.

词义辨析

创作、创造

1、作为动词,"创作"和"创造"都表示制作出以前没有过的事物,"创造"的宾语可以是抽象的,也可以是具体的;但"创作"的宾语往往指艺术作品,如音乐、绘画、小说等。例如:创造纪录。有些人相信上帝创造了世界。这位诗人创作了一首新诗。

As verbs, both 创作 and 创造 mean to create something. The objects of 创作 can be something concrete or abstract; while the objects of 创作 are often artistic works, such as music, paintings and novels. For example: to create a record. Some people believe that God created the world. The poet composed a new work.

2、作为名词,"创作"也与艺术有关,"创造"表示制造新事物的行为或结果。例如:艺术创作,发明创造。

As nouns, 创作 also concerns art, while 创造 indicates the act of creating, or the fact or state of having been created. For example: artistic creation, invention and creation.

练习

练习一、根据拼音写汉字,根据汉字写拼音

chuàng（　）pí（　）（　）gù dòng（　）pí（　）
（　）造　（　）劳　事（　）（　）摇　（　）气

练习二、搭配连线

(1) 童话　　　　　　A. 驾驶
(2) 动员　　　　　　B. 故事
(3) 交通　　　　　　C. 群众
(4) 自我　　　　　　D. 认识
(5) 疲劳　　　　　　E. 事故

练习三、从今天学习的生词中选择合适的词填空

1. 这_____街道两旁有很多树,所以我喜欢在那儿散步。
2. 孩子说他睡不着,要我给他讲个_____。
3. 这位作家正在_____一部长篇小说。
4. 看书看了6个小时,他觉得眼睛有点_____。
5. 想问题不能以_____为中心。
6. 现在的一些孩子都是今天花明天的钱,_____花将来的钱。
7. 《圣经》上说,是上帝_____了世界。
8. 在一次_____中,他失去了父母。
9. 繁忙的工作让这个父亲的_____变坏了。
10. 她_____条件好,又很努力,所以很快就成了有名的舞蹈演员。

 答案

练习一:
略

练习二:
(1) B　　(2)C　　(3)E　　(4)D　　(5)A

练习三:
1. 条　　2. 故事　　3. 创作　　4. 疲劳　　5. 自我
6. 现在　7. 创造　　8. 事故　　9. 脾气　　10. 自身

星期三

yīnwèi
因为 （甲）连
① because ② because of

常用搭配
他因为太忙而不能回家。
He was too busy to go home.
因为堵车，所以他迟到了。
He was late because of a traffic jam.

用法示例
李林没有出席会议，因为他病了。
Li Lin didn't attend the meeting because he was ill.
我批评他，不是因为我恨他，而是因为我爱他。
I criticized him, not because I hate him, but because I love him.
这名记者因为试图揭露一个阴谋而被杀害。
The reporter was killed because he tried to expose a plot.

kōngqì
空气 （甲）名
air

常用搭配
新鲜空气 fresh air　空气污染 air pollution

用法示例
新鲜空气有益于健康。
Fresh air is beneficial to our health.
他打开窗户，放出污浊的空气。
He opened the window to let out the foul air.
当我们吸气时，空气会被吸入肺里。
When we breathe, we draw air into our lungs.

yóuyú
由于 （乙）介
① due to ② because of

常用搭配
由于粗心而犯错误
make a mistake due to carelessness
由于高速开车而引起的事故
accidents due to driving at high speed

用法示例
由于有病，我不能参加了。
I couldn't attend, owing to an illness.
由于天气恶劣，许多选民今天没有投票。
Many electors didn't vote today because of the bad weather.

shíjì
实际 （乙）名/形
① reality; fact ② actual

常用搭配
实际上 in fact　在实际生活中 in real life

用法示例
我说那天是星期二，实际上是星期一。
I said it was Tuesday, but in fact it was Monday.
他说他要给钱，可实际上他没有钱。
He said he would pay, but in reality he has no money.
我们的计划必须与当前的实际相结合。
Our plans have to be in accord with the present realities.

kōngjiān　　　　　　　　dìfang
空间　　 ⊜ 地方 （乙）名
space

常用搭配
生存空间 living space

用法示例
这里有很大的活动空间。
There is plenty of space here to move about.
那张安乐椅占用了太多的空间。
That easy chair takes up too much room.
没有挪动的空间。
There's no room to move.

kōngqián　　　　　　　chángjiàn
空前　　 ⊝ 常见 （乙）形
unprecedented; unparalleled

常用搭配
空前的成功 an unprecedented success
空前的胜利 an unparalleled victory
以空前的规模 on an unheard-of scale

用法示例
敌人的轰炸对这个国家造成了空前的破坏。
The enemy's bombardment caused unprecedented destruction in the country.
开销达到空前的水平。
Expenditure rapidly rose to an unprecedented level.

kèfú　　　　　　　　qūfú
克服　　 ⊝ 屈服 （乙）动
overcome; surmount

常用搭配
克服困难 overcome a difficulty
克服缺点 overcome one's shortcomings

用法示例
我认为大多数障碍都是可以克服的。
I think most of the obstacles can be surmounted.
她克服了恐惧，自己走过了摇摇晃晃的桥。
She conquered her fear and crossed the shaking bridge by herself.
只要我们紧密团结就能克服困难。
We can surely overcome these difficulties as long as we are united.

yuànwàng
愿望　◎ 心愿　（乙）名
desire; wish

常用搭配
满足某人的愿望 gratify one's wish
美好的愿望 good wishes

用法示例
他想当演员的愿望实现了。
His wish to be an actor has come true.
据说如果你在看见流星时许个愿,愿望就会实现。
It is said that if you make a wish when you see a falling star, your wish will come true.
既然现在她在法国工作,那就可以实现她游览欧洲的愿望了。
Now that she has a job in France she can gratify her desire to see Europe.

tiānkōng
天空　（丙）名
sky

常用搭配
蔚蓝的天空 blue sky

用法示例
暴风雨来临时,天空转暗。
The sky turned dark as the storm neared.
他抬起头,凝望着天空。
He lifted his head and stared into the sky.
暴风雨过后,天空明朗了。
After the storm the sky cleared.

kěwàng
渴望　（丙）动
thirst for; long for; yearn for

常用搭配
渴望休息 yearn for rest　充满渴望的眼睛 wistful eyes

用法示例
许多男孩都渴望冒险。
Many boys have a thirst for adventure.
我心中充满了回家的渴望。
I am filled with a desire to go back home.
演员渴望喝彩。
Actors thirst for fame.

kē
颗　（甲）量
measure word for grain or small spheres

常用搭配
一颗种子 a seed　一颗子弹 a bullet

用法示例
他买了三颗大珍珠。
He bought three big pearls.
她有一颗善良美好的心。
She has a kind and beautiful heart.

kē
棵　（乙）量
measure word for plants

常用搭配
一棵树 a tree　一棵草 a blade of grass

用法示例
那棵植物开着鲜艳的小紫花。
The plant has a brilliant purple flower.
这些树是每隔3米栽种一棵的。
The trees were planted at 3 meter intervals.

词义辨析

因为、由于

1、"因为"和"由于"都表示原因或理由,但"因为"是连词,用在因果复句中,可以用于第一分句,也可以用于第二分句,如:"因为……,所以……","之所以……,是因为……"。

Both 因为 and 由于 mean "because" or "for the reason that". 因为 is a conjunction, and can be used in the first or second clause of a complex sentences, such as "因为……,所以……","之所以……,是因为……".

2、"由于"一般用作介词,通常用于第一分句,除了能与"所以"搭配,还能与"因此"、"因而"搭配使用,"因为"不可以与"因此"、"因而"搭配使用。如:①因为/由于现在是收获期,所以我们都非常忙。②由于他太累了因此他不想跟我们一起去。

由于 is usually used as a preposition, and used in the first clause of complex sentences. 由于 can used together with 因此,因而 as well as 所以, while 因为 can not be used together with 因此 and 因而. For example:① We are all very busy because it's harvest time.　② He is very tired, so he does not want to go with us.

 **练习**

练习一、根据拼音写汉字，根据汉字写拼音
kě（　）（　）jì　kè（　）（　）jiān（　）wèi
（　）望　实（　）（　）服　空（　）　因（　）

练习二、搭配连线
(1) 晴朗的　　　　　A. 情况
(2) 空前的　　　　　B. 天空
(3) 实际的　　　　　C. 成功
(4) 新鲜的　　　　　D. 愿望
(5) 美好的　　　　　E. 空气

练习三、从今天学习的生词中选择合适的词填空
1. ＿＿＿＿ 近期下大雨，有些航班取消了。
2. 他昨天拔了一 ＿＿＿＿ 牙。
3. ＿＿＿＿ 上，校长早就知道了班里发生的事，他是故意装出吃惊的样子的。
4. 如果把床放到窗户旁边，＿＿＿＿ 看起来会更大一点。
5. 这个国家正在经历一场规模 ＿＿＿＿ 的运动，几乎每个人都受到了影响。
6. 校园里有两 ＿＿＿＿ 苹果树。
7. 我今天不能去了，＿＿＿＿ 我家里有点事儿。
8. 父母最大的 ＿＿＿＿ 是孩子一生平安、幸福。
9. 十三岁的儿子 ＿＿＿＿ 得到家人的理解与支持。
10. 父亲教育儿子要学会自己 ＿＿＿＿ 困难，不要遇到困难就想后退。

 **答案**

练习一：
略

练习二：
(1) B　　(2) C　　(3) A　　(4) E　　(5) D

练习三：
1. 由于　2. 颗　3. 实际　4. 空间　5. 空前
6. 棵　7. 因为　8. 愿望　9. 渴望　10. 克服

 星期四

háishi
还是　　　（甲）连
① or　② still　③ all the same
【常用搭配】
还是戒不了烟 still haven't quit smoking
真的还是假的 true or false
【用法示例】
那幅画是原作还是复制品？
Is that painting authentic or a reproduction?
你是赞成还是反对？
Are you for or against?
尽管我们尽力了，我们还是输掉了比赛。
Despite all our efforts, we still lost the game.

huòzhě
或者　　　（甲）连
① or　② either… or…
【常用搭配】
回家或者留下 either go home or stay here
忍耐或者反抗 submit or resist
【用法示例】
回答是或者不是。
Answer either yes or no.
我们或者寻求供货，或者自己制造。
Either we will find a supplier, or we will make the goods ourselves.
归结起来有两个选择：你或者改进工作，或者辞职。
It comes down to two choices: you either improve your work, or you leave.

dàpī　　　　　　**dàliàng**
大批　　◎ 大量　　（乙）形
large quantity
【常用搭配】
大批学生 a number of students
大批购买 bulk purchase
【用法示例】
春天有大批的鸟飞到这里。
Vast multitudes of birds fly here in spring.
他已经收到了大批信件。
He has received a pile of letters.

yánsù
严肃　　（乙）形/动
① serious; solemn　② enforce
【常用搭配】
严肃的气氛 serious atmosphere
严肃的面孔 a solemn face

请严肃！ Be serious, please!

用法示例
他是个严肃的老师。
He is a serious teacher.
我不是在开玩笑，这是一个严肃的问题。
I am not joking. It is a serious question.
他表情严肃地望着她。
He looked at her with a solemn expression.

yánzhòng
严重　　反 轻微　　（乙）形
severe; serious

常用搭配
严重的后果 a serious consequence
严重的疾病 a serious illness
伤得很严重 be seriously hurt

用法示例
这错误不太严重。
The mistake is not very serious.
这家公司陷入了严重的财政困难。
This company was in serious financial difficulties.
情况比我原来料想的严重。
The condition was more serious than I expected.

zhòngdà
重大　　（乙）形
critical; very important

常用搭配
重大决定 a critical decision
重大意义 great significance

用法示例
这对她意义重大。
It means a great deal to her.
我们遇到了重大的问题。
We encountered major problems.
这是本世纪最重大的发现之一。
It was one of the most important discoveries this century.

zhòngdiǎn
重点　　同 要点　　（乙）名
stress; emphasis; main points

常用搭配
报告的重点(内容) main points of a report

用法示例
道德是他讲话的重点。
Morality was the main focus of his speech.
他介绍了计划的重点内容。
He introduced the main points of his proposal.
法官把重点放在了法律和秩序上。
The judge stresses law and order.

tánpàn
谈判　　（乙）动
negotiate; talk

常用搭配
与敌人谈判 parley with one's enemies
贸易谈判 trade negotiation
谈判技巧 negotiation skill

用法示例
谈判正处于关键阶段。
The negotiations were at a crucial stage.
资方和工会的谈判失败了。
Talks between management and the unions have collapsed.
我们决定就工资问题与雇主谈判。
We've decided to negotiate with the employers over our wage claim.

fúhé
符合　　反 违背　　（乙）动
conform; coincide

常用搭配
符合要求 conform to requirements
符合标准 meet the standard

用法示例
他讲的与事实相符合。
The story he told us coincides with the facts.
这家旅馆符合你的要求吗？
Does the hotel meet your expectations?
这座建筑物不符合安全规定。
The building does not conform to safety regulations.

tánlùn
谈论　　（丙）动
talk

常用搭配
谈论音乐 talk about music　　谈论战争 talk about war
谈论天气 talk about the weather

用法示例
我姐姐总是谈论她的工作。
My sister always talks about her work.
我们不能公开谈论这个话题。
We cannot talk about this matter in public.
你们在谈论什么？
What are you talking about?

tánhuà
谈话　　（丙）名
talk; conversation

常用搭配
总统的谈话 the President's speech

用法示例
我听到了他们的谈话。
I listened to their conversation.
我和你们老师进行了长时间的谈话。
I had a long conversation with your teacher.
他关于种族的谈话引起了骚动。
His talk about race caused agitation.

piān 篇 (甲) 量

measure word for articles

常用搭配
这篇文章 this article
一篇论文 a dissertation

用法示例
她将宣读一篇英语教学的论文。
She will read a paper on the teaching of English.
这期的周刊上有一篇有趣的文章。
There is an interesting article in this weekly.
她约他每两周写一篇有关欧洲情况的文稿。
She asked him to contribute an article biweekly on European affairs.

或者、还是

1、作为连词，"或者"和"还是"表示选择关系，"或者"常用于叙述，"还是"用于询问或含有问题的句子。比如：①他想当医生或者经商。②我们坐吸烟车厢还是非吸烟车厢？③我在考虑去还是不去。

As conjunctions, both 或者 and 还是 mean "alternative relationships". 或者 is often used in declarative sentences, while 还是 is often used in questions, or statements which contain a question. For example: ① He wants to be a doctor or go into business. ② Shall we sit in a smoking or non-smoking? ③ I am thinking whether to go there or not.

2、"还是"还有仍然、照旧的意思，"或者"没有，如：①我病了，但还是完成了工作。②老师又解释了一遍，可我还是不明白。

还是 has another meaning of "still", "all the same"; 或者 does not. For example: ① I was ill, but I finished the job all the same. ② The teacher explained it once more, but I was still confused.

练习一、根据拼音写汉字，根据汉字写拼音
( )sù　　( )diǎn　　( )hé　　( )pàn　　huò( )
严( )　　重( )　　附( )　　谈( )　　( )者

练习二、搭配连线
(1) 愉快的　　　　A. 决定
(2) 重大的　　　　B. 面孔
(3) 严重的　　　　C. 物资
(4) 严肃的　　　　D. 后果
(5) 大批的　　　　E. 谈话

练习三、从今天学习的生词中选择合适的词填空
1. 你要红的_____绿的？
2. 大家都没想到问题这么_____。
3. 星期天我通常做作业_____出去玩。
4. 双方_____了三个小时还是没有结果。
5. 小明昨天没来上课,今天老师找他_____了。
6. 老师要求我们每星期写一_____作文。
7. 战争使_____难民无家可归。
8. 爸爸是个_____认真的人，很少开玩笑。
9. 男人们在一起总是喜欢_____女人。
10. 对不起,你的条件不_____我们的要求。

答案

练习一：
略
练习二：
(1) E　　(2)A　　(3)D　　(4)B　　(5)C
练习三：
1. 还是　2. 严重　3. 或者　4. 谈判　5. 谈话
6. 篇　　7. 大批　8. 严肃　9. 谈论　10. 符合

星期五

zhēn
真 （甲）形/副
① real ② truly

常用搭配
真皮 genuine leather　真的吗？Really?
真好玩儿!How amusing!　真好！It's so nice !

用法示例
那是一只真狗,不是玩具狗。
That is a real dog, not a toy.
这张画真的很美。
This picture is truly beautiful.
说真的,你不该干那件事。
Really, you shouldn't have done it.
这枚戒指是真金的。
This ring is genuine gold.

zhēnzhèng
真正　　　反虚假　（甲）形
true; real; genuine

常用搭配
真正的朋友 a real friend
真正的宝石 real diamond

用法示例
她是个真正的专家。
She is a real professional.
真正的权力属于人民。
The real power resides with the people.
这次比赛中真正的英雄是我们的守门员。
The real hero of the match was our goalkeeper.

shìxiān
事先　　　反事后　（乙）名
① beforehand ② in advance

常用搭配
事先通知 inform in advance
事先安排 be arranged beforehand

用法示例
为了确定他在家,我事先给他打了电话。
I called him in advance, to make sure that he was at home.
事先把一切准备好。
Get everything ready beforehand.
我们事先就意识到这个问题了。
We were aware of the problem beforehand.

jiégòu
结构 （乙）名
structure

常用搭配
三角形结构 triangular structure.
语法结构 grammatical structure
产业结构 industrial structure

用法示例
你能分析这个句子的结构吗？
Can you analyze the structure of the sentence?
这座建筑物的结构很坚固。
The building is structurally sound.
那是一座钢铁结构的桥梁。
It's a bridge made of a steel frame.

jiāohuàn
交换 （乙）动
exchange

常用搭配
交换礼物 exchange gifts　交换意见 exchange ideas

用法示例
在会上,我们就此事交换了意见。
We exchanged our opinions about the events of the meeting.
既然你喜欢我的连衣裙而我也喜欢你的,咱们交换好吗？
Since you like my dress, and I like yours, shall we swap?
他们相互交换了人质。
They exchanged hostages with each other.

jiāojì
交际 （乙）名/动
social intercourse

常用搭配
交际舞 ballroom dancing　交际花 social butterfly
交际广泛 socialize broadly

用法示例
工作时间不得进行交际活动。
No socializing is allowed during business hours.
她善于交际。
She is good at social intercourse.

jiāoliú
交流 （乙）动/名
① exchange ② interflow

常用搭配
文化交流 cultural exchanges
交流思想 exchange of thoughts

用法示例
在会上,我们将交流经验。
We will share our experiences in the meeting.
经常的文化交流肯定有助于发展我们两校之间的友好关系。
Frequent cultural exchanges will certainly help foster friendly relations between our two universities.

zīliào
资料　　　同材料　（乙）名
data; material

常用搭配
查资料 look up data　　收集资料 collect data

用法示例
谢谢你给我提供这么多的资料。
Thank you for furnishing me with so much data.
我们所收集的资料还不够。
The data we have collected is not enough.
这份资料是从参考书中摘录的。
The information has been culled from various reference books.

guàng
逛　　　　　　　　　　　　（乙）动
stroll; ramble

常用搭配
逛商场 look round the shop　　逛公园 go over to the park

用法示例
我们逛了逛公园。
We strolled through the park.
我的朋友爱逛旧货市场。
My friend likes to prowl around the flea market.

jiélì　　　　　　　jìnlì
竭力　　　　　≡尽力　　　（丙）副
do one's best

常用搭配
竭力帮助他 try one's best to help him

用法示例
我们总要竭力改进自己的工作。
We must always endeavor to improve our work.
他将竭力完成这份工作。
He will do his best to finish the task.
推销员竭力说服我买他的产品。
The salesman tried to persuade me to buy his products.

zīběn
资本　　　　　　　　　　　（丙）名
capital

常用搭配
资本主义 capitalism　　注册资本 registered capital

用法示例
有人说资本主义和社会主义最终会合而为一。
Some say that capitalism and socialism will eventually converge.
公司的注册资本最少是五百万元。
The registered capital of the company is at least five million yuan.

píng
瓶　　　　　　　　　　　　（甲）名/量
① bottle ② a measure word

常用搭配
花瓶 vase　　饮料瓶 beverage bottle
一瓶啤酒 a bottle of beer
两瓶牛奶 two bottles of milk

用法示例
我需要一个热水瓶。
I need a thermos flask.
他打翻了一瓶墨水。
He upset a bottle of ink.
医生给他一瓶药水。
The doctor gave him a bottle of elixir.

 词义辨析

真、真正

1、形容词"真"和"真正"都表示真实的,不是假的。但"真正"还有名实相符的意思。比如:这是一把真枪(不是玩具枪);他是真正的专家(不只有专家的称号)。

　　As adjectives 真 and 真正 mean "real", "not false". 真正 also indicates "being no less than what is stated; worthy of the name", e.g. This is a real gun (not a toy). He is a real expert (who is worthy of his title).

2、"真正"不能修饰单音节词,"真"能修饰单音节词,也能修饰多音节词。作为副词,"真"还表示确实、十分的意思,经常用于口语;"真正"很少这样用。比如:真冷! 真恶心! 真有意思!

　　真正 can not modify monosyllabic nouns, but 真 can modify monosyllabic and polysyllabic words. As an adverb, 真 indicates "really", "very", and is often used in spoken languages. 真正 is rarely used in this way. For example: It's terribly cold! It's really disgusting! It's very interesting!

 练习

练习一、根据拼音写汉字，根据汉字写拼音

jiāo（　）　jié（　）　jié（　）　zī（　）　（　）xiān
（　）换　（　）构　（　）力　（　）本　　事（　）

练习二、搭配连线

(1) 交换　　　　　　A. 安排
(2) 事先　　　　　　B. 礼物
(3) 收集　　　　　　C. 思想
(4) 交流　　　　　　D. 说服
(5) 竭力　　　　　　E. 资料

练习三、从今天学习的生词中选择合适的词填空

1. 我可以借给你笔记，但作为_____条件，你得陪我去看场电影。
2. 他这个人有很多的朋友，他的_____能力很强。
3. 由于父母工作太忙，跟孩子缺少_____，孩子变得很内向。
4. 父亲常说，在困难的时候帮助你、没有离开你的人才是_____的朋友。
5. 这些复习_____是给你的，你好好看看。
6. 我说的都是_____话，不信你可以问他。
7. 不是所有的女孩子都喜欢_____街、买东西，我女朋友就不喜欢。
8. 年轻是一种_____，但一个人不会永远年轻。
9. 听到这个坏消息，他想_____表现得轻松一点，但人们还是看出了他的心情很沉重。
10. 中国现在的很多家庭是2·1·4_____，即夫妻二人、一个孩子、四个老人。

答案

练习一：
略

练习二：
(1) B　　(2) A　　(3) E　　(4) C　　(5) D

练习三：
1. 交换　2. 交际　3. 交流　4. 真正　5. 资料
6. 真　　7. 逛　　8. 资本　9. 竭力　10. 结构

第2月,第4周的练习

练习一、根据词语给加点的字注音
1.（ ）　2.（ ）　3.（ ）　4.（ ）　5.（ ）
竭力　　严肃　　呼吸　　符合　　渴望

练习二、根据拼音填写词语
1.（ pí ）劳　2.（ pí ）气　3.大（ pī ）　4.（ yáo ）言　5.动（ yáo ）

练习三、辨析并选择合适的词填空
1. 这次出（ ）考察的目的是学习发达（ ）的先进的管理经验。（国、国家）
2. 国家领导人去欧洲访问了四个（ ），并与这四（ ）签署了合作协议。（国、国家）
3. 这幅画是由四名作家共同（ ）的。（创作、创造）
4. 这名运动员在奥运会上（ ）了两项新的世界纪录。（创作、创造）
5.（ ）明天有大雨,因而比赛的时间改在后天了。（因为、由于）
6. 她之所以没参加昨晚的活动,是（ ）她陪妈妈去医院看病了。（因为、由于）
7. 明天去逛街（ ）去旅游,我还没有决定。（或者、还是）
8. 我明天（ ）去逛街（ ）去旅游。（或者、还是）
9. 这位音乐家（ ）了不起,他唱得（ ）棒。（真、真正）
10. 在你最困难的时候和你在一起的那个人,才是你（ ）的朋友。（真、真正）

练习四、选词填空
严格　　严重　　交际　　交流　　空前
严肃　　实际　　交换　　提前　　空间
1. 医生说他的病不（ ）,吃点药,休息两天,就会好了。
2. 刚工作的时候,我发现在学校里学习的理论跟（ ）情况有很大的不同。
3. 他总是很（ ）,很少和我们开玩笑,自己也很少笑。
4. 坐飞机旅行时,一般要（ ）两个小时到机场。
5. 他和父亲的关系很好,两个人经常（ ）思想。
6. 这个足球队取得了（ ）的成功,第一次赢得世界杯冠军。
7. 在分别的时候,我们与外国朋友彼此（ ）有本国特色的礼品作为留念。
8. 她想买一架钢琴,可是她家的房子太小了,没有足够的（ ）,放不下钢琴。
9. 她特别善于（ ）,能很快适应新环境,结交新朋友。
10. 这个老师对学生要求很（ ）,学生开始有些怕他,后来发现他对同学们的帮助最大。

练习五、选择量词填空
篇　　棵　　头　　颗　　瓶　　条
1. 外出参观的时候,老师给我们每人一（ ）矿泉水。
2. 他写了一（ ）作文,题目是《我和我的祖国》。
3. 山坡上有两（ ）牛在吃草。
4. 我喜欢钓鱼,曾在这（ ）河里钓到过一（ ）4斤重的大鱼。
5. 她的戒指上有一（ ）漂亮的大钻石。
6. 我家门前有两（ ）高大的松树。

练习六、写出下列词语的同义词
1. 着急（　　）　　2. 脾气（　　）
3. 愿望（　　）　　4. 资料（　　）
5. 重点（　　）

练习七、写出下列词语的反义词
1. 推迟（　　）　　2. 动摇（　　）
3. 严重（　　）　　4. 符合（　　）
5. 真正（　　）

　答案

练习一：
1. jié　2. sù　3. xī　4. fú　5. kě

练习二：
1. 疲　2. 脾　3. 批　4. 谣　5. 摇

练习三：
1. 国,国家　2. 国家,国　3. 创作　4. 创造　5. 由于
6. 因为　7. 还是　8. 或者,或者　9. 真,真
10. 真正

练习四：
1. 严重　2. 实际　3. 严肃　4. 提前　5. 交流
6. 空前　7. 交换　8. 空间　9. 交际　10. 严格

练习五：
1. 瓶　2. 篇　3. 头　4. 条,条　5. 颗
6. 棵

练习六：
1. 焦急　2. 性格　3. 心愿　4. 材料　5. 要点

练习七：
1. 提前　2. 坚定　3. 轻微　4. 违背　5. 虚假

3月 第1周的学习内容

xíguàn
习惯 （甲）名/动
① habit ② to be used to

常用搭配
吸烟的习惯 the habit of smoking　好习惯 a good habit
你会习惯的。You'll get used to it.

用法示例
熬夜是个坏习惯。
It is a bad habit to sit up late at night.
对于学生来说,养成良好的学习习惯很重要。
It's important for a student to develop good study habits.
你习惯吃这儿的饭菜吗?
Are you used to the food here?

biérén
别人 （甲）代
others; other people

常用搭配
为别人做好事 do good for others
别人的想法 other people's ideas

用法示例
不要干涉别人的事情。
Don't meddle with other men's business.
不仅要想到自己,也要想到别人。
Think of others as well as yourself.
她很关心别人。
She showed great concern for others.

duì
对 （甲）介
to; toward

常用搭配
对……感兴趣 be interested in sth
对他说 said to him

用法示例
别对你的父母这么没礼貌!
Don't be so rude to your parents!
吸烟对健康有害。
Smoking is harmful to one's health.
我想知道他们对这件事的看法。
I'd like to know their opinions on the issue.

lìliang
力量 （乙）名
power; strength; force

常用搭配
军事力量 military power
榜样的力量 force of example
力量的源泉 source of our strength

用法示例
知识就是力量。
Knowledge is power.
新生力量是不可战胜的。
The new emerging forces are invincible.
那次示威游行显示了我们的力量。
That demonstration showed our power.

duìyú
对于 （乙）介
in regard to; as to

常用搭配
对于这件事的看法 viewpoint on the matter

用法示例
对于音乐,她没有什么兴趣。
She shows little interest in music.
对于我来说,得到驾驶执照很容易。
It is easy for me to get a driving license.
这些价值观对于我们的生活方式是至关重要的。
Such values are central to our way of life.

guānzhào
关照 同 照顾 （乙）动
look after; care

常用搭配
请多多关照。
I'd appreciate your consideration.

用法示例
当我不在的时候,请你关照好我的妹妹。
Take care of my sister while I am away.
你去英格兰上学的时候,我那里的朋友会关照你。
When you study in England, my English friend will take care of you.

zìdòng
自动 反 手动 （乙）形
automatic

常用搭配
自动洗衣机 automatic washing machine
自动报警 automatic alarm
自动拨号 speeddial

【用法示例】
旅馆里的取暖系统是自动调控的。
The heating system in the hotel has an automatic temperature control.
超级市场的门是自动关闭的。
The supermarket doors shut automatically.

自费 zìfèi （乙）形
at one's own expense
【常用搭配】
自费留学 study abroad at one's own expense
【用法示例】
我要自费留学。
I will study abroad at my own expense.
你学习计算机是自费还是公费?
Did you learn computer science at your own expense, or at the public's expense?

恢复 huīfù （乙）动
restore; recover
【常用搭配】
恢复名誉 restore one's reputation
恢复健康 recover from an illness
【用法示例】
她恢复得那么快,我们感到很吃惊。
We are surprised by the speed of her recovery.
军队的任务是要去恢复公共秩序。
The army's task was the restoration of public order.
假期过后,我觉得身体恢复得相当不错。
I feel restored to health by my holiday.

辉煌 huīhuáng （丙）形
splendid; glorious
【常用搭配】
辉煌的成就 splendid achievements
辉煌的胜利 glorious victory
【用法示例】
他们获得了辉煌的胜利。
They won a glorious victory.
对您取得的辉煌成绩致以诚挚的祝贺。
My sincerest congratulations on your splendid success.

关怀 guānhuái 同 关心 guānxīn （丙）动
① show loving care for ② solicitude
【常用搭配】
受到关怀 be cared for
【用法示例】
在妻子的悉心关怀下,他很快就痊愈了。
He soon recovered under his wife's tender loving care.
爷爷总是很关怀我。
Grandfather always shows such solicitude for me.

自豪 zìháo  羞愧 xiūkuì （丙）形
pride
【常用搭配】
为自己的成就而自豪 pride in one's achievements
为孩子而感到自豪 proud of one's child
【用法示例】
他为自己所做的事感到自豪。
He was proud of what he had done.
她自豪地看着自己的工作成果。
She looked with pride at the result of her work.
士兵应为能报效国家而感到自豪。
Soldiers should be proud to serve their country.

词义辨析

对于、对

1、作为介词,"对于"和"对"都用于引出动作的对象,"对"几乎可以代替"对于",只是"对于"多用于句首,"对"多用于句中;"对于"多用于书面语,"对"多用于口语。

As prepositions, 对于 and 对 are used to introduce the object of an action, and 对于 can be substituted by 对. 对于 is usually used in the beginning of a sentence, while 对 is mostly used in the middle of a sentence; 对于 is usually used in written language, while 对 is used in spoken language.

2、在助动词和副词之后和表示向或面对的意思时用"对"不用"对于"。例如:恐怕他会对我发脾气。他对我说……。这个窗户对着公园。

对 can follow modal verbs or adverbs, 对于 can not; 对 also means "toward" or "face", 对于 does not have this meaning. For example: I am afraid he will get angry with me. He said to me... The window faces the park.

3、"对"还是动词,意思是"对待";"对"也是形容词,意思是"正确";"对于"没有这样的用法和意思。

对 is also a verb or adjective, meaning "to treat" and "correct". 对于 does not have these usages and meanings.

练习

练习一、根据拼音写汉字，根据汉字写拼音

zì（　）huī（　）huī（　）（　）zhào（　）guàn
（　）豪　（　）复　（　）煌　关（　）　习（　）

练习二、搭配连线

(1) 自费　　　　　A. 自豪
(2) 感到　　　　　B. 留学
(3) 学习　　　　　C. 报警
(4) 自动　　　　　D. 健康
(5) 恢复　　　　　E. 习惯

练习三、从今天学习的生词中选择合适的词填空

1. 我刚来这个公司时什么都不懂，好在经理对我比较_____。
2. 我们一齐_____他说：祝你生日快乐！。
3. _____她来说，今天的幸福生活真的来之不易。
4. 新买的洗衣机是全_____的。
5. 我的祖国有着悠久的历史和丰富的文化，我为此感到_____。
6. 孩子们应该从小就养成良好的生活_____。
7. 灾区的人们感受到了总理的亲切_____。
8. 团结就是_____。
9. 爸爸上大学的时候不用交学费，现在上大学都是_____。
10. 快说吧，房间里只有我们俩，没有_____。

答案

练习一：
略

练习二：
(1) B　　(2) A　　(3) E　　(4) C　　(5) D

练习三：
1. 关照　2. 对　3. 对于／对　4. 自动　5. 自豪
6. 习惯　7. 关怀　8. 力量　9. 自费　10. 别人

星期二 Tuesday

改变 gǎibiàn　≈ 变化　（甲）动／名
① alter ② change

常用搭配
改变主意 change one's mind　　改变计划 change the plan
改变发型 change the hairstyle

用法示例
习俗随着时代而改变。
Customs vary with the times.
经历和环境改变了他的性格。
Experience and environment transformed his character.
他建议做一些改变。
He proposed that a change should be made.

自己 zìjǐ　（甲）代
① own ② oneself (reflexive pronoun)

常用搭配
我自己 myself　　自己做主 be one's own master
自己生活 live on one's own

用法示例
管好你自己的事！
Mind your own business!
他已建立了自己的公司。
He has established his own firm.
每个人都是自己命运的创造者。
Everyone is the architect of his own fortune.

艺术 yìshù　（甲）名
art

常用搭配
艺术品 works of art　　艺术家 artist
雕塑艺术 statuary art

用法示例
他爱好艺术。
He has a talent for art.
她加入了大学里的艺术协会。
She joined the university art society.
这家博物馆收藏了许多艺术珍品。
This museum has many art treasures.

转变 zhuǎnbiàn　（乙）动
transform; change

常用搭配
转变态度 change one's attitude
转变立场 change one's position

【用法示例】
她昨天的讲话标志着她的观点已经转变了。
Her speech yesterday was a sign that her views have changed.
他以前灰心丧气,不过现在有了明显的转变。
He was discouraged then, but these days he has changed.

qítā
其它　　　　　　　　　　　　(乙)代
① other (things) ② anything else
【常用搭配】
其它地方 other places　　其它事 other things
【用法示例】
除了拜访朋友,你去上海还有其它事吗?
Besides visiting your friends, what else will you do in Shanghai?
我们只去了博物馆,没做其它事。
We only went to the museum and did nothing else.

dúlì　　　　　zìlì
独立　　⊜ 自立　　　　　　(乙)动
be independent
【常用搭配】
独立思考 independent thinking
独立的国家 independent country
独立日 independence day
【用法示例】
这个国家在 1960 年获得了独立。
This country gained its independence in 1960.
男孩子大学毕业开始赚钱时,便可独立生活了。
When a boy leaves college and begins to earn money, he can live a life of independence.
她很独立,拒绝一切资助。
She is so independent that she refused all pecuniary aid.

huìjiàn　　　huìmiàn
会见　　⊜ 会面　　　　　　(乙)动
to meet with (someone who is paying a visit)
【常用搭配】
会见记者 interview reporters
会见来访的人 meet visitors
【用法示例】
法官在他的办公室里会见了两位律师。
The judge met the two lawyers in his office.
早餐时总统会见了他的高级助手。
The President met with his senior aides at breakfast.

huìyì
会议　　　　　　　　　　　　(乙)名
conference; meeting
【常用搭配】
参加会议 attend a meeting　　召集会议 call a conference
召开会议 hold a meeting　　紧急会议 emergency meeting

【用法示例】
我们已做好会议的全部筹备工作。
We have made all the arrangements for the conference.
本次会议将处理这些问题。
The meeting will deal with these problems.
下月将在北京举行一个国际会议。
An international conference will be held in Beijing next month.

wùlǐ
物理　　　　　　　　　　　　(甲)名
physics
【常用搭配】
物理变化 physical change
物理特性 physical character
【用法示例】
他在大学主修物理学。
He majored in physics in university.
物理学研究力学、热学、光学、声学等。
Physicists studies mechanics, heat, light, and sound etc.

shùlì
树立　　　　　　　　　　　　(丙)动
set up; establish
【常用搭配】
树立榜样 set an example
【用法示例】
他为我们树立了一个好榜样。
He set a fine example to all of us.
她的勤奋为其他人树立了榜样。
Her diligence has set an example to the others.
上大学的时候,他树立了一种伟大的人生观。
He established an unusual life philosophy when he studied at college.

dìlǐ
地理　　　　　　　　　　　　(丙)名
geography
【常用搭配】
地理书 geography book
【用法示例】
他研究自然地理。
He studied physical geography.
我觉得地理试题很难。
I think the geography paper was rather difficult.
他正在看一本地理杂志。
He is reading a geographical magazine.

dúzì　　　　　dāndú
独自　　⊜ 单独　　　　　　(丙)形
alone
【常用搭配】
她独自生活。She lived alone.

109

> 用法示例

你不该让孩子独自去旅行。
You should not allow the child to travel alone.
晚上我不敢独自呆在家里。
I dare not stay home alone at night.
他独自一人回去了。
He went back alone.

 词义辨析

改变、转变

动词"改变"和"转变"都表示与以前相比发生变化的意思。但"改变"多指外界影响导致的变化,"改变"的对象可以是具体的也可以是抽象的;"转变"多指自身发生的变化,一般是向好的方面发展,"转变"的对象一般是抽象的。如:①什么也改变不了他,他始终是那个样子。②我发觉她态度上有所转变,也许她会帮助我们。

As verbs, both 改变 and 转变 mean "to change, to be different from before". 改变 often indicates to be changed owing to an outside influence; the object of 改变 can be either concrete or abstract. 转变 mostly refers to changing, or changes from the inside, usually indicating to become better; the object of 转变 is often something abstract. For example: ① Nothing will change him; he will always be the same. ② I detected a change in her attitude, maybe she will help us.

 练习

练习一、根据拼音写汉字,根据汉字写拼音

( )biàn yì( )   ( )lǐ   ( )lì   huì( )
转( )   ( )术   物( )   独( )   ( )议

练习二、搭配连线

(1) 改变   A. 榜样
(2) 树立   B. 计划
(3) 转变   C. 记者
(4) 会见   D. 会议
(5) 召开   E. 态度

练习三、从今天学习的生词中选择合适的词填空

1. 晚上,我经常_____在家,但我并不感到寂寞。
2. 听了他的话,小王_____了原来的想法。
3. 他长大想当个_____家。
4. 大使_____了在中国的留学生。
5. 只有这个答案是正确的,_____的都不对。
6. 大学毕业以后,我能自己挣钱,已经能够_____生活了。
7. 中学时他最喜欢上的课是中国_____。
8. 对于新事物,我们要_____旧有的观念。
9. 刚才的_____开了三个小时。
10. 妈妈让哥哥好好学习,给弟弟们_____好的榜样。

答案

练习一:
略

练习二:
(1) B   (2)A   (3)E   (4)C   (5)D

练习三:
1. 独自   2. 改变   3. 艺术   4. 会见   5. 其它
6. 独立   7. 地理   8. 转变   9. 会议   10. 树立

zánmen
咱们　　　　　　　　　　　　　　　（甲）代
① we (including the person addressed) ② us

常用搭配
咱们学生 we students　　咱们走吧。Let's go.

用法示例
你去开会之前,咱们能谈谈吗?
Could we have a word with you before you go to the meeting?
天气多好哇,咱们为什么不到海边玩玩?
It's a lovely sunny day; why don't we go to the coast?
别忘了咱们的约定。
Don't forget our appointment.
这样的形势对咱们不利。
This situation is not favorable for us.

wǒmen
我们　　　　　　　　　　　　　　　（甲）代
① we ② us

常用搭配
我们自己 ourselves
我们大家 all of us

用法示例
我们在这儿玩,好不好?
Let't play here, shall we?
我们按时到达了演讲厅。
We made it to the lecture hall on time.
他们带我们去看马戏。
They took us to the circus.

qǔdé　　　　　huòdé
取得　　　同获得　　　　　　　　（甲）动
acquire; obtain

常用搭配
取得文凭 to acquire a diploma
取得成功 to gain success

用法示例
她为自己的孩子取得的成绩感到十分骄傲。
She takes great pride in her children's success.
他在物理学方面已经取得了巨大成就。
He has made brilliant achievements in the field of physics.

guójì
国际　　　　　　　　　　　　　　　（乙）名
international

常用搭配
国际形势 international situation
国际贸易 international trade
国际事务 international affairs

用法示例
在国际交往中英语比德语使用得更加广泛。
English is used more in international contacts than German.
他正在国际贸易系学习国际法。
He is studying international law in the International Trade Department

shìchǎng
市场　　　　　　　　　　　　　　　（乙）名
market

常用搭配
国外市场 foreign market　　跳骚市场 flea market
批发市场 wholesale market

用法示例
那家公司要开辟新的市场。
The company will expand into new markets.
在国际市场上,我们的商品不亚于任何公司。
Our goods are second to none in the world market.
石油市场欣欣向荣。
The oil market is enjoying a boom.

kěndìng　　　　fǒudìng
肯定　　　反否定　　　　　　（乙）动/形
① be sure ② certain; affirmative

常用搭配
那是肯定的。That's for sure.
肯定的答复。an affirmative reply.
你能肯定吗? Are you sure?

用法示例
这次考试她肯定考得好。
She's certain to do well in the examination.
我们肯定会获胜。
We'll win for sure.
我肯定他是对的。
I am sure that he is right.

shìjiè
世界　　　　　　　　　　　　　　　（甲）名
world

常用搭配
世界冠军 a world champion
世界地图 map of the world

用法示例
全世界都知道这件事。
The whole world knows about it.
全世界都使用这种小汽车。
This kind of car is used all over the world.
这个事件震惊了世界。
The event shocked the world.

wèishēng　　　　gānjìng
卫生　　　同干净　　　　　　（乙）形/名
sanitation; hygiene; health

常用搭配
环境卫生 environmental sanitation
食品卫生 food sanitation
心理卫生 mental health

用法示例
经常洗澡以保证个人卫生。
Showering often can ensure personal hygiene.
卫生当局正调查这件事。
The health authorities are investigating the matter.
公共卫生部门的官员定期前来检查这个餐馆。
This restaurant is visited regularly by public health officers.

wèixīng
卫星 （乙）名
satellite

常用搭配
人造卫星 man-made satellite
通讯卫星 communications satellites

用法示例
月球是地球的卫星。
The moon is a satellite of the earth.
他们通过人造卫星接收电视图像。
They receive television pictures by satellite.
他们成功地发射了一颗人造卫星。
They have launched a man-made satellite successfully.

quèdìng
确定 （乙）动
fix; confirm

常用搭配
确定身份 to confirm one's identity

用法示例
我们开会的时间已经确定了。
The time for our meeting has already been fixed.
为了确定他在家,我先给他打了个电话。
I called him in advance to make sure that he was at home.
他四处张望,以确定周围没人。
He looked around to make sure that he was alone.

guójí
国籍 （丙）名
nationality

常用搭配
双重国籍 dual nationalities　　中国国籍 Chinese national

用法示例
理查德是美国人,我是中国人,我们的国籍不同。
Richard is American, I am Chinese — we have different nationalities.
他去年申请加入英国国籍。
He applied for British citizenship last year.
她在德国出生但现在是法国国籍。
She was German by birth, but is now a French citizen.

quánlì
权利  （丙）名
right

常用搭配
公民的权利 citizen's rights
发表意见的权利 right to be heard

用法示例
改变主意是我的权利。
It is my right to change my mind.
权利和职责是分不开的。
Rights are inseparable from duties.
你一定要维护自己的权利。
You must stand up for your rights.

词义辨析

咱们、我们

"咱们"和"我们"都是代词,表示复数第一人称。但"咱们"包括对话双方,一般用于口语;"我们"多指说话人这一方,一般不包括对方。比如:①你要是愿意的话,咱们今天晚上出去。②我们的汽油用完了,你能帮帮我们吗?

Both 咱们 and 我们 are pronouns, meaning "we or us". 咱们 indicates both sides in the conversation, and is more colloquial; 我们 mostly indicates the speaker's side, and generally does not include the other side. For example: ① If you like, we could go out this evening. ② Our petrol has run out, can you help us?

练习

练习一、根据拼音写汉字，根据汉字写拼音

( ) jí　　què ( )　　wèi ( )　　qǔ ( )　　zán ( )
国( )　　( )定　　( )星　　( )得　　( )们

练习二、搭配连线

(1) 通讯　　　　　　　A. 地图
(2) 世界　　　　　　　B. 卫星
(3) 取得　　　　　　　C. 市场
(4) 批发　　　　　　　D. 贸易
(5) 国际　　　　　　　E. 成功

练习三、从今天学习的生词中选择合适的词填空

1. 这个运动员参加了很多国内比赛，他希望有一天能参加 _____ 比赛。
2. 由于孩子是在美国出生的，所以他有美国 _____。
3. 他喜欢地理，房间里挂着一张 _____ 地图。
4. 离学校不远有个水果批发 _____，那儿的水果又新鲜又便宜。
5. 他的工作得到了大家的 _____。
6. 每个孩子都有受教育的 _____。
7. 通过 _____，我们向全世界转播了奥运会开幕式的盛况。
8. 这个答案对不对我不太 _____。
9. 夏天吃东西一定要注意 _____。
10. 这次考试她 _____ 了全班第一名的好成绩。

答案

练习一：
略

练习二：
(1) B　　(2) A　　(3) E　　(4) C　　(5) D

练习三：
1. 国际　　2. 国籍　　3. 世界　　4. 市场　　5. 肯定
6. 权利　　7. 卫星　　8. 确定　　9. 卫生　　10. 取得

星期四　Thursday

家 jiā　　（甲）名
home; family

常用搭配
回家 go home　　在家 at home　　家人 family member

用法示例
她到家了吗？
Is she home yet?
他的家在伦敦。
His home is in London.
代我向你们全家问好。
Give my best to your family.

家庭 jiātíng　　（甲）名
family

常用搭配
大家庭 a large family　　家庭作业 homework
家庭成员 family member

用法示例
孩子们需要温暖的家庭环境才能健康地成长。
Children need a warm home environment for healthy growth.
他的行为给他的家庭带来了耻辱。
His behavior has brought dishonor to his family.
战争使许多家庭妻离子散。
The war separated many families.

态度 tàidu　　（甲）名
attitude; manner

常用搭配
对……的态度 attitude to
态度热情 warmhearted manner
友好的态度 friendly manner

用法示例
她对工作的态度很积极。
She shows a very positive attitude to her work.
困扰我的不是他的工作，而是他的态度。
It's not his work that bothers me; it's his attitude.
她用轻蔑的态度和我们说话。
She talked to us in a defiant manner.

大家 dàjiā　　（甲）代
everyone; all

常用搭配
我们大家 all of us　　大家好！Hello! Everybody.

用法示例
我们大家都不喜欢早起。
None of us enjoy getting up early.
请大家保持安静。
Please keep quiet everybody!
大家都同意。
All are agreed.

shǔyú
属于 (乙)动
belong to
常用搭配
属于中国 belong to China
属于我 belong to me
用法示例
这块地依法属于政府所有。
The land legally belongs to the Government.
真正的权力属于人民。
The real power resides with the people.
你和我属于不同的党派。
You and I belong to different parties.

xiànzhì
限制 (乙)动/名
① limit; restrict ② limitation
常用搭配
受时间限制 be restricted by time
进口限制 import restriction
重量限制 weight restriction
用法示例
我母亲限制我的饭量。
My mother limits the amount of food that I eat.
他限制自己每天只吸两根烟。
He limits himself to two cigarettes a day.

huánjìng
环境 (乙)名
surroundings; environment
常用搭配
家庭环境 home environment
环境污染 environmental pollution
适应新的环境 adjust to a new environment
用法示例
这座房屋四周的环境很优美。
The house is in beautiful surroundings.
农村的环境有助于他恢复健康。
The rural environment lent itself to the restoration of his health.
我们生活在舒适的环境中。
We are living in pleasant surroundings.

fēnxī   pōuxī
分析   ⊜ 剖析   (乙)动
analyze

常用搭配
分析问题 analyze issues
化学分析 chemical analysis
对牛奶的分析 an analysis of the milk
用法示例
教练分析了我们失败的原因。
The coach analyzed the cause of our defeat.
经过化学分析,我们知道了矿石的构成。
After chemical assay, we know the composition of the ore.
分析这个句子的成份。
Analyze the constituent parts of the sentence.

fēnpèi   fēnpài
分配   ⊜ 分派   (乙)动
distribute; assign; allocate
常用搭配
分配任务 allot tasks
分配红利 allot the profits of the business
用法示例
这两间大教室已经分配给我们了。
The two large classrooms have been assigned to us.
经理向职员们分配各项任务。
The manager set the clerks various tasks.

zìxìn   zìbēi
自信   ⊘ 自卑   (丙)动/形
① believe in oneself ② self-confident
常用搭配
自信的男孩 a confident boy   缺乏自信 lack confidence
用法示例
我们自信能成功。
We are confident of success.
她显得很自信。
She appeared very confident.
她充满自信。
She has a lot of confidence.

bǎoyǎng   huǐhuài
保养   ⊘ 毁坏   (丁)动
take care of (one's health); maintain
常用搭配
保养汽车 maintain an automobile
保养公路 maintain a highway
日常保养 daily maintenance
用法示例
这些机器需要经常保养。
The machinery requires constant maintenance.
这辆汽车一直保养得很好。
The car has always been properly maintained.
她身体保养得很好,看上去还像五年前那样年轻。
She takes good care of her health, and she looks as young as she did five years ago.

保健 bǎojiàn
(丁) 动
health care

常用搭配
保健食品 health food　　保健设施 healthcare facility

用法示例
这对老夫妇喜欢买保健食品。
The old couple liked to buy health food.
李教授是著名的保健专家。
Professor Li is a famous health expert.

家、家庭

作为名词，"家"和"家庭"都可以表示以婚姻和血缘关系为基础的社会生活单位。"家庭"比较正式，常用于书面语，及一些习惯搭配，如：家庭作业，家庭住址，家庭和睦等；"家"比较口语化，还可以表示生活的地方，如：回家，搬家等。"家"还是量词，如：一家公司。

As nouns, 家 and 家庭 mean family. 家庭 is more formal, and is often used in written language. It has some customary collocations such as homework, home address, harmonious family, etc. 家 is more colloquial, and it also means home or house, e.g. go home, move house. 家 is also a measure word, e.g. a company.

练习

练习一、根据拼音写汉字，根据汉字写拼音
bǎo（　）（　）xī（　）zhì（　）jìng tài（　）
（　）养　分（　）　限（　）　环（　）（　）度

练习二、搭配连线
(1) 幸福的　　　　A. 态度
(2) 优美的　　　　B. 家庭
(3) 严格的　　　　C. 分析
(4) 友好的　　　　D. 环境
(5) 详细地　　　　E. 限制

练习三、从今天学习的生词中选择合适的词填空
1. 他们对这些数据作了认真_____，然后修改了原来的方案。
2. 她_____就在学校附近，她每天走路来学校。
3. 这对老夫妇已经七十多岁了，但是他们很健康，身体_____得很好。
4. 这对夫妻有一个三岁的女儿，_____很幸福。
5. 有问题_____一起想办法。
6. 这位服务员_____很好。
7. 不_____我的东西我不要。
8. 这个地方周围_____不错，旁边是山，山下有一条河。
9. 人不能骄傲，但也要有_____。
10. 资源的过度开发受到了政府的_____。

答案

练习一：
略

练习二：
(1) B　　(2)D　　(3)E　　(4)A　　(5)C

练习三：
1. 分析　　2. 家　　3. 保养　　4. 家庭　　5. 大家
6. 态度　　7. 属于　　8. 环境　　9. 自信　　10. 限制

yìyì
意义 （甲）名
sense; significance

常用搭配
历史意义 historic meaning   生活的意义 meaning of life

用法示例
去那里没有任何意义。
It doesn't make any sense to go there.
这是一个具有重大意义的问题。
This is a matter of great significance.
在某种意义上，他说的是对的。
In a sense, what he said is right.

yìsi
意思 （甲）名
meaning

常用搭配
一个词的意思 meaning of a word
我明白你的意思。I see what you mean.

用法示例
我不明白你的意思。
I can't catch your meaning.
你那样说是什么意思？
What do you mean by saying that?
你能解释这些生词的意思吗？
Can you explain the meaning of these new words?

wénhuà
文化 （甲）名
culture

常用搭配
中国文化 Chinese culture   外国文化 foreign culture
古代文化 ancient culture

用法示例
这两个国家有着不同的文化。
These two countries have different cultures.
这些是文艺复兴时期的文化遗产。
These are the cultural legacies of the Renaissance.

wénxué
文学 （甲）名
literature

常用搭配
英国文学 English literature   古代文学 ancient literature

用法示例
今年春天我要修两门课——文学和数学。
I shall take two courses this spring —— literature and mathematics.

这些年轻人对文学很感兴趣。
These young people are interested in literature.

gōngyè
工业 （甲）名
industry

常用搭配
重工业 heavy industry   工业污染 industrial pollution
工业革命 industrial revolution

用法示例
英国是一个发达的工业国家。
England is an advanced industrial country.
她是工业设计师。
She is an industrial designer.
汽车工业把许多人吸引到了这个城市。
The auto industry has brought many people to this city.

shāngyè
商业 （乙）名
commerce; business

常用搭配
商业信函 business letters   商业贷款 a commercial loan
商业银行 commercial bank

用法示例
这家商业公司成立于1724年。
This company was founded in 1724.
他的公司坐落在北京的商业中心。
His company is located in the commercial center of Beijing.

rèliè
热烈 冷淡 （乙）形
warm (welcome, etc.)

常用搭配
热烈鼓掌 warm applause   热烈的讨论 a lively discussion
热烈欢呼 rousing cheers

用法示例
她赢得了热烈的掌声。
She was received with warm applause.
他的讲话受到了热烈的欢迎。
His talk met with a warm reception.
你将受到热烈欢迎。
A warm welcome awaits you.

tǔdì
土地 （乙）名
land

常用搭配
肥沃的土地 fertile land   土地法 land laws

用法示例
土地很干旱，很久没有下雨了。
The land is very dry; there has been no rain for long time.
土地是宝贵的，一寸土地也不能荒废。
Land is valuable. Not an inch of land is allowed to lie in waste.

fāyán
发言　≈ 讲话　（乙）名
speech

常用搭配
发言人 spokesman　简短的发言 short speech

用法示例
他把发言内容归纳成四个主要方面。
He arranged his speech under four main headings.
她坐在那里努力集中思想准备发言。
She sat trying to gather her thoughts before making her speech.
所有参加辩论的人都有机会发言。
All the participants in the debate had an opportunity to speak.

fāyáng
发扬　反 克服　（乙）动
develop

常用搭配
发扬民主精神 develop the spirit of democracy
发扬优良传统 carry forward traditions

用法示例
我们应该发扬优良传统。
We shall carry forward the traditions.
这种精神应该得到充分的发扬。
The spirit should be fully developed.

tǔrǎng
土壤　（丙）名
soil

常用搭配
土壤改良 soil improvement

用法示例
这种土壤含沙很多。
This soil is very sandy.
她把种子种进土壤里。
She put the seeds in the earth.

bǐcǐ
彼此　≈ 互相　（丙）代
one another; each other

常用搭配
彼此帮助 help each other　彼此信任 trust each other

用法示例
他们彼此憎恨。
They hate each other.
他们彼此不和。
They are at odds with each other.
他们俩彼此尊重对方。
Both of them respect the other.
他们彼此相处得很愉快。
They get along well with one another.

 词义辨析

意思、意义

1、"意思"和"意义"都是名词,都指所表达的内容。但"意思"往往指一般的内容或字面含义,"意义"则强调重要的、深刻的内容,常用于书面语。

意思 and 意义 are nouns, meaning "meaning", "something that is conveyed or signified". But 意思 usually means the common meaning or literal meaning; while 意义 indicates the important and profound content, usually used in written language.

2、"意思"还有其它含义如：愿望、用意、趣味、趋势等,"意义"没有这些用法。例如：他还没有要结婚的意思。我觉得这个故事没意思。

意思 has other meanings, such as wishes, intentions, interests, tendencies, etc; 意义 does not have these meanings. For example: He has no intention of marrying yet. I don't think the story is interesting.

3、"意义"多指事物的价值、作用、影响等,"意思"没有这种用法。例如：大学生打工的意义还不仅在于钱和经验。

意义 mostly indicates value; significance; importance and effect, 意思 does not have these meanings. For example: The significance for college students of doing a part-time job means more than money and experience.

 练习

练习一、根据拼音写汉字，根据汉字写拼音

( )yì　　shāng( )( )liè　( )yáng　bǐ( )
意( )　　( )业　热( )　发( )　( )此

练习二、搭配连线
(1) 工业　　　　　A. 交流
(2) 文化　　　　　B. 欢迎
(3) 商业　　　　　C. 污染
(4) 热烈　　　　　D. 信任
(5) 彼此　　　　　E. 信函

练习三、从今天学习的生词中选择合适的词填空

1. 这次会议有着十分深远的历史_____。
2. 他们的节目非常受欢迎,演出结束的时候,观众都站起来_____地鼓掌。
3. 这个国家拿_____换和平，战争结束了。
4. 我们要_____团结精神,大家一起和困难作斗争。
5. 他们吵架了,_____谁也不理谁。
6. 我们对_____特别感兴趣,最喜欢鲁迅和莎士比亚。
7. 这句话的_____我看不懂,我想请老师再解释一下。
8. 老师让大家在课堂上多_____,这样汉语水平才能提

高得快。
9. 每个国家都有自己不同的历史_____。
10. 这个地方的_____很肥沃(fertile)。

 答案

练习一：
略

练习二：
(1) C　　(2) A　　(3) E　　(4) B　　(5) D

练习三：
1. 意义　　2. 热烈　　3. 土地　　4. 发扬　　5. 彼此
6. 文学　　7. 意思　　8. 发言　　9. 文化　　10. 土壤

第3月，第1周的练习

练习一、根据词语给加点的字注音
1.(　)　2.(　)　3.(　)　4.(　)　5.(　)
自豪　　国籍　　分配　　土壤　　彼此

练习二、根据拼音填写词语
　　huī　　huī　　yì　　yì　　yì
1.(　)复　2.(　)煌　3.会(　)　4.(　)思　5.(　)术

练习三、辨析并选择合适的词填空
1. 迈克觉得，学校的老师们(　)留学生很好。(对于、对)
2. (　)这个问题，我们要认真对待。(对于、对)
3. 十几年来，小城的面貌没有大的(　)。(改变、转变)
4. 就业形势不好，大学生们的就业观念也发生了(　)。(改变、转变)
5. (　)家有四口人，你们家呢？(咱们、我们)
6. 安娜，这次留学生运动会(　)班都有谁参加游泳比赛？(咱们、我们)
7. 我们(　)有四口人，爸爸、妈妈、我和皮特。皮特是一只小狗。(家、家庭)
8. 我们班像一个大(　)，同学们就像兄弟姐妹一样。(家、家庭)
9. 这句话是什么(　)？(意思、意义)
10. 2008年对他来说是(　)重大的一年。(意思、意义)

练习四、选词填空
独自　　国际　　自信　　发言　　分析
独立　　国籍　　自动　　发扬　　分配
1. 奥运会是一项(　)性的比赛，世界各国的运动员都可以参加。
2. 孩子从小就有(　)精神，能自己做的事情就不麻烦别人。
3. 我同学拥有美国和加拿大两个(　)。
4. 商店安装了(　)门，有人走近它的时候，它就开开，走远了就关上。
5. 为了办好这次活动，经理给每个人都(　)了任务。
6. 虽然现在生活好了，但我们仍然需要(　)艰苦奋斗的作风。
7. 相信自己的能力是好事，但过于(　)就会变成骄傲，所以年轻人要谦虚一点。
8. 我正在准备明天在大会上的(　)。
9. 李丽对这次考试失败的原因进行了认真的(　)和总结。
10. 晚上她不敢(　)回家，我去送她回去吧。

练习五、写出下列词语的同义词
1. 独自(　)　　2. 关怀(　)
3. 取得(　)　　4. 发言(　)
5. 分配(　)

练习六、写出下列词语的反义词
1. 热烈(　)　　2. 自豪(　)
3. 自信(　)　　4. 权利(　)
5. 发扬(　)

 答案

练习一：
1. háo　　2. jí　　3. pèi　　4. rǎng　　5. bǐ

练习二：
1. 恢　　2. 辉　　3. 议　　4. 意　　5. 艺

练习三：
1. 对　　2. 对于/对　　3. 改变　　4. 转变/改变
5. 我们　　6. 咱们　　7. 家　　8. 家庭
9. 意思　　10. 意义

练习四：
1. 国际　　2. 独立　　3. 国籍　　4. 自动　　5. 分配
6. 发扬　　7. 自信　　8. 发言　　9. 分析　　10. 独自

练习五：
1. 单独　　2. 关心　　3. 获得　　4. 讲话　　5. 分派

练习六：
1. 冷淡　　2. 羞愧　　3. 自卑　　4. 义务　　5. 克服

3月 第2周的学习内容

wēixiǎn
危险 ⊙ 安全 （甲）形/名
dangerous; danger

常用搭配
有……的危险 be in danger of
脱离危险 out of danger
冒……的危险 run the danger of

用法示例
他们说那是一项危险的投资。
They said that it was a hazardous investment.
有发生火灾的危险吗？
Is there any danger of fire?
医生说他已脱离生命危险了。
The doctor said that his life was out of danger.

nǎlǐ
哪里 （甲）代
where; wherever

常用搭配
去哪里？ Going to where?
从哪里来？ Coming from where?

用法示例
你是从哪里学会说英语的？
Where did you learn to speak English?
你计划去哪里度假？
Where do you plan to spend your holiday?
学生在哪里实习，教师们就在哪里上课。
Teachers teach wherever their pupils are studying.

pīpíng
批评 ⊙ 表扬 （甲）动/名
① criticize ② criticism

常用搭配
严厉地批评 be severely criticized
自我批评 self-criticism
文学批评 literary criticism

用法示例
他批评了我的冒险行为。
He criticized my risk taking.
这位足球教练受到了当地电视台的批评。
The football coach was criticized by the local TV station.
他因未对事故进行汇报而受到了委员会的批评。
He was criticized by the committee for failing to report the accident.

zhēnshí   zhēnzhèng
真实 ⊙ **真正** （乙）形
true; real

常用搭配
真实的身份 true identity　真实的经历 real experience

用法示例
他那快活的样子掩饰了他真实的感情。
His cheerful manner belied his real feelings.
告诉我你的真实想法。
Tell me what you really think.

shízài
实在 （乙）形
real; honest

常用搭配
一个实在的人 an honest person
实在受不了 really can't tolerate
实在太棒了。It's really very great.

用法示例
实在不值一提。
It really isn't worth mentioning.
说实在的，你不该做那件事。
Really, you shouldn't have done it.

xiǎoshuō
小说 （乙）名
novel

常用搭配
侦探小说 detective novel　科幻小说 science fiction
小说家 novelist

用法示例
狄更斯写了许多小说。
Dickens wrote many novels.
我业余时间喜欢读短篇小说。
I like reading short stories in my spare time.

jiējìn   kàojìn
接近 ⊙ **靠近** （乙）动
near; approach

常用搭配
接近500万 approaching 5 million
接近敌舰 approach the enemy ship

用法示例
那位友善的领导很容易接近。
That friendly leader is easy to approach.

孩子们的年龄很接近。
The children are close to each other in age.
船已接近陆地。
The ship was nearing land.

pīzhǔn
批准　　　　　　　　　　　　　（乙）动
approve; ratify

常用搭配
正式批准 official approval
未经……的批准 without the approval of

用法示例
国会批准了预算。
Congress approved the budget.
政府已经批准了这个项目。
The government has ratified the project.
这些文件已获得批准。
These files have been ratified.

wèizhi
位置　　　　　　　　　　　　　（乙）名
position; location

常用搭配
学校的位置 location of the school
准确的位置 accurate position

用法示例
你知道中国在世界地图上的位置吗？
Do you know the location of China on the world map?
他们确定这座新建筑的位置了吗？
Have they decided on the location of the new building yet?
电话放的位置不好，我够不着它。
The telephone is in a bad position — I cannot reach it.

wèiyú
位于　　　　　　　　　　　　　（丙）动
locate; stand

常用搭配
位于山脚下 be located at the foot of the mountain
位于市中心 be located in the center of city

用法示例
希腊位于欧洲的东南部。
Greece is located in the southeast of Europe.
这座城市位于中国的西北。
The city is located in the northwest part of China.
新体育馆位于城市的东端。
The new gymnasium is situated at the eastern end of the city.

bǎoxiǎn
保险　　　　　　　　　　　　　（丙）名/形
① insurance ② safe

常用搭配
汽车保险 automobile insurance
意外保险 accident insurance

用法示例
他悄悄地把钱放在保险箱里了。
He put the money in a secret coffer.
保险公司将赔偿他的损失。
The insurance company will recompense him his loss.
古玩是一种非常保险的投资途径。
Antiques are a very safe investment.

bǎomì
保密　　　　　　　　　　　　　（丙）动/名
① keep secret ② secrecy

常用搭配
严格保密 keep sth a strict secret

用法示例
这里说的话必须保密。
Whatever is said here must be kept secret.
他已经发誓对这件事保密。
He has been sworn to secrecy about this.
不要对任何人讲我们的计划，要保密。
Don't tell anyone about our plan, keep it a secret.

词义辨析

位于、位置

"位置"和"位于"都表示地点、方位，但"位于"是动词，其宾语是具体的地点和方位；"位置"是名词，指人或物所在的地点。如：①小镇位于河的左岸。②这所房子的位置很好。③你能告诉我你所在的位置吗？

位置 and 位于 mean location or situation. But 位于 is a verb, its objects are concrete locations or situations; while 位置 is a noun, and means "a place where something or somebody is situated". For example: ① The town stands on the left bank of the river. ② The house has a fine position. ③ Can you tell me where you are?

 **练习**

练习一、根据拼音写汉字，根据汉字写拼音
( ) jìn　　( ) zhi　　pī ( )　　nǎ ( )　　wēi ( )
接( )　　位( )　　( )准　　( )里　　( )险

练习二、搭配连线
(1) 遭到　　　　　　A. 保险
(2) 获得　　　　　　B. 批评
(3) 侦探　　　　　　C. 批准
(4) 脱离　　　　　　D. 小说
(5) 意外　　　　　　E. 危险

练习三、从今天学习的生词中选择合适的词填空
1. 这家餐厅的饭菜质量很好，只是所在的_____不太好，离市中心比较远。
2. 酒后开车很_____，为了自己和他人的生命安全，一定不要酒后开车。
3. 不好意思，这几天_____是太忙了，一直没有给你打电话。
4. 这个星期他天天迟到，老师_____了他。
5. 为了得到姑娘的爱，这个小伙子想了很多办法_____她。
6. 她觉得把这么多钱放在家里不_____，还是存到银行的好。
7. 这些资料以前都是_____的，最近才刚刚公开。
8. 他们公司地理位置很好，_____CBD商务区。
9. 报纸上的这些事情都是_____的吗？
10. 明天我有事不能来上班，我向经理请假，经理_____了。

答案

练习一：
略

练习二：
(1) B　　(2) C　　(3) D　　(4) E　　(5) A

练习三：
1. 位置　　2. 危险　　3. 实在　　4. 批评　　5. 接近
6. 保险　　7. 保密　　8. 位于　　9. 真实　　10. 批准

 星期二

tīngjiàn
听见　　tīngdào ≈ 听到　　（甲）动
hear

常用搭配
听得见吗？ Can you hear it？

用法示例
大点儿声，我听不见。
It's so loud! I can't hear anything.
她注意听了，但什么也听不见。
She listened, but could hear nothing.
昨晚我们听见了火警声。
The sound of the fire-alarm was heard by us yesterday evening.

tīngshuō
听说　　jùshuō ≈ 据说　　（甲）动
hear of

常用搭配
我听说过他。I've heard of him.

用法示例
我听说她出车祸的事了。
I heard about her accident.
我从没听说有人做那种事。
I've never heard of anyone doing that.
听说他病了。
I heard that he was ill.

jùshuō
据说　　（乙）副
① it is said that　② reportedly

常用搭配
据说他们离婚了。
It is said that they divorced.

用法示例
据说暴风雨明天就要来了。
It is said that the storm will come tomorrow.
据说上帝是万能的。
It is said that God is almighty.
据说法国是世界上最浪漫的地方之一。
It is said that France is one of the most romantic places in the world.

nǎge
哪个　　（乙）代
which

常用搭配
你要哪个？ Which do you want?
哪个国家？ Which country?
哪一个？ Which one?

用法示例
你想要哪个,苹果还是橘子?
Which one would you prefer, an apple or an orange?
你支持哪个足球队?
Which football team do you support?
你的房间朝哪个方向?
Which direction does your room face?

guānchá
观察　◎ chákàn 察看　(乙)动
observe; watch

常用搭配
观察孩子的行为 observe a child's behavior
观察天气的变化 observe the changes in the weather

用法示例
他观察她的变化,并向她的医生报告。
He observed the changes in her and told her doctor.
他被送进医院观察。
He was taken into hospital for observation.
他们派她去那里做观察员。
They sent her there as an observer.

kāifàng
开放　(乙)动
open

常用搭配
思想开放 an open mind
对公众开放 open to the public

用法示例
展览会每周末开放。
The exhibition is open on weekends.
城里的花园应该对公众免费开放。
The town gardens must be open to the public free of charge.
这些玫瑰花还没有完全开放。
These roses haven't fully opened.

zhuāngjia
庄稼　(乙)名
crops

常用搭配
播种庄稼 sowing crops　庄稼人 peasant, farmer

用法示例
他种的是什么庄稼?
Which crops does he grow?
你们收割庄稼了吗?
Have you harvested your crops?

shénjīng
神经　(乙)名
nerve

常用搭配
神经病 neuropathy　神经系统 nervous system
神经中枢 nerve centre

用法示例
她神经过敏。
She is all nerves.
她患有神经衰弱症。
She suffers from neurasthenia.

qíyú
其余　(乙)代
the others; remainder

常用搭配
其余的钱 the remainder of the money
其余的人 the other people

用法示例
她走之后,其余的人继续讨论。
After her departure the others resumed their discussion.
我先离开,其余的人可以在这里等着。
I will leave first, and the remainder of you can wait here.
来了十个人,其余的没来。
Ten people came, but the others stayed away.

qítā
其他　(乙)代
other

常用搭配
其他国家 other countries
其他学生 other students

用法示例
李林比班上其他的同学用功。
Li Lin is more diligent than anyone else in his class.
他超过了同时期的其他作曲家。
He excels beyond all other composers of his period.

shìchá
视察　(丙)动
inspect

常用搭配
视察学校 inspect a school　视察工厂 inspect a factory

用法示例
督学下周要来视察。
The school inspector is visiting next week.
市长视察了我们公司。
The mayor inspectored our company.

shénqíng
神情　◎ shéntài 神态　(丙)名
expression; look

常用搭配
迷惑的神情 a confused expression
愤怒的神情 an angry look

用法示例
他脸上显出严肃的神情。
A serious look crossed his face.
他忘不了女孩眼中的孤独的神情。
He can't forget the lonely expression in the girl's eyes.

他一脸吃惊的神情。
He had a startled look on his face.

kāifā
开发　　　　　　　　　　　　（丙）动
exploit; develop

常用搭配
开发石油 to exploit the oil
开发新产品 develop new products

用法示例
在开发自然资源前，人们应该先了解相关的规定。
People should read the related regulations before they exploit natural resources.
教育能开发人的潜能。
Education develops potential.
她的工作是开发计算机软件。
Her work is to develop software for computers.

据说、听说

1、"听说"和"据说"都表示从别人那里得知消息，用于句首的时候可以互换使用，两个词中间都可以插入名词表示消息的来源，如：听说／据说她结婚了。听／据朋友说……

As verbs, 听说 and 据说 mean to get information from other people, they are interchangeable when used at the beginning of a sentence, and both of them can be used as nouns that indicate the sources of the information. For example: I heard she got married. I heard from my friend that …

2、"听说"可以有主语，可以用于疑问句；"已经"、"曾经"、"没有"等副词可以修饰"听说"，"听说"也可以跟"了"、"过"。"据说"不能。例如：你有没有听说她到中国来了？他是谁？——我从没听说过他。

听说 can have a subject, can be used in a question, and can be modified by adverbs like 已经，曾经，没有，and can be followed by 了 and 过；but 据说 can not. For example：Have you heard about her coming to China? Who's he?—I have never heard of him.

练习一、根据拼音写汉字，根据汉字写拼音
(　)chá　zhuāng(　)(　)jīng　jù(　)(　)yú
视(　)　　(　)稼　　神(　)　　(　)说　　其(　)

练习二、搭配连线
(1) 开发　　　　　A. 变化
(2) 视察　　　　　B. 资源
(3) 神经　　　　　C. 庄稼
(4) 观察　　　　　D. 工厂
(5) 播种　　　　　E. 系统

练习三、从今天学习的生词中选择合适的词填空
1. 这两个房间_____更大？
2._____这个商场的服装在打折，我们下班去逛逛吧。
3. 这位老人在陪小孙子做游戏，看上去_____很愉快。
4. 不知为什么，他总头疼，父母决定带他去医院的_____科检查。
5. 前年这儿还是庄稼地，今年就成了经济_____区。
6. 我要回国了，除了房间里的书我要带走以外，_____的东西都送给别人。
7. 除了北京和上海，我没去过_____地方。
8. 在办公室里骂老板的话被老板_____了，奇怪的是他没生气。
9. 北京的很多公园向游客免费_____。
10._____这个女演员原来是个服务员。

答案

练习一：
略

练习二：
(1) B　　(2)D　　(3)E　　(4)A　　(5)C

练习三：
1. 哪个　2. 听说　3. 神情　4. 神经　5. 开发
6. 其余　7. 其他　8. 听见　9. 开放　10. 据说

liǎojiě
了解 （甲）动
know

常用搭配

了解她 know about her　　了解事实 know the facts
了解中国文化 know about Chinese culture

用法示例

你完全了解事实吗？
Are you fully acquainted with the facts?
所有了解他的人都对他非常尊敬。
He commands the respect of all who know him.
他了解这里的地形。
He knows the lay of the land here.

zěnyàng
怎样 （甲）代
how

常用搭配

我怎样做呢？ How shall I do it?
你感觉怎样？ How do you feel?
他是怎样的人？ What is he like?

用法示例

他不知道怎样使用计算机。
He doesn't know how to use a computer.
我怎样才能跟你联络呢？
How can I get in touch with you?

péngyou
朋友 （甲）名
friend

常用搭配

交朋友 make friends　　好朋友 close friend
老朋友 old friend

用法示例

他是我的朋友。
He is my friend.
我们是朋友。
We are friends.
李明是刘娜的男朋友，刘娜是李明的女朋友。
Li Ming is Liu Na's boyfriend; Liu Na is Li Ming's girlfriend.

lǐjiě　　　　liàngjiě
理解　　同谅解 （乙）动/名
① understand ② understanding; comprehension

常用搭配

阅读理解 reading comprehension
互相理解 to understand each other

用法示例

虽然我不同意你的观点但我理解你。
I understand you even though I disagree with your point of view.
我并不是责怪你，因为我理解你当时的难处。
I didn't mean to blame you, I understood your difficulties at that moment.
她觉得很难理解他。
She found great difficulties in understanding him.

wèilái　　　　jiānglái
未来　　同将来 （乙）名
① future ② in the future ③ aftertime

常用搭配

未来的家 future home
预测未来 predict the future

用法示例

他对未来充满信心。
He felt very confident about the future.
我们应该展望未来。
We should look forward to the future.

dírén
敌人 （乙）名
enemy

常用搭配

抵抗敌人 fight against the enemy
歼灭敌人 annihilate the enemy

用法示例

骄傲是进步的敌人。
Conceit is the enemy of progress.
他把我们当作敌人。
He looks at us as his enemy.
他们把箭射向敌人。
They fired their arrows at the enemy.

kǎolǜ
考虑 （乙）动
① think over ② consider

常用搭配

认真考虑 consider seriously
考虑问题 consider a problem

用法示例

给你点儿时间考虑考虑。
I'll give you some time to consider this.
我正在考虑出国。
I am considering going abroad.
经过慎重考虑，我们决定接受他们的提议。
After careful consideration, we've decided to accept their offer.

huópō　　　　dāibǎn
活泼　　反呆板 （乙）形
lively; vivacious

【常用搭配】
活泼的男孩 a lively boy　　活泼的曲调 a vivacious tune
【用法示例】
她是个活泼的孩子，大家都喜欢她。
She's a lively child and popular with everyone.
他很活泼又很幽默。
He's very lively and humorous.
那个女孩的活泼与善良令他着迷。
He was charmed by the girl's vivacity and kindness.

huóyuè
活跃　　⊖ 沉闷　　（乙）形／动
① active ② enliven
【常用搭配】
思想活跃 an active mind
活跃气氛 enliven the atmosphere
【用法示例】
她非常活跃。
She is very active.
他是俱乐部的活跃分子。
He is an active member of the club.
李林女士在晚会上很活跃。
Ms. Li Lin is active in the party.

wǎnglái
往来　　（丙）动
dealings or communications between persons or groups.
【常用搭配】
友好往来 fraternization　　业务往来 business dealings
互相往来 to communicate with each other
【用法示例】
我们以前和这家公司没有商业往来。
We've had no previous dealings with this company.
我们两国之间的往来可以追溯到上个世纪。
The relationship between our two countries can be traced back to last century.
军职人员常被禁止与平民百姓友好往来。
Army personnel are often forbidden to fraternize with the civilian population.

kǎochá
考察　　（丙）动
① explore ② make an on-the-spot investigation
【常用搭配】
科学考察 a scientific expedition
考察南极 explore the South Pole
【用法示例】
你真的考察那座山了吗？
Have you really explored the mountain?
总理正在上海考察。
The premier is making an on-the-spot investigation in Shanghai.

dútè
独特　　（丙）形
unique; distinct
【常用搭配】
独特的风味 distinct flavor
【用法示例】
那座建筑很独特，因为其他像它那样的建筑都被毁坏了。
That building is unique because all the others like it were destroyed.
他在英国文学中占有独特的地位。
He occupies a unique place in English literature.

 词义辨析

了解、理解

1、"了解"和"理解"都可以用作动词，都有懂和知道的意思。但"理解"一般强调深刻地领会了道理和用意；"了解"表示知道或掌握了情况。比如：如果你了解了作者的生平，就更容易理解他的作品。

As verbs, both 了解 and 理解 mean "to know or understand." But 理解 indicates "to have a deep understanding of the meaning or intention"; 了解 means to know something or somebody in detail. For example: You often find a writer's books more comprehensible if you know about his life.

2、"理解"还表示懂得别人内心的感受或处境；"了解"还表示调查、询问的意思。这两个用法是不能相互替代的。比如：①我理解你当时的心情。②我马上去了解情况。

理解 also means "to understand one's feelings"; 了解 means "to try to know something through investigation or inquiry". In these cases, the two words are not interchangeable. For example: ① I understood your feeling at that time. ② I will try to understand the situation.

练习一、根据拼音写汉字，根据汉字写拼音
( )jiě ( )lǜ ( )pō dú( ) ( )yàng
了( ) 考( ) 活( ) ( )特 怎( )

练习二、搭配连线
(1) 独特的　　　　A. 未来
(2) 活跃的　　　　B. 地位
(3) 真诚的　　　　C. 气氛
(4) 活泼的　　　　D. 朋友
(5) 美好的　　　　E. 曲调

练习三、从今天学习的生词中选择合适的词填空
1. 这种咖啡味道很_____，跟以前喝过的都不一样。
2. 结婚后，安娜和朋友们很少_____。
3. 她在大学里是学生会主席，非常_____。
4. 我_____他当时的心情，如果我是他，我也会很生气。
5. _____穿衣服才能让自己看起来更瘦一点呢？
6. 公司在来中国发展前，先对中国的市场作了_____。
7. 姐姐的孩子很_____好动。
8. 为了孩子们有个美好的_____，很多家长把孩子送到国外读书。
9. A：那件事是你干的吗？
　 B：当然不是，你还不_____我这个人吗？
10. _____到自己未来的前途，他没有答应老板的条件。

答案
练习一：
略
练习二：
(1) B　(2) C　(3) D　(4) E　(5) A
练习三：
1. 独特　2. 往来　3. 活跃　4. 理解　5. 怎样
6. 考察　7. 活泼　8. 未来　9. 了解　10. 考虑

---

xīwàng
希望　　　　　　　　　　　（甲）动/名
① hope ② desire

常用搭配
希望成功。Success is our desire.
有一线希望。There is a ray of hope.

用法示例
希望你能原谅我。
I hope you'll forgive me.
囚犯们希望重获自由。
The prisoners wish to be free again.
这支队伍是获胜的唯一希望。
This team has the only hope for victory.

zěnme
怎么　　　　　　　　　　　（甲）代
① how (to do) ② how (can it be that)

常用搭配
怎么做 how to do something
怎么说 how to say something
怎么了？ what's wrong?

用法示例
这个词怎么念？
How is this word pronounced?
这台机器是怎么运转的？
How does this machine work?
你怎么会来得这么晚？
How come you're so late?

juédìng
决定　　　　　　　　　　　（甲）动/名
① decide ② decision

常用搭配
做出决定 come to a decision
英明的决定 a wise decision
重大的决定 a big decision

用法示例
他决定学医。
He decided to study medicine.
我们决定早动身。
We are determined to start early.
我们一致赞成你的决定。
We all applaud you for your decision.

pànwàng　　　　qīwàng
盼望　　　　回 期望　　　（乙）动
① long for (to) ② look forward to

【常用搭配】
盼望着毕业 looking forward to graduation.
【用法示例】
我们都盼望着假期。
We are all looking forward to our holiday.
人们盼望和平。
People are longing for peace.
我盼望着今年暑假见到你。
I'm looking forward to seeing you this summer vacation.
我们盼望她早日康复。
We expect she'll recover soon.

bǎochí
保持 （乙）动
keep; maintain
【常用搭配】
保持冷静 maintain calm   保持干燥 be kept dry
保持室内清洁 keep the room clean
【用法示例】
车辆之间应保持适当的间距。
The proper amount of space should be maintained between vehicles.
如果你被捕，你有权保持沉默。
If you are arrested, you have the right to remain silent.
孩子骑在自行车上不能保持平衡。
The child can't keep his balance on his bicycle.

bǎocún   xiāohuǐ
保存 反 销毁 （乙）动
conserve; preserve
【常用搭配】
保存体力 conserve one's physical strength
被妥善保存 be properly preserved
【用法示例】
你可以用冰箱保存肉或鱼。
You can preserve meat or fish in a refrigerator.
我保存着旧书信。
I keep old letters.

juéxīn
决心 （乙）名／动
① determination; resolution ② determine
【常用搭配】
下决心 to make up one's mind
决心做某事 be determined to do sth.
【用法示例】
这则消息坚定了我的决心。
The news confirmed my decision.
他决心成立一个俱乐部。
He decided to form a club.
他下决心每天要读一小时书。
He made a resolution to read for one hour every day.

juéduì   xiāngduì
绝对 反 相对 （乙）形
① absolute ② absolutely
【常用搭配】
绝对信任 absolute trust
绝对有把握。Absolutely certain.
这绝对不可能！It's absolutely impossible!
【用法示例】
我觉得这是绝对必要的。
I feel it is absolutely necessary.
我认为你绝对错了。
I think you're absolutely wrong.

pòqiè   jíqiè
迫切 同 急切 （乙）形
pressing; urgent
【常用搭配】
迫切需求 pressing need.
迫切需要解决的问题 urgent problem
【用法示例】
开拓新的市场是我们最迫切需要解决的问题。
Developing new markets is our most pressing concern.
他们迫切地需要你的帮助。
They need your help urgently.

pòhài
迫害 （丙）动
persecute
【常用搭配】
遭受迫害 suffer persecution
【用法示例】
她认为自己受到了迫害。
She believes that she is being persecuted.
犹太人在希特勒的统治下受到了残酷的迫害。
The Jews suffered terrible persecution under Hitler's rule.
他们因宗教信仰而受到了迫害。
They were persecuted for their religious beliefs.

juéwàng
绝望 （丁）动
despair; be hopeless
【常用搭配】
绝望的神情 a despairing look
他感到绝望。He despaired.
【用法示例】
我陷入绝望。
I have reached the point of desperation.
他绝望地叹了口气。
He sighed with despair.
那个绝望的人跳下了悬崖。
The despairing man jumped off the cliff.

wèibì
未必 （丙）副
① may not ② not necessarily

常用搭配

有钱人未必快乐。The rich are not necessarily happy.

用法示例

最强壮的人未必活得最久。
The strongest man does not necessarily live the longest.
好书未必畅销。
A good book does not necessarily sell well.
有学问的人未必都是聪明人。
Learned men are not necessarily wise.

词义辨析

希望、盼望

1、作为动词，"希望"和"盼望"都表示愿意某事的发生或出现。"盼望"程度更深，心情更殷切，"盼望"后面往往跟"着"，表示期待的心情；"希望"使用比较广，往往用于表达一般的愿望。比如：①我希望你更健壮。②我们盼望着早日看见你。

As verbs, both 希望 and 盼望 mean "to wish for the probable occurrence or appearance of". However 盼望 expresses a higher degree of desire and is more ardent, and it is often followed by "着", indicating "looking forward to"; while 希望 is used more widely, and often expresses an ordinary wish. For example: ① I hope you'll be strong. ② We are longing to see you as soon as possible.

2、"希望"可用于句首，也可用作名词；"盼望"没有这样的用法。例如：希望你们互相帮助。没有希望了。

希望 can be used at the beginning of a sentence, and can be used as a noun; 盼望 usually can not. For example: I hope you can help each other. There is no hope.

练习

练习一、根据拼音写汉字，根据汉字写拼音

pàn（　　）　pò（　　）　jué（　　）　jué（　　）　（　　）bì
（　　）望　（　　）切　（　　）对　（　　）心　未（　　）

练习二、搭配连线

(1) 感到　　　　　　　　A. 体力
(2) 迫切　　　　　　　　B. 清洁
(3) 保存　　　　　　　　C. 需要
(4) 保持　　　　　　　　D. 必要
(5) 绝对　　　　　　　　E. 绝望

练习三、从今天学习的生词中选择合适的词填空

1. 听到这个消息，他彻底_____了。
2. 这只是大家的猜测，结果_____是这样。
3. 经过认真考虑，我_____到另一家公司工作。
4. 你_____了？生病了吗？
5. 听了健康讲座以后，他下_____不再抽烟了。
6. 一到星期三，我就开始_____周末快点到来。
7. 世界上没有完全_____的事情。
8. 不要在楼道里大声说话，请_____安静。
9. 难民们_____需要食物和药品。
10. 二十年来，朋友们给我写的信我都_____着。

练习一：
略
练习二：
(1) E　　(2)C　　(3)A　　(4)B　　(5)D
练习三：
1. 绝望　2. 未必　3. 决定　4. 怎么　5. 决心
6. 盼望　7. 绝对　8. 保持　9. 迫切　10. 保存

wǎngwǎng
往往 (乙)副
often; usually

常用搭配
如果发烧,往往会觉得冷。
You usually feel cold if you have a fever.

用法示例
他往往会提前几分钟上班。
He usually goes to work a few minutes early.
初学者往往觉得汉语难学。
Chinese is usually hard to learn for beginners.
他一忙起来,往往忘了吃饭。
He usually forgot his meals if he was busy.

chángcháng
常常 (甲)副
often; usually

常用搭配
他常常迟到。He often arrives late.

用法示例
她常常一边看电视一边织毛衣。
She often knits while watching TV.
微笑常常表示高兴和友善。
A smile often denotes pleasure and friendship.
红灯常常是危险的信号。
A red lamp is often a danger signal.

zhōngxué
中学 (甲)名
middle school

常用搭配
中学生 middle school students
职业中学 vocational middle school

用法示例
她是一名中学教师。
She is a teacher in a middle school.
我妹妹在读中学。
My sister studies in middle school.
他在一所中学工作。
He works in a secondary school.

duōshǎo
多少 (甲)代
① how much/many ② which (number)

常用搭配
多少钱? How much money?
多少人? How many people?
你买多少? How much/many do you want to buy?

用法示例
你们班有多少个学生?
How many students are there in your class?
出国要花多少钱?
How much does it cost to go abroad?
把这些数字加起来,告诉我总数是多少。
Add these numbers together and give me the total.

tiān
添 (乙)动
① add ② increase ③ to replenish

常用搭配
给你添麻烦 cause you trouble

用法示例
她用火钳往炉火中添煤。
She uses tongs to add coals to the fire.
新来的学生给你添了不少麻烦吧?
Did the new student give you much trouble?

jiēshi　　　　láogù
结实 ⑥ 牢固 (乙)形
strong; rugged; sturdy

常用搭配
结实的绳子 a strong rope　结实的帆布 sturdy canvas

用法示例
孩子们需要结实的鞋子。
Children need sturdy shoes.
这根绳子不够结实,所以我们用金属线。
The rope was not strong enough, so we used wire.
你一定要把房屋建得尽可能地结实。
You must make the houses as sturdy as possible.

tián
填 (乙)动
to fill in

常用搭配
填空 fill in the blanks　填表 fill in forms

用法示例
申请人得填写几种表格。
The applicants have to fill in several forms.
你能把墙上的那条裂缝填上吗?
Can you fill that crack in the wall?
他是填补这一空缺的最佳人选。
He's the best person to fill this position.

lǎoshi　　　　jiānzhà
老实 ⑥ 奸诈 (乙)形
honest; frank

常用搭配
老实讲 frankly speaking
他很老实。He is well-behaved.

用法示例
在这个问题上你能不能跟我说老实话?
Will you be frank with me on this matter?

老实讲,我不同意你的计划。
Frankly, I don't agree with your plan.
我告诉那孩子要老实点儿。
I told the child to behave himself.

zīyuán
资源  能源 （乙）名
resources

常用搭配
自然资源 natural resources　　人力资源 human resources

用法示例
资源管理是一项重要的经营技能。
Resource management is an important business skill.
现在大多数人已认识到保护自然资源的必要性。
Most people have come to accept the need for the conservation of natural resources.

bìxiū
必修 （丙）形
compulsory; obligatory

常用搭配
必修课 compulsory subjects

用法示例
英语是必修科目吗?
Is English a compulsory subject?
在你们学校里,哪些课程是必修的?
Which subjects are compulsory in your school?

zìyuàn
自愿  被迫 （丙）动
volunteer

常用搭配
自愿献血 volunteer to donate blood
自愿参加 volunteer to attend
自愿捐款 voluntary contribution

用法示例
我们都自愿帮助警察维持秩序。
We all volunteered to help the police keep order.
慈善事业依靠自愿捐赠。
Charities rely on voluntary contributions.
他们都是自愿的,完全是因为喜欢而做的。
They're all volunteers, doing it just for the love of it.

xuǎnxiū
选修 （丙）动/形
① take as an elective course ② elective

常用搭配
选修课 elective subjects

用法示例
她明年选修法语。
She is taking French as an elective next year.
中文在我们学校是选修课。
Chinese is an elective subject in our college.

这个学期他选修了泛读课程。
He selected an extensive reading course this term.

词义辨析

往往、常常

作为副词,"往往"和"常常"都可以表示反复发生。"往往"表示在一定条件下,或有一定的规律性,不用于主观愿望和将来;"常常"表示经常的或习惯性的,没有条件限制的,可以用于主观愿望和将来。比如:①他常常去阅览室。②下午有空的时候,他往往/常常在图书馆看书。③希望你们能常常来图书馆看书。

　　As adverbs, 往往 and 常常 mean "usually, or happen repeatedly". 往往 indicates something that happens under a certain condition, or happens regularly, and is not used to express a wish or a future occurence. 常常 indicates to "happen usually or habitually", and is not limited by any conditions. It can be used to express current, or future wishes. For example: ① He often goes to the reading room. ② He usually goes to the library if he is free in the afternoon. ③ I hope you can often come to the library.

练习

练习一、根据拼音写汉字,根据汉字写拼音
(　)xiū　(　)yuán　(　)yuàn　(　)shí　tián(　)
选(　)　资(　)　自(　)　结(　)　(　)空

练习二、搭配连线
(1) 选修　　　　　A. 资源
(2) 自愿　　　　　B. 课程
(3) 常常　　　　　C. 捐献
(4) 自然　　　　　D. 中学
(5) 职业　　　　　E. 迟到

练习三、从今天学习的生词中选择合适的词填空
1. 这些事不是别人让他干的,都是他_____做的。
2. 亚洲一些国家存在水_____短缺的问题。
3. 不用担心,这根绳子很_____。
4. 今年我_____了一门中国古代文学课。
5. 今年夏天,北京_____下雨。
6. 这门课是_____课,虽然很难,但是大家都得学。
7. _____说,我不喜欢吃北京烤鸭。
8. 考试一开始,老师说先在卷子上_____上姓名。
9. 现实_____不像人们想象的那样美好。
10. 服务员,请给这桌_____双筷子,我们又增加了一个人。

 答案

练习一：
略
练习二：
(1) B (2)C (3)E (4)A (5)D
练习三：
1.自愿 2.资源 3.结实 4.选修 5.常常
6.必修 7.老实 8.填 9.往往 10.添

第3月，第2周的练习

练习一、根据词语给加点的字注音
1.( ) 2.( ) 3.( ) 4.( ) 5.( )
考虑 迫害 自愿 神经 危险

练习二、根据拼音填写词语
　　　lǐ　　lǐ　　jué　　jué　　zī
1.哪( ) 2.( )解 3.( )望 4.( )心 5.( )源

练习三、辨析并选择合适的词填空
1. 他的别墅( )香山附近。（位于、位置）
2. 他一直在谋求公司总经理的( )。（位于、位置）
3. ( )，这种草药能治胃病。（据说、听说）
4. 我( )学校最近要来一位新院长。（据说、听说）
5. 明天老板要来我们部门( )情况，大家要做好准备。（了解、理解）
6. 对于你的选择我们表示( )。（了解、理解）
7. 这次旅行孩子( )了一年了。（希望、盼望）
8. ( )在新的一年里同学们能取得更大的进步。（希望、盼望）
9. 父母离婚，( )对孩子产生不好的影响。（常常、往往）
10. 姑姑希望我( )去她家玩，她一个人生活很寂寞。（常常、往往）

练习四、选词填空
决定　保存　活泼　观察　批评
决心　保持　活跃　视察　批准
1. 他想请一个月的假来陪他生病的母亲，可是领导觉得时间太长，没( )。
2. 他在关键时刻做了一个非常正确的( )。
3. 老师说，写好文章的秘诀就在于善于( )生活。
4. 这唯一的一张全家福照片，她一直( )着。
5. 他暗暗下( )，一定要好好学习，不辜负父母对他的期望。
6. 孩子考试没考好，父亲严厉地( )了孩子一顿。
7. 这些小猫都非常( )可爱，经常在一起玩耍。

8. 这个老师上课时，课堂气氛非常( )。
9. 总理( )了灾区，对灾后重建工作做了重要批示。
10. 考一次第一名不难，难的是一直( )这个名次。

练习五、选择疑问代词填空
哪里　哪个　怎样　怎么　多少
1. 这里有红的和绿的，你喜欢( )？
2. 路上碰见他时，他问我去( )，我说去参加朋友的生日晚会。
3. 你在北京一个月大概花( )钱？
4. 刚来北京时，我不知道( )使用 ATM 机。
5. 你觉得那个姑娘( )？你要是喜欢，我给你介绍介绍。

练习六、写出下列词语的同义词
1. 未来( )　　2. 迫切( )
3. 结实( )　　4. 神情( )
5. 接近( )

练习七、写出下列词语的反义词
1. 保存( )　　2. 危险( )
3. 老实( )　　4. 活泼( )
5. 批评( )

 答案

练习一：
1.lù　　2.pò　　3.yuàn　　4.shén　　5.xiǎn
练习二：
1.里　　2.理　　3.绝　　4.决　　5.资
练习三：
1.位于　2.位置　3.据说　4.听说　5.了解
6.理解　7.盼望　8.希望　9.往往　10.常常
练习四：
1.批准　2.决定　3.观察　4.保存　5.决心
6.批评　7.活泼　8.活跃　9.视察　10.保持
练习五：
1.哪个　2.哪里　3.多少　4.怎么　5.怎样
练习六：
1.将来　2.急切　3.牢固　4.神态　5.靠近
练习七：
1.销毁　2.安全　3.奸诈　4.呆板　5.表扬

3月 第3周的学习内容

hùxiāng
互相 （甲）副
① each other ② mutually

常用搭配
互相帮助 help each other
互相学习 learn from each other
互相尊重 mutual respect

用法示例
我们互相拥抱。
We embraced each other.
他们举起帽子互相致意。
They saluted each other by raising their hats.

zhèyàng
这样 （甲）代
① this way ② like this ③ such

常用搭配
这样读。Read like this.
这样一个大家庭 such a large family

用法示例
你应该这样操作机器。
You should operate the machine in this way.
像他这样的好学生一定会成功。
A good student such as he will succeed.
这样的局面对我们很有利。
This situation is favorable for us.

nàyàng
那样 （甲）代
① that kind ② that way

常用搭配
你不能那样做。You can't do it like that.
她是那样的迷人。She is so attractive.

用法示例
就英文而言，它并不像你所认为的那样难。
As far as English is concerned, it is not as difficult as you might think.
她真是那样说的吗？
Did she really say it like that?
我不喜欢那样长时间的等待。
I dislike such long waits.

xiānghù
相互 （乙）形
① mutual ② each other

常用搭配
相互交往 to communicate with each other
相互矛盾 contradict each other

用法示例
你能解释一下人与环境之间的相互关系吗？
Can you explain the relationship between people and the environment?
这两个事件是相互联系的。
These two events were related to each other.
我们初次见面时相互打量。
We sized each other up at our first meeting.

děngdài   **děnghòu**
等待   同 等候   （乙）动
① wait for ② await

常用搭配
等待消息 wait for news
等待时机 wait for an opportunity
长时间的等待 a long wait

用法示例
我们正等待着王明的到来。
I'm waiting for Wang Ming to arrive.
光明的前程在等待你。
A great future awaits you.
摩托车手们正在等待比赛开始。
Motorcyclists are awaiting the start of the race.

gōngfu
功夫 （乙）名
① skill ② kung fu

常用搭配
功夫片 kung fu movies
练功夫 kung fu exercises

用法示例
他的中国功夫很棒。
His Chinese kung fu is wonderful.
我没功夫（工夫）看电视。
I have no time to watch television.

gōngfu   **shíjiān**
工夫   同 时间   （乙）名
① time ② effort ③ skill

常用搭配
下工夫 make a great effort
没工夫（功夫） have no time

【用法示例】
你下了这么大工夫，一定能通过考试。
You've done so much work that you're bound to pass the exam.
请你在学业上多下点儿工夫。
Please put more effort into your school work.
如果你忙得没工夫笑，那你就真是太忙了。
If you are too busy to laugh, you are just too busy.

普遍 pǔbiàn （乙）形
① widespread ② general

【常用搭配】
普遍认为…… It is generally believed that ...
普遍现象 common phenomenon

【用法示例】
这个建议得到了普遍的赞同。
The proposal was met with general acceptance.
人们普遍认为她是一位优秀的作家。
She is generally regarded as an excellent writer.
那是一种普遍的误解。
It is a widespread misunderstanding.

污染 wūrǎn 反 净化 jìnghuà （乙）动
pollute

【常用搭配】
污染空气 polluted air   环境污染 environmental pollution
噪声污染 noise pollution

【用法示例】
油轮沉没了，石油污染了海面。
The tanker sank, and the oil polluted the sea.
科学家们认为北极面临着被污染的危险。
Scientists think that the Arctic is endangered by pollution.
因为污染严重，许多美丽的鱼正面临灭绝。
Many beautiful fish are quickly disappearing due to severe pollution.

功劳 gōngláo （丙）名
① merit ② contribution

【常用搭配】
功劳大 great contribution

【用法示例】
他是有功劳的人。
He is a man of merit.
这个发明是他的功劳。
He is credited with the invention.
我讨厌他把全部功劳归于自己。
I didn't like him taking all the credit.

普及 pǔjí （丙）动／形
① popularize ② popular; widespread

【常用搭配】
普及科学知识 popular science

【用法示例】
如今移动电话已经非常普及了。
Mobile telephones are very popular nowadays.
这个软件已经在全国普及了。
The software has been popularized throughout the country.
随着电视的普及，电视广告发展得很快。
With the prevalence of TV, TV advertisements have developed greatly.

诬蔑 wūmiè  澄清 chéngqīng （丙）动
slander; vilify

【常用搭配】
诬蔑他的名声 slander his reputation

【用法示例】
他在我的朋友面前诬蔑我。
He slandered me in front of my friend.
你不能诬蔑好人。
You shouldn't slander a good person.

词义辨析

互相、相互

"相互"和"互相"都表示两个或两个以上的个体之间彼此同等对待对方。"相互"是形容词，可以充当状语和定语；"互相"是副词，只能充当状语，如：他们相互／互相交换了礼物。这个试验证明了这两种物质的相互作用。

相互 and 互相 are used to describe a reciprocal relationship between two or more things or people. But 相互 is an adjective, and can function as an adverbial or an attributive; while 互相 is an adverb and can only function as an adverbial, e.g. They exchanged gifts with each other. The experiment proves the interaction between the two substances.

练习一、根据拼音写汉字，根据汉字写拼音
wū（ ） wū（ ） pǔ（ ）（ ） dài hù（ ）
（ ）染 （ ）蔑 （ ）遍 等（ ）（ ）相

练习二、搭配连线
(1) 互相　　　　　　A. 环境
(2) 等待　　　　　　B. 关心
(3) 普遍　　　　　　C. 时机
(4) 污染　　　　　　D. 好人
(5) 诬蔑　　　　　　E. 现象

练习三、从今天学习的生词中选择合适的词填空
1. 我教小王英语，小王教我汉语，我们＿＿＿＿＿帮助。
2. 信任是＿＿＿＿＿的，不是单方面的。
3. 来中国以前，马克以为所有中国人都会中国＿＿＿＿＿。
4. 不到半个小时的＿＿＿＿＿，饭就做好了。
5. 面试结果还没出来，大家都在静静地＿＿＿＿＿。
6. 很久以前，人们＿＿＿＿＿认为地球是宇宙的中心。
7. 电脑已经在中国很＿＿＿＿＿了，几乎每个年轻人都会使用电脑。
8. 北京市政府想了很多办法治理空气＿＿＿＿＿。
9. 这位作家说他成功的一半＿＿＿＿＿属于妻子。
10. 请你不要＿＿＿＿＿我，我根本没有说过那样的话。

答案

练习一：
略

练习二：
(1) B　　(2) C　　(3) E　　(4) A　　(5) D

练习三：
1. 互相　　2. 相互　　3. 功夫　　4. 工夫／功夫
5. 等待　　6. 普遍　　7. 普及　　8. 污染
9. 功劳　　10. 诬蔑

星期二

确实　　例 的确　（甲）形
① indeed　② real

常用搭配
确实是我的错。It's indeed my fault.
确实不喜欢他 really dislike him

用法示例
我确实得走了。
I really have to be going.
我确确实实很好，谢谢您。
I'm very well indeed, thank you.
她确实很害羞。
She really is shy.

这里　（甲）代
here

常用搭配
请到这里来。Come here please.
我住在这里。I live here.

用法示例
这里不许吸烟。
Smoking is not allowed here.
我吃完晚饭就来这里了。
I came here immediately after having dinner.
你在这里多久了？
How long have you been here?

那里　（甲）代
① there　② that place

常用搭配
别再去那里了。Don't go there again.
我喜欢那里。I like that place.

用法示例
你能告诉我到那里怎么走吗？
Can you tell me how to get there?
他是第一个到达那里的。
He was the first to arrive.
以前我去过那里。
I have been there before.

的确　（乙）副
really; indeed

常用搭配
的确非常感谢你。Thank you very much indeed.
的确非常冷 very cold indeed

用法示例
我的确说了真话。
I did tell the truth.
他的确没想伤害你。
He certainly means you no harm.
我听到这条消息的确很高兴。
I was indeed very glad to hear the news.

lǎngdú
朗读 ◎ lǎngsòng 朗诵 （乙）动
read out
常用搭配
朗读课文 read out the text
大声朗读 read aloud
用法示例
请大声朗读，好让我能听到。
Please read aloud so that I can hear you.
看着课文，听我给你朗读。
Follow the text while I read it out to you.
他每天晚上给他的孩子们朗读文章。
He reads to his children every night.

gǎnxìngqù
感兴趣 （乙）
be interested
常用搭配
对……感兴趣 be interested in…
用法示例
她对音乐感兴趣。
She is interested in music.
我对这些不感兴趣。
I have no interest in such things.

sòngxíng
送行 ◎ sòngbié 送别 （乙）动
to see someone off
常用搭配
在飞机场为她送行 see her off at the airport
用法示例
我们去车站为她送行。
We went to the station to see her off.
她兴高采烈地为他送行。
She sent him off in high spirits.
如果我们事先知道你要离开，我们将到机场送行。
If we had known of your departure, we would have seen you off at the airport.

chéngdù
程度 （乙）名
level; degree
常用搭配
很大程度上 to a high degree
在一定程度上 to a certain degree
到……的程度 to the extent of…

用法示例
学生们做实验时，表现出不同程度的技巧。
The students show various levels of skill in doing the experiments.
水源污染已经达到危及居民健康的程度。
Pollution of the water supply reached a level dangerous to the health of the population.
国民财富在很大程度上取决于一个国家的教育水准。
National wealth depends to a high degree on a country's educational standard.

yuèdú
阅读 ◎ yuèlǎn 阅览 （乙）动
read
常用搭配
阅读能力 reading ability
阅读理解 reading comprehension
用法示例
他通过阅读来提高自己的汉语水平。
He improved his Chinese through reading.
我计划在假期阅读一些中国历史方面的书籍。
I plan to read some books about Chinese history over the holidays.

lǎngsòng
朗诵 （丙）动
① read aloud with expression ② recite
常用搭配
朗诵诗歌 recite poems   朗诵者 reciter
用法示例
他抑扬顿挫地朗诵了一首诗。
He read a poem with cadence.
他们将举办一个关于莎士比亚作品的朗诵会。
They will hold a recitation party for Shakespeare's works.
我不喜欢当众朗诵。
I don't like reciting in public.

xíngzhèng
行政 （丙）名
administration
常用搭配
行政单位 administrative unit
行政责任 administrative responsibilities
用法示例
这个公司大约有50个行政人员。
There are about fifty administrative staff in this company.
他在一个行政部门工作。
He works in an administrative department.

chéngxù
程序 （丙）名
① procedures ② program
常用搭配
法律程序 legal procedure   设计程序 to design programs.

计算机程序 computer program

用法示例

他对进口程序很熟悉。
He is familiar with import procedure.
他们得遵循通常的程序。
They have to follow the usual procedure.
他的工作是编制电脑程序。
His job is to program computers.

词义辨析

的确、确实

1、"的确"和"确实"有真实、确切的意思,都可以重叠使用。但"的确"往往用于加重肯定的语气;"确实"则强调客观情况的真实性,如:我的确 / 的确确没打算去。医生说他确实 / 确确实实是感冒了。

Both 的确 and 确实 mean "truthfully", "accurately", and can be used in a repeated form. However 的确 is usually used to stress a positive mood; while 确实 is used to stress a fact, e.g. I really did not mean to go. The doctor said that he had caught a cold.

2、"的确"是副词,只能做状语;"确实"是形容词,在句子中除了充当状语,还可以做定语、谓语等,如:确实的消息。这些数字不确实。

的确 is an adverb, and can only function as an adverbial in a sentence. 确实 is an adjective, it can function as an attributive, a predicate, and an adverbial, e.g. reliable information. These figures are not precise.

练习

练习一、根据拼音写汉字,根据汉字写拼音

( )xù   ( )zhèng ( )sòng ( )qù ( )què
程( )   行( )   朗( )   兴( )   的( )

练习二、搭配连线

(1) 大声   A. 部门
(2) 大量   B. 朗读
(3) 设计   C. 阅读
(4) 行政   D. 程序
(5) 朗诵   E. 诗歌

练习三、从今天学习的生词中选择合适的词填空

1. 安妮,请你_____一下课文的第二段。
2. 山田要回日本了,同学们到机场为她_____。
3. 我喜欢做生意,不喜欢做_____工作。
4. 根据法律_____,律师将审查该公司的法人资格和财务情况。
5. 真对不起,我_____没时间参加这次活动,我们下周就要考试了。
6. 我对哲学和历史很_____,买了很多这方面的书。
7. _____,我们应该重视这个问题。
8. 一般来说,日本学生和韩国学生的汉语_____水平较高。
9. 他的病已经到了很危险的_____,必须马上做手术。
10. 晚会上有一个节目是诗_____。

练习一:
略

练习二:
(1) B   (2)C   (3)D   (4)A   (5)E

练习三:
1. 朗读   2. 送行   3. 行政   4. 程序   5. 确实
6. 感兴趣   7. 的确   8. 阅读   9. 程度   10. 朗诵

星期三

nàme
那么　　　　　　　　　　（甲）代
so; such

常用搭配
那么高的建筑物 such tall buildings　　那么黑 so dark

用法示例
别那么大声地说话。
Don't talk so loudly.
那么早起来没有任何意义。
It doesn't make any sense to get up so early.
别那么敏感，我不是在批评你。
Don't be so sensitive, I was not criticizing you.

zhème
这么　　　　　　　　　　（甲）代
so; such

常用搭配
这么长的时间 such a long time　　这么多 so much

用法示例
你为什么这么说？
Why do you say that?
别对你的父母这么没礼貌。
Don't be so rude to your parents!
没有这么大的地方来放这些书。
There is not much room for these books.

gōngzuò
工作　　　同 职业　　　　（甲）动/名
① work ② job

常用搭配
工作服 work clothes　　找工作 look for job

用法示例
我在一家小公司工作。
I work in a small company.
你做什么工作？
What's your job?
你在三个小时内完成了一天的工作。
You have done a day's work in three hours.

xiàndài
现代　　　反 古代　　　　（甲）名
modern times

常用搭配
现代社会 modern society　　现代化 modernization
现代汉语语法 modern Chinese grammar

用法示例
她不太了解现代艺术。
She knows little about modern art.

他在大学主修现代文学专业。
He majored in modern literature at university.

réngrán
仍然　　　　　　　　　　（乙）副
still; yet

常用搭配
仍然记得…… still remember…
仍然不明白 still confused

用法示例
这些法律仍然有效。
The laws are still in effect.
几十年了，她仍然住在那所房子里。
For decades she has lived in the same house.
尽管遇到很多困难，他仍然很乐观。
Though he faced a lot of obstacles, he remained optimistic.

bǎoliú
保留　　　反 撤销　　　　（乙）动
maintain; reserve; continue to have

常用搭配
毫无保留地 without reservation
保留意见 reserve one's opinion

用法示例
我将保留我的权力。
I will retain my rights.
我们装修房间时保留了原有的壁炉。
We retained the original fireplace when we renovated the room.
他毫无保留地述说了他在监狱中的事。
He spoke without reserve of his time in prison.

gōngzī
工资　　　同 薪水　　　　（乙）名
wages; salary

常用搭配
领工资 draw one's salary　　月工资 monthly pay
给工人发工资 pay the workers

用法示例
他们的工资高，物价也高。
Their wages are high, but prices are high, too.
我的周工资是多少？
What is my weekly wage?
铁路工人要求增加工资。
The railroad workers asked for a wage increase.

hùzhào
护照　　　　　　　　　　（乙）名
passport

常用搭配
美国护照 an American passport

用法示例
我持有法国护照。
I hold a French passport.

请出示护照。
Show me your passport, please.
我的护照再过两个月就到期了。
My passport is due to expire in two months.
我的护照已经办完了。
My passport has been seen to.

糊涂 hútu （乙）形
confused; muddled

常用搭配
头脑糊涂 muddleheaded
被……搞糊涂了 be confused by…

用法示例
他的解释令我更加糊涂了。
His explanation just confused me more.
我完全糊涂了。
My mind was in a complete daze.
她糊涂了,甚至记不起那是哪一天。
She was in a muddle; she couldn't even remember what day it was.

功课 gōngkè （丙）名
school work; academic work

常用搭配
做功课 do homework
复习功课 review lessons that were studied in school

用法示例
我要着手做功课了。
I will go now to do my lessons.
她的功课不大符合要求。
Her school work isn't quite up to standard.
我能在两小时内把功课做完。
I can finish my homework in two hours.

头脑 tóunǎo （丙）名
mind; brains

常用搭配
他很有头脑。He's got brains.
头脑不健全 of unsound mind

用法示例
她头脑十分敏锐。
She has a very complex mind.
他已年过八十,但头脑仍然十分机敏。
Although he's over eighty his mind is still remarkably alert.
我觉得这个年轻人没有头脑。
I don't think the young man has a brain in his head.

保管 bǎoguǎn （丙）动
① take care of ② keep safe ③ be sure

常用搭配
保管文件 keep files safe

用法示例
我把钥匙交给你保管。
I'll leave the keys in your keeping.
驾驶执照一定要妥善保管。
Always keep your driving license in a safe place.
他保管会失败。
He'll surely fail.

词义辨析

这么,那么

1、"这么"和"那么"都是代词,都可以指代程度或方式,如:这双鞋这么／那么贵。这么写这个字,别那么写。

Both 这么 and 那么 are pronouns, indicating degree, manner or way of doing something, e.g. The shoes are so expensive. Write the Chinese character like this, don't write it like that.

2、"这么"多用于指示离说话人近的事物或说话人认为与他更近的事物;"那么"则指示相对远的事物。例如:北京没有哈尔滨这么冷(说话人在哈尔滨)。北京没有哈尔滨那么冷(说话人不在哈尔滨)。

这么 indicates something or somebody that is close to the speaker; while 那么 indicates something or somebody relatively far from the speaker, e.g. It is not so cold in Harbin as it is in Beijing. 北京没有哈尔滨这么冷 (The speaker is in Harbin). 北京没有哈尔滨那么冷 (The speaker is not in Harbin).

3、"那么"还可以做连词,"这么"不可以。如:既然他不来了,那么你也别等了。

那么 can be used as a conjunction, meaning "then"; 这么 can not. For example: Since he hasn't come, you are dismissed.

练习

练习一、根据拼音写汉字，根据汉字写拼音
hú（　）　（　）nǎo　hù（　）　réng（　）　（　）dài
（　）涂　头（　）　（　）照　（　）然　现（　）

练习二、搭配连线
(1) 办理　　　　　　　A. 文件
(2) 复习　　　　　　　B. 工资
(3) 保管　　　　　　　C. 功课
(4) 现代　　　　　　　D. 护照
(5) 增加　　　　　　　E. 社会

练习三、从今天学习的生词中选择合适的词填空
1. 放学了，孩子们先做＿＿＿＿再吃饭。
2. 各宿舍的钥匙统一由赵老师＿＿＿＿。
3. 在国外旅行时，一定要照看好自己的手机、钱包和＿＿＿＿。
4. 他们那里的东西都比较贵，确实不像咱北京＿＿＿＿便宜。
5. 我看他当时＿＿＿＿忙，就没把这件事告诉他。
6. 这位总统在上大学的时候就表现出了非凡的政治＿＿＿＿。
7. 在那个公司工作需要经常加班，但是＿＿＿＿很高。
8. 他越解释我就越＿＿＿＿，我还是去问老师吧。
9. 分手后那个小伙子＿＿＿＿爱着这个姑娘。
10. 关于这件事我有权利＿＿＿＿我的意见。

答案

练习一：
略

练习二：
(1) D　　(2) C　　(3) A　　(4) E　　(5) B

练习三：
1. 功课　2. 保管　3. 护照　4. 这么　5. 那么
6. 头脑　7. 工资　8. 糊涂　9. 仍然　10. 保留

---

rènshi
认识　　　　　　　　　　（甲）动/名

① know; recognize　② knowledge

常用搭配
认识她 know her
对自然的认识 knowledge of nature

用法示例
我认识她好几年了。
I've known her for years.
他认识到他的错误了吗？
Has he realized his error yet?
随着年龄的增长，人们的自我认识在不断加深。
Self knowledge increases as one gets older.

zhījiān
之间　　　　　　　　　　（甲）名

between

常用搭配
师生之间 between teachers and students
6 点到 7 点之间 between 6:00 and 7:00
两山之间 between two mountains

用法示例
他们之间的交易告吹了。
The deal between them was called off.
我坐在他们两人之间。
I sat between them.
在两个城市之间有一条铁路。
There is a railroad between the two cities.

jiànkāng　　　　　　　xūruò
健康　　反 虚弱　　（甲）名/形

① health　② healthy

常用搭配
心理健康 mental health　　祝你健康！Here's to your health!
健康的样子 a healthy appearance

用法示例
走路对健康有益。
Walking is good for one's health.
一般人都相信健康重于财富。
It is believed that health is above wealth.
你看上去很健康。
You look very healthy.

rènde
认得　　　　　　　　　　（乙）动

know; recognize

常用搭配
认得某人的笔迹 recognize one's handwriting

认得某人 recognize one's face
用法示例
我不认得这个单词,它是什么意思?
I don't know this word, what does it mean?
我认得她,但想不起她的名字了。
I recognize her face, but I can't recall her name.
他不认得他的邻居。
He doesn't know his neighbors.

lìjí
立即 ◎ 立刻 (乙)副
immediately
常用搭配
立即采取行动 take immediate action
立即答复 reply immediately
立即离开 leave immediately
用法示例
你得立即处理这件工作。
This work demands your immediate attention.
你必须立即向他道歉。
It's imperative that you apologize to him immediately.
他看到我,立即从车上下来了。
He saw me and got out of the car immediately.

lìchǎng
立场 (乙)名
position; standpoint
常用搭配
改变立场 modify its position
他对此事的立场 his standpoint on it
用法示例
他总是坚持自己的立场。
He always stands his ground.
他对这个问题持什么立场?
Where does he stand on this matter?
是否从纳税人的立场上考虑过这个问题?
Has the matter been considered from the taxpayers' standpoint?

chèdǐ
彻底 (乙)形
thorough; complete
常用搭配
彻底搜查 a thorough search
彻底改变 to change completely
用法示例
把房间彻底打扫一下。
Give the house a thorough cleaning.
他感到这次他彻底失败了。
He felt he had failed completely this time.
他想要彻底忘了她。
He wanted to forget her completely.

jiànquán　　　　shāngcán
健全 ❷ 伤残 (丙)形/动
① healthy and strong ② elaborate
常用搭配
健全的体质 sound constitution
用法示例
健全的身体比金子更有价值。
A good healthy body is worth more than gold.
健全的体魄是心灵的家园;衰弱的身体则是牢狱。
A healthy body is the home of the soul; a sick one, its prison.
健全的精神是与健康的身体不可分割的。
A sound mind is inseparable from a sound body.

hǎiyáng
海洋 (乙)名
ocean; sea
常用搭配
海洋生物 marine creatures　　海洋性气候 sea climate
用法示例
海洋几乎占地球表面的四分之三。
The sea covers nearly three-fourths of the earth's surface.
人们认为海洋曾经是生命的发源地。
The sea is thought to have been the cradle of life.
他们致力于开发海洋资源。
They are working on utilising oceanic resources.

lìqiú　　　　jǐnliàng
力求 ◎ 尽量 (丙)动
make every effort to; do one's best
常用搭配
力求满足他们的需要 try to satisfy their needs
力求完美 try to perform perfectly
用法示例
我们要力求增加出口。
We must aim to increase exports.
他爱家庭,但也喜欢高尔夫球,并力求两全其美。
He loves his family, but he also likes golf, and tries to make the best of both worlds.
要力求两天内完成这项工作。
Try and finish the work in two days.

zhèshí
这时 (丙)代
at the moment
常用搭配
到这时 by this time
用法示例
这时,有人敲门。
Just then, someone knocked on the door.
到这时他已经烂醉如泥了。
By this time, he was in a hopeless pickle.
这时演讲人停下来喝了一口水。
Here the speaker paused to have a drink.

那时 nàshí (丁)代
at that time; then

常用搭配
那时我还年轻。I was still young then.
那时正在打仗。The war was on then.

用法示例
那时我们住在乡下。
We lived in the country then.
那时罗马人统治着一个很大的帝国。
At that time the Romans controlled a vast empire.
那时我还没有结婚。
I was still unmarried then.

词义辨析

认识、认得

1、作为动词，"认识"和"认得"都有分辨或确定某人某事物的意思，有时可以互换使用。例如：我不认识/认得这个单词，它是什么意思？

As verbs, both 认识 and 认得 mean "to know or be able to recognize". 认识 and 认得 can sometimes be interchangeable, e.g. I don't recognize this word -- what does it mean?

2、"认识"还有了解、懂得的意思，强调经过了观察、分析的过程，"认识"还可以用作名词，"认得"没有此类用法。例如：他似乎还没有认识到这个问题的紧迫性。我们对宇宙的认识还很有限。

认识 also means to understand, stressing the process of observation and analysis; 认识 can be used as a noun too. 认得 has no such usage. For example: He doesn't seem to realize the immediacy of the problem. Our knowledge about the universe is still quite limited.

练习

练习一、根据拼音写汉字，根据汉字写拼音
jiàn（ ） lì（ ） lì（ ） chè（ ） rèn（ ）
（ ）康 （ ）即 （ ）求 （ ）底 （ ）识

练习二、搭配连线
(1) 身体　　　　A. 搜查
(2) 立即　　　　B. 健康
(3) 力求　　　　C. 立场
(4) 彻底　　　　D. 答复
(5) 改变　　　　E. 完美

练习三、从今天学习的生词中选择合适的词填空
1. 我觉得女孩子的身高在一米六五到一米七 _____ 是最理想的。
2. 这位老人病得很重了，已经不 _____ 家人了。
3. 我一接到电话就 _____ 去医院了。
4. 事情到这一步已经 _____ 没有希望了。
5. 我们看问题时应该常常站在别人的 _____ 上想想。
6. 人们把 _____ 时间很短就结婚的现象叫闪婚，就是结婚像闪电一样快的意思。
7. 这位老奶奶八十岁了，身体很 _____。
8. 丈夫说生个男孩女孩都没关系，只要是个 _____ 的婴儿就好。
9. 地球上71%的面积是 _____。
10. 他对自己要求很高，做什么都 _____ 完美。

答案

练习一：
略

练习二：
(1) B　　(2)D　　(3)E　　(4)A　　(5)C

练习三：
1. 之间　　2.认得　　3. 立即　　4. 彻底　　5. 立场
6. 认识　　7. 健康　　8. 健全　　9. 海洋　　10. 力求

星期五

biǎoshì
表示 (甲) 动/名
① denote; indicate ② indication

常用搭配
点头表示同意 indicate approval with a nod
表示感谢 express one's thanks
表示不满 show one's dissatisfaction

用法示例
她戴着结婚戒指,表示她已结婚了。
She wears a wedding ring to show that she's married.
他们表示愿意与我们合作。
They expressed their willingness to cooperate with us.
这个符号表示删掉了某个词。
This mark denotes that a word has been deleted.

zhège
这个 (甲) 代
this

常用搭配
这个人 this person　这个星期 this week

用法示例
这个词是什么意思?
What does this word mean?
我已在这个旅馆里订了房间。
I have booked a room at this hotel.
这个港口是天然港。
This is a natural harbor.

nàge
那个 (甲) 代
that

常用搭配
那个男孩 that boy　那个国家 that country
那个教堂 that church

用法示例
我并不崇拜那个影星。
I am not a fan of that film star.
那个学生昨天丢了书。
That student lost his book yesterday.
这是我的碗;那个是你的。
This is my bowl; that bowl is yours.

biǎomíng
表明 (乙) 动
make clear; show; express

常用搭配
表明态度 show one's attitude
表明立场 make clear one's standpoint

用法示例
市长已经表明了对该问题的立场。
The mayor has made clear his stance on the problem.
那个姑娘被太阳晒黑了的脸表明她喜欢户外运动。
That girl's sun-tanned face suggests that she likes outdoor sports.
他的态度表明他对这个问题不感兴趣。
His attitude is indicative of his lack of interest in it.

shíqī
时期 (乙) 名
a period in time or history

常用搭配
法国大革命时期 the period of the French Revolution
经济繁荣时期 a period of economic prosperity
困难时期 a difficult period

用法示例
那是她生命中最困难的时期。
That was one of the most difficult periods of her life.
幼年是生长迅速的时期。
Childhood is a period of rapid growth.
她对这段时期的情况了解得相当详细。
She has a detailed knowledge of this period.

kāibàn　　　　chuàngbàn
开办 ≈ 创办 (丙) 动
start (a business, etc); set up

常用搭配
开办一家公司 start up a company

用法示例
我们决定开办一家公司。
We decided to start up a company.
开办这样的买卖有点冒险。
Setting up this business was a bit of a gamble
这个企业为工人的孩子开办了一所幼儿园。
The enterprise set up a nursery school for its workers' children.

wúxiàn
无限 (乙) 形
unlimited; boundless

常用搭配
无限的想象力 boundless imagination
无限的爱 boundless love

用法示例
他的无限慷慨深深地感动了我们。
His boundless generosity moved us deeply.
无限的耐心使她成为这个医院最好的护士。
Her endless patience made her the best nurse in the hospital.
我祝你有无限美好的前程。
I wish you a future of incomparable brightness.

jiàzhí
价值 (乙) 名
worth; value

【常用搭配】
有价值的情报 valuable information
没有价值的资料 priceless data
使用价值 usage value

【用法示例】
你应该多读些真正有价值的书。
You should read more books of real worth.
你的建议很有价值。
Your advice has been of great value.
那件古董的价值无法估量。
The value of that antique is inestimable.

价格 jiàgé 同 价钱 jiàqián （乙）名
price

【常用搭配】
商品价格 price of commodities
价格上涨 rise in price
出厂价格 cost price

【用法示例】
这只钻戒的价格是多少？
What is the price of this diamond ring?
这件衣服的价格不合理。
The price of this dress is unreasonable.
这些商品供应不足,价格会上涨。
These goods are in short supply; the price will be high.

开除 kāichú 同 除名 chúmíng （丙）动
expel; dismiss

【常用搭配】
被开除学籍 be expelled from school
他被开除了。He was dismissed.

【用法示例】
他被他的老板开除了。
He was dismissed by his boss.
今年学校已开除了三名学生。
There have been three expulsions from the school this year.
他因玩忽职守而被开除了。
He was dismissed for neglecting his duties.

时光 shíguāng 同 光阴 guāngyīn （丁）名
time; period of time

【常用搭配】
消磨时光 kill time　珍惜时光 to treasure time

【用法示例】
他经常回忆起年轻时代的幸福时光。
He often recalls the happy times of his youth.
我们在海边度过了愉快的时光。
We had a glorious time at the seaside.
不要虚度时光。
Don't loiter your time away.

有限 yǒuxiàn （丙）形
limited

【常用搭配】
有限的资金 limited funds　有限公司 limited company

【用法示例】
他知道自己的能力有限。
He knows his limitations.
我必须告诉你,我的耐心是有限的。
I must tell you that my patience has its limits.
他的经验相当有限。
His experience is rather limited.

表示、表明

1、"表示"是凭借语言等事物来表达一定的意思,它的宾语通常是双音节的动词、形容词及其扩展。如：闪烁的黄灯表示警告。表示赞成；表示气愤；表示十分愤慨。

表示 means "to express a certain meaning by words or something else", it's objects can be a disyllabic verb, disyllabic adjective or one of their expansions. For example: A flashing yellow light denotes caution. To show one's approval, to show one's indignation, to show one's extreme indignation.

2、"表明"的意思是表示明白,它的宾语通常是名词或一个句子,其宾语不能是动词或形容词。如：表明观点,这本书表明他是一个有创造力的作家。

表明 means to make clear, or to express clearly. The object of it is usually a noun or a clause, it can not be a verb or an adjective. For example: to express one's opinion, This book shows that he is an ingenious author.

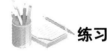

练习一、根据拼音写汉字，根据汉字写拼音
( )zhí   ( )xiàn   biǎo( )   nà( )   ( )chú
价( )   无( )   ( )明   ( )个   开( )

练习二、搭配连线
(1) 表示　　　　A. 学籍
(2) 珍惜　　　　B. 时期
(3) 困难　　　　C. 时光
(4) 开办　　　　D. 满意
(5) 开除　　　　E. 工厂

练习三、从今天学习的生词中选择合适的词填空
1. 他的发言_____他的态度已经发生了转变。
2. 我在这里向帮助过我的人们_____感谢。
3. 她很怀念童年的美好_____。

4. 那段_____他写了很多优秀的作品。
5. 他说自己的汉语水平_____,还不能当翻译。
6. 这个学生因为打架被学校_____了。
7. 市场里水果的_____比超市里的便宜。
8. 我认为他提供的信息很有_____,我们应该重视。
9. 他和几个朋友_____了一个工厂,他成了工厂的老板。
10. 人的生命是有限的,但为人民服务是_____的。

答案

练习一:
略

练习二:
(1) D (2) C (3) B (4) E (5) A

练习三:
1. 表明 2. 表示 3. 时光 4. 时期 5. 有限
6. 开除 7. 价格 8. 价值 9. 开办 10. 无限

第3月,第3周的练习

练习一、根据词语给加点的字注音

1.( ) 2.( ) 3.( ) 4.( ) 5.( )
送行   朗诵   彻底   糊涂   等待

练习二、根据拼音填写词语

　　wū　　wū　　shí　　shí　　shi
1.( )染 2.( )蔑 3.确( ) 4.( )期 5.认( )

练习三、辨析并选择合适的词填空

1. 尊重是( )的,不是单方面的。(互相、相互)
2. 大家要( )帮助,直到胜利到达终点。(互相、相互)
3. ( ),他是一个非常懂事的孩子。(确实、的确)
4. 我们得到了( )的消息,银行将提高利率。(确实、的确)
5. 我觉得去年夏天好像没有今年夏天( )热!(这么、那么)
6. 从这儿到超市( )远,我可不想走着去。(这么、那么)
7. 三十年后再见面,我们变化都很大,有的都不( )了。(认识、认得)
8. 来,我来介绍你们( )一下。(认识、认得)
9. 公司领导对我们的改革方案( )赞成。(表示、表明)
10. 研究( ),男女在智力方面并没有差异。(表示、表明)

练习四、选词填空

价值　健康　保管　程度　普遍
价格　健全　保留　程序　普及

1. 电脑还没有在中国家庭完全( )。
2. 我祝大家在新的一年里身体( ),万事如意!
3. 地震中,这个国家捐了( )五百万的物资。

4. 医生,能不能告诉我,我的病严重到了什么( )?
5. 在公共场合,请( )好贵重物品。
6. 他把自己的学习经验毫无( )地介绍给了大家。
7. 新出的这款手机( )太贵,过两个月再买可能会便宜点。
8. 你要想申请奖学金,就得填表、申报,每个人都要按( )办事。
9. 这种现象很( ),没什么大惊小怪的。
10. 作为( )的人,很难理解残疾人的感受,所以和他们打交道时要特别注意。

练习五、选择指示代词填空

这样　这里　这么　这是　这个
那样　那里　那么　那时　那个

1. 我希望以后不要再出现像今天( )的情况。
2. ( )地方很远,我看你还是别去了。
3. ( )我们都还年轻,还不懂得珍惜时光。
4. 他说,既然如此,( ),就按合同上写的办吧。
5. 明天是周末,我要去朋友( )玩,或者让他来我( )。

练习六、写出下列词语的同义词

1. 立即( )　　2. 开办( )
3. 工作( )　　4. 朗读( )
5. 等待( )

练习七、写出下列词语的反义词

1. 健全( )　　2. 诬蔑( )
3. 现代( )　　4. 保留( )
5. 污染( )

答案

练习一:
1. sòng 2. sòng 3. chè 4. hú 5. dài

练习二:
1. 污 2. 诬 3. 实 4. 时 5. 识

练习三:
1. 相互 2. 互相 3. 的确 4. 确实 5. 这么
6. 那么 7. 认得 8. 认识 9. 表示 10. 表明

练习四:
1. 普及 2. 健康 3. 价值 4. 程度 5. 保管
6. 保留 7. 价格 8. 程序 9. 普遍 10. 健全

练习五:
1. 这样 2. 那个 3. 那时 4. 那么
5. 那里,这里

练习六:
1. 立刻 2. 创办 3. 职业 4. 朗诵 5. 等候

练习七:
1. 伤残 2. 澄清 3. 古代 4. 撤销 5. 净化

3月 第4周的学习内容

zhèngquè
正确　　　　　　　反 错误　　　　（甲）形
correct; proper
【常用搭配】
正确的答案 a correct answer
正确的读音 proper pronunciation
【用法示例】
你对这个问题的回答是正确的。
Your answer to the question is correct.
只有时间才能证明你是否正确。
Only time will tell if you are right.
我认为他对这个问题的评论不正确。
I think his commentary on this issue is incorrect.

zhǒng
种　　　　　　　　　　　　　　（甲）名/量
① seed ② kind
【常用搭配】
多种…… many kinds of...
各种书 books of all sorts
【用法示例】
你最喜欢哪一种肥皂？
What kind of soap do you like the best?
世界上有多少种动物？
How many kinds of animals are there in the world?
棉花是一种材料。
Cotton is a type of material.

zhòng
种　　　　　　　　　　　　　　（甲）动
plant
【常用搭配】
种庄稼 seed corn　　种树 plant a tree
【用法示例】
你种蔬菜了吗？
Have you planted any vegetables yet?
他在大门前种了两棵松树。
He planted two pine trees in front of the gate.

cuòwù
错误　　　　　　　　　　　　　（甲）名
error; mistake
【常用搭配】
拼写错误 spelling mistake　　犯错误 make mistakes
承认错误 admit a mistake　　错误的见解 a wrong opinion
【用法示例】
这种错误会有损于你的事业。
Such a mistake would mar your career.
他没意识到他的错误。
He was unconscious of his mistake.
有很多错误是由疏忽造成的。
Many errors are caused by oversights.

quēfá　　　　　　　chōngzú
缺乏　　　　　　　反 充足　　　　（乙）动/形
① lack ② be short of
【常用搭配】
缺乏经验 lack of experience
【用法示例】
他工作不错，但似乎缺乏信心。
He is good at his job, but he seems to lack confidence.
她因缺乏营养而身体虚弱。
She is weak from lack of sustenance.
因为他们对对手缺乏了解，所以他们输了。
They lost the game, because they knew little about their rivals.

quēshǎo
缺少　　　　　　　　　　　　　（乙）动
lack
【常用搭配】
缺少资金 lack of funds
【用法示例】
我们的主要问题就是缺少时间。
Our principal problem is a lack of time.
缺少雨水庄稼就不会长得好。
The crops will not grow well for lack of rain.
这家公司的主要问题是缺少技术人员。
The company's main problem is their shortage of skilled personnel.

shíkè
时刻　　　　　　　　　　　　　（乙）名
moment
【常用搭配】
时刻表 timetable
幸福的时刻 a happy moment
【用法示例】
那个时刻我永远都不会忘记。
That was a moment that I shall never forget.

圣诞节应是欢乐的时刻。
Christmas should be a time of great cheer.

开辟 kāipì 〔同〕开拓 kāituò （乙）动
open up; start

常用搭配
开辟新市场 open up new markets
开辟一条新路 open a new road

用法示例
销售经理想在中国开辟更加广阔的市场。
The sales manager wants to open up a bigger market in China.
应该开辟更多的公交路线，因为公共汽车载客多。
More bus routes should be added because buses can accommodate more passengers.
他们开辟了一条穿过森林的新路。
They opened a new road that passes through the forest.

成熟 chéngshú （乙）动/形
① mature ② ripe

常用搭配
成熟的桃子 ripe peaches　　成熟的经验 ripe experience

用法示例
这水果还没有成熟，我们不能吃。
This fruit isn't ripe yet — we can't eat it.
社会变革的时机已经成熟了。
The time is ripe for societal changes.
他对生活有成熟的看法。
He has a mellow attitude to life.

沉默 chénmò 〔同〕缄默 jiānmò （乙）形
silent

常用搭配
保持沉默 keep silent　　沉默寡言的人 a man of few words

用法示例
【谚】雄辩是银，沉默是金。
Speech is silver; silence is gold.
我们认为他沉默是表示拒绝。
We interpreted his silence as a refusal.
他唯一的反应是一阵沉默。
His only reaction was silence.

开设 kāishè （丙）动
offer (course); open; establish

常用搭配
开设中文课程 to offer a Chinese course
开设一家医院 to establish a hospital

用法示例
这所学院开设英语速成课。
The college offers a crash course in English.

今年将为儿童开设一家图书馆。
A childrens' library will open this year.

时节 shíjié （丙）名
season; time

常用搭配
农闲时节 farming's quiet season

用法示例
收获的时节快到了。
The harvest season nears.
在农忙时节，他们得帮助父母干活。
They will help their parents work during the busy farming season.

沉思 chénsī （丙）动
meditate; muse; contemplate

常用搭配
他陷入沉思。He is deep in meditation.

用法示例
每天早晨神父要沉思一个小时。
Each morning the priest spent an hour in quiet contemplation.
她躺着沉思了一会儿。
She lay there musing for a while.
这个女孩陷入了沉思。
The young girl was lost in a reverie.

词义辨析

缺乏、缺少

1、动词"缺乏"和"缺少"都表示应该有而没有或不足，"缺少"多用于人或具体事物的数量不足。例如：缺少人手，缺少食物；"缺乏"一般用于抽象的事物，还可以与动词搭配；另外，缺乏还可以用作形容词。如：怯懦的人缺乏勇气。我觉得你缺乏锻炼。

The verbs 缺乏 and 缺少 mean "to be without" or "to have less than enough of". 缺少 is mostly used for people, or something concrete, e.g. lack of men, lack of food; 缺乏 is mostly used for something abstract, and it can be followed by verbs. Also 缺乏 can serve as an adjective; 缺少 can not. For Example: A coward lacks courage. I think you don't exercise enough.

练习一、根据拼音写汉字，根据汉字写拼音
quē（ ）（ ）shú　chén（ ）kāi（ ）（ ）jié
（ ）乏　成（ ）　（ ）默　（ ）辟　时（ ）

练习二、搭配连线
(1) 陷入　　　　　A. 沉默
(2) 农闲　　　　　B. 沉思
(3) 保持　　　　　C. 经验
(4) 缺乏　　　　　D. 错误
(5) 承认　　　　　E. 时节

练习三、从今天学习的生词中选择合适的词填空
1. 夏秋 _____ 水果最多。
2. 这学期我们新 _____ 了一门中国文化课。
3. 农民在院子里新 _____ 出一块地方种西红柿。
4. 努力是成功不可 _____ 的条件。
5. 如果你认为你的选择是 _____ 的，你就要坚持。
6. 他不爱说话，是个 _____ 的人。
7. 经历了这么多事以后，这个年轻人变得 _____ 多了。
8. 他要去旅行，买了一本列车 _____ 表。
9. 因为 _____ 经验，他刚到公司的时候，常常遭到领导的批评。
10. 每个人都有可能犯 _____，关键是发现了自己的问题，就要及时改正。

答案
练习一：
略

练习二：
(1) B　(2)E　(3)A　(4)C　(5)D

练习三：
1. 时节　2. 开设　3. 开辟　4. 缺少　5. 正确
6. 沉默　7. 成熟　8. 时刻　9. 缺乏　10. 错误

shì
事　　　　　　　　　　　（甲）名
thing; affair

常用搭配
私事 a personal matter　蠢事 stupid thing
有什么事？What's the matter?

用法示例
说是一回事，做又是另一回事。
Saying it is one thing, and doing it is another.
还有一件事我想问你。
There is another thing I want to ask you about.
这不是我的事。
It's not my business.

shìqíng
事情　　　　　　　　　　（甲）名
matter; affair

常用搭配
重要的事情 important matter
讨论事情 talk about one thing

用法示例
事情进行得怎么样了？
How are things going?
关于这件事情你应该请教你的律师。
You should seek advice from your lawyer on this matter.
不要过于匆忙地对重要的事情作决定。
Don't decide on important matters too quickly.

chǎng
场　　　　　　　　　　（甲）名/量
① field; place ② measure word, used for sport, recreation, etc.

常用搭配
战场 battle field　一场音乐会 a concert
一场运动 a campaign

用法示例
他们画出了足球场地的边界。
They marked the boundaries of the football field.
一场示威游行将要发生。
A demonstration will take place.
谁赢了那场网球赛？
Who won the tennis match?

lèguān　　　　　　　　　bēiguān
乐观　　　反悲观　　　　（乙）形
optimistic

常用搭配
乐观的性格 a sanguine nature

对事情乐观的看法 an optimistic view of events

用法示例

我们对未来十分乐观。
We are very optimistic about the future.
股东对公司的前景很乐观。
The stockholders are optimistic about the company's future.
她即使在最糟糕的时候也总是很乐观。
She was always optimistic, even when things were at their worst.

bǎowèi
保卫 同 捍卫(hànwèi) （乙）动
safeguard; defend

常用搭配

保卫祖国 defend the motherland

用法示例

他们拿起武器保卫国家。
They took up arms in defense of their country.
这些士兵的职责是保卫岛屿不受侵犯。
The duty of these soldiers is to defend the island against invasion.

wénmíng
文明 反 野蛮(yěmán) （乙）名/形
① civilization ② civilized

常用搭配

文明世界 the civilized world
精神文明 spiritual civilization
西方文明 Western civilization

用法示例

古埃及人曾经拥有高度文明。
The ancient Egyptians had an advanced civilization.
讲话要文明！
Keep a civil tongue in your head!
从某些方面看,上个世纪文明似乎进步不大。
In some ways, civilization does not seem to have progressed much in the last century.

jìlǜ
纪律 同 规定(guīdìng) （乙）名
discipline

常用搭配

纪律严明 be strict in discipline
遵守纪律 abide by discipline
军事纪律 military discipline

用法示例

那位老师无法维持课堂纪律。
The teacher can't keep discipline in her class.
在敌人的炮火下,那些士兵显示了良好的纪律。
The soldiers showed perfect discipline under enemy fire.
一到周末纪律往往涣散下来。
Discipline is often relaxed on the weekends.

jìjié
季节 （乙）名
season

常用搭配

收获的季节 harvest season　季节性商品 seasonal goods
多雨的季节 rainy season

用法示例

春天和秋天是我喜欢的季节。
Spring and autumn are my favorite seasons.
大衣是季节性商品。
Overcoats are seasonal goods.
秋天比任何季节都适合读书。
Autumn is better for reading than any other season.

jíshí
及时 （乙）形
① in time ② timely

常用搭配

及时帮助 timely help　及时到达 arrive in time

用法示例

我们能及时到达车站吗?
Will we get to the station in time?
我们希望的是及时付款。
What we expected was nothing less than a timely payment.
感谢你及时提醒我。
Thank you for your reminding me in time.

wénmíng
闻名 （丙）动
be well-known; be famous

常用搭配

举世闻名 world-famous
因/以……而闻名 be famous for…

用法示例

埃及以巨大的金字塔而闻名。
Egypt is famous for its grand pyramids.
长城举世闻名。
The Great Wall is world-famous.
圣保罗教堂的圆顶闻名于世。
The dome of St. Paul's Cathedral is well known in the world.

bēiguān
悲观 （丙）形
pessimistic

常用搭配

悲观的态度 pessimistic attitude

用法示例

他对未来感到悲观。
He is pessimistic about the future.
她对经济状况持悲观的看法。
She takes a pessimistic view of the state of the economy.
向悲观的人推销保险很容易。
It's easy to sell insurance to a pessimist.

保守 bǎoshǒu (丙) 动/形

① keep (secret) ② (politically) conservative

常用搭配
保守秘密 keep a secret
保守的估计 conservative estimate
保守党 Conservative Party

用法示例
你会保守秘密的,是吧!
You'll keep it to yourself, won't you?
老年人通常比年轻人保守。
Old people are usually more conservative than young people.
她在穿着方面很保守。
She is conservative in the way she dresses.

事、事情

1、"事"和"事情"都是名词,表示社会、生活中的活动或现象。比较正式的、重大的通常用"事情";"事"一般比较口语化,比较随意,并且常用于习惯用语。如:我要和你谈一件事 / 事情。这不关你的事。万事如意。

事 and 事情 are nouns, meaning "thing or matter". 事情 is usually used for formal and important things; 事 is more colloquial, and often used in idioms. For example: I have a matter to talk to you about. That's none of your business. Everything is as one wishes.

2、"事"能被单音节词修饰,也能被多音节词修饰;"事情"往往不被单音节词修饰,"事情"还强调情形、过程。如:重要的事 / 事情。告诉我们事情的经过。

事 can be modified by monosyllabic and polysyllabic words, 事情 can not be modified by monosyllabic words. 事情 also stresses the condition or process of one thing. For example: An important matter. Tell us all about the matter.

练习一、根据拼音写汉字,根据汉字写拼音

wén (　) wén (　) (　) guān jì (　) (　) shǒu
(　)明　(　)名　悲(　)　(　)律　保(　)

练习二、搭配连线
(1) 讨论　　　　A. 秘密
(2) 遵守　　　　B. 闻名
(3) 举世　　　　C. 事情
(4) 保守　　　　D. 祖国
(5) 保卫　　　　E. 纪律

练习三、从今天学习的生词中选择合适的词填空
1. 他很 _____,从来不说脏话。
2. 今年九月我来到了中国,并且游览了世界 _____ 的万里长城。
3. 很多人认为西方人比较开放,东方人比较 _____。
4. 面对困难,不要 _____,而要积极地想办法解决困难。
5. 幸亏警察 _____ 赶到,要不然,小偷就跑掉了。
6. 你最喜欢哪个 _____,春天还是秋天?
7. 你现在有时间吗? 我有件急 _____ 要跟你商量。
8. _____ 的经过就是这样的。
9. _____ 的人给人带来快乐和信心。
10. 那些 _____ 祖国的边防战士们是当代最可爱的人。

答案

练习一:
略

练习二:
(1) C　(2) E　(3) B　(4) A　(5) D

练习三:
1. 文明　2. 闻名　3. 保守　4. 悲观　5. 及时
6. 季节　7. 事　8. 事情　9. 乐观　10. 保卫

星期三

shíhou
时候 （甲）名
time; moment

常用搭配
什么时候 what time   有时候 sometimes
我年轻的时候 when I was young

用法示例
我们什么时候走？
When will we leave?
爱迪生小时候是一个成绩不好的学生。
Edison was not a good student when he was young.
当他开门的时候，电话响了。
Just as he was unlocking the door, the telephone rang.

shíjiān
时间 （甲）名
time

常用搭配
这需要时间。It takes time.　没有时间 have no time
到……的时间了 it's time for ...

用法示例
别再浪费我的时间了！
Don't waste anymore of my time!
时间就是金钱。
Time is money.
你在家里怎么打发时间？
How do you spend your time at home?

zhāng
张 （甲）量
piece(s)

常用搭配
一张报纸 a sheet of newspaper   两张地图 two maps
三张照片 three photos

用法示例
她把一张白纸插入打字机里。
She inserted a new sheet of paper into the typewriter.
这张旧桌子是一件很珍贵的家具。
This old table is a valuable piece of furniture.
请递给我一张纸巾。
Please pass me a tissue.

bǎoguì   zhēnguì
宝贵 ≈ 珍贵 （乙）形
① precious ② valuable

常用搭配
宝贵经验 precious experience   宝贵的时间 precious time
宝贵资源 precious resources

用法示例
我的时间很宝贵，我只能见你几分钟。
My time is precious; I can only give you a few minutes.
真正的友谊比金钱更宝贵。
Real friendship is more valuable than money.
你应很好地利用宝贵的时间去学习。
You should make good use of this precious time to study.

ránshāo
燃烧 （乙）动
burn; ignite

常用搭配
燃烧的木柴 burning wood

用法示例
火在炉条上燃烧着。
A fire was burning in the grate.
人们总是把老师比喻为燃烧的蜡烛。
Teachers are often compared to burning candles.
他们从燃烧的房子里逃了出来。
They fled from the blazing house.

jiǎnqīng   jiāzhòng
减轻 ⊘ 加重 （乙）动
mitigate; ease

常用搭配
减轻痛苦 mitigate suffering
减轻压力 relieve pressure

用法示例
这能减轻他的负担吗？
Will this ease him of his burden?
她的话减轻了我的痛苦。
Her words eased my suffering.
这将会在一定程度上减轻火车的压力。
This will relieve pressure on the trains to some extent.

jiǎnshǎo
减少 （乙）动
decrease; reduce

常用搭配
减少开支 reduce expenditure
他的收入减少了。His income diminished.

用法示例
工人要求减少工作时间并增加工资。
The workmen want to decrease working hours and increase pay.
今年在校的学生人数减少了。
The number of students in the school has decreased this year.
我在练习上花的时间逐渐减少了。
The time I spent exercising gradually diminished.

guòchéng   jìnchéng
过程 ≈ 进程 （乙）名
process; course of events

【常用搭配】
生产过程 manufacturing process
反应过程 chain reaction
在……的过程中 in the course of...
【用法示例】
改革教育制度将是一个艰难的过程。
Reforming the education system will be a difficult process.
这位作家叙述了创作这部小说的过程。
The writer described the process of writing this novel.

jiànlì
建立 （乙）动
establish; set up
【常用搭配】
建立业务关系 establish business relations
建立一座纪念碑 erect a monument
【用法示例】
他们建立了一个学生组织。
They have established a student organization.
他已建立起自己的公司。
He has established his own firm.
这座楼前将要建立一座雕像。
A statue will be erected in front of the building.

ránliào
燃料 （丙）名
fuel
【常用搭配】
燃料短缺 shortage of fuel
【用法示例】
煤气和煤都是燃料。
Gas and coal are fuels.
煤是矿物燃料。
Coal is a fossil fuel.
有些国家的燃料供应非常有限。
There are some countries where the supply of fuel is very limited.

péngzhàng
膨胀  （丙）动
expand; inflate; swell
【常用搭配】
通货膨胀率 rate of inflation
人口膨胀 a swell in population
金属遇热膨胀。Metals expand with heat.
【用法示例】
铁受热时就会膨胀。
Iron expands when it is heated.
政府正力求缓和通货膨胀的影响。
The government is trying to ease the effects of inflation.

guòfèn
过分 （丙）形
excessive; extravagant

【常用搭配】
过分的要求 extravagant claims
【用法示例】
别对他的私事过分关心。
Don't have such an excessive interest in his private matters.
我觉得她慷慨得过分了。
I think she is generous to a fault.
影片结尾的暴力场面太过分了。
The film's violent ending is completely over the top.

词义辨析

时候、时间

1、时候和时间都是名词，都可以表示时点或时段。但"时候"主要是相对某项活动而言的，常用作"（当）……的时候"、"这时候"、"那时候"等；"时间"多表示具体的时刻或时段，可以与量词搭配，还可以作定语。如：一段时间，两年的时间，时间观念。

Both 时候 and 时间 are nouns, indicating a point in time or a period of time. 时候 mainly indicates "at the time that", used as "（当）……的时候" (when, while), "这时候" (at this moment), "那时候" (at that moment), etc. 时间 mostly indicates a certain time; it can be used together with quantifiers, and can function as an attributive, e.g. a period of time, two-year's time, the concept of time.

2、"时候不早了，我该回去了"，"时间不早了，我该回去了"两句话意思相同，但第一句比较口语化，第二句可以用于书面语也可以用于口语。"有时候"，"有时间"，意思不同，也可以说"没时间"，不能说"没时候"。

"时候不早了，我该回去了"，"时间不早了，我该回去了"（It's quite late, I have to go home）Both mean the same, but the first one is more colloquial than the second one. Also the second one can be used in spoken language or written language. "有时候" means "sometimes"; while "有时间" means "have enough time"; "没时间" means "have no time" while we can not say "没时候".

练习

练习一、根据拼音写汉字，根据汉字写拼音

rán（　）（　）qīng　guò（　）（　）zhàng（　）guì
（　）烧　减（　）　（　）分　膨（　）　宝（　）

练习二、搭配连线

(1) 年轻的　　　　　A. 蜡烛
(2) 宝贵的　　　　　B. 时候
(3) 过分的　　　　　C. 时间
(4) 燃烧的　　　　　D. 过程
(5) 反应的　　　　　E. 要求

练习三、从今天学习的生词中选择合适的词填空

1. _____ 还早，再睡一会儿吧。
2. 我小的 _____ 是跟奶奶一起生活的。
3. 请大家多提 _____ 意见。
4. 大火 _____ 了三天三夜才被扑灭。
5. 请你讲讲这个实验的 _____。
6. 高温下，金属会 _____。
7. 他的要求真的有点 _____，老板一定不会同意。
8. 她减肥成功了，体重 _____ 了二十斤。
9. 发生那件事后去法国旅行的中国人 _____ 了。
10. 这个公司出钱 _____ 了一所希望小学。

答案

练习一：
略

练习二：
(1) B　　(2) C　　(3) E　　(4) A　　(5) D

练习三：
1. 时间　2. 时候　3. 宝贵　4. 燃烧　5. 过程
6. 膨胀　7. 过分　8. 减轻　9. 减少　10. 建立

---

kāishǐ
开始　　　　　反 结束　　　（甲）动/名
① start ② beginning

常用搭配
开始比赛 began the race　开始时 in the beginning

用法示例
他十六岁开始在这里工作。
He started working here when he was sixteen.
树叶已开始变色，很快就是冬天了。
The leaves have started to change color; it will soon be winter.
认识从实践开始。
Knowledge begins with practice.

kǒu
口　　　　　　　　　　　　　（甲）量/名
① A measure word for family members, knives, etc.
② mouth

常用搭配
三口人 three family members
一口水 a mouthful of water
洞口 entrance to a cave

用法示例
我吸了一口新鲜的空气。
I gulped a mouthful of sweet air.
我吃得太饱了，一口也不能多吃了。
I'm so full I couldn't eat another bite.
火山口很大。
The mouth of a volcano is very large.

kēxué
科学　　　　　　　　　　　　（甲）名/形
① science ② scientific

常用搭配
社会科学 social science　科学研究 scientific research
科学实验 scientific experiment　科学家 scientist

用法示例
他们计划组织一次科学考察。
They planned to organize a scientific expedition.
我喜欢自然科学，不喜欢人文科学。
I prefer science to the humanities.
他们的方法很科学。
They are very scientific in their approach.

réngōng
人工　　　　　　　　　　　　（乙）形
artificial

常用搭配
人工降雨 artificial rain　人工呼吸 artificial respiration

用法示例
人工供暖能促进植物生长。
Artificial heating hastens the growth of plants.
这种橙汁饮品不含人工调味料。
This orange drink contains no artificial flavorings.

jiāgōng
加工　　　　　　　　　　　　（乙）动
process; manufacture
常用搭配
加工奶酪 process cheese
精密加工 precision machining
粗加工 rough machining
用法示例
这种金属易于加工。
This metal machines easily.
我的工作是加工玉米。
My job is to process corn.

jìyì
记忆　　　　　　　　　　　　（乙）名
memory
常用搭配
令人不愉快的记忆 unpleasant memories
他记忆力好。He has a good memory.
用法示例
他对数字的记忆力很差。
He has a bad memory for figures.
那天晚上是我记忆中最快乐的时光之一。
That evening is one of my happiest recollections.
他对竞选的记忆不是那么清晰。
His recollection of the campaign is not very clear.

jìde
记得　　　　　　　　　　　　（乙）动
remember
常用搭配
记得清清楚楚 remember quite clearly
你还记得我吗？ Do you remember me?
用法示例
我记得见过他一次。
I remember seeing him once.
你记得她的名字吗？
Do you recollect her name?
我记得他这样讲过。
I recollect having heard him say so.

huíyì　　　　　　　huíxiǎng
回忆　　　同 回想　　　　　　（乙）动
recall; recollect
常用搭配
回忆起学生时代 recall one's schooldays
回忆往事 the remembrance of things past

用法示例
你能回忆起事故是如何发生的吗？
Can you recall how the accident happened?
让我回忆一下他说过什么。
Let me recall what he said.
这件事唤起了他对过去苦难经历的回忆。
The incident stirred up memories of his past sufferings.

huàichù　　　　　　hàichù
坏处　　　同 害处　　　　　　（乙）名
harm; disadvantage
常用搭配
对……有坏处 do harm to…
用法示例
早起对你没有坏处。
Getting up early won't harm you!
试一下不会有什么坏处的。
No harm can come of trying.
这不会对你有什么坏处。
It will not do you any harm.

kējì
科技　　　　　　　　　　　　（丙）名
science and technology
常用搭配
科技部 Ministry of Science and Technology
随着科技的发展……
With the development of science and technology…
用法示例
这所大学的主要任务是教授科技知识。
The main task of this university is to teach science and technology.
现代科技发展得十分迅速。
Modern science and technology develop very rapidly.

kāitóu　　　　　　jiéwěi
开头　　　反 结尾　　　　　　（丁）名/动
① beginning ② begin
常用搭配
文章的开头部分 the beginning of an article
用法示例
我们通常用称呼作为一封信的开头。
We usually begin a letter with a salutation.
电影的开头部分我没有看到。
I missed the beginning of the film.

xuékē
学科　　　　　　　　　　　　（丙）名
subject
常用搭配
一门学科 a subject
用法示例
计算机科学目前已是一门成熟的学科。
Computer science is now a fully-fledged academic subject.

他对这个学科很熟悉。
He is quite familiar with this subject.
他对这门学科的兴趣逐渐减退。
His interest in this subject is gradually decreasing

 词义辨析

开始、开头

1、名词"开始"和"开头"都表示初始阶段,"开头"比"开始"更常用,更口语化。如:你会发现这本书的结尾比开头好。

As nouns, 开始 and 开头 mean "beginning", 开头 is more colloquial and more widely used than "开始". For example: You will find that the end of the book is better than the beginning.

2、动词"开始"的意思是着手进行,从某一点起;"开头"作为动词没有开始使用得广泛,往往强调进行动作的第一步,如:我的演讲怎么开头呢?今年九月,我开始在北京学习汉语。

As a verb, 开始 means "to start", "to start from a point". As a verb 开头 is now used as widely as 开始, and usually indicates "to take the first step in performing an action", e.g. How can I begin my speech? In September I began to learn Chinese in Beijing.

 练习

练习一、根据拼音写汉字,根据汉字写拼音
( )shǐ ( )yì ( )jì jì( ) huài ( )
开( ) 回( ) 科( ) ( )得 ( )处

练习二、搭配连线
(1) 开始　　　　A. 呼吸
(2) 人工　　　　B. 比赛
(3) 社会　　　　C. 往事
(4) 加工　　　　D. 科学
(5) 回忆　　　　E. 玉米

练习三、从今天学习的生词中选择合适的词填空
1. 你还_____那个人长得什么样吗?
2. 听说这种食物能增强_____力。
3. 电影是从这位老人的_____展开的。
4. 他的提醒是善意的,你别往_____想。
5. 这儿有个服装_____厂。
6. 儿子长大了想当个_____家。
7. 电影七点_____,九点半结束。
8._____使人类的生活发生了翻天覆地的变化。
9. 九十年代后,这个_____发展很得快。
10. 这篇文章的结尾非常精彩,但是_____写得不太好。

答案

练习一:
略
练习二:
(1) B　　(2)A　　(3)D　　(4)E　　(5)C
练习三:
1. 记得　2. 记忆　3. 回忆　4. 坏处　5. 加工
6. 科学　7. 开始　8. 科技　9. 学科　10. 开头

zhī
支 (甲)量

a measure word for pen, song, troops, etc.

常用搭配
一支铅笔 a pencil
一支队伍 a troop
一支歌 a song

用法示例
在聚会时,他唱了一支流行歌曲。
He sang a popular song at the party.
她送给他一支钢笔作为生日礼物。
She gave him a pen as a birthday gift.

zhī
只 (甲)量

A measure word for one of a pair, certain animals or birds, etc.

常用搭配
一只鞋 one shoe　一只鸟 a bird
一只老虎 a tiger　一只船 a boat

用法示例
我养了一只猫和一只狗,但它们老是打架。
I have a dog and a cat, but they fight all the time.
她在农场养了几只鸡和两只鸭子。
She raises some hens and two ducks on the farm.

shíxiàn
实现 (甲)动

① achieve ② come true

常用搭配
实现理想 to realize an ambition
实现现代化 realize modernization

用法示例
他想当演员的愿望实现了。
His wish to be an actor has come true.
今年这个大学已经实现了所有的奋斗目标。
The university has achieved all its goals this year.
他的梦想实现了。
His dream came true.
他很高兴他的理想实现了。
The realization of his ambition makes him very happy.

yùnshū
运输 (乙)动/名

① transport ② transportation

常用搭配
运输货物 carry goods
铁路运输 rail transportation

用法示例
这艘货轮能够运输五万吨货物。
This freighter can carry a 50000-ton cargo.
将用卡车运输这批货物。
The goods will be transported by truck.
用火车运输货物更方便。
It is more convenient to transport the goods by train.

guāndiǎn　　　　kànfǎ
观点　◎看法 (乙)名

viewpoint

常用搭配
从医生的观点来看 from the point of view of a doctor
表达观点 express one's viewpoint

用法示例
我们之间的观点不一致。
Our views are very different.
老师向我讲述了他的教育观点。
Our teacher explained his views on education to me.
我们的观点存在着严重的分歧。
Our views diverged greatly.

jìsuàn
计算 (乙)动

count; calculate; compute

常用搭配
计算机 computer　计算器 calculator
计算税款 compute the tax due

用法示例
他们在试图计算光的速度。
They are trying to calculate the velocity of light.
你能计算这个容器的容积吗?
Can you compute the volume of the container?
我们的价格是经过精密计算的,没有降低的余地。
The price has already been carefully calculated. There is no room for reduction.

jìzhě
记者 (乙)名

reporter; journalist

常用搭配
记者招待会 press conference
体育记者 sports journalist

用法示例
是两名年轻的记者揭露了全部阴谋。
It was two young reporters who uncovered the whole plot.
两名记者负责报导这则新闻。
Two reporters covered the news story.
最优秀的记者被派去作战地报道了。
The best reporters were sent to cover the war.

jítǐ
集体 (乙)名

collective; collectivity

【常用搭配】
集体行动 collective action　　班集体 class collective
集体主义 collectivism
【用法示例】
我认为集体利益永远高于个人利益。
I think collective interests are always superior to private interests.
那项发明是集体努力的成果。
The invention was a collective effort.
我认识到了集体的力量。
I learned the strength of the collective.

实行 shíxíng ⊜ 施行 shīxíng （乙）动
implement; carry out
【常用搭配】
实行一个计划 carrying out a plan
【用法示例】
实行一项新政策。
Implement a new policy.
不久将会实行新的规则。
The new regulation will be implemented soon.
政府将实施开放政策。
The government will implement their new policy of openness.

观测 guāncè ⊜ 观察 guānchá （丙）动
observe; make a systematic or scientific observation
【常用搭配】
观测月球 observe the moon
观测气候的变化 observe the changes in climate
【用法示例】
科学家们在观测这个星球的轨道。
Scientists are observing the orbit of the star.
他们将公布环境观测报告。
They will publish the observational report on the environment.

面孔 miànkǒng ⊜ 面容 miànróng （丙）名
face
【常用搭配】
英俊的面孔 a handsome face
熟悉的面孔 a familiar face
【用法示例】
上课第一天我们看到了许多新面孔。
We saw many new faces on the first day of class.
他渴望见一见那些熟悉的老面孔。
He yearned for a glimpse of the old, familiar faces.
讲演的人俯视着下面无数的面孔。
The lecturer looked down at the sea of faces beneath him.

输送 shūsòng （丁）动
transport; carry

【常用搭配】
输送煤气的管道 pipes that carry gas
【用法示例】
管道把水从这里输送到田间。
Pipes convey water from here to the fields.
主动脉将血液由心脏输送到其它器官。
The main arteries carry blood from the heart to other organs.

词义辨析

运输、输送

"运输"和"输送"都是动词，表示移送人或物。"运输"的对象多为具体物资，还可以用作名词；"输送"往往强调通过特殊的方式送达，或表示一定的抽象意义。如：①铁路及船舶是用来运输物资的。②输油管把石油输送到东部。③这所大学为社会输送了大批人才。

Both 运输 and 输送 are verbs, meaning "to transport people or things from one place to another place." The object of 运输 is usually concrete goods, and it also can be used as a noun; while 输送 indicates to carry by specific means, and it can be used in the abstract. For example: ① Railways and ships are to carry goods. ② Pipes carry oil to the east. ③ The university has provided the society with large numbers of talented menbers.

练习

练习一、根据拼音写汉字，根据汉字写拼音
jǐ (　) 　shū (　) 　jì (　) 　jí (　) kǒng
(　)者　　(　)送　　(　)算　　(　)体　面(　)

练习二、搭配连线
(1) 实现　　　　　A. 行动
(2) 公路　　　　　B. 理想
(3) 表达　　　　　C. 观点
(4) 计算　　　　　D. 运输
(5) 集体　　　　　E. 税款

练习三、从今天学习的生词中选择合适的词填空
1. 卡车司机负责_____货物。
2. 他这个人总是听别人的，没有自己的_____。
3. 他们家有一_____可爱的小狗。
4. 警察在他的车里搜出了一_____猎枪。
5. 为了维护_____的利益，他牺牲了个人利益。
6. 中国_____八小时工作制。
7. 通过_____成本，我们认为这样的价格不合适。
8. 参加晚会的人中有一些我不认识的_____。
9. 天文学家正在_____月球表面的环境变化。
10. 天然气通过管道从俄罗斯_____到欧洲。

 答案

练习一：
略

练习二：
(1) B　　(2)D　　(3)C　　(4)E　　(5)A

练习三：
1. 运输　　2. 观点　　3. 只　　4. 支　　5. 集体
6. 实行　　7. 计算　　8. 面孔　　9. 观测　　10. 输送

第3月，第4周的练习

练习一、根据词语给加点的字注音
1.(　)　2.(　)　3.(　)　4.(　)　5.(　)
过分　　输送　　开辟　　闻名　　膨胀

练习二、根据拼音填写词语
　　bǎo　　　bǎo　　　jì　　　jì　　　jì
1.(　)守　2.(　)贵　3.(　)者　4.(　)律　5.(　)算

练习三、辨析并选择合适的词填空
1. 由于营养过剩和（　）锻炼，很多小学生都成了小胖子。（缺乏、缺少）
2. 我们一共需要十个人，还（　）两个。（缺乏、缺少）
3. 中国人认为结婚是人生大（　），一定要慎重。（事、事情）
4. （　）比我想象的复杂，我不知该怎么办。（事、事情）
5. 我小的（　）喜欢吃甜食，所以牙不好。（时候、时间）
6. 开车去那个地方需要多长（　）？（时候、时间）
7. 这位钢琴家三岁就（　）学钢琴了。（开始、开头）
8. 这篇文章的（　）写得不好，中间部分和结尾写得不错。（开始、开头）
9. 航空（　）的速度很快，但是运费比较贵。（运输、输送）
10. 俄罗斯向欧洲各国（　）石油和天然气。（运输、输送）

练习四、选词填空
实现　　回忆　　减轻　　文明　　沉默
实行　　记忆　　减少　　闻名　　沉思
1. 闲暇的时间，她喜欢（　）以前的美好时光。
2. 老人闭上双眼，陷入了（　）。
3. 这个运动员夺得了奥运金牌，他的梦想终于（　）了。
4. 父母对孩子要求很严格，不允许他有任何不（　）的举止。
5. 为了（　）父母的负担，他自己打工挣学费。
6. 她这样做的目的是为了（　）麻烦。
7. 听说，多吃核桃能增强（　）力。
8. 当别人误会他时，他总是报以（　），从来不辩解。
9. 长城是世界（　）的建筑，每年都接待很多来自各国的游客。
10. 中国（　）每周五天的工作制。

练习五、量词填空
种　　只　　支　　口　　张　　场
1. 这（　）小狗受伤了，我们把它送到了宠物医院。
2. 请借给我一（　）铅笔和两（　）纸，我忘记带了。
3. 这（　）植物生长在热带。
4. 我不能喝酒，喝一（　），脸就红。
5. 今晚我要去看（　）电影。

练习六、写出下列词语的同义词
1. 观点(　　)　　2. 实行(　　)
3. 回忆(　　)　　4. 宝贵(　　)
5. 保卫(　　)

练习七、写出下列词语的反义词
1. 正确(　　)　　2. 乐观(　　)
3. 膨胀(　　)　　4. 开头(　　)
5. 开始(　　)

 答案

练习一：
1.fèn　　2.shū　　3.pì　　4.wén　　5.zhàng

练习二：
1. 保　　2. 宝　　3. 记　　4. 纪　　5. 计

练习三：
1. 缺乏　　2. 缺少　　3. 事　　4. 事情　　5. 时候
6. 时间　　7. 开始　　8. 开头　　9. 运输　　10. 输送

练习四：
1. 回忆　　2. 沉思　　3. 实现　　4. 文明　　5. 减轻
6. 减少　　7. 记忆　　8. 沉默　　9. 闻名　　10. 实行

练习五：
1. 只　　2. 支,张　　3. 种　　4. 口　　5. 场

练习六：
1. 看法　　2. 施行　　3. 回想　　4. 珍贵　　5. 捍卫

练习七：
1. 错误　　2. 悲观　　3. 收缩　　4. 结尾　　5. 结束

4月 第1周的学习内容

星期一 Monday

mǎshàng
马上 同 立刻 （甲）副
immediately; soon
(常用搭配)
我马上就做。I will do it at once.
(用法示例)
请马上离开这儿!
Please leave here immediately!
她马上就回来。
She will be back soon.
我听到这个消息就马上来了。
I came as soon as I heard the news.

lìkè
立刻 （甲）副
at once; forthwith
(常用搭配)
叫他立刻来。Tell him to come forthwith.
立刻停止抽烟! Stop smoking immediately!
(用法示例)
你们必须立刻开始工作。
You must start working at once.
我们决定立刻去火车站。
We decided to go to the railway station at once.
我一进去,他立刻停止了弹琴。
He stopped playing the piano as soon as I entered.

wénzhāng
文章 （甲）名
article; essay
(常用搭配)
写一篇文章 write an article
读文章 read an article
关于……的文章 an article on（about）
(用法示例)
你细读这篇文章了吗?
Have you perused this article?
她写了一篇题为《我的家庭》的文章。
She wrote an essay titled My Family.
这期的周刊上有一篇有趣的文章。
There is an interesting article in this publication.

jiājù
家具 （乙）名
furniture
(常用搭配)
一件家具 a piece of furniture　办公家具 office furniture
家具店 furniture shop
(用法示例)
这张旧的中国八仙桌是一件很珍贵的家具。
This old Chinese square table is a very valuable piece of furniture.
这对新婚夫妇花了一些钱购买家具。
The new couple spent some money on furniture.
这件古老的家具是1700年制作的。
This antique furniture was made in 1700.

yángguāng
阳光 （乙）名
sunlight; sunshine
(常用搭配)
在阳光下 under the sun
(用法示例)
阳光很明亮。
The sunlight was very bright.
孩子们在阳光下玩耍。
The children played in the sunshine.
我坐在庭院里享受阳光。
I was sitting in the garden enjoying the sunshine.

bùxǔ　　　**bùzhǔn**
不许 同 不准 （乙）动
① not to allow ② must not
(常用搭配)
不许讲话! No talking!
(用法示例)
我这次就原谅你,你可不许再犯错误了。
I'll forgive you this time, but you must not make that mistake again.
这里不许吸烟。
Smoking is not allowed here.
不许他们使用武器。
They were not allowed to use arms.
她不许家中有狗。
She won't permit dogs in the house.

jǐnliàng　　　**jìnlì**
尽量 同 尽力 （乙）副
① as much as possible ② try one's best

【常用搭配】
尽量早来。Come as early as possible.
尽量快点儿 as soon as possible
【用法示例】
精明的人尽量不得罪人。
A politic man tries not to offend people.
要尽量客观地对待这件事。
Try to be more objective about it.
在有关钱的问题上,我总是尽量小心谨慎。
Where money is concerned, I always try to be very careful.

wénjiàn
文件　　　　　　　　　　　（乙）名
file; document
【常用搭配】
机密文件 secret document　　文件夹 a file folder
保存文件 save a file
【用法示例】
这些文件已经得到批准。
These files have been ratified.
我用这张磁盘拷不了文件,这张盘满了。
I can't copy the file with this disc; it's full.
别乱动我桌上的文件。
Don't disturb the paper on my desk.

wénwù
文物　　　　　　　　　　　（乙）名
cultural artifact; historical relic
【常用搭配】
出土文物 unearthed artifacts
【用法示例】
该博物馆收藏了很多珍贵的文物。
The museum has many precious cultural artifacts.
博物馆展出了许多出土文物。
Many unearthed cultural artifacts were exhibited at the museum.

jìnlì
尽力　　　　　　　　　　　（丙）动
① do one's best ② endeavor
【常用搭配】
尽力提供帮助 endeavor to accommodate
我会尽力而为。I will do my best to do it.
【用法示例】
我正在尽力学汉语。
I'm trying to learn Chinese.
他从不尽力帮助任何人。
He never exerts himself to help anyone.
我们一定要尽力改进工作。
We must endeavor to improve our work.

yàobúshì
要不是　　　　　　　　　　（丙）连
① but for ② if it were not for

【常用搭配】
要不是下雨了…… But for the rain…
要不是我有病…… Only that I am ill…
【用法示例】
要不是你的忠告,我会失败的。
But for your advice, I should have failed.
要不是他在场,我会处罚你的。
If it were not for his presence, I would punish you.
要不是为了他,我不会到这里来。
If not for him, I would not be here.

yàobùrán　　　　　fǒuzé
要不然　　否则　　（丙）连
otherwise; or
【常用搭配】
快点儿吧,要不然就迟到了。Hurry up or we'll be late.
【用法示例】
你得去上班了,要不然就要失去这份工作了。
You must go to work or else you'll lose your job.
我们得早一点去,要不然就没有座位了。
We should go early, otherwise we may not get a seat.
要抓住机会,要不然你会后悔的。
Seize the chance, otherwise you will regret it.

词义辨析

立刻、马上

　　"立刻"和"马上"都是副词,表示很快,不耽搁。"立刻"往往带有命令的语气,而"马上"有时含有将来、最近的意思。例如:①他们到家后马上/立刻打了电话。②你必须立刻停止吸烟。③晚饭马上就好了。

　　Both 立刻 and 马上 are adverbs, meaning "immediately, without delay". 立刻 usually indicates an imperative mood; while 马上 sometimes means "at the nearest point in the future". For example: ① They phoned immediately after they reached home. ② You must stop smoking at once. ③ Dinner will be ready soon.

 练习

练习一、根据拼音写汉字，根据汉字写拼音
jìn（　）　yáng（　）（　）jù（　）zhāng（　）kè
（　）量　（　）光　家（　）　文（　）　立（　）

练习二、搭配连线
(1) 一篇　　　　　　A. 捣乱
(2) 不许　　　　　　B. 家具
(3) 两件　　　　　　C. 文件
(4) 文物　　　　　　D. 文章
(5) 三份　　　　　　E. 展览

练习三、从今天学习的生词中选择合适的词填空
1. _____ 他提醒我，我还不知道我的签证快过期了。
2. 我们在电影院门口见面吧，_____ 我去你家找你，然后一起去。
3. 领导 _____ 就到了，你们怎么还没准备好？
4. 一分钟都不要等，_____ 行动。
5. 这件事情我会 _____ 的，你放心吧。
6. 新房子里还没添 _____ 呢。
7. 这是个朝南的房间，下午的时候，_____ 能照到床上。
8. 这是会上要发的 _____，请拿到会议室去。
9. 最近在这个地方发现了一批 500 年前的珍贵 _____。
10. 我 _____ 快点做，如果做不完，请你理解。

 答案

练习一：
略

练习二：
(1) D　　(2) A　　(3) B　　(4) E　　(5) C

练习三：
1. 要不是　2. 要不然　3. 马上　4. 立刻 / 马上
5. 尽力　　6. 家具　　7. 阳光　8. 文件　9. 文物
10. 尽量

 星期二

复杂 fùzá　　反 简单 jiǎndān　（甲）形
complex; complicated

常用搭配
复杂的机器 a complicated machine
情节复杂 The plot is intricate.
情况复杂 The situation is complex.

用法示例
这是一个复杂的问题，你的回答太简炼了。
It's a complex question and your answer was too simple.
生活正在变得越来越复杂和艰难。
Life is getting more complex and difficult.
我们经常思考人生的美丽与复杂。
I often reflect on the beauty and complexity of life.

容易 róngyì　（甲）形
easy

常用搭配
容易解决的问题 an easy problem　容易做 be easy to do

用法示例
这次考试很容易。
The exam was quite easy.
那人容易打交道。
That man is easy to deal with.
他长相奇特，人们很容易认出他。
He is easily distinguished by his strange appearance.

方便 fāngbiàn　反 麻烦 máfan　（甲）形
convenient

常用搭配
为了方便起见 for the convenience of
方便面 instant noodles
在……方便的时候 at one's (own) convenience

用法示例
住在大城市里很方便。
It's a great convenience to live in a big city.
你上午来方便吗？
Will it be convenient for you to come in the morning?
这些冷冻食品很方便。
These frozen foods are very convenient.

面积 miànjī　（乙）名
area

常用搭配
农场的面积 area of a farm

三角形的面积 area of the triangle
面积 100 平方米 an area of 100 sq. meters

用法示例

这个房间的面积是多少？
What are the dimensions of the room?
厨房的面积是 24 平方米，办公室的面积是 35 平方米。
The kitchen is 24 square meters; the area of the office is 35 square meters.
我们能用半径计算出圆的面积。
We can compute the circular area using the radius.

jìrán
既然 （乙）连
since; now that

常用搭配

既然如此 since that is so

用法示例

既然有空，我们可以享受一下音乐。
Now that we have free time, we can enjoy listening to music for a while.
既然雨下得这么大，你今晚就住在这儿吧。
Since it is raining hard, you'd better stay here tonight.
你既然问，我就告诉你。
Since you ask, I will tell you.

lùxù
陆续 （乙）副
successively; continually

常用搭配

陆续离开 leave successively
陆续到达 arrive successively

用法示例

人们陆续进入教堂。
The procession moved into the church.
早晨 7:30 到 8:00 学生们陆续来到学校。
Students come pouring in to the school from 7:30 to 8:00 in the morning.

liánxù　　　　 jiànduàn
连续　　反 间断　（乙）副/动

① continuously ② continue

常用搭配

连续下了一个星期雨 a week of incessant rain
电视连续剧 television series

用法示例

周一周二连续两天我们都得开会。
We shall have meetings on two consecutive days, Monday and Tuesday.
经过连续几次的失败，他最后终于通过了驾驶考试。
After a series of unsuccessful attempts, he has finally passed his driving test.
连续三天的飞行之后，飞行员和他的助手都很疲惫。
After three days' of continuously flying, the pilot and his assistant were very tired.

liánmáng
连忙 （乙）副
promptly; at once

常用搭配

连忙回答 to answer promptly

用法示例

看见老太太站在那里，他连忙起来让座。
Upon seeing an old lady standing there, he immediately stood up and offered his seat to her.
他意识到自己错了，连忙向大家道歉。
As soon as he realized it was his fault, he made an apology.

nuǎnqì
暖气 （乙）名
heating system

常用搭配

暖气装置 a heating apparatus
电暖器 electric heater

用法示例

我房间里的暖气出了点毛病。
The heater in my car doesn't work properly.
这种暖气能自动调节温度。
This heating system has an automatic temperature control.

lùdì
陆地 （丙）名
land

常用搭配

陆地环境 terrestrial environment

用法示例

当看见陆地时，那水手发出一声欢呼。
When land was sighted, the sailor let out a whoop of joy.
船已接近陆地。
The ship was nearing land.
象是最大的陆地动物。
The elephant is the biggest terrestrial animal.
我们在海上航行了十天，终于看见了陆地。
The land came in to view after ten days of sailing.

miànduì
面对 （丙）动
confront; face

常用搭配

面对现实 to face reality
面对危险 to confront danger

用法示例

他勇敢地面对困难。
He faced the challenge courageously.
他在面对危险的时候表现出了非凡的勇气。
He showed remarkable courage when faced with danger.

她必须面对自己已不再年轻的事实。
She must face the fact that she is no longer young.

连接 lián jiē　反 断开 duànkāi　(丙) 动

link; attach

常用搭配
连接管道 connect pipes
将东西连接在一起 link things together

用法示例
新的大桥把这个岛与大陆连接在一起。
The new bridge links the island to the mainland.
将煤气炉和煤气管连接起来。
Connect the gas stove with the gas pipe.
他能告诉你怎么连接打印机线。
He can tell you how to attach a line printer.

词义辨析

陆续、连续

　　副词"陆续"和"连续"都有接连发生的意思，但"陆续"强调有先有后，可以间断，只能作状语；"连续"则指一个接一个，没有间断，"连续"还是动词。例如：演讲很乏味，不久，听众就开始陆续离开了。他已经连续工作了12个小时。

　　As adverbs, 陆续 and 连续 mean "to happen continually". 陆续 is used as an adverbial in sentences, indicating "to happen in turn" or "to happen successively", it indicates there may be a break in the flow. 连续 indicates "one after another" or "continuously" without a break, and can be used as a verb. For example: The lecture was so dull that soon the audience began to trickle out. He has been working for 12 hours straight.

练习

练习一、根据拼音写汉字，根据汉字写拼音
fù(　) (　)xù　nuǎn(　)　lián(　)　jì(　)
(　)杂　陆(　)　(　)气　(　)忙　(　)然

练习二、搭配连线
(1) 情况　　　　A. 很大
(2) 考试　　　　B. 很复杂
(3) 交通　　　　C. 很容易
(4) 面积　　　　D. 很广阔
(5) 陆地　　　　E. 很方便

练习三、从今天学习的生词中选择合适的词填空
1. 宿舍和教室在一个楼里，上课很_____。
2. 我觉得汉字比较难，但是语法比较_____。
3. 孩子的世界很简单，大人的世界则比较_____。
4. 春节的时候，我家的_____坏了，家里特别冷。
5. 在机场，我认错了人，_____说"对不起,对不起"。
6._____一个星期，都在下雨。
7. 开会的人_____到了。
8._____他来了，那我们还是热情招待吧。
9. 投资失败了，他觉得无法_____妻子。
10. 四通八达的地铁把北京各地_____起来了,去哪儿都很方便。

答案

练习一：
略
练习二：
(1) B　　(2)C　　(3)E　　(4)A　　(5)D
练习三：
1. 方便　2. 容易　3. 复杂　4. 暖气　5. 连忙
6. 连续　7. 陆续　8. 既然　9. 面对　10. 连接

biǎoyǎn
表演 (甲) 动/名
① perform ② performance

常用搭配
表演独奏 give a recital
表演艺术 performing arts

用法示例
魔术师表演了一些令人惊叹的戏法。
The magician performed some astonishing tricks.
我们喜欢看海豚的表演。
We like to see the dolphins perform.
她在剧中的表演非常好。
Her performance in the play was very good.

yǎnchū
演出 (甲) 动/名
① perform ② (acting) play

常用搭配
演出很成功。The performance was successful.
一场演出 a performance

用法示例
他们的演出太精彩了。
Their performance was marvelous.
乐队解散之前,在这家剧院作了最后一次演出。
The band played a final gig in this theatre before splitting up.
在我看来,这次演出恐怕不能算是完全成功的。
I'm afraid that the performance was not a total success.

duànliàn
锻炼 (甲) 动
take exercise

常用搭配
加强锻炼 to exercise more
锻炼身体 to do physical training

用法示例
他每天在健身房锻炼一个小时。
He does an hour of vigorous daily exercise at a gym.
你越来越胖了,应该多锻炼。
Your weight is increasing. You should exercise more.
你锻炼得不够。
You don't exercise enough.
你应当加强锻炼以保持精力充沛。
You should exercise more so as to keep energetic.

kuòdà
扩大 (乙) 动
expand; enlarge

常用搭配
扩大生产规模 enlarge the scale of production
扩大经营范围 extend one's business

用法示例
我想把草坪扩大。
I want to enlarge the lawn.
进入黑暗的房间时,瞳孔就会扩大。
The pupils of your eyes dilate when you enter a dark room.
她另加了一间房以扩大她的商店。
She expanded her store by adding another room.

zànshí yǒngjiǔ
暂时 反 永久 (乙) 形
provisional; temporary

常用搭配
暂时的需要 temporary needs
暂时的困难 temporary difficulty

用法示例
因为私事,刘先生将暂时离开我们。
Mr. Liu will leave us for a while because of private issues.
这部影片分散了我的注意力,让我暂时忘记了这些烦恼。
The film managed to distract me from my troubles for a while.
在找到合适的工作之前,他暂时住在我家。
He stayed in my home temporarily before he found a proper job.

búguò
不过 (乙) 连
① merely ② but; however

常用搭配
我只不过看看,并不想买。
I merely looked at it; I did not want to buy.
很好,不过很贵。
It's quite good, but it's rather expensive.

用法示例
别责备他,他只不过是个孩子。
Don't scold him; he is a mere child.
这本书很贵;不过很值。
The book is expensive; however, it's worth it.
我们要走了,不过我们还会回来的。
We are going; nevertheless we shall return.

qiántú qiánjǐng
前途 同 前景 (乙) 名
prospects; future

常用搭配
前途远大 have a great future   没前途 have no future

用法示例
我们有美好的前途。
We have good prospects.
他因疏忽大意而断送了前途。
He ruined his prospects by carelessness.

我为前途而忧虑。
I'm uneasy about the future.

前进 qiánjìn （乙）动
advance; go forward

常用搭配
缓慢前进 advance slowly
向（朝）……前进 advance towards…

用法示例
我军前进,敌军后退。
The enemy fell back as our troops advanced.
指挥官命令他们前进。
The officer directed them to advance.
轮船在大海中缓慢前进。
The ship made progress across the sea.

先进 xiānjìn 反 落后 luòhòu （乙）形
advanced

常用搭配
先进的技术 advanced technology
先进的教学方法 advanced teaching methods
先进的制度 advanced system

用法示例
先进的文化必然战胜没落的文化。
Advanced cultures are bound to triumph over declining cultures.
我们的生产线是世界上最先进的。
Our processing line is the most advanced in the world.

利用 lìyòng （甲）动
make use of; utilize

常用搭配
利用太阳能 to use solar energy
利用每一个机会 to exploit every opportunity
被利用 be made use of…

用法示例
你应该好好利用这个机会。
You should take advantage of the opportunity.
充分利用自然资源的愿望终究会实现。
The dream of fully utilizing natural resources will eventually come true.
我们应该更好地利用现有的设备。
We should make better use of the existing equipment.

免得 miǎnde 同 以免 yǐmiǎn （丙）连
① so as not to ② lest

常用搭配
安静！免得打扰他。
Be quiet so as not to disturb him.

用法示例
把它藏起来免得被他看见。
Hide it lest he should see.
她把裙子往上提起,免得弄湿。
She hitched up her skirt so as not to get it wet.
我服从她,免得她生气。
I obeyed her lest she should get angry.

事迹 shìjì （丙）名
(good) deeds

常用搭配
英雄事迹 heroic deeds　英勇事迹 brave deeds

用法示例
他的勇敢事迹为他带来了荣耀。
His brave deeds earned him honor.
报纸称赞了他们的英雄事迹。
The newspapers glorified their heroic deeds.

词义辨析

表演、演出

1、作为名词,"表演"指演员在舞台、电影上的表现和运用的技巧;"演出"强调为观众表演(技艺或角色)。如：表演艺术,表演技巧。这个剧场一天有两场演出。

As nouns, 表演 indicates the performance or performing skill of actors on stage or in a movie; while 演出 indicates to enact (a feat or role) before an audience. For example: performing arts, performing skill. The theater gives two performances a day.

2、作为动词,"演出"往往不接宾语,"表演"常常接宾语,如：表演京剧,表演节目等。

As verbs, 演出 is not followed by an object; while 表演 is usually followed by an object, e.g. to perform a Beijing Opera, to perform a program, etc.

 **练习**

练习一、根据拼音写汉字，根据汉字写拼音
( )yǎn　( )liàn　( )tú　( )jì　miǎn( )
表( )　锻( )　前( )　事( )( )得

练习二、搭配连线
(1) 精彩的　　　　　A. 困难
(2) 暂时的　　　　　B. 前程
(3) 先进的　　　　　C. 事迹
(4) 美好的　　　　　D. 技术
(5) 英勇的　　　　　E. 演出

练习三、从今天学习的生词中选择合适的词填空
1. 人们在这个地方_____风能发电。
2. 公司在中国发展得很好，业务范围_____了三倍。
3. 前面的桥坏了，汽车无法_____。
4. 春节晚会上，那个明星_____的节目最受欢迎。
5. 中国京剧团最近要到美国_____。
6. 他自身条件好，又努力，是个很有_____的演员。
7. _____先不要跟他说这事，等他心情好了再谈。
8. 欧洲制造飞机的技术很_____。
9. 这个战士的英雄_____传遍了全中国。
10. 做这件事前，我先跟你解释一下，_____发生误会。

 **答案**

练习一：
略
练习二：
(1) E　　(2) A　　(3) D　　(4) B　　(5) C
练习三：
1. 利用　　2. 扩大　　3. 前进　　4. 表演　　5. 演出
6. 前途　　7. 暂时　　8. 先进　　9. 事迹　　10. 免得

guānxì
关系　　　同 liánxì **联系**　　（甲）名
relation; relationship
■ 常用搭配
国际关系 international relations
公共关系 public relations
母女关系 mother-daughter relationship
■ 用法示例
他们之间的关系正在改善。
The relationship between them is improving.
这两个国家已经断绝关系了。
The two countries have severed their relations.
这位老师和学生们的关系很好。
The teacher has a very good relationship with her students.

jīběn
基本　　　（甲）形
basic; fundamental
■ 常用搭配
基本概念 elementary concept
基本需要 elementary need
基本上 on the whole
■ 用法示例
我们已经学习了语法的基本规则。
We have already studied the fundamental rules of grammar.
衣、食、住所是生活的基本必需品。
Food, clothing and shelter are all basic necessities of life.
我基本上同意你的建议，但是有几个小问题有待讨论。
Overall I agree with your proposals, but there are a few small points I'd like to discuss.

tiānqì
天气　　　（甲）名
weather
■ 常用搭配
炎热的天气 hot weather　　天气预报 the weather forecast
好天气 fine weather
■ 用法示例
天气怎么样？
What's the weather like?
寒冷的天气不利于植物的生长。
Cold weather is bad for plant's growth.
因为天气不好，他们取消了旅行计划。
Their travel plans were cancelled because of the bad weather.

gēnběn
根本　（乙）形
① at all ② fundamental

常用搭配
根本变化 a fundamental change
我根本不遗憾。I am not at all sorry.

用法示例
事实上，我根本不认识他。
As a matter of fact, I didn't know him at all.
我根本不喜欢他。
I don't like him at all.
这两位政治家的态度有着根本的区别。
There is a fundamental difference in attitude between these two politicians.

bùguǎn
不管　同 无论　（乙）连
① regardless of ② no matter

常用搭配
不管怎样 no matter how　　不管谁 no matter who

用法示例
不管他工作多努力，他就是得不到提升。
No matter how hard he works, he can not get a promotion.
不管他来不来，我们仍按原计划进行。
Whether or not he comes, we will continue with our plan.
他怎么想就怎么说，从来不管别人的感受。
He always says what he thinks, regardless of other people's feelings.

lìngwài
另外　（乙）连
① other ② besides

常用搭配
那完全是另外一回事。That's quite another matter.
另外想办法 find another way

用法示例
这座房子太小，另外离我们公司也太远。
The house is too small, and furthermore, it's too far from our company.
对一些人来说，人生是快乐，对另外一些人来说则是苦难。
To some, life means pleasure; to others, suffering.
他还申请了另外两份工作，以防这次面试不合格。
He's applying for two other jobs as insurance against not succeeding the interview for this one.

jiāotōng
交通　（乙）名
traffic

常用搭配
交通规则 traffic rules
交通银行 Bank of Communications
交通部 the Ministry of Communications

用法示例
他的左膝在一次交通事故中受伤了。
His left knee was hurt in a traffic accident.
交通标志应该明显。
A traffic sign should be conspicuous.
假日的车辆造成了交通堵塞。
The holiday traffic is jamming up the roads.

qìhòu
气候　（乙）名
climate

常用搭配
海洋性气候 sea climate　　温和的气候 mild climate
干燥的气候 arid climate

用法示例
气候影响了他的健康。
The climate affected his health.
我不适应这里的气候。
The climate disagrees with me.
草原的气候变化无常。
The climate on the grasslands is capricious.

jùlí
距离　（乙）名
distance

常用搭配
两座城市间的距离 the distance between two cities
零距离 zero distance

用法示例
你到学校要走多远的距离？
How far do you have to walk to school?
请保持在听得见的距离之内。
Please keep within earshot.
在英国测量距离用英里，不用公里。
In England distance is measured in miles, not in kilometers.

jiāoyì
交易　同 买卖　（丙）名
transaction; business deal

常用搭配
公平交易 fair dealings　　股票交易 standard deal
现金交易 cash transactions

用法示例
他们之间的交易告吹了。
The deal between them was called off.
这家商店因公平交易而获得了好名声。
This store has an excellent reputation for fair dealing.
他们拒绝同恐怖分子做交易。
They refused to deal with the terrorists.

guānkàn
观看　同 观赏　（丙）动
watch; to view

常用搭配

观看一场比赛 to watch a game
观看一幅画 to view a picture

用法示例

我们将去体育场观看足球比赛。
We will go to the stadium to watch a football match.
这些女孩在溜冰,而这些男孩在观看。
The girls are skating and the boys (are) watching.
清晨,她喜欢在沙滩上观看日出。
Early in the morning, she likes to watch the sunrise on the beach.

guānniàn
观念 (丙)名
concept; idea

常用搭配

伦理观念 ethical concept
是非观念 sense of what is right and just

用法示例

他总有一些奇怪的政治观念。
He has always had some strange political ideas.
我们不应该受错误观念的影响。
We should not be influenced by erroneous ideas.
我们从前的一些观念正在转变。
Some of our previous ideas are now in the melting pot.

词义辨析

基本、根本

"基本"和"根本"都是形容词。"基本"强调事物基础的必要的部分,做状语时往往表示大体上的意思;"根本"强调事物本质的有决定性意义的部分,做状语时往往表示彻底地、完全地意思,多用于否定式。例如:基本原理,根本原因;这个月的天气基本上是好的。我根本不知道。

Both 基本 and 根本 are adjectives. 基本 usually indicates the basic and necessary elements of something, and as an adverbial, means "generally or basically"; while 根本 indicates the essential and decisive element or entity, as an adverbial, means "thoroughly or completely", and often is used in the negative form. For example: basic principle, a fundamental cause; The weather this month has been good on the whole. I don't know at all.

练习

练习一、根据拼音写汉字,根据汉字写拼音
jī(　　) (　　)xì (　　)tōng (　　)hòu jù(　　)
(　　)本 关(　　) 交(　　) 气(　　) (　　)离

练习二、搭配连线
(1) 公共　　　　　A. 规则
(2) 天气　　　　　B. 关系
(3) 基本　　　　　C. 预报
(4) 是非　　　　　D. 概念
(5) 交通　　　　　E. 观念

练习三、从今天学习的生词中选择合适的词填空
1. 我提醒过他好几次,可他_____不听。
2. 毕业后,他_____上两年回一次家乡。
3. _____怎么说,打架是不对的。
4. 因为海南的_____好,很多人冬天去那儿度假。
5. 我想在中国学习汉语,了解中国文化,_____,还想交更多的中国朋友。
6. 自己骑车上学,一定要注意_____安全。
7. 她不想拿自己的婚姻做_____。
8. 农村的人和城里的人_____不同。
9. 这场比赛,没有多少人_____。
10. 最近,老板和经理的_____很紧张。

练习一:
略
练习二:
(1) B　　(2) C　　(3) D　　(4) E　　(5) A
练习三:
1. 根本　　2. 基本　　3. 不管　　4. 气候　　5. 另外
6. 交通　　7. 交易　　8. 观念　　9. 观看　　10. 关系

huānyíng
欢迎　　　　　　　　　　　　（甲）动
welcome
常用搭配
欢迎你回来 welcome back
热烈欢迎 warm welcome
受欢迎的客人 a welcome guest
用法示例
欢迎你到北京来。
Welcome to Beijing.
你在我家总是受欢迎的。
You are always welcome in my home.
欢迎你加入到我们当中来。
You are welcome to join us.

suǒyǐ
所以　　　　　　　　　　　　（甲）连
therefore; so
常用搭配
因为……，所以……（Because）… so…
之所以……，是因为…… The reason why…is that…
用法示例
下雪了，所以我无法外出。
It was snowing, so I could not go out.
这种汽车之所以畅销是因为价格合理。
The reason why the car sells well is that its price is reasonable.

yīncǐ
因此　　　　　　　　　　　　（乙）连
therefore; for this reason
他摔坏了腿，因此，不能走路了。
He has broken his leg and therefore he can't walk.
他是唯一的候选人，因此，他当选了。
He was the only candidate; therefore, he was elected.

yīnér
因而　　　　　　　　　　　　（乙）连
therefore; thus
他那么努力，因而能够顺利地通过考试。
He studied hard so that he could easily pass the examination.
经济前景暗淡，因而股票价格大跌。
Share prices plunged as a result of the gloomy economic forecast.

tóu
投　　　　㊌扔　　　　　　　（乙）动
throw
常用搭配
投汽油弹 to throw a petrol bomb
投篮 throw a goal
用法示例
那个可怜的农民被投进了地牢。
The poor peasant was thrown into the dungeon.
他把信投进邮筒。
He put the letter into the mailbox.

tōu　　　　　dào
偷　　　　㊌盗　　　　　　　（乙）动
steal
常用搭配
偷汽车 steal a car　　偷工减料 to jerry-build
用法示例
他偷了那笔钱。
He stole the money.
真不幸，我的钱包被偷了！
It's bad luck, my wallet was stolen!
谁偷了我的包?
Who stole my bag?

jiǎnghuà
讲话　　　　　　　　　　　　（乙）名/动
① a speech ② to speak
常用搭配
发表讲话 to make a speech　　大声讲话 speak loudly
用法示例
他的讲话赢得了听众的掌声。
His speech drew the applause of the audience.
我心情不好，不想和任何人讲话。
I am out of spirits and don't want to speak to anyone.
电影开演后，他们还在大声讲话。
They went on talking loudly after the film had started.

píngjūn
平均　　　　　　　　　　　　（乙）动/形
average
常用搭配
平均年龄 average age
平均寿命 average length of life
用法示例
4,6,8 的平均数是 6。
The average of 4, 6 and 8 is 6.
我们每天平均工作八个小时。
We average 8 hours' work a day.
他的收入大大低于平均水平。
His income is well below the average.

yìshí
一时　　　　　　　　　　　　（乙）名
momentary; temporary
常用搭配
一时的快乐 temporary pleasure

用法示例

他激动得一时说不出话来了。
He was so excited, momentarily unable to speak.
她一时思想紊乱,犹豫不定。
She hesitated in momentary confusion.
我气得一时忘了他的名字。
I was too angry to remember his name for a moment.

灵巧 língqiǎo ⊜灵敏 língmǐn (丁)形
dexterous; nimble

常用搭配

灵巧的手指 deft fingers
像鹿一样灵巧 as nimble as a deer

用法示例

她观察那个工人,想模仿他灵巧的动作。
She watched the worker and tried to copy his dexterous movements.
她用灵巧的手指解开了绳子。
With deft fingers she untangled the rope.

讲解 jiǎngjiě ⊜解说 jiěshuō (丁)动
explain

常用搭配

讲解数学题 explain a math problem
耐心地讲解 explain patiently

用法示例

请把这个问题给我讲解一下。
Please explain this problem to me.
给我们讲解一下第三段,好吗?
Will you explain the third paragraph to us?
请为我讲解从哪里开始以及怎样做。
Please explain to me where to begin and how to do it.

平衡 pínghéng (丙)形/动
equilibrium; balance

常用搭配

保持平衡 keep in balance
与……平衡 be in equilibrium with…
心理平衡 mental equilibrium

用法示例

他失去平衡,跌倒了。
He lost his balance and fell over.
他骑自行车时不能保持平衡。
He can't maintain enough equilibrium to ride a bike.
人类采用一切手段保持生态平衡。
Mankind tries every means to maintain the balance of nature.

词义辨析

所以、因此、因而

1、三个连词都可以在因果关系的复句中引出结果或结论。"所以"往往与"因为"搭配使用,如"因为……,所以……","之所以……,是因为……";"因此"和"因而"常与"由于"搭配,不能与"因为"搭配,也常常独立使用,多用于书面语。如:我之所以迟到是因为堵车。

The three words are conjunctions used to introduce consequences or conclusion clauses. 所以 is usually used with 因为, such as "因为……,所以……","之所以……,是因为……"; 因此 and 因而 are used with 由于, and can not be used with 因为, and they are often used independently between two clauses in written language. For example: I was late due to the traffic jam.

2、"因此"和"因而"的不同在于:"因此"强调"因为这个"引出的结果,可以连接分句、句子或段落,后面往往有停顿;"因而"强调逻辑推理,只连接复句中的分句,一般不连接句子和段落,后面也没有停顿。例如:这个国家的人口在增长,因此,他们需要更多的食物。我病了,因而没能来。

The difference between 因此 and 因而: 因此 indicates "because of it", stressing the result, and it also can be used between two clauses, sentences, or paragraphs, and there is often a pause after it. 因而 stresses the logical consequence, only used between two clauses of a complex sentence, but not sentences or paragraphs, and there is no pause after it. For example: The population is increasing in that country, and therefore they need more food. I was ill, and therefore could not come.

练习一、根据拼音写汉字,根据汉字写拼音

( )qiǎo　( )héng　( )yǐ　( )jiě　( )yíng
灵( )　　平( )　　所( )　　讲( )　　欢( )

练习二、搭配连线

(1) 保持　　　　A. 讲话
(2) 大声　　　　B. 水平
(3) 平均　　　　C. 平衡
(4) 欢迎　　　　D. 讲解
(5) 耐心　　　　E. 光临

练习三、从今天学习的生词中选择合适的词填空

1. 他_____入了很多时间和精力来做这件事。
2. 身体_____能力好的人学滑冰比较快。
3. 他之_____没出国是因为要照顾年老的父母。
4. 由于是第一次在这么多人面前发言,_____她有点儿紧张。
5. 老板在大会上的_____让员工充满信心。

6. 他＿＿＿＿高兴,喝了很多酒。
7. 小偷正在＿＿＿＿钱时被警察抓住了。
8. 新郎和新娘的父母站在大门口,＿＿＿＿来参加婚礼的客人。
9. 这次去长城,全班＿＿＿＿每个人花了 200 元。
10. 博物馆里专门有工作人员＿＿＿＿。

答案

练习一:
略
练习二:
(1) C　　(2) A　　(3) B　　(4) E　　(5) D
练习三:
1. 投　　2. 平衡　　3. 所以　　4. 因此　　5. 讲话
6. 一时　　7. 偷　　8. 欢迎　　9. 平均　　10. 讲解

第4月,第1周的练习

练习一、根据词语给加点的字注音
1.(　)　2.(　)　3.(　)　4.(　)　5.(　)
陆续　　免得　　距离　　平衡　　家具

练习二、根据拼音填写词语
　　　　jì　　　jì　　　guān　　guān　　guǎn
1. 事(　) 2.(　)然　3.(　)系　4.(　)念　5. 不(　)

练习三、辨析并选择合适的词填空
1. 我刚回到家,经理就打电话,让我(　)去公司一趟。(立刻、马上)
2. (　)要开学了,我的作业还没做完。(立刻、马上)
3. 我们将(　)工作三个星期,一天也不准休息。(陆续、连续)
4. 观众(　)进场,演出快开始了。(陆续、连续)
5. 国家芭蕾舞团下周将赴欧洲(　)。(表演、演出)
6. 晚会上,他(　)了一个魔术。(表演、演出)
7. 那个地方很冷,你穿这么少(　)不行。(基本、根本)
8. 这件事情到现在已经(　)完成了。(基本、根本)
9. 那里正在修路,堵车堵得厉害,(　),我们迟到了二十分钟。(所以、因此、因而)
10. 因为今天下雨了,(　)爬山比赛取消了。(所以、因此、因而)

练习四、选词填空
气候　　讲话　　连续　　文章　　前途
天气　　讲解　　连接　　文件　　前进
1. 这位医生为了抢救病人的生命,(　)工作了 48 小时。
2. 这是一份保密(　),请尽快交给市长。
3. 这个地方(　)好,适合老年人居住。
4. 在(　)的道路上可能会有困难,但我们不怕。

5. 参观故宫时,导游给我们做了详细的(　)。
6. 这座跨海大桥把两个城市(　)了起来,促进了两个城市的经济发展和交流。
7. 他聪明能干,公司领导一致认为他(　)光明。
8. 这几天(　)闷热,要是下场大雨就好了。
9. 下面我们有请公司王总经理给大家(　)。
10. 我经常能在报纸上读到他写的(　)。

练习五、选择连词填空
要不是　　既然　　要不然　　不管　　不过　　免得
1. (　)是出来旅游,那就把工作上的事完全忘掉吧。
2. (　)报纸报道了这位老人,谁也想不到他曾经是个百万富翁。
3. 我以为这个专业以后好找工作呢,(　)我就不学这个专业了。
4. 我告诉你一个秘密,(　)你可千万别告诉别人。
5. 外边冷,多穿点,(　)感冒。
6. 现在很难找工作,所以(　)你喜欢不喜欢这份工作,你都要尽量做好。

练习六、写出下列词语的同义词
1. 前途(　)　　2. 尽量(　)
3. 交易(　)　　4. 灵巧(　)
5. 不许(　)

练习七、写出下列词语的反义词
1. 暂时(　)　　2. 复杂(　)
3. 先进(　)　　4. 连接(　)
5. 方便(　)

答案

练习一:
1. xù　　2. miǎn　　3. jù　　4. héng　　5. jù
练习二:
1. 迹　　2. 既　　3. 关　　4. 观　　5. 管
练习三:
1. 立刻　　2. 马上　　3. 连续　　4. 陆续　　5. 演出
6. 表演　　7. 根本　　8. 基本　　9. 因此　　10. 所以
练习四:
1. 连续　　2. 文件　　3. 气候　　4. 前进　　5. 讲解
6. 连接　　7. 前途　　8. 天气　　9. 讲话　　10. 文章
练习五:
1. 既然　　2. 要不是　　3. 要不然　　4. 不过　　5. 免得
6. 不管
练习六:
1. 前景　　2. 尽力　　3. 买卖　　4. 灵敏　　5. 不准
练习七:
1. 永久　　2. 简单　　3. 落后　　4. 断开　　5. 麻烦

4月 第2周的学习内容

bāngzhù
帮助 （甲）动
① help ② assistance
常用搭配
在……帮助下 with the help of
对……有帮助 be helpful for
用法示例
我帮助她找到了那本书。
I helped her find the book.
我会尽一切可能帮助你。
I'll do everything possible to help you.
你的建议对我有很大的帮助。
Your advice was of great help to me.

tígāo　　　　　jiàngdī
提高　　反 降低 （甲）动
enhance; improve; increase
常用搭配
提高能力 improve abilities
提高道德意识 enhance one's moral consciousness
提高工资 have a rise in wages
用法示例
去年的国民生产总值提高了百分之五。
The gross national product increased 5 percent last year.
棉花的价格虽然提高了,但消耗也增加了。
Consumption of cotton increased even after it rose in price.
我们必须提高生产水平。
We must increase production levels.

wúlùn
无论 （乙）连
no matter what; regardless of
常用搭配
无论你在哪里 No matter where you are…
无论我怎么做 No matter how I do it…
用法示例
无论发生什么事都要保持冷静。
Keep calm, whatever happens.
不论你来还是留在家中,我都要去。
I shall go whether you come or stay at home.

miànmào　　　　miànmù
面貌　　同 面目 （乙）名
appearance; look
常用搭配
城市的面貌 appearance of a city
学生的面貌 the look of students
用法示例
这个城镇的面貌变化很大。
The appearance of the town is quite changed.
旧城换上了新面貌。
The old city has taken on a new look.

gǎnjǐn　　　　gǎnkuài
赶紧　　同 赶快 （乙）副
hurriedly
常用搭配
赶紧来。 Make haste to come.
赶紧说／走 hasten to say/ walk
用法示例
他把事故的经过告诉了她,但赶紧补充说没有人受伤。
He told her about the accident, but hastened to add that no one was hurt.
我答应赶紧写好报告,今天就给他们送去。
I promised to hurry up with the report and send it to them today.
她赶紧把好消息告诉她母亲。
She made haste to tell her mother the good news.

lǐxiǎng
理想 （乙）名／形
ideal
常用搭配
实现理想 realize one's ideals
度假的理想场所 an ideal place for a holiday
用法示例
他对人生抱有崇高的理想。
He has lofty ideals about life.
这是一个出外野餐的理想日子。
It is an ideal day for a picnic.
新房子的位置十分理想。
The location of the new house is ideal.

lǐyóu
理由 （乙）名
reason; excuse
常用搭配
不学习的理由 excuse for not studying
离开的理由 reason for leaving

【用法示例】
无知不能成为违反法律的理由。
Ignorance is no excuse for breaking the law.
他有理由认为我不喜欢他。
He thinks, with reason, that I don't like him.
你迟到的理由是什么？
What' your justification for being late?

jiàngdī
降低　　　　　　　　　　　　（乙）动
to lower; bring down
【常用搭配】
降低利率 to lower the interest rate
降低要求 reduce one's demands
【用法示例】
这个月气温渐渐降低了。
The temperature has gradually fallen this month.
政府决心降低通货膨胀率。
The government is determined to bring down inflation.
降低工资的决定激怒了工人。
The decision to reduce pay levels incensed the work force.

sùdù
速度　　　　　　　　　　　　（乙）名
speed
【常用搭配】
以惊人的速度
at an astonishing speed
以每小时 80 英里的速度
at a speed of eighty miles an hour
【用法示例】
这架飞机的速度非常快。
The speed of this aircraft is very fast.
当我们快到车站时，火车减慢了速度。
The train lessened its speed as we approached the station.
他以极快的速度开车。
He is driving at a terrific speed.

sùchéng
速成　　　　　　　　　　　　（丙）动
crash (course)
【常用搭配】
速成课程 crash course
【用法示例】
这所大学开设了英语速成班。
The college offers a crash course in English.
他正在学习一门速成课程。
He is learning through a crash course.

yuánzhù
援助　　　　　　　　　　　　（丙）动/名
① aid ② help
【常用搭配】
国际援助 international aid　　技术援助 technical aid

无偿援助 non-reimbursable assistance
【用法示例】
他们将尽力援助遭受水灾的灾民。
They will try their best to aid flood victims.
他们请求经济援助。
They've made a request for economic aid.
他们在走投无路的情况下恳求援助。
They asked for help in the desperate situation.

gǎnshàng　　　　　　　luòxià
赶上　　　落下　　　（丙）动
catch up with
【常用搭配】
赶上头班车 to catch the first bus
【用法示例】
我们正好赶上了火车。
We're just in time to catch the train.
我得跑才能赶上他。
I had to run to catch up with him.
要想赶上其他同学，我得特别努力才行。
I have to work hard to catch up with the other students.

词义辨析

帮助、援助

　　"帮助"和"援助"都是动词，都有帮别人解决困难的意思。"帮助"多用于日常生活、工作和学习等，还可以用作"对……有帮助"；而"援助"多用于经济、军事等大的方面，多用于官方语言。"援助"还经常用作定语，如：援助物资，救援设备，援助部队等。

　　As verbs, 帮助 and 援助 mean "to help others". 帮助 is mostly applied to daily life, work, and study, and can be used as "对……有帮助" ("be helpful to…"); while 援助 is usually applied to economic or military affairs, and mostly used in official language. 援助 can function as an attributive, such as the aided material, the rescue aid, assisted army.

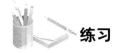 练习

练习一、根据拼音写汉字，根据汉字写拼音

yuán（　）（　）dī（　）yóu sù（　）（　）mào
（　）助　降（　）　理（　）　（　）度　面（　）

练习二、搭配连线

(1) 城市的　　　　　　A. 援助
(2) 惊人的　　　　　　B. 面貌
(3) 无偿的　　　　　　C. 理由
(4) 崇高的　　　　　　D. 速度
(5) 离开的　　　　　　E. 理想

练习三、从今天学习的生词中选择合适的词填空

1. 不要为自己的错误找＿＿＿＿了，关键是不要再犯同样的错误了。
2. 五年后再来，发现这个城市的＿＿＿＿焕然一新。
3. ＿＿＿＿怎么解释，她再也不相信他的话了。
4. 与二十年前相比，中国人民的生活水平有了很大＿＿＿＿。
5. 暑假，我报了个汉语口语＿＿＿＿班。
6. 这名运动员跑步的＿＿＿＿很快，所以人们叫他"飞人"。
7. 他跑得慢了点，公共汽车开走了，他没＿＿＿＿。
8. 东南亚发生了海啸，中国提供了很多＿＿＿＿物资。
9. 我对您的＿＿＿＿表示深深地感谢。
10. 老师发现这些学生学得比较慢，所以＿＿＿＿了对他们的要求。

 答案

练习一：
略
练习二：
(1) B　　(2)D　　(3)A　　(4)E　　(5)C
练习三：
1. 理由　　2. 面貌　　3. 无论　　4. 提高　　5. 速成
6. 速度　　7. 赶上　　8. 援助　　9. 帮助　　10. 降低

 星期二

liànxí
练习　　　　　　　　　　　　　（甲）动/名

① exercise ② drill; practice

▸ 常用搭配
练唱歌 practice singing
练习本 exercise book
拼写练习 spelling exercises

▸ 用法示例
她在练习弹钢琴。
She is practicing the piano.
我们经常做这种练习。
We often do this kind of exercise.
你应该在课堂上完成语法练习。
You should finish your English grammar drills in class.

jiànshè
建设　　　　　　　　　　　　　（甲）动/名

① build ② construction

▸ 常用搭配
经济建设 economic construction
建设新学校 build a new school

▸ 用法示例
他们正在建设一条海底隧道。
They are building a submarine tunnel.
中国在经济建设方面有很大进步。
China is rapidly progressing in her economic construction.
新机场仍在建设中。
The new airport is still under construction.

fǎnduì　　　　　zànchéng
反对　　反 赞成　　　　　　　（甲）动

oppose; object to

▸ 常用搭配
我反对这个提议。I object to the proposal.
投反对票 to vote against
强烈反对 a strong objection to

▸ 用法示例
父亲反对儿子的婚事。
The father opposed his son's marriage.
我反对他的计划。
I object to his plan.
许多居民反对修建那条公路的计划。
Many residents are opposed to the plan of building the road.

yǒushí
有时　　　　　　　　　　　　　（乙）连

sometimes

常用搭配

有时刮风,有时下雨
It is sometimes windy, sometimes rainy.

用法示例

作为消防队员有时会有危险。
Being a fireman may sometimes be dangerous.
他有时忙,有时闲。
He is sometimes busy, sometimes idle.
命运有时是残酷的。
Destiny is sometimes cruel.

rán ér
然而 同 可是 (乙)连
yet; but

常用搭配

他很努力,然而他失败了。
He worked hard, yet he failed.

用法示例

现在是 5 月了,然而天气还像冬天一样冷。
It is May, yet it is almost as cold as winter.
林莉很开心,然而我却很尴尬。
Lin Li was amused, but I was very embarrassed.
我给他写了封长信,然而他一直没有回信。
I wrote him a long letter, but he never wrote back.

lián hé
联合 反 分裂 (乙)动
unite; ally

常用搭配

联合国 United Nations
与……联合 ally oneself with

用法示例

他们联合起来抵御共同的敌人。
They made an alliance against the common enemy.
两个政党已经联合起来组成政府。
The two political parties have combined to form a government.
他是大学教师联合会的一名成员。
He is a member of the Association of University Teachers.

hé lǐ
合理 (乙)形
reasonable

常用搭配

合理的解释 a reasonable explanation
合理的要求 a reasonable demand
价格合理。The price is reasonable.

用法示例

我认为他的解释是合理的。
I think that his explanation is reasonable.
我觉得这是个合理的建议,但他不同意。
I thought it was a reasonable proposal, but he didn't agree.

这不是很合理吗?
Isn't it reasonable?

jiǎng zuò
讲座 (乙)名
lecture

常用搭配

做讲座 give a lecture   参加讲座 attend a lecture
关于……的讲座 a lecture on/about sth.

用法示例

教授将要做关于太阳系的讲座。
The professor will give a lecture on the solar system.
这个系列讲座可分为三部分。
The lecture series falls into three parts.
讲座取消了,我们昨天下午去看电影了。
The lecture was cancelled, and we went to the cinema yesterday afternoon.

fǎn fù
反复 (乙)副/名
① repeatedly ② relapse

常用搭配

反复警告 repeat a warning   病情有反复 relapse of an illness

用法示例

父亲对我反复强调了努力工作的重要意义。
My father repeatedly impressed upon me the value of hard work.
反复听到同样的抱怨,你难道不烦吗?
Don't you weary of hearing the same complaints over and over again?
这种衣料经得住反复洗涤。
This dress material will withstand repeated washing.

jiǎng kè   shòu kè
讲课   同 授课   (丙)动
teach

常用搭配

给外国人讲课 give lectures for foreigners

用法示例

她讲课前把讲稿匆匆看了一遍。
She ran over her notes again before giving the lecture.
今天上午他已经讲了四个小时的课了。
He has been teaching for four hours already this morning.

shí shí
时时 (丙)副
① at all times ② constantly ③ often

常用搭配

时时都要小心 Be careful at all times.

用法示例

你应当时时注意礼节。
You ought to be courteous at all times.
把词典时时放在手边。
Always keep your dictionary close to hand.

他时时提醒自己要努力学习。
He often reminds himself to work hard.

miànlín
面临　　　　　　　　　　　　　（丙）动
to face; to be confronted with

常用搭配
我们面临危机。We faced a crisis.

用法示例
即使面临危险,你也要保持镇静。
You should keep calm even in the face of danger.
我面临很多困难。
I am faced with many difficulties.
现代社会的每个人都面临着激烈的竞争。
Everyone in modern society faces keen competition.

 词义辨析

有时、时时

"有时"和"时时"都是副词,但含义不同。"有时"表示有时候或有一部分时间;"时时"表示每时每刻,一直,经常等意思。例如:①有时她帮助妈妈做家务。②他时时关注科学的最新发展。

Both 有时 and 时时 are adverbs, but they are different in meaning. 有时 means "sometimes" or "now and then"; 时时 means "at every moment, always, often". For example: ① Sometimes she helps her mother in the house. ② He always pays attention to the latest developments in science.

 练习

练习一、根据拼音写汉字,根据汉字写拼音

lián（　　）　miàn（　　）（　　）kè（　　）fù（　　）jiàn（　　）
（　　）合　（　　）临　讲（　　）　反（　　）　（　　）设

练习二、搭配连线

(1) 面临　　　　　A. 反对
(2) 坚决　　　　　B. 建设
(3) 价格　　　　　C. 危险
(4) 经济　　　　　D. 练习
(5) 语法　　　　　E. 合理

练习三、从今天学习的生词中选择合适的词填空

1. 有人_____这个计划,可是老板支持我们。
2. 出院没多久,他的病情又出现了_____。
3. 她平常住在学校,_____去她姐姐家度周末。
4. 他_____刻刻记得妈妈的话。
5. 本来大家以为这个队胜利了,_____没想到的是在最后三分钟,对方踢进了两个球。
6. 老师_____时,有的人认真听,有的人不认真听。
7. 明天下午有个"中国经济形势"的_____。
8. 这个公司的产品卖不出去,很多员工_____失业。
9. 留学生要多跟当地人交谈,以便有更多_____口语的机会。
10. 顾客要求无条件退货,服务员觉得不_____,他认为是顾客把商品弄坏的。

 答案

练习一:
略

练习二:
(1) C　　(2)A　　(3)E　　(4)B　　(5)D

练习三:
1. 反对　　2. 反复　　3. 有时　　4. 时时　　5. 然而
6. 讲课　　7. 讲座　　8. 面临　　9. 练习　　10. 合理

告诉 gàosu (甲) 动
tell; inform

常用搭配
告诉某人某事 to tell sb about sth

用法示例
你能告诉我你的电话号码吗?
Will you tell me your phone number?
告诉我发生了什么事。
Tell me what happened.
他把他的决定告诉了我。
He informed me of his decision.
校长告诉我们下星期学校将停一天课。
The headmaster informed us that the school would be closed for one day next week.

使用 shǐyòng (甲) 动
to use

常用搭配
使用助听器 use a hearing aid
使用计算机 use the computer
使用武力 employ force

用法示例
政府已经禁止使用化学武器。
The government has banned the use of chemical weapons.
这家公司现在使用电脑来计算所有的账目。
The company now uses a computer to do all its accounts.
我们应该使用无烟煤以防止空气污染。
We should use anthracite to avoid air pollution.

支持 zhīchí (乙) 动
support

常用搭配
互相支持 support each other

用法示例
别担心,我们都会支持你的。
Do not fear; all of us will support you.
你支持哪一方?
Which side do you support?
他的话给了我很大支持。
His words supported me greatly.
没有你们的支持,我是不会成功的。
I wouldn't have succeeded without your support.

支付 zhīfù 反 领取 lǐngqǔ (丁) 动
pay; defray

常用搭配
支付罚金 pay the penalty
支付工人工资 pay workers
用支票支付 pay by check

用法示例
考察队的费用由校方支付。
The cost of the expedition was defrayed by the college.
政府每年为教育支付大笔资金。
The government disburses a large amount of money for education every year.

实用 shíyòng (乙) 形
practical

常用搭配
实用的方法 a practical method
不实用的工具 an impractical tool

用法示例
这个发明不实用。
This invention is not practical.
这本书理论性太强,我需要一本实用的书。
This book is too theoretical, I need a practical one.

利益 lìyì (乙) 名
interest; advantage

常用搭配
公共利益 public interests 个人利益 personal interest

用法示例
我们通过立法保护投资者的利益。
We protect the interests of investors through legislation.
我们为了双方的利益签订这项合同。
We entered into this contract in the interests of both parties.
个人利益必须服从集体利益。
The interests of the individual must be subordinate to the interests of the collective.

礼貌 lǐmào (乙) 名
manners; civility

常用搭配
对人有礼貌 be polite to sb.
有礼貌的回答 a polite reply

用法示例
打断别人说话是不礼貌的。
It is bad manners to interrupt others.
王强在他父母的朋友面前表现得很有礼貌。
Wang Qiang displays his good manners for his parents' friends.
你应该对每个人都有礼貌。
You should be polite to everyone.

礼物 lǐwù 同 礼品 lǐpǐn (甲) 名
gift

【常用搭配】
生日礼物 a birthday gift
圣诞礼物 a Christmas gift
【用法示例】
每个孩子给母亲带来一件礼物。
Each child brought a present for their mothers.
他给了妻子一个小礼物。
He gave his wife a little present.

zhīyuán
支援　　　　　　　　yuánzhù
　　　　　　　　⦿ 援助　　　　　　（乙）动
support; provide assistance or backing
【常用搭配】
互相支援 support each other
技术支援 technical aid
【用法示例】
没有你们的支援,我是不会成功的。
I wouldn't have succeeded without your support.
我们都支援灾区的建设。
We all gave aid to the reconstruction of the disaster area.

lìrùn
利润　　　　　　　kuīsǔn
　　　　　　　　⦶ 亏损　　　　　　（丙）名
profit
【常用搭配】
获得利润 gain a profit
【用法示例】
我们公司的利润在这两年中增至三倍。
Profits in our company have tripled in the last two years.
这项新发明会给你们带来丰厚的利润。
This new invention will bring you great profits.
现在卖报纸利润很少。
There is very little profit in selling newspapers at present.

jíshǐ
即使　　　　　　　　　　　（丙）连
even though; even if
【常用搭配】
即使下雨我也要去。I'll go even if it rains.
【用法示例】
即使你不喜欢这工作,你也得做。
Even though you do not like it, you must do it.
即使下雨,他也会准时来的。
He will come on time even though it is raining.
即使他知道自己错了,也从不道歉。
He never apologizes, even when he knows that he is in the wrong.

lǐjié
礼节　　　　　　　　　　　（丁）名
etiquette
【常用搭配】
外交礼节 diplomatic etiquette
繁琐的礼节 trivial formality

【用法示例】
我们应该遵守礼节。
We should observe the proprieties.
在日常生活中没有时间讲礼节。
There's no time for etiquette in everyday life.
她不喜欢宴会的礼节。
She didn't like the formality of the banquet.

 词义辨析

支持、支援

"支持"和"支援"都是动词,都有为别人提供帮助的意思。"支持"可以是物质的也可以是精神的援助,其对象多是事业或人,往往用作"支持某事","支持某人"或"支持某人做某事";"支援"往往是用人力、物力、财力等具体形式援助,其对象往往是地区、组织或群体,一般不用于个人之间的帮助。如:我支持这个建议。我们支持你。我们支持你执行这个计划。支援灾区。基金会支援非洲两架飞机。例句中的"支持"和"支援"都不能相互替换。

　　Both 支持 and 支援 are verbs, meaning to give assistance to others. 支持 indicates "to support with something concrete, or to support morally". The object of 支持 is a person or a cause, usually used as "支持某事" (support something), "支持某人" (support somebody) or "支持某人做某事" (support somebody to do something). 支援 indicates "to help with manpower, material or financial aid", the object of 支援 often is an area, organization or entity, it is not applied to individual assistance. For example: I support this proposal. We will support you. We will support you in carrying out the plan. To aid the disaster area. The foundation will supply Africa with two planes. In the examples above, 支持 and 支援 can not replace each other.

 练习

练习一、根据拼音写汉字，根据汉字写拼音
( )rùn ( )shǐ shí( ) ( )chí gào
利( ) 即( ) ( )用 支( ) ( )诉

练习二、搭配连线
(1) 实用的   A. 利益
(2) 个人的   B. 利润
(3) 繁琐的   C. 礼物
(4) 丰厚的   D. 礼节
(5) 珍贵的   E. 方法

练习三、从今天学习的生词中选择合适的词填空
1. 他_____孩子的计划，并且愿意帮助他。
2. 麦克买完衣服用银行卡_____。
3. 朋友给我的电脑安装了新软件，可我不知道怎么_____。
4. 这个电子辞典不贵，但是非常_____。
5. 人多的地方，大声说话很没_____。
6. 年轻人结婚前，双方父母要见面，这是中国人的_____。
7. 圣诞节就要到了，我得为孩子们准备一些_____。
8. 这件事没有那么简单，这里面有很复杂的_____关系。
9. _____你不喜欢他，也要对他有礼貌。
10. 这笔生意将给公司带来丰厚的_____。

答案

练习一：
略

练习二：
(1) E (2) A (3) D (4) B (5) C

练习三：
1. 支持 2. 支付 3. 使用 4. 实用 5. 礼貌
6. 礼节 7. 礼物 8. 利益 9. 即使 10. 利润

 星期四 Thursday

复习 fùxí   ≡ 温习 wēnxí   （甲）动
review; go over

常用搭配
复习功课 review lessons
复习生词 go over new words

用法示例
张林在考试前复习功课。
Zhang Lin went over the lessons before the exam.
把课文再复习一遍。
Go over the text again.
我整个星期都在复习。
I've been revising all week.

但是 dànshì   ≡ 可是 kěshì   （甲）连
but; however

常用搭配
他很善良，但是很固执。
He is very kind, but rather stubborn.

用法示例
我打过电话了，但是没有人接。
I've called but nobody answered.
他很穷，但是很快乐。
He was poor, yet happy.
我想把机器修好，但是失败了。
I tried to fix the equipment but I failed.

车站 chēzhàn   （甲）名
station

常用搭配
公共汽车站 bus stop　　火车站 railway station
在车站 at the station

用法示例
我们能及时到达车站吗？
Will we get to the station in time?
我们决定立刻去火车站。
We determined to go to the railway station at once.
从车站走到这里只有十分钟的路程。
It is no more than ten minutes' walk from the station.

准 zhǔn   （乙）形
accurate

常用搭配
发音准 precise pronunciation
猜得准 guess accurately

用法示例
这只表准吗？ Is this watch accurate?
他打枪打得准。 He can shoot the target accurately.

zhǔnquè
准确　　　反 含糊　　　（乙）形
precise; accurate

常用搭配
准确的答案 an accurate answer
词的准确含义 the exact meaning of a word
准确的尺寸 precise measurements

用法示例
他能准确流利地说英语。
He can speak English fluently and accurately.
他的报告不够准确。
His report lacks precision.
他对事件报道的每个细节都是准确的。
His report of the event was accurate in every detail.

mǎhu
马虎　　　反 细心　　　（乙）形
careless

常用搭配
马虎的学生 a careless student
马马虎虎的校对 careless proofreading

用法示例
他父亲提醒他别马虎。
His father reminded him not to be careless.
由于马虎,他数学考试没及格。
He failed his math's examination because of his careless work.
我游得马马虎虎,但比昨天好一些。
I swam ok, but better than yesterday.

mǎtóu
码头　　　（乙）名
wharf; dock

常用搭配
码头工人 dock worker

用法示例
货轮停泊在码头边。
The freighter moored alongside the wharf.
船在码头停着。
The ship lies at the pier.
轮船正靠近码头。
The ship is nearing the wharf.
允许那艘船在码头上卸货。
The ship was allowed to unload cargo on the wharf.

chējiān
车间　　　（乙）名
workshop

常用搭配
加工车间 processing workshop
车间主任 workshop director

用法示例
这个车间里有五十多个工人。
There are more than fifty workers in this workshop.
这些都是在这个车间制造的吗?
Are these toys made in this workshop?

fùyìn
复印　　　（乙）动
copy; xerox

常用搭配
复印机 photocopier
复印文件 copy the file

用法示例
你把日程表复印二十份好吗?
Could you run off twenty copies of the agenda?
请为我复印一下这封信。
Copy this letter for me please.
我比较了复印件和原件,但是差别不大。
I compared the copy with the original, but there was not much difference.

yìnshuā
印刷　　　（乙）动
print

常用搭配
印刷厂 printing plant
印刷工人 printing worker

用法示例
这篇文章是用粗黑体字印刷的。
This article is printed in Gothic script.
这台自动印刷机每分钟能印刷二百页。
This automatic printer can print 120 pages a minute.
现在正在印刷今天的报纸。
Today's newspaper is being printed now.

yàoshi
钥匙　　　（丙）名
key

常用搭配
一把钥匙 a key
一串钥匙 a bunch of keys

用法示例
我们有教室门的钥匙。
We have a key to the door of the classroom.
我在找我的车钥匙。
I am looking for the key to my car.

fùzhì
复制　　　（丙）动
duplicate; make a copy of

常用搭配
复制一张画 to reproduce a picture
复制一盘磁带 to duplicate a tape

用法示例

录音磁带的复制质量有了很大改进。
The reproductive quality of audio tapes has improved enormously.
这是复制品,不是原作。
This is a reproduction, not the original.
他们复制了这个古董以防意外。
They make copies of the antiques as a safeguard against accidents.

词义辨析

准、准确

"准"和"准确"都是形容词,都有正确无误的意思。"准"强调没有误差,比较口语化,在句子中常作补语和谓语;"准确"强调符合标准,常用作书面语,在句子中可做补语和谓语,也常作定语和状语。比如:①这个温度计不准。②他发音很准/准确。③准确的发音对学生很重要。④你能准确地读出这些单词吗?

Both 准 and 准确 are adjectives, meaning "accurate". 准 stresses "to be without mistake or error", is more colloquial, and often functions as a predicate or a complement; while 准确 stresses "standard", is often used in written language, and functions as a predicate, a complement, an attributive or an adverbial. For example: ① This thermometer is inaccurate. ② His pronunciation is very standard. ③ Accurate pronunciation is important for students. ④ Can you read these words correctly?

练习

练习一、根据拼音写汉字,根据汉字写拼音
zhǔn(　) mǎ(　) (　)tóu (　)shuā(　) shi
(　)确　 (　)虎　码(　)　印(　)　钥(　)

练习二、搭配连线
(1) 复习　　　　　　　A. 答案
(2) 加工　　　　　　　B. 功课
(3) 复印　　　　　　　C. 文件
(4) 复制　　　　　　　D. 车间
(5) 准确　　　　　　　E. 磁带

练习三、从今天学习的生词中选择合适的词填空
1. 老板说,我知道你努力了,_____ 这远远不够。
2. 船停在 _____ 上,游客下船参观。
3. 马克写汉字很 _____。把"太"写成了"大"。
4. 这么复杂的数学题,不到30秒,这个小女孩就 _____ 地说出了计算结果。
5. 下个星期就要考试了,同学们都在抓紧时间 _____。
6. 这件文物不是真的,是 _____ 品。
7. 我了解我的女儿,我给她买的衣服,她 _____ 喜欢。
8. 请把这个文件帮我 _____ 两份。
9. 当天的报纸,是在头天晚上 _____ 的。
10. _____ 里,工人们正在组装零件。

答案

练习一:
略
练习二:
(1) B　　(2) D　　(3) C　　(4) E　　(5) A
练习三:
1. 但是　2. 码头　3. 马虎　4. 准确　5. 复习
6. 复制　7. 准　8. 复印　9. 印刷　10. 车间

星期五

jīngjì
经济 (甲) 名/形
① economy ② economic

常用搭配
知识经济 knowledge economy
商品经济 commercial economy
经济危机 economic crisis
计划经济体制 planned economy

用法示例
不断发展的经济使农民富裕起来了。
The expanding economy enriched the peasants.
经济正在萎缩而不是在增长。
The economy is shrinking instead of growing.
他在大学攻读经济学。
He majors in economics at university.
贪污是一种经济犯罪。
Corruption is a type of economic crime.

kěshì
可是 (甲) 连
however; but

常用搭配
这本书很贵,可是很值。
The book is expensive; however, it's worth it.

用法示例
我本来要写信的,可是把你的地址弄丢了。
I was going to write to you, but I lost your address.
演说很好听,可是没什么内容。
It's a clever speech, but there was no real depth to it.
他们说要帮助我们,可是他们食言了。
They said they'd help but they've ratted on us.

kòngzhì　　　　　cāozòng
控制　　 ◎ 操纵　　　　(乙) 动
control

常用搭配
控制通货膨胀 control inflation　　控制火势 control a fire

用法示例
这座城市处于敌军的控制之下。
The city is under the control of enemy forces.
火势已得到控制。
The fire has been brought under control.
通货膨胀已失去了控制。
Inflation has gotten out of control.

shìdàng　　　　　qiàdàng
适当　　 ◎ 恰当　　　　(乙) 形
proper; appropriate

常用搭配
在适当的时候 at a proper time
适当的时机 proper occasion

用法示例
在适当的时候将把详情告诉你。
You will be informed of the details at the appropriate time.
如果我们的产品适当加以推销,销路应该很好。
If our product is properly marketed, it should sell very well.
到了适当的年龄,就要鼓励孩子们独立生活。
Upon reaching an appropriate age, children are encouraged to live independently.

duó
夺 (乙) 动
snatch; rob

常用搭配
夺高产 strive for high yield

用法示例
他从我的手里夺走了书。
He snatched the book from my hands.
你争我夺是粗鲁的行为。
It's rude to snatch.
我们队夺得了游泳冠军。
Our team won the swimming championships.

lǐlùn
理论 (乙) 名
theory

常用搭配
把理论应用于实践 apply theory to practice
理论联系实际 integrate theory with practice
学习理论 theory of learning

用法示例
这种理论与已知事实不符。
This theory is at variance with the known facts.
老教授主持了一次理论物理学家的研讨会。
The old professor had presided over a seminar for theoretical physicists.
那个理论的精髓是为人民服务。
The core of that theory is about serving the people.

hézuò　　　　　xiézuò
合作　　 ◎ 协作　　　　(乙) 动
cooperate

常用搭配
与……合作 cooperate with…

用法示例
如果我们合作,很快就能完成。
If we all cooperate, we'll soon finish it.
感谢你们的合作。
Thank you for your cooperation.

英、法两国合作制造了这种新式轮船。
The British cooperated with the French in building the new ship.
资方要感谢全体员工的通力合作。
The management would like to thank the staff for being so cooperative.

hétong
合同　　　　　　　　　　（乙）名
contract

常用搭配
撕毁合同 break the contract　履行合同 keep a contract
代理合同 agency contract

用法示例
他们签了建造新桥的合同。
They were contracted to build the new bridge.
根据我们的合同,你每年有十五天的带薪假期。
According to our contract, you get 15 days' paid holiday a year.
你们的合同已经被终止了。
Your contract has been terminated.

lǐpǐn
礼品　　　　　　　　　　（丁）名
gift; present

常用搭配
礼品店 present store　购买礼品 to buy presents

用法示例
这家商店有各式各样的礼品。
There are a wide assortments of gifts in the shop.
春节前,她要给公司的老主顾们购买礼品。
Before the New Year, she will buy presents for customers of her company.

yìzhì
抑制　　　　（丙）动
inhibit; restrain

常用搭配
抑制邪念 inhibit wrong desires

用法示例
我无法抑制我的愤怒。
I couldn't restrain my anger.
我简直无法抑制我的好奇心。
I could hardly contain my curiosity.

shìwēi
示威　　　　　　　　　　（丙）动
① demonstrate ② display by a rally or march:

常用搭配
举行示威 hold demonstrations　示威者 demonstrators
和平示威 peaceful demonstrations

用法示例
他们决定示威反对增加税收。
They decided to protest against the tax hikes.

警方说参加游行示威的人超过了十万。
The police said over 100,000 people had taken part in the demonstration.
在这两个城市同时举行了示威游行。
The simultaneous demonstrations were held in these two cities.

qiǎngjié
抢劫　　　　　　　　　　（丁）动
rob

常用搭配
抢劫银行 rob a bank　遭到抢劫 be robbed

用法示例
银行遭到抢劫的消息很快传开了。
The news of the bank robbery spread quickly.
他在回家的路上遭到了抢劫。
He was mugged on his way home.

词义辨析

控制、抑制

"控制"和"抑制"都是动词。"控制"的意思是掌握住对象,不让它任意发展或超出范围,"控制"的对象多是人或事,有时也可以是感情;"抑制"的意思是约束、压制,其对象多是内心的活动等比较抽象的事物,有时用于医学术语。例如:①局势已发展得难以控制了。②那时,他无法控制/抑制心中的怒火。③这种药能够抑制病菌的生长。

Both 控制 and 抑制 are verbs. 控制 means "to control something within a certain scope", the object of 控制 is a person or thing, and sometimes emotions. 抑制 means "to hold in restraint", the object of 抑制 is something abstract such as emotions, and is sometimes used as medical term. For example: ① The situation is out of control now. ② At that moment, he couldn't restrain his anger. ③ This medicine can inhibit the growth of bacteria.

练习一、根据拼音写汉字,根据汉字写拼音
lǐ（　）　shì（　）　shì（　）　kòng（　）（　）jì
（　）论　（　）威　（　）当　（　）制　经（　）

练习二、搭配连线
(1) 抑制　　　　　　A. 危机
(2) 经济　　　　　　B. 游行
(3) 示威　　　　　　C. 合同
(4) 抢劫　　　　　　D. 银行
(5) 履行　　　　　　E. 邪念

练习三、从今天学习的生词中选择合适的词填空

1. 麦克觉得这件礼物很漂亮,买了送给女朋友,_____女朋友不喜欢。
2. 小偷一把_____过那个女孩的钱包就跑了。
3. 通货膨胀很厉害,政府_____地提高了工资。
4. 他们_____写了一本书。
5. 公司和当地政府签署了一份_____,合作开发这里的石油资源。
6. 见到巧克力,她就_____不住自己的嘴巴了。
7. 中国的_____发展得很快。
8. 搞学术研究一定要_____联系实际。
9. 面对这个傲慢无礼的客人,服务员难以_____住愤怒,跟他争吵了起来。
10. 和平爱好者在政府门前_____,反对向别的国家发起战争。

练习一:
略

练习二:
(1) E　　(2) A　　(3) B　　(4) D　　(5) C

练习三:
1. 可是　　2. 夺　　3. 适当　　4. 合作　　5. 合同
6. 控制　　7. 经济　　8. 理论　　9. 抑制　　10. 示威

第4月,第2周的练习

练习一、根据词语给加点的字注音

1.(　) 2.(　) 3.(　) 4.(　) 5.(　)
抑制　利润　援助　印刷　面貌

练习二、根据拼音填写词语

　　shi　　shì　　shì　　shí　　shǐ
1. 钥(　) 2.(　)当 3.(　)威 4.(　)用 5. 即(　)

练习三、辨析并选择合适的词填空

1. 我非常感谢那些曾经(　)过我的老师和同学们。(帮助、援助)
2. 中国政府为灾区送去了大量的(　)物资。(帮助、援助)
3. 我们(　)都要记得那些在困难时向我们伸出援手的人们。(有时、时时)
4. 周末我一般都在家休息,(　)也出去看场电影什么的。(有时、时时)
5. 那里发生了森林大火,政府派去了军队去(　)消防队。(支持、支援)
6. 全家都反对我的选择,只有姐姐一个人(　)我。(支持、支援)

7. 考试考得这么差,他(　)没好好复习。(准、准确)
8. 我只记得大概的路线,不能(　)地说出来。(准、准确)
9. 政府想了很多办法来(　)通货膨胀进一步升级。(控制、抑制)
10. 骑马的时候,她没有(　)好马奔跑的速度,从马背上摔了下来。(控制、抑制)

练习四、选词填空

理想　　合理　　合作　　合同　　反复
理论　　理由　　礼物　　礼貌　　反对

1. 他们俩在工作上(　)得很愉快。
2. 在公共场合大声说话不太(　)。
3. 你请假的(　)不够充分,因此不能批准。
4. 这个孩子的(　)是长大了当一名医生,挽救病人的生命。
5. 孩子丢了,妈妈急疯了,她每天什么也不做,只是(　)叫着孩子的名字。
6. 这两个单位签了一个为期五年的(　)。
7. 他的这个要求不(　),我们不能满足他。
8. 母亲节那天,我给妈妈买了一件(　),她特别喜欢。
9. 他们俩的婚事遭到双方父母的(　)。
10. 当代大学生不仅要有较高的(　)水平,还要有良好的实践能力。

练习五、写出下列词语的同义词

1. 面貌(　)　2. 礼物(　)　3. 复习(　)
4. 抑制(　)　5. 讲课(　)

练习六、写出下列词语的反义词

1. 利润(　)　2. 马虎(　)　3. 联合(　)
4. 提高(　)　5. 反对(　)

答案

练习一:
1. yì　　2. rùn　　3. yuán　　4. shuā　　5. miàn

练习二:
1. 匙　　2. 适　　3. 示　　4. 实　　5. 使

练习三:
1. 帮助　　2. 援助　　3. 时时　　4. 有时　　5. 支援
6. 支持　　7. 准　　8. 准确　　9. 抑制　　10. 控制

练习四:
1. 合作　　2. 礼貌　　3. 理由　　4. 理想　　5. 反复
6. 合同　　7. 合理　　8. 礼物　　9. 反对　　10. 理论

练习五:
1. 面目　　2. 礼品　　3. 温习　　4. 克制　　5. 授课

练习六:
1. 亏损　　2. 细心　　3. 分裂　　4. 降低　　5. 赞成

4月 第3周的学习内容

 星期一 Monday

líkāi
离开　　　fēnkāi
　　　　　　同 分开　　　　　　（甲）/ 动
leave; to part

常用搭配
离开这个国家 leave the country
离开故乡 depart from one's hometown
离不开妈妈 cannot part with one's mother

用法示例
直到他来我才离开。
It was not until he came that I left.
我不完全理解他离开的理由。
I don't fully understand his reasons for leaving.
你认为他真要离开公司吗？
Do you think he is serious about leaving the company?

yúkuài
愉快　　　bēishāng
　　　　　　反 悲伤　　　　　　（甲）形
pleasant; cheerful; delightful

常用搭配
愉快的心情 a cheerful mood
愉快地讨论 discuss pleasantly
感到愉快 feel happy

用法示例
祝你旅途愉快。
I wish you a pleasant trip.
我们在海滨玩得很愉快。
We had a delightful time by the seashore.
她脸上露出愉快的微笑。
There is a merry smile on her face.

zǔzhī
组织　　　　　　　　　　　（甲）动 / 名
① organize ② organization

常用搭配
组织罢工 organize a strike　　组织聚会 organize a party
慈善组织 benevolent organization

用法示例
他们计划组织一次科学考察。
They planned to organize a scientific expedition.
组织这样大规模的聚会要花费许多时间和精力。
The organization of such a large-scale party takes a lot of time and energy.

这个慈善团体是个非盈利性组织。
This charity is a nonprofit organization.

bāngmáng　　　bāngzhù
帮忙　　　同 帮助　　　　　　（乙）动
help; do a favor

常用搭配
要我帮忙吗？ Can I help?
能请您帮个忙吗？ May I ask you a favor?

用法示例
如果你需要我帮忙,就请给我打电话。
If you need me to help, please call me.
他们不大愿意帮忙。
They were reluctant to help.
只要有可能,他总是设法帮忙。
He tries to help, wherever possible.

shìjì
世纪　　　　　　　　　　　（乙）名
century

常用搭配
21 世纪 21st century
在 20 世纪 80 年代 in the 1980s
半个世纪 half a century

用法示例
这座教堂是 19 世纪建造的。
The church was built in the 19th century.
我们生活在 21 世纪。
We are living in the 21st century.
上个世纪我们已经经历了两次世界大战。
We have had two world wars in the last century.

tiāo
挑　　　　　　　　　　　（乙）动
choose; select

常用搭配
挑走 pick off　　挑出较小的苹果 pick out smaller apples
从六个里挑一个 choose one out of the six

用法示例
他从书架上挑了一本书。
He chose a book from the shelves.
小刘挑了一件红衬衣,因为他喜欢红颜色。
Xiao Liu picked a red shirt because he liked red.
他们是从许多报名者当中挑出来的。
They were selected from many applicants.

táo
逃　　　　　　　　　　　（乙）动
escape; flee

常用搭配
逃走(跑) run away 逃课 skip classes
逃犯 escaped criminal

用法示例
小偷被逮住了,但他的同伙逃了。
The thief was arrested, but his accomplice escaped.
这三兄弟不久就从敌营逃走了。
The three brothers soon escaped from the enemy's camp.
居民被迫逃离这座被围困的城市。
Citizens were forced to flee the besieged city.

píngjìng
平静 (乙)形
undisturbed; tranquil; calm

常用搭配
平静的生活 a tranquil life
平静的湖面 the calm surface of the lake

用法示例
当他平静下来时,我开始告诉他实情。
When he had calmed down, I began to tell him the truth.
在外表上她保持着平静,但实际上她生气极了。
She maintained a calm exterior, though really she was furious.
当我告诉他这个坏消息时,他很平静。
He was calm when I told him the bad news.

jǐnguǎn
尽管 (乙)连
① feel free to ② although ③ despite

常用搭配
有要求尽管提 feel free to demand

用法示例
如果你需要什么东西,尽管对我说。
If you need anything, please don't hesitate to ask me.
尽管他们老了,却很快乐。
Though they are old they are happy.
尽管她已经四十岁了,看上去还很年轻。
She seemed young, although she was already forty.

píngfán wěidà
平凡 反 伟大 (丙)形
commonplace; ordinary

常用搭配
平凡人 an ordinary person

用法示例
他的工作很平凡。
His job is quite ordinary.
他们过着平凡而幸福的生活。
They lead an ordinary and happy life.

bāng
帮 (丙)动
help

常用搭配
帮她买书 help her buy books
请帮帮我。Help me, please.

用法示例
我帮她找到了那本书。
I helped her find the book.
他帮我穿好大衣。
He helped me into my coat.
我举不动这个箱子,请你帮我一下好吗?
I can't lift this box — can you please help me?

yǐbiàn
以便 (丙)连
so as to...; so that

常用搭配
我留下来以便能照顾你。
I stayed so I could look after you.

用法示例
我们打开灯,以便看清它是什么。
I turned on the light so that we could see what it was.
他调小了收音机的音量,以便不打扰其他人。
He turned down the radio so as not to disturb the others.
大点声,以便大厅里的人能听清楚。
Speak louder so that the people in the hall can hear you.

词义辨析

帮、帮忙、帮助

1、三个动词都表示协助别人做事或解决困难。"帮忙"是具体的协助的行为,多指在生活和工作中用人力相助;而"帮"和"帮助"可以是物质方面也可以是精神方面的协助。

They are verbs, indicating "to help". 帮忙 indicates "actual physical help", mostly used to refer to manual assistance or a favor given in life or at work; while 帮 and 帮助 mean to support somebody materially or spiritually.

2、"帮"和"帮助"经常带宾语,如"帮/帮助某人","帮/帮助某人做某事";而"帮忙"不能接宾语,可以说"给/为某人帮忙"。

帮 and 帮助 often take an object, such as "帮/帮助某人" (to help somebody), "帮/帮助某人做某事 (to help somebody to do something)"; while 帮忙 is not followed by an object, and can be used like "给/为某人帮忙" (to help somebody).

3、"帮忙"是离合词,可以说"帮个忙"、"帮倒忙";"帮助"没有这样的用法。但"帮助"可以做名词,如"感谢你的帮助!","帮忙"和"帮"不可以。

帮忙 is a separable word, and another word or phrase can be put between them, thus 帮忙 can be used as "帮个忙" (give assistance to)、"帮倒忙" (when trying to help somebody, one makes trouble); while 帮助 can not be used like this. 帮助 is also a noun, e.g. "感谢你的帮助！" (Thank you for your help!), 帮 and 帮忙 are not used like this.

练习一、根据拼音写汉字，根据汉字写拼音
yú（　）（　）jǐ（　）guǎn píng（　）（　）zhī
（　）快　　世（　）尽（　）（　）凡　　组（　）

练习二、搭配连线
(1) 组织　　　　　　A. 愉快
(2) 离开　　　　　　B. 聚会
(3) 旅途　　　　　　C. 平静
(4) 热心　　　　　　D. 学校
(5) 态度　　　　　　E. 帮忙

练习三、从今天学习的生词中选择合适的词填空
1. 你能 _____ 我翻译一下这句话吗？
2. 这次演讲比赛是汉语中心 _____ 的。
3. 谢谢您，要不是您 _____，这孩子到现在还找不到工作。
4. 我在中国生活得很好，心情很 _____。
5. 表演节目时，我帮她 _____ 了一件红色的礼服。
6. 据说罪犯已经 _____ 到了另一个城市了。
7. 现在是二十一 _____。
8. 他很 _____ 地接受了这个事实。
9. 他不想活得太累，只想做一个 _____ 人。
10. 老师说，有什么不明白的问题 _____ 问。

练习一：
略
练习二：
(1) B　　(2) D　　(3) A　　(4) E　　(5) C
练习三：
1. 帮　　2. 组织　　3. 帮忙　　4. 愉快　　5. 挑
6. 逃　　7. 世纪　　8. 平静　　9. 平凡　　10. 尽管

guānxīn
关心　　　　　　　　　　　　　　（甲）动
care; concern

常用搭配
互相关心 care about each other
对……关心 be concerned about...
护士对病人的关心 a nurse's concern for a sick man

用法示例
她不关心儿子到什么地方去。
She didn't care where her son went.
我们都非常关心他的健康。
We are all concerned about his health.
这个老师很关心她的学生。
The teacher is very concerned about her students.

jīngyàn
经验　　　　　　　　　　　　　　（甲）名
experience

常用搭配
丰富的经验 rich experience
缺乏经验 lack of experience
获得经验 gain experience

用法示例
他教英语的经验很丰富。
He has much experience in teaching English.
你有工作经验吗？
Have you had previous career experience?
对于这种职位，他没有足够的经验。
He has not enough experience for the position.

jīngshén
精神　　　　　　　　　　　　　　（甲）名／形
① spirit ② spiritual

常用搭配
进取精神 a spirit of enterprise　　精神好 in good spirits
精神生活 the spiritual life
精神文明 spiritual civilization

用法示例
这条好消息使我精神大振。
The good news lifted my spirits.
我们应该学习她那种不屈不挠的精神。
We should learn from her indefatigable spirit.
很多年轻人不能抵制精神污染。
Many young people can not resist spiritual pollution.

zǐxì
仔细　　　　　　　　　　　　　　（乙）形
careful

【常用搭配】
仔细研究 careful study　仔细检查 careful examination
仔细听！Listen carefully!
【用法示例】
这篇文章值得仔细研究。
The article deserves careful study.
他非常仔细，把每一个细节都核对过了。
He was careful enough to check every detail.

xīxīn
细心　⊝ 粗心 cūxīn　（乙）形
careful; attentive
【常用搭配】
细心的姑娘 a careful girl　细心观察 observe carefully
【用法示例】
细心的人总是把东西放得很整齐。
Attentive people usually put everything in order.
你应该再细心些。
You should be more careful.
老王做事很细心。
Lao Wang is a careful worker.

chuántǒng
传统　（乙）名
tradition
【常用搭配】
传统服装 traditional costume
传统文化 traditional culture
保持传统 keep up tradition
【用法示例】
我们应该发扬优良传统。
We shall carry forward the tradition.
他们决心要打破传统。
They decided to break with tradition.

fēngsú
风俗　⊜ 习俗 xísú　（乙）名
custom
【常用搭配】
风俗习惯 habits and customs
【用法示例】
国家不同，风俗各异。
So many countries, so many customs.
我想这些风俗会逐渐消失。
I think such customs will die out.
坏的风俗应当废除。
Bad customs should be abolished.

fēngjǐng
风景　（乙）名
landscape; scenery
【常用搭配】
春天的风景 the spring landscape
美丽的风景 beautiful scenery

【用法示例】
我要能看到风景的双人房间。
I want a double room with a view.
这些村舍与周围的风景十分协调。
The cottages harmonize well with the landscape.
山里的风景非常美。
The scenery in the mountains is very beautiful.

fǎnkàng　　　　　　fúcóng
反抗　⊝ 服从　（乙）动
revolt; resist
【常用搭配】
反抗统治者 rebel against a ruler
【用法示例】
他们无力反抗。
They were powerless to resist.
奴隶们反抗奴隶主并把他们都杀了。
The slaves rebelled against their masters, and killed them all.
人民反抗他们的君主。
The people revolted against their king.

fǎnjī　　　　　　huíjī
反击　⊜ 回击　（丙）动/名
① counterattack ② a resistance attack
【常用搭配】
反击敌人 counterattack the enemy
【用法示例】
到反击敌人的时候了。
It's time to counterattack the enemy.
我们在寻找机会反击他们。
We are seeking a chance to counterattack them.

xìzhì
细致　（丙）形
careful; meticulous
【常用搭配】
她很细致。She is very meticulous.
【用法示例】
这件服装的手工非常细致。
The handwork of the suit is very delicate.
她描述得很细致。
She described it in detail.
大夫为他作了细致的检查。
The doctor made a careful examination of him.

yǐmiǎn
以免　（丁）连
① lest ② so as not to
【常用搭配】
以免出差错 so as not to make a mistake
【用法示例】
我们小声说话以免吵醒孩子。
We talked in a low voice lest we should wake the baby up.

他仔细检查,以免出错。
He checked it carefully so as not to make any mistakes.
他们晚上走,以免被人看到。
They left at night so as not to be seen.

 **词义辨析**

仔细、细心、细致

1、"仔细"、"细心"和"细致"都是形容词,都有心思细密周到的意思。"仔细"一般用于形容做事的态度,因此经常用作状语或补语;"细致"和"细心"通常强调人的个性就是用心细密,连小的地方都能注意到,往往作定语、补语、谓语等,很少做状语。例如:他很马虎,不像他姐姐那么仔细/细心/细致。仔细地检查试卷。她做得又快又仔细。她是一个细心/细致的姑娘。

They are all adjectives, meaning "careful, considerate". 仔细 is mostly applied to one's attitude to work, so it often functions as an adverbial or a complement; while 细致 and 细心 are often applied to one's character that is always careful, so they usually function as an attributive, a complement, or a predicate. For example: He is very careless, and he is not as careful as his sister. Go over your exam paper carefully. She did it quickly and carefully. She is a careful girl.

2、"仔细"可以重叠使用,如:"仔仔细细";"细心"和"细致"不能这样用。"仔细"和"细心"主要用来形容人或人做事的状态;"细致"则可以用来形容物,比如:他要仔仔细细地检查作业。那种布织得很细致。

仔细 can be reduplicated into "仔仔细细"; 细心 and 细致 can not be reduplicated. 仔细 and 细心 are mostly applied to a person, or to one's way of doing something; while 细致 can be applied to something. For example: He examined his homework very carefully. The cloth is woven very fine and close.

 **练习**

练习一、根据拼音写汉字,根据汉字写拼音

jīng( ) jīng( ) ( )zhì ( )tǒng)sú
( )神   ( )验   细( )   传( )   风( )

练习二、搭配连线
(1) 精神   A. 经验
(2) 风俗   B. 检查
(3) 仔细   C. 敌人
(4) 缺乏   D. 文明
(5) 反击   E. 习惯

练习三、从今天学习的生词中选择合适的词填空
1. 经过_____检查,我们发现有一个机器的零件坏了。
2. 这件衣服的做工很_____。
3. 她是个_____的女孩,特别善于照顾他人。
4. 你们最好早点儿去机场,_____赶不上航班。
5. 他拿起一根棍子_____欺负他的人。
6. 颐和园的_____很美,我们照了许多照片。
7. 每个国家都有自己的_____习惯。
8. 她的家庭很_____,不希望她当演员。
9. 穿着这身运动衣,小伙子看上去很_____。
10. 他汉语学得很好,老师请他为新同学介绍了他学习汉语的_____。

 **答案**

练习一:
略
练习二:
(1) D   (2)E   (3)B   (4)A   (5)C
练习三:
1. 仔细   2. 细致   3. 细心   4. 以免   5. 反击
6. 风景   7. 风俗   8. 传统   9. 精神   10. 经验

星期三

yàoshi
要是 （甲）连
if

常用搭配
要是……就 If... , then ...

用法示例
你要是想回家就回家吧。
If you want to go home, then go.
要是你想得到一份报酬，你就必须做好你该分担的那一份工作。
If you want your share of the profit, you'll have to do your fair share of the work.
要是你不去看他，我也不去了。
If you don't go to see him, I won't go either.

fúwù
服务 （甲）动
service; serve

常用搭配
为人民服务 serve the people
提供服务 provide service
服务员 waiter (or waitress)

用法示例
他们想方设法为居民服务。
They are doing everything to serve the residents.
账单中包含服务费吗？
Is service included in the bill?
这个饭店的服务质量已经有了很大改善。
The quality of service in this restaurant has improved a lot.

rúguǒ   yàoshì
如果 ≈要是 （乙）连
if

常用搭配
如果我是你…… if I were you…
如果明天下雨…… if it rains tomorrow…

用法示例
如果我再有一次机会就好了。
If only I had another chance.
我想如果我坚持下去就会成功。
I thought if I kept at it I should succeed.
如果他现在回来怎么办？
What if he comes back now?

gèrén
个人 （乙）名

① individual ② personal

常用搭配
个人主义 individualism   个人卫生 personal hygiene

用法示例
我个人最喜欢蓝色。
Personally, I like blue best.
我个人并不介意。
Personally, I didn't mind.
就我个人而言，我认为他不诚实，可是有许多人信任他。
Personally, I think he is dishonest, but many people trust him.

rúhé
如何 （乙）代
how

常用搭配
事情进行得如何？ How are things going?
球赛结果如何？ How did the game turn out?

用法示例
我应该如何理解这话？
How should I take that remark?
我们不知道这些鸟如何认路。
We have no idea how the birds find their way.
我很想知道如何才能做好这件事。
I should like to know how to do it well.

jīdòng   píngjìng
激动   反平静 （乙）动
excite

常用搭配
别激动！ Don't get so excited!
令人激动的故事 an exciting story
我太激动了。 I was too excited.

用法示例
这个英雄的故事使他激动不已。
The story about the hero moved him greatly.
他的声音因激动而颤抖。
His voice shook with emotion.
我看到雪时，激动得连寒冷都不在乎了。
I was so excited to see snow that I was indifferent to the cold.

jīnglì
经历 （乙）动/名
experience

常用搭配
经历苦难 to experience hardships
难忘的经历 memorable experience

用法示例
昨天我经历了一件不寻常的事。
I had an unusual experience yesterday.
这些国家经历过多次战争。
These countries have gone through many wars.
那是一次有趣的经历。
It is an interesting experience.

jīnglǐ
经理 （乙）名
manager

常用搭配
银行经理 bank manager　　总经理 general manager

用法示例
他已被提升为经理了。
He has been promoted to manager.
他哥哥是一家大公司的经理。
His brother is a manager of a big company.
我们的经理很年轻但很能干。
Our manager is young but very capable.

gètǐ
个体　　反 集体 （乙）名
individual

常用搭配
个体经济 individual economy
个体差异 individual difference

用法示例
她把她的学生视为不同的个体。
She treats her students as different individuals.
他在研究儿童的个体差异。
He is researching the individual differences of children.

rúcǐ
如此 （丙）代
① so　② in this way

常用搭配
正是如此！Just so!　　虽然如此 even so

用法示例
真奇怪，她竟然会如此粗鲁。
It's strange for her to be so rude.
她是如此的疲惫以致于病倒了。
She was so weary that she fell ill.
她喜欢狗，他也如此。
She likes dogs; so does he.

jiǎrú
假如 （丙）连
if

常用搭配
假如我是你……
If I were you…

用法示例
假如我可以选择，我三十岁就退休。
If I had the choice, I would retire at thirty.
假如没下雨我就去。
I shall go, provided that it doesn't rain.

cìhou
伺候　　同 服侍 （丙）动
care for; look after

常用搭配
伺候病人 care for a patient　　伺候老人 care for the old

用法示例
我奶奶年纪大了，需要人伺候。
My grandmother is so old that she needs someone to look after her.
当他生病时，他的儿子伺候他。
His son cared for him when he was ill.

 词义辨析

如果、假如、要是
　　三个词意思和用法基本相同，通常可以互换使用。"假如"是书面语，强调条件是假设的，往往用于虚拟语气。"要是"比较口语化，主要强调条件可能是真实的，往往用于将来的时间。"如果"在以上两种情况中都可以代替"假如"和"要是"。例如：假如/如果你是我，你会怎么回答？要是/如果下雨，他们就不能去了。

　　Generally speaking, the three words have the same usage and meaning, and they are interchangeable in a sentence. 假如 is often used in writing, mainly indicating a hypothesis in a subjunctive mood; while 要是 is mostly colloquial, generally emphasising a condition in a future tense; 如果 can replace 假如 and 要是 in the cases above. For example: If you were me, how would you answer? If it rains, they can't go.

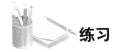

练习

练习一、根据拼音写汉字，根据汉字写拼音
fú（ ）（ ）lǐ（ ）cǐ jī（ ）cì（ ）
（ ）务 经（ ） 如（ ） （ ）动 （ ）候

练习二、搭配连线
(1) 个人　　　　A. 服务
(2) 个体　　　　B. 老人
(3) 提供　　　　C. 坎坷
(4) 伺候　　　　D. 卫生
(5) 经历　　　　E. 经济

练习三、从今天学习的生词中选择合适的词填空
1. 学习是_____的事情，不是老师的事情，也不是父母的。
2. 他爸爸是个_____户。
3. _____你不来，请告诉我一声。
4. 你总下决心要改掉坏习惯，可总改不了，你让我_____相信你？
5. 既然_____，那我们就没什么可说的了。
6. 你_____他，你怎么做？
7. 这些老人都_____过战争，知道战争意味着什么。
8. 父母老了，身体不好，身边需要有人_____。
9. 看到自己的儿子从战场上平安回来，母亲_____得抱着儿子哭了。
10. _____生命只剩三天了，你打算做点什么呢？

答案

练习一： 略

练习二：
(1) D　(2)E　(3)A　(4)B　(5)C

练习三：
1. 个人　2. 个体　3. 如果/要是　4. 如何
5. 如此　6. 要是　7. 经历　8. 伺候
9. 激动　10. 假如

星期四

tóngyì
同意　　　　　　　　　　　　（甲）动
agree; approve

常用搭配
同意某人的观点 agree with sb.
双方同意 by mutual consent
我完全同意。I couldn't agree more.

用法示例
我完全同意你的看法。
I entirely agree with you.
我的父母亲同意我们去。
My parents agreed that we should go.
部长已同意印发他的讲话了吗？
Has the minister consented to have his speech printed?

chúle
除了　　　　　　　　　　　　（甲）介
besides; apart from

常用搭配
除了……，都/没有…… apart from; except for
除了……，还/也…… in addition to; besides

用法示例
除了我们之外他没有什么朋友。
He had few friends besides us.
除了这本，我还有五本别的书。
I have five other books besides this one.
我除了要通过考试之外，没有别的心愿。
I have no other wish except to pass the examination.

wěidà
伟大　　　　　　　　　　　　（甲）形
great

常用搭配
伟大的政治家 a great statesman
伟大的将领 a great general

用法示例
贝多芬是一位伟大的音乐家。
Beethoven was a great musician.
孔子是一位伟大的教育家。
Confucius was a great educator.
毛泽东作为伟大的领袖而被载入史册。
Mao Zedong went down in history as a great leader.

liánghǎo　　　　　yōuliáng
良好　　　　⊜ 优良　　　　（乙）形
fine; good

常用搭配
良好的关系 good relationship

良好的开端 good beginning

用法示例

没有良好的经营管理,事业就不会兴旺发达。
A business cannot thrive without good management.
他有良好的视觉记忆力。
He has a good visual memory.
天气情况良好。
Weather conditions are good.

yèlǐ
夜里　≡晚上　（乙）名
nighttime

常用搭配

昨天夜里 last night

用法示例

你夜里一定要将东西放好,这里有人偷东西。
Make sure you put your things away at night; some people round here are light-fingered.
昨天夜里你听到叫喊声了吗?
Did you hear that scream last night?
那天夜里我做了个恶梦。
I had a nightmare that night.

yèwǎn
夜晚　（乙）名
night

常用搭配

漆黑的夜晚 dark night

用法示例

夜晚我们可以看见星星。
We can see the stars at night.
猫头鹰是一种能在夜晚飞行的鸟。
An owl is a bird that flies at night.
他在家里度过了一个寂寞的夜晚。
He spent a lonely evening at home.

kěkào
可靠　（乙）形
reliable

常用搭配

可靠的消息来源 reliable source of information
可靠的工人 dependable worker

用法示例

他不太可靠。
He's not very reliable.
单凭外貌来判断一个人是不可靠的。
It's not reliable to judge a man solely by his appearance.
她是一名可靠的助手。
She is a reliable assistant.

guǎnggào
广告　（乙）名
advertisement

常用搭配

商业广告 commercial advertisement
电视广告 TV advertisement

用法示例

我们决定为我们的新产品做广告。
We decided to advertise our new product.
这个电视节目中的广告太多了。
There are too many TV advertisements in the program.
墙上贴满了广告。
The wall was covered with advertisements.

guǎngkuò
广阔　⊠狭小　xiáxiǎo　（乙）形
wide; vast

常用搭配

广阔的沙漠 a vast expanse of desert
广阔的海洋 the wide ocean

用法示例

亚洲的平原非常广阔。
The Asiatic plains are very broad.
展现在我们面前的是一片广阔的土地。
A wide stretch of land lay in front of us.

yèjiān
夜间　⊠白天　báitiān　（丙）名
nighttime

常用搭配

今天夜间有雨。It will be raining tonight.

用法示例

蝙蝠在夜间飞行。
Bats fly at night.
夜间会更冷。
It will be colder during the night.
小偷在夜间盗窃。
The thief stole during the night.

chúfēi
除非　（丙）连
unless

常用搭配

我会来的,除非下雨。I will come, unless it is raining.

用法示例

除非你改变想法,否则我帮不了你。
Unless you change your mind, I won't be able to help you.
除非下雨,要不然这位退休工人每天都锻炼。
The retired worker does exercises every day except on rainy days.
你永远都不会成功,除非你努力工作。
You will never succeed unless you work hard.

kějiàn
可见　（丙）连
it is obvious that; it is thus clear that

用法示例

她擅长数学和物理学,还是个有名的发明家,可见,她很聪明。
She is good at math and physics, and she is a famous inventor. It is obvious that she is very clever.

这里的植物种类在减少,而且鱼和鸟也比以前少了,可见,这个地区的污染很严重。
The number of plant species is decreasing, and there are fewer birds and fishes than before. It is clear that the pollution is very serious in this area.

除非、除了

"除非"是连词,引出唯一的前提,往往连接两句话,不能连接单个的词。"除了"是介词,表示除去个别的或补充,如这两个结构"除了……都/全""除了……还/也","除了"的宾语往往是一个词,很少是一个句子。如:①除了小李,我们都到那儿去了。②除了牛奶,我们还需要蔬菜。③除非我有很多钱,否则我是不会买房子的。

除非 is a conjunction, introducing the only prerequisite condition. It is often used to connect two sentences, but not words. 除了 is a preposition, indicating "except" or "besides", such as the two structures "除了……都/全" (except) and "除了……还/也" (besides). The object of 除了 is usually a word, rarely a sentence. For example: ① We all went there except Xiao Li. ② Besides milk, we need vegetables. ③ Unless I am rich, I am not going to buy a house.

练习一、根据拼音写汉字,根据汉字写拼音

yè(　)　(　)kuò　liáng(　)chú(　)(　)kào
(　)晚　广(　)　(　)好　(　)非　可(　)

练习二、搭配连线
(1) 良好的　　　A. 夜晚
(2) 商业的　　　B. 关系
(3) 广阔的　　　C. 广告
(4) 可靠的　　　D. 海洋
(5) 漆黑的　　　E. 朋友

练习三、从今天学习的生词中选择合适的词填空

1. 昨天_____,我们邻居的小孩一直哭,把我吵醒了。
2. 秋天的_____,凉风习习,繁星点点,真是美极了。
3. 高考期间,为了让学生能够休息好,所有的_____施工都停了。
4. 我喜欢看有思想、有创意的_____。
5. 我喜欢海,每当看到_____的大海,就忘记了一切烦恼。
6. 他是个_____的人,女儿和他结婚,你就放心吧。
7. _____中国以外,山本还去过欧美一些国家。
8. _____他自己跟我说这事,否则我不相信。
9. 这个人总是自我感觉_____,从来不知道谦虚。
10. 昨天夜里刮风了,把有些树和广告牌都破坏了,_____,风一定很大。

答案

练习一:
略

练习二:
(1) B　(2)C　(3)D　(4)E　(5)A

练习三:
1.夜里　2.夜晚　3.夜间　4.广告　5.广阔
6.可靠　7.除了　8.除非　9.良好　10.可见

星期五 Friday

jiǎndān
简单 ⊜ 容易 （甲）形
simple; brief

常用搭配
一项简单的任务 simple task　简单的问题 simple question
简单的手续 straightforward procedure

用法示例
那小男孩已经能做简单的算术题了。
The little boy can already do simple arithmetic problems.
和面的方法很简单,只要把水和在面粉里就行了。
The way to make dough is very simple as you only need to mix flour with water.
这个家伙很笨,连一件简单的工作也做不好。
The guy is so impotent that he can't even do a simple job well.

suīrán
虽然 （甲）连
although; even though

常用搭配
他虽然老了却很健壮。Though he was old, he was strong.

用法示例
虽然那篇文章很短,但很重要。
The article is very important though it is short.
虽然当时正下着雨,他还是到那里去了。
Though it was raining, he still went there.
虽然汤药很苦,我还是得喝。
I had to take the herb tea even though it's bitter.

xìngfú
幸福 ⊝ 痛苦 （甲）形
happy

常用搭配
幸福的家庭 happy family　幸福的时光 happy days

用法示例
金钱买不来幸福。
Money can't buy happiness.
他们的婚姻生活很幸福。
They have a happy marriage.
中国老百姓现在过着幸福的生活。
China's population live a happy life now.

qǐngkè
请客 （乙）
stand treat; invite to dinner

常用搭配
这次由我请客。This is my treat.
该我请客了。It is my shout.

用法示例
这顿饭我请客。
This meal is my treat.
今天我请客。我来付。
It's my shout today. I'll pay.
下次该谁请客了?
Whose round is it next?

pǐnzhǒng
品种 （乙）名
variety; breed

常用搭配
新品种 a new breed　小麦的品种 varieties of wheat

用法示例
他的马是最好的品种。
His horse is of the best breed.
大多数西红柿成熟时是红色的,但有些品种是黄色的。
Most tomatoes are red when ripe, but some kinds are yellow.
你能辨别这两个品种吗?
Can you differentiate between the two varieties?

kào
靠 （乙）动/介
① lean against; depend upon ② near; by

常用搭配
他靠打猎谋生。He earns a living by hunting.
把它靠在墙上。Lean it against the wall.
靠边站 stand aside

用法示例
我们全靠自己完成了这项工作。
We finished the job all by ourselves.
她靠父母生活。
She lives off her parents.
他把自行车靠在篱笆上。
He propped his bicycle up against the fence.

yīkào
依靠 ⊜ 依赖 （乙）动
rely on; depend on

常用搭配
依靠自己的努力 rely on one's own efforts

用法示例
既然你长大了,就不应该依靠你的父母了。
Now that you are grown up, you should not rely on your parents.
他们依靠努力工作而获得成功。
They succeeded through hard working.

nánguò
难过 ⊝ 高兴 （乙）动/形
① feel sorry ② sad

常用搭配
令人难过的消息 sad news

用法示例

我的小猫死了,我很难过。
My kitten's death made me sad.
我对他的失明深表难过。
I pitied his blindness.
听说他生了重病,我感到很难过。
I'm sorry to hear that he has been seriously ill.

língqián
零钱 (乙)名
change; small change

常用搭配

你有零钱吗？ Do you have any change?
我没有零钱。I've no small change.

用法示例

你能换5块钱的零钱吗？
Do you have change for five yuan?
别忘了数数你的零钱。
Don't forget to count your change.
我需要些零钱。
I need some change.

pǐnzhì
品质 (丙)名
quality; moral character

常用搭配

生活品质 living quality
品质差的布料 poor quality material
她的高贵品质 her noble quality

用法示例

她最主要的品质是善良。
Her most essential quality is kindness.
他看上去粗鲁,但有许多优秀品质。
He had many good qualities, despite his apparent rudeness.
他具有教师应有的一切优秀品质。
He embodies all the best qualities of a teacher.

gùrán
固然 (丙)连
① admittedly ② it's true that...

用法示例

临终前的悔过固然不错,但对受害者又有什么用处呢？
A death-bed repentance is all very well, but what good will it do for the victims?
她固然很好,但有必要那样表扬她吗？
She was good, but was it necessary to praise her quite like that?

qǐngjiào
请教 (丙)动
consult

常用搭配

请教专家
to consult an expert

用法示例

我能向您请教一个学术问题吗？
May I ask you an academic question?
这件事情你应该请教你的律师。
You should seek advice from your lawyer on this matter.
我得向老师请教那件事。
I have to consult my teacher about this matter.

 词义辨析

虽然、固然

"虽然"和"固然"都是连词,都表示转折的关系。"虽然"常用于从句的句首,所引的句子的意思往往与主句的意思相反；"固然"常常用于从句的主语后边,该句的意思有时与主句的意思不一定相反。如：①你的想法固然很好,但是我还想听听老师的想法。②虽然这项工作很费力,但是他很快就做完了。

虽然 and 固然 are conjunctions, meaning "although", and indicating a concession. 虽然 is usually used at the beginning of a clause, the meaning of which is opposite to the meaning of the main clause. 固然 is usually used after the subject of the clause, the meaning of which may or may not be opposite to the main clause. For example: ① Your idea is really good, but I hope to ask for advice from my teacher. ② Although the work was arduous, he finished it in a short amount of time.

 练习

练习一、根据拼音写汉字，根据汉字写拼音

qǐng ( ) gù ( ) pǐn ( ) ( ) fú jiǎn ( )
( )教 ( )然 ( )种 幸( ) ( )单

练习二、搭配连线

(1) 手续   A. 很幸福
(2) 感到   B. 很丰富
(3) 品质   C. 很简单
(4) 品种   D. 很优秀
(5) 生活   E. 很难过

练习三、从今天学习的生词中选择合适的词填空

1. 这种郁金香花是从荷兰引进的新_____。
2. 大学时,我的生活很_____,每天都是在宿舍、教室、食堂三个地方。
3. 我最大的愿望就是孩子们能够生活得_____。
4. 别_____在墙上,墙面的油漆还没干。
5. 父母都在老家,在这座城市里,她没有_____。
6. 听到她意外受伤的消息,大家都很_____。
7. 我拿到了第一笔工资,所以今天吃饭我_____。
8. 这个人_____不错,就是做事慢一点。

9. 一次付清房款 _____ 好，但谁有那么多钱呢！
10. 王教授,有个问题我想 _____ 您一下,不知您现在有没有时间。

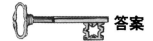 **答案**

练习一：
略
练习二：
(1) C (2)E (3)D (4)B (5)A
练习三：
1. 品种 2. 简单 3. 幸福 4. 靠 5. 依靠
6. 难过 7. 请客 8. 品质 9. 固然 10. 请教

第4月，第3周的练习

练习一、根据词语给加点的字注音
1.( ) 2.( ) 3.( ) 4.( ) 5.( )
尽管 传统 伺候 广阔 固然

练习二、根据拼音填写词语
1. 细( ) zhì 2. 品( ) zhì 3. 世( ) jì 4. 反( ) jī 5. ( )动 jī

练习三、辨析并选择合适的词填空
1. 你( )我把洗衣机里的衣服晾到阳台上去吧。（帮、帮助、帮忙）
2. 他回老家找工作的话,父母可以( ),不过,他想在北京找工作。（帮、帮助、帮忙）
3. 那段困难的日子里,我们互相( )、互相鼓励,从来没有放弃理想。（帮、帮助、帮忙）
4. 答完卷子的同学请再( )检查一遍。(仔细、细心、细致)
5. 这件衣服做工非常( )。（仔细、细心、细致）
6. 一般来说,女孩子比男孩子( )一点。(仔细、细心、细致)
7. ( )你是老师,你会怎么处理这件事呢？（如果、假如、要是）
8. ( )明天下雨的话,篮球赛就在室内举行。（如果、假如、要是）
9. ( )搬家,否则就只能忍受附近的飞机场的噪音。（除了、除非）
10. ( )会说汉语,他还会讲西班牙语和英语。（除了、除非）
11. 一边工作一边学习的想法( )不错,可实际上,可能工作和学习都搞不好。（虽然、固然）
12. 我( )去过几次上海,但还是会迷路。（虽然、固然）

练习四、选词填空
以便 风俗 经历 经验 可见
以免 风景 经理 依靠 可靠
1. 年轻人要学会独立,特别是工作后经济上不要再( )父母了。
2. 我们要总结( )教训,不要再犯同样的错误。
3. 下那么大的雨,她都按时来赴约,( )她是个守信的人。
4. 公司任命小王为业务( ),负责业务部的工作。
5. 把两个闹钟都给我定好闹铃,( )我早晨起不来。
6. 到了西藏,就要尊重当地少数民族的( )习惯。
7. 这个地方( )优美,气候宜人,真是度假的好地方。
8. 把垃圾放到门口,( )下楼时顺手拿下去。
9. 他以前做过很多不同的工作,丰富的人生( )为他的成功打下了基础。
10. 他是个( )的人,我从没怀疑过他。

练习五、写出下列词语的同义词
1. 伺候( ) 2. 帮忙( )
3. 风俗( ) 4. 依靠( )
5. 良好( )

练习六、写出下列词语的反义词
1. 激动( ) 2. 广阔( )
3. 愉快( ) 4. 夜间( )
5. 细心( )

 **答案**

练习一：
1.jǐn 2.tǒng 3.cì 4.kuò 5.gù
练习二：
1. 致 2. 质 3. 纪 4. 击 5. 激
练习三：
1. 帮 2. 帮忙 3. 帮助 4. 仔细 5. 细致
6. 细心 7. 假如／如果 8. 如果／要是
9. 除非 10. 除了 11. 固然 12. 虽然
练习四：
1. 依靠 2. 经验 3. 可见 4. 经理 5. 以免
6. 风俗 7. 风景 8. 以便 9. 经历 10. 可靠
练习五：
1. 服侍 2. 帮助 3. 习俗 4. 依赖 5. 优良
练习六：
1. 平静 2. 狭小 3. 悲伤 4. 白天 5. 粗心

第4周的学习内容

fǔdǎo
辅导 （甲）动
coach; tutor
常用搭配
辅导学生 to tutor a pupil　个别辅导 individual tutorial
辅导课 tutorial class
用法示例
他给这小孩辅导物理。
He tutored the child in physics.
我为准备汉语考试的人做辅导。
I coach people for their Chinese exams.
如果班上的人数多,老师就不能给予个别辅导了。
A teacher can't give individual attention to each pupil if his class is large.

dùn
顿 （甲）量
measure for meal, beating, etc.
常用搭配
一顿饭 a meal　打他一顿 give him a beating
用法示例
那顿饭简直好极了。
That meal was simply delicious!
他爸爸用棍子痛打他一顿。
His father beat him with a stick.
他们遭到老师的一顿批评。
They received criticism from their teacher.

xiāomiè
消灭 （乙）动
annihilate
常用搭配
消灭敌人 annihilate the enemy
用法示例
侵略者被消灭了。
The invaders were annihilated.
自从岛上蚊子被消灭后,那儿成了更加美好的居住地。
Since the mosquitoes were exterminated, the island had become a more pleasant place to live in.
这种杀虫剂可以消灭苍蝇。
This kind of insecticide can kill off flies.

xiāoshī　　　　**chūxiàn**
消失　　反 **出现** （乙）动
disappear; fade away
常用搭配
彩虹消失了。The rainbow disappeared.
用法示例
男孩在拐弯处消失了。
The boy disappeared round the corner.
那些轮船似乎已经从地球表面消失了。
Those ships seem to have disappeared from the face of the earth.
旋风消失了。
The whirlwind disappeared.

kàojìn
靠近 （丙）动
be near; approach
常用搭配
向敌舰靠近 approach the enemy ship
用法示例
这里是禁区不许靠近。
It is forbidden to approach the restricted area.
这是一家靠近机场的旅馆。
This hotel is close to the airport.
我们的国家靠近太平洋。
Our country is near the Pacific Ocean.

xíngchéng
形成 （乙）动
form; come into being
常用搭配
性格的形成 formation of one's character
用法示例
地球是什么时候形成的?
When was the earth formed?
云是由空中极细微的水滴形成的。
Clouds are formed up of tiny drops of water in the sky.
水沿山泻下,形成了一条瀑布。
The water created a waterfall down the mountain.

yīngyǒng　　　**yǒnggǎn**
英勇　　同 **勇敢** （乙）形
valiant; brave
常用搭配
英勇的行为 valiant deed
英勇的事迹 valiant record
英勇的战士 brave soldier

【用法示例】
士兵们为了赢得胜利进行了英勇的斗争。
The soldiers put up a valiant fight for victory.
这名士兵由于英勇而受到国王的嘉奖。
The soldier was cited by the king for his bravery.
他英勇无比。
He is unrivaled in bravery.

yīngxióng
英雄 （乙）名
hero
【常用搭配】
英雄崇拜 hero worship
民族英雄 national hero
英雄的故事 heroic myths
【用法示例】
有许多关于古代英雄的传说。
There are many legends about the heroes of yore.
这次比赛中真正的英雄是我们的教练。
The real hero of the match was our coach.
奥狄修斯是传说中的希腊英雄。
Odysseus was a legendary Greek hero.

zhuǎngào　　　　　　　zhuǎndá
转告　　　同 转达　　（乙）动
send word; pass on (a message)
【常用搭配】
请转告他…… Please tell him…
他让我转告你…… He told me to inform you…
【用法示例】
请转告他，叫他务必按时到会。
Tell him that he must be at the meeting on time.
请把这个消息转告给她。
Please pass the news on to her.
他让我一定转告你,他得知你的病情好转后十分高兴。
He says he is delighted to hear about your fine progress.

zhuǎnbō
转播 （丙）动
relay broadcasting; broadcast (on radio or TV)
【常用搭配】
实况转播 outside broadcast
转播一场比赛 broadcast a game
【用法示例】
将通过电台和电视转播这场比赛。
The match will be broadcast on the radio and TV.
地方电视台转播了开幕仪式。
The local TV station relayed the broadcast of the opening ceremony.

xíngtài
形态 （丙）名
shape; form

【常用搭配】
形态特征 morphological character
生物的形态 morphology of organisms
物质的形态 form of the substance
【用法示例】
冰、雪和蒸汽是水的不同形态。
Ice, snow and steam are different forms of water.
蝌蚪是青蛙的幼年形态。
Tadpoles are the infant forms of frogs.

yāsuō　　　　　　kuòchōng
压缩  扩充 （丙）动
compress
【常用搭配】
压缩开支 reduce expenditure
压缩文件 compressed files
【用法示例】
把三集的节目内容压缩成了一集。
Three episodes have been combined to form a single program.
他们把两个月的工作压缩成了一个月。
They compressed two months' work into one.
战士们午餐吃压缩食品。
These soldiers have compressed food for their lunch.

词义辨析

消失、消灭

　　"消失"和"消灭"都是动词。但"消失"是指人或物主动地或自然地或逐渐地看不到或不存在了；"消灭"是指彻底除掉有害的或认为不好的人或物。例如：①随着太阳的升起,星星从天边渐渐消失了。②我们消灭了敌人。

　　消失 and 消灭 are verbs. However 消失 means "disappear", indicating that something or somebody "passes out of sight or cease to exist" actively, naturally or gradually; while 消灭 means "to completely destroy something or somebody that is bad or harmful". For example: ① The stars faded from the sky when the sun rose. ② We annihilated the enemy.

 **练习**

练习一、根据拼音写汉字，根据汉字写拼音
( )bō　　( )tài　　( )yǒng　xiāo ( )( )dǎo
转( )　　形( )　　英( )　　( )灭　辅( )

练习二、搭配连线
(1) 消灭　　　　　　A. 转播
(2) 民族　　　　　　B. 文件
(3) 实况　　　　　　C. 敌人
(4) 形态　　　　　　D. 英雄
(5) 压缩　　　　　　E. 特征

练习三、从今天学习的生词中选择合适的词填空
1. 他才是真正的_____，他没有消灭敌人，但是使我们的国家避免了战争。
2. 星期天下午一个老师来给他_____汉语，他准备参加HSK考试。
3. 中国人一般一天吃三_____饭，分别是早饭、午饭和晚饭。
4. 这种药水能快速地_____细菌。
5. 出了国以后，我再也没有他的消息，他好像从地球上_____了一样。
6. 这位_____的解放军战士牺牲在了战场上。
7. 这个想跳楼自杀的人告诉人们别_____他，要不他就真的跳了。
8. 地球上的陆地是怎么_____的？老师给我们介绍了最新的研究结果。
9. 麻烦您，请_____一下王平，我来找过他。
10. CCTV5_____了这次的欧洲杯足球赛。

答案

练习一：
略
练习二：
(1) C　　(2)D　　(3)A　　(4)E　　(5)B
练习三：
1. 英雄　　2. 辅导　　3. 顿　　4. 消灭　　5. 消失
6. 英勇　　7. 靠近　　8. 形成　　9. 转告　　10. 转播

zuò
座　　　　　　　　　　　　　　　　　（甲）量
measure word for massive or fixed objects
常用搭配
一座山 a mountain　　一座桥 a bridge
一座纪念碑 a monument
用法示例
我们学校后边有一座小山。
There is a small hill behind our school.
这座纪念碑是献给所有在国内战争中牺牲的人的。
This pillar is a monument to those who died in the civil war.

lǚxíng　　　　　　　　lǚyóu
旅行　　　　 同 **旅游**　　　　　　　（甲）动
① travel ② trip
常用搭配
长途旅行 a long journey　　到非洲旅行 travel to Africa
用法示例
我做好了旅行的所有准备。
I have got everything ready for the trip.
经过这么长时间的旅行，我感到很累。
I feel weary after such a long journey.
我们将到那个城市去旅行。
We will go on an excursion to that city.

duìfu　　　　　　　　yìngfù
对付　　　　 同 **应付**　　　　　　　（乙）动
handle; deal with
常用搭配
她能对付他。She can deal with him.
难对付的顾客 a tough customer
用法示例
你怎样对付持有武器的盗贼？
How would you deal with an armed burglar?
他是个很难对付的人。
He was a difficult man to deal with.

shìshí　　　　　　　　zhēnxiàng
事实　　　　 同 **真相**　　　　　　　（乙）名
fact
常用搭配
事实上 as a matter of fact　　面对事实 face the fact
用法示例
我们迟早会查明事实真相。
We shall find out the truth sooner or later.
这不是想象，是事实。
This is not just my imagination, but reality.

事实胜于雄辩。
Facts speak louder than words.

shìwù
事物 (乙)名
thing

常用搭配
美的事物 beautiful things　新事物 new things

用法示例
你不该以那种眼光看待事物。
You should not look at things that way.
作为作家，你得善于观察事物。
Being a writer, you should be good at observing things.
他参观了许多地方并且了解了许多事物。
He visited many places and knew many things.

lǚguǎn
旅馆 (乙)名
hotel

常用搭配
汽车旅馆 motel　经营一家旅馆 keep an inn

用法示例
我已在这家旅馆订了一个房间。
I have booked a room at this hotel.
这家旅馆为旅客提供订票服务。
The hotel provides a ticket booking service for its guests.
这家旅馆有 80 位客人。
This hotel has eighty guests.

jiānjù
艰巨 (乙)形
arduous; strenuous

常用搭配
一项艰巨的任务 a strenuous task

用法示例
这是件艰巨的工作，但她是能胜任的。
It's a difficult job but she's the person to get it done.
虽然任务艰巨，他们还是设法及时完成了。
Difficult though the task was, they managed to accomplish it in time.
这就是我们面临的艰巨任务。
This is a hard task that is ahead of us.

jiānkǔ
艰苦 (乙)形
hard (life, work)

常用搭配
艰苦的工作 hard work
艰苦的生活 hard life

用法示例
在困难时期我们过着艰苦的生活。
We led a hard life in times of difficulty.
多年艰苦的劳动使他丧失了健康。
His health suffered due to his years of hard work.

艰苦奋斗是事业成功的唯一途径。
Hard work is the only way to succeed in business.

kèkǔ
刻苦 (乙)形
hardworking; assiduous

常用搭配
刻苦学习 study hard

用法示例
他哥哥正刻苦学习数学。
His brother is assiduous in the study of math.
大部分学生都有礼貌而且学习刻苦。
Most students are polite and hardworking.
她学习非常刻苦。
She studies very hard.

yìngchou
应酬 (丙)动
① treat with courtesy ② social intercourse
③ engage in social activities

常用搭配
应酬客人 treat guests with courtesy

用法示例
她善于应酬。
She is good in social situations.
今晚，我有应酬。
Tonight I have to attend a dinner party.
她厌倦了各种应酬。
She is tired of engaging in various social activities.

lǚxíng　　　　　zhíxíng
履行　　◎执行 (丁)动
fulfill; carry out

常用搭配
履行职责 carry out one's duties　履行诺言 fulfill one's promise

用法示例
他们履行合同后，我才付款。
I withheld payment until they had fulfilled the contract.
你们必须履行义务。
You must fulfill your obligations.

yìngfu
应付 (丙)动
cope; deal with

常用搭配
难以应付 hard to deal with

用法示例
他们已准备好应付这种局面。
They were ready to deal with the situation.
准备应付意想不到的困难。
Be prepared to deal with unexpected difficulties.
我们经理善于应付各种人。
Our manager is good at dealing with various types of people.

词义辨析

艰巨、艰苦

"艰巨"和"艰苦"都是形容词。但是"艰巨"强调艰难而繁重的意思,往往修饰任务、责任(艰巨的任务,艰巨的责任)等;而"艰苦"强调艰难和困苦,往往用于描述环境或生存状态,如:艰苦的生活,艰苦的工作等。

艰巨 and 艰苦 are adjectives. 艰巨 indicates "arduous and hard to do", usually modifying a task or responsibility（艰巨的任务 or 艰巨的责任）; while 艰苦 indicates "hardships and poverty-stricken", and is often used to describe an environment or state of life and work, e.g. hard life, hard work, and so on.

练习

练习一、根据拼音写汉字,根据汉字写拼音
(　)xíng　yìng(　)　jiān(　)　lǚ(　)　duì(　)
履(　)　(　)酬　(　)苦　(　)馆　(　)付

练习二、搭配连线
(1) 长途　　　　　　　A. 诺言
(2) 汽车　　　　　　　B. 真相
(3) 事实　　　　　　　C. 旅行
(4) 刻苦　　　　　　　D. 学习
(5) 履行　　　　　　　E. 旅馆

练习三、从今天学习的生词中选择合适的词填空
1. 我想去西藏＿＿＿＿,听说那里的风景特别美。
2. 公民在拥有权利的同时也要无条件地＿＿＿＿自己的职责。
3. 这是一项＿＿＿＿的任务,他们完成得非常出色。
4. 父母那一代的人,生活大都很＿＿＿＿。
5. 这个女孩学习很＿＿＿＿,因为她想考北大外语系。
6. 对于朋友,我们用鲜花迎接;对于敌人,我们用枪炮＿＿＿＿。
7. 他只是＿＿＿＿我,没有认真考虑我说的话。
8. 每当有＿＿＿＿的时候,经理就叫上他,因为他能喝酒。
9. 旅行时,住＿＿＿＿比住酒店便宜很多。
10. 那＿＿＿＿山上有条大瀑布。

答案

练习一:
略

练习二:
(1) C　　(2)E　　(3)B　　(4)D　　(5)A

练习三:
1. 旅行　　2. 履行　　3. 艰巨　　4. 艰苦　　5. 刻苦
6. 对付　　7. 应付　　8. 应酬　　9. 旅馆　　10. 座

yìjiàn
意见 (甲) 名
opinion; complaint

常用搭配
一条意见 a piece of advice
对……发表意见 express one's opinion on

用法示例
在会上,我们就此事交换了意见。
We exchanged our ideas about the event at the meeting.
他们对你很有意见,你对他们太苛刻了。
They have a lot of complaints about you. You are too hard on them.

jié
节 (甲) 量
measure word for parts or sections of sth.

常用搭配
三节课 three classes
一节电池 a battery
两节车厢 two carriages of the train

用法示例
我们在倒数第二节车厢里。
We'll be sitting in the second carriage from the back of the train.
星期五,我们只有上午四节课,下午没有课。
On Friday we only have four classes in the morning and none in the afternoon.

kànfǎ
看法 (乙) 名
opinion; view

常用搭配
对某事的看法 view on sth
坚持对某事的看法 assert his view of the matter

用法示例
我能知道你对这件事的看法吗?
May I know your views on it?
我们的看法相似。
We have similar opinions.
他并不在乎我对此事的看法。
He doesn't care for my opinion on it.

shìjiàn
事件 (乙) 名
event; incident

常用搭配
国际事件 an international incident
历史事件 historic events

用法示例
我们将按照历史上的先后顺序研究这些事件。
We will study these events in their historical sequence.
我们已观看了这一事件的图片记录。
We have watched the visual records of the event.
警方认为这次事件和上周的恐怖分子爆炸事件有关。
The police are connecting this incident with last week's terrorist bombing.

zhēngqiú
征求 ⊜ 征询 zhēngxún (乙) 动
seek; ask for

常用搭配
征求意见 ask for advice

用法示例
我想征求一下你对这个计划的建议。
I'd like to ask for your advice on the plan?
他写了这封信打算征求一些意见。
He wrote the letter with the intention of asking for advice.
我征求了老师的意见。
I asked the teacher for his advice.

quánmiàn
全面 ⊜ 片面 piànmiàn (乙) 形
overall; comprehensive

常用搭配
全面的规划 comprehensive planning
全面的教育 an all-around education
全面调查 an overall survey

用法示例
她已全面掌握了这一学科。
She has a comprehensive grasp of the subject.
记者已做了全面的报道。
The reporter has made a comprehensive report.
您介绍得非常全面。
You gave it a very comprehensive introduction.

yíngjiē
迎接 ⊜ 送别 sòngbié (乙) 动
meet; greet

常用搭配
迎接朋友 greet guests   迎接春天的到来 salute the spring

用法示例
我们将到火车站迎接李教授。
We will meet Professor Li at the station.
他去机场迎接英国来的朋友。
He went to the airport to meet his friend from England.
人群走出城迎接英雄。
The crowds poured forth from the town to meet the hero.

piànmiàn
片面 (乙) 形
one-sided; unilateral

【常用搭配】
片面的观点 a one-sided argument
【用法示例】
我认为他的看法是片面的。
I think his opinion is one-sided.
片面的看法会导致片面的行为。
One-sided opinions lead to one-sided action.

zhuānyè
专业　　　　　　　　　　　　（乙）名
specialized field; specialty
【常用搭配】
专业知识 specialized knowledge
专业技能 specialized skill
【用法示例】
他大学时的专业是国际贸易。
He majored in international commerce in college.
他的专业是生物学，我的专业是物理学。
His specialty is biology, mine is physics.
她是法语专业的学生。
She is a French major.

huòwù
货物　　　　　　　　　　　　（丙）名
goods; cargo
【常用搭配】
空运货物 the transportation of goods by air
【用法示例】
装载这些货物时必须小心。
This freight must be handled carefully when being loaded.
他的工作是在港口装卸货物。
His work is to load or unload cargo in the port.
这批货物的质量很好。
The batch of goods is of high quality.

shìwù　　　　　shìqíng
事务　　　 ⊜ 事情　　　　　（丙）名
work; affair
【常用搭配】
国际事务 international affairs　　日常事务 daily routine
【用法示例】
这位副总理负责国内事务。
The vice-premier is in charge of domestic affairs.
她每周六还要处理公司的事务。
She has to cope with her company affairs that are held every Saturday.

zhēngfú
征服　　　　　　　　　　　　（丙）动
vanquish; conquer
【常用搭配】
征服一个国家 conquer a country

【用法示例】
现代医学征服了许多疾病。
Modern medical science has conquered many diseases.
这位演员用他精彩的表演征服了观众。
The actor won over the audience with his attractive performance.
这位钢琴家的演奏征服了每一位听众。
The pianist won over every audience for whom she played.

 词义辨析

看法、意见
　　"看法"和"意见"都是名词，表示对事物所持的见解。"看法"可以不太具体，感情色彩不强；而"意见"则往往针对具体的对象，有时含有不满意的意思。如：①这个编辑常对一些时事问题发表意见/看法。②他对老板有意见，觉得他不公正。③我们每个人都对事物有自己的看法。
　　看法 and 意见 are nouns, meaning "to have views about…". 看法 may not be very concrete and is neutral; while 意见 is usually applied to concrete objects, and sometimes has a derogatory sense. For example: ① The editor often gives his opinions on topical issues. ② He is not satisfied with his boss, he thinks his boss is unfair. ③ We each have our private views on the matter.

 **练习**

练习一、根据拼音写汉字，根据汉字写拼音
( )qiú ( )jiē huò ( )( )wù yì ( )
征( ) 迎( ) ( )物 事( ) ( )见

练习二、搭配连线
(1) 装卸　　　　　A. 意见
(2) 全面　　　　　B. 事件
(3) 历史　　　　　C. 事务
(4) 日常　　　　　D. 货物
(5) 征求　　　　　E. 调查

练习三、从今天学习的生词中选择合适的词填空
1. 接下来的十分钟，请大家发表自己的_____。
2. 不顾环保，_____追求经济的高增长，是不对的。
3. 他想问题很_____，可能遇到的麻烦几乎都想到了。
4. 关于这个问题，我想_____一下各位老师的意见。
5. 通过武力_____一个国家是野蛮的行为。
6. 他每天要处理很多公司的_____，根本没有时间照顾家庭。
7. 这些_____商店里放不下了，放到后面的仓库里吧。
8. 他在大学时学的是经济_____，可二十年后却成了作家。
9. 我们每天上午要上四_____课。
10. 这次和平抗议活动最终变成了暴力_____。

答案

练习一：
略

练习二：
(1) D　　(2) E　　(3) B　　(4) C　　(5) A

练习三：
1. 看法　2. 片面　3. 全面　4. 征求　5. 征服
6. 事务　7. 货物　8. 专业　9. 节　10. 事件

 星期四 Thursday

精彩 jīngcǎi　（甲）形
wonderful; splendid

常用搭配
精彩的故事 a wonderful story
精彩的演出 a brilliant performance

用法示例
刘教授作了精彩的长篇演说。
Professor Liu launched into a brilliant tirade.
独奏演员做了精彩的表演
The soloist gave a brilliant performance.

形状 xíngzhuàng　同 形态 xíngtài　（乙）名
shape; form

常用搭配
蛋糕的形状 shape of a cake　奇怪的形状 strange shapes

用法示例
这茶壶把儿的形状真别扭。
The handle of this teapot has an awkward shape.
塔的形状就像一口钟。
In shape, the tower was like a bell.
他喜欢收集各种形状的瓶子。
He collects bottles of all kinds and shapes.

形式 xíngshì　（乙）名
form

常用搭配
内容和形式的统一 unity of content and form
复数形式 plural form

用法示例
他好像讨厌任何形式的运动。
He seems to dislike any form of exercise.
这个问题又以新的形式出现了。
The problem has assumed a new form.

形势 xíngshì　（乙）名
situation; circumstances

常用搭配
国际形势 international situation
经济形势 economic situation

用法示例
形势很复杂。
The situation was complicated.
他似乎没有意识到形势的严重性。
He doesn't seem to understand the gravity of the situation.

这个办法不受欢迎,但形势需要这样做。
It's an unpopular measure, but the situation necessitates it.

主人 zhǔrén 反 客人 (乙)名
host; master

常用搭配
女主人 hostess　鱼塘的主人 the owner of a fish pond
农场的主人 master of a farm

用法示例
女主人招待得十分周到。
The hostess is indefatigable in her hospitality.
这只狗听主人的话。
The dog obeyed his master.
他是那条船的主人。
He is the captain of the boat.

补习 bǔxí (乙)动
take lessons after school or work

常用搭配
补习班 extension class

用法示例
她正在成人学校补习法语。
She's brushing up on her French at an adult school.
我的儿子每晚都去补习英语。
My son takes English lessons after school every evening.

客人 kèrén (乙)名
guest

常用搭配
招待客人 entertain guests
受欢迎的客人 a welcome guest
美国客人 an American guest

用法示例
她把食物和饮料放在客人面前。
She set the food and drink before the guest.
他们将作为我的客人出席晚会。
They are coming to the party as my guests.
这些印度客人对这本书很熟悉。
These Indian guests are familiar with this book.

主观 zhǔguān 反 客观 (乙)名/形
subjective

常用搭配
人的主观能动性 man's subjective nature
主观印象 subjective impression
主观感受 subjective sensation

用法示例
评论她的作品不要过于主观。
Don't judge her work too subjectively.

她的主观印象并不可靠。
Her subjective impressions are not dependable.

客观 kèguān (丙)名/形
objective

常用搭配
客观现实 objective reality　客观事物 objective things
客观的评论家 an objective critic

用法示例
尽量客观地对待此事吧。
Try to be objective about it.
客观地说,他绝不可能成功。
Objectively speaking, he can't possibly succeed.

严禁 yánjìn 同 禁止 jìnzhǐ (丙)动
strictly prohibit

常用搭配
严禁吸烟。Smoking is strictly prohibited.

用法示例
严禁在教堂内照相。
Photography is strictly forbidden in the cathedral.
在处理易爆物时,严禁吸烟。
Smoking is strictly prohibited in the process of handling explosive materials.
此段河流严禁捕鱼。
The fishing in this stretch of the river is tightly restricted.

风格 fēnggé (丙)名
style

常用搭配
写作风格 writing style　建筑风格 the style of a building
艺术风格 artistic style

用法示例
我不喜欢他演讲的风格。
I don't like his style of speaking.
这块地毯是俄罗斯风格的。
This carpet is in the Russian style.
这种建筑风格起源于古希腊。
The style of architecture originated from the ancient Greeks.

封 fēng (甲)量/动
① word for letter ② to seal

常用搭配
寄一封信 to post a letter　封信 to seal (up) a letter

用法示例
我想给我的朋友写一封信。
I want to write a letter to my friend.
我们把信封的背面封上。
We sealed the back of the envelopes.

警察正在箱子上贴封条。
The police are putting seals on the boxes.

 词义辨析

形状、形式、形势

　　这三个词都是名词,但意思和用法有差别。"形状"多指物的外形和模样,用于具体事物,是书面语;"形式"指事物的表现形式或外观,可以用于具体事物,也可以用于抽象的事物;"形势"指事态发展的状况或在特定时刻各种情况的总体态势。如:①盒子里有各种形状的饼干。②相声是一种有趣的艺术形式。③目前的国际形势极其微妙。

　　The three words are nouns, but they have different meanings and usages. 形状 means "outward shape, or appearance of something concrete", and is usually used in writing; 形式 means "form, or the way to manifest something concrete or abstract"; while 形势 means "situation, state of affairs, or the combination of circumstances at a given moment". For example: ① There are biscuits of all shapes in the box. ② Comic dialogues are an interesting art form. ③ The international situation is very delicate at present.

 练习

练习一、根据拼音写汉字,根据汉字写拼音

xíng(　　)(　　)guān　bǔ(　　)(　　)cǎi(　　)gé
(　　)势　　客(　　)　　(　　)习　　精(　　)　　风(　　)

练习二、搭配连线

(1) 复数　　　　　　　A. 形势
(2) 写作　　　　　　　B. 形式
(3) 国际　　　　　　　C. 印象
(4) 主观　　　　　　　D. 现实
(5) 客观　　　　　　　E. 风格

练习三、从今天学习的生词中选择合适的词填空

1. 因为明天家里要来_____,所以夫妻俩准备了很多好吃的。
2. _____地讲,你的行为伤害了我,尽管你不是有意的。
3. 为了确保公正,大家分析问题时尽量不要带_____色彩。
4. 这个杯子的_____很特别。
5. 老板已经决定要他了,面试只是个_____而已。
6. 这几年,中国经济的_____很好,年增长速度一直在8%以上。
7. 春节联欢晚会的节目都很_____,我特别喜欢看。
8. 这个作家的作品很有自己的_____,一看就知道是他写的。
9. 小王去年考大学考得不理想,_____了一年,今年考上北大了。
10. 你不能在这里抽烟,没看到墙上写着"库房重地,_____吸烟"吗?

答案

练习一:
略

练习二:
(1) B　　(2)E　　(3)A　　(4)C　　(5)D

练习三:
1. 客人　　2. 客观　　3. 主观　　4. 形状　　5. 形式
6. 形势　　7. 精彩　　8. 风格　　9. 补习　　10. 严禁

星期五

xiāngxìn
相信 （甲）动
believe; be convinced

常用搭配
我相信你。I believe you.
别相信他的话。Don't believe what he said.

用法示例
别相信他,他像老狐狸一样狡猾。
Don't trust him, he is a sly old fox.
你相信有鬼吗?
Do you believe in ghosts?
我相信他是诚实的。
I believe him to be honest.

gēn
根 （甲）量/名
① measure word for long things ② root

常用搭配
一根筷子 a chopstick
两根电线 two wires
牙根 the root of a tooth

用法示例
我们操场有一根旗杆。
There is a flag pole in our playground.
我要去超市买两根葱。
I want to buy two shallots in the supermarket.
他们砍断了树根。
They cut off the root of the tree.

méiyòng
没用 ⊘有用 （乙）形
useless

常用搭配
没用的自行车 useless bike

用法示例
这是把没用的小刀,刀把坏了。
This is a useless knife — the handle has been broken!
对不信上帝的人引用《圣经》的话是没用的。
It's no use citing the Bible to somebody who doesn't believe in God.
她发现和他们争论没用。
She finds it useless to argue with them.

mìqiè
密切 （乙）形
intimate; close

常用搭配
保持密切接触 maintain close contact with

用法示例
他们和我保持着密切联系。
They keep in close contact with me.
味觉与嗅觉是密切相关的。
Taste and smell are closely connected.
我们虽算不上关系密切,但还常见面。
We're not exactly on intimate terms, but we see each other fairly often.

miànqián   bèihòu
面前 ⊘背后 （乙）名
in front of

常用搭配
在父母面前 facing one's parents
他面前的桌子 the desk in front of him

用法示例
他在生人面前总是不知要说什么。
He is always at a loss as to what to say when in front of strangers.
老师把男孩叫到前面。
The teacher called the boy up to the front.
展现在我们面前的是一片绿色的草地。
A green grassland spread itself before our eyes.

yǒuyòng
有用 （乙）形
useful

常用搭配
这东西有什么用? Is it of any use?
有用的字典 useful dictionary

用法示例
这本参考书对你有用吗?
Is this reference book of any use to you?
等她有什么用?
What is the use of waiting for her?
自行车可能对她有用。
A bike may be useful to her.

jiědá   huídá
解答 ◎回答 （乙）动
answer

常用搭配
解答问题 answer one's question

用法示例
我解答不了这个难题。
I can't solve the problem.
一个好老师应该尽力解答学生的问题。
A good teacher should try his best to answer his students' questions.
抱歉,不过那个接待员能回答你们的问题。
Sorry, but the desk clerk can answer your question.

kāiyǎn
开演 （乙）动
(of a play, movie, etc.) to begin

【常用搭配】
电影已经开演了。The film has already begun.
八点开演的节目 a play that begins at eight o'clock
【用法示例】
话剧两点钟开演。
The drama begins at two o'clock.
我们可以在电影开演前一小时去取票。
We can pick up the tickets an hour before the film begins.
在等待开演的时候,演员们十分紧张。
The performers were edgy as they waited for the show to begin.

kāizhǎn
开展 （乙）动
(begin to) develop; launch
【常用搭配】
开展禁酒运动 start a prohibition movement
开展商业活动 launch a commercial campaign
【用法示例】
他们开展了一项阻止人们吸烟的运动。
They launched a campaign to stop people smoking.
我们将开展一项全国性的调查。
We will begin a national investigation.

zhuǎnwān   guǎiwān
转弯 ◎拐弯 （丙）动
turn
【常用搭配】
向左转弯 Turn left.
【用法示例】
如果要避开市中心,请从这里向右转弯。
To avoid the city center, turn right here.
在街道的转弯处有一个食品店。
There's a grocer's at the corner of the street.
卡车转弯时,车上的货物掉了下来。
The lorry turned, and its load slipped down.

xìnrèn
信任 （丙）动/名
trust
【常用搭配】
可以信任的人 a dependable friend
我不信任他。I don't trust him.
【用法示例】
我的丈夫信任我,我不想失去这种信任。
My husband trusts me and I don't intend to lose his trust.
不要辜负人民对你的信任。
Don't betray the people's trust in you.
我认为他值得信任。
I judge him to be worthy of trust.

zhuǎnyí
转移 （丙）动
transfer; divert

【常用搭配】
战略转移 strategic shift
转移注意力 divert one's attention
【用法示例】
一阵喧闹声转移了我的注意力。
A loud noise caught my attention.
军营从这里转移到了山后边。
The army camp transferred from here to the back of the mountain.

 词义辨析

相信、信任

作为动词,"相信"和"信任"都有不怀疑的意思,但"相信"强调作为事实或真理接受,它的宾语可以是人,也可以是事物;可以是别人,也可以是自己;可以是一个词,也可以是一句话。"信任"强调因为相信而感到放心,认为可以依靠,"信任"的宾语一般是人或组织(但不用于自己),只能是名词或代词,不能是句子。另外,"信任"还是名词,可以在句子中作主语和宾语。如:①我们相信他会成功。②我相信我有能力解决这个问题。③他是骗子,谁能信任这种人呢?④他靠欺骗获取了我们的信任。

As verbs, both mean "not to doubt". 相信 indicates 'to accept as true or real', and its object can be people or things, others or oneself, a word or a clause. 信任 indicates "to trust", "one feels at ease because one believes in somebody". The object of 信任 is either people or organizations (it can not be oneself), either a noun or a pronoun, it can not be a clause. For example: ① We believe that he will succeed. ② I believe in my ability to solve the problem. ③ He is a cheat. Who can rely on such a man? ④ He gained our trust through deception.

 练习

练习一、根据拼音写汉字,根据汉字写拼音

mì( ) ( )dá ( )zhǎn ( )wān ( )rèn
( )切 解( ) 开( ) 转( ) 信( )

练习二、搭配连线

(1) 相信   A. 信任
(2) 解答   B. 转移
(3) 值得   C. 联系
(4) 密切   D. 朋友
(5) 战略   E. 问题

练习三、从今天学习的生词中选择合适的词填空

1. 别动,你有一_____白头发,我给你拔了。
2. 如果你骗过别人,就很难让人再_____你了。
3. 现在摆在我们_____的问题是什么?
4. 这些旧信封还_____,别把它们扔了。
5. 都过了十分钟了,电影还没_____,怎么回事?
6. 别指望他会改变主意,既然他已经决定了,别人怎么劝也_____。
7. 记者问的问题他都一一作了_____。
8. 植物的生长与气候和土壤有_____的关系。
9. 非常感谢您对我的_____。
10. 最近学校_____了一项"关于学生业余生活的调查"活动。

答案

练习一:
略

练习二:
(1) D (2) E (3) A (4) C (5) B

练习三:
1. 根 2. 相信 3. 面前 4. 有用 5. 开演
6. 没用 7. 解答 8. 密切 9. 信任 10. 开展

第4月，第4周的练习

练习一、根据词语给加点的字注音
1.( )　2.( )　3.( )　4.( )　5.( )
压缩　应酬　艰苦　严禁　转播

练习二、根据拼音填写词语
　　xíng　　xíng　　fu　　fú　　fǔ
1.( )态　2.旅( )　3.应( )　4.征( )　5.( )导

练习三、辨析并选择合适的词填空
1. 这种农药药性很强,倒一点儿就能把害虫( )干净。(消失、消灭)
2. 过了一会儿,天空中的那个亮点( )了,有人说那个亮点是飞碟(UFO)。(消失、消灭)
3. 尽管任务十分( ),我们还是按时完成了。(艰巨、艰苦)
4. 边远山区的条件( ),有时没有充足的食物,大家要有心理准备。(艰巨、艰苦)
5. 这只是我个人对那件事的( ),说得不对的地方还请大家原谅。(看法、意见)
6. 要是你对我有( ),请直接提出来,不要去经理那儿说我坏话。(看法、意见)
7. 这件艺术品的( )和颜色很特别,我很喜欢。(形状、形势、形式)
8. 今年的就业( )不好,大学毕业生很难找到好工作。(形状、形势、形式)
9. 我不愿在那个公司,我发现在那里人与人之间缺乏( )。(相信、信任)
10. 不管别人信不信,反正我( )你的话。(相信、信任)

练习四、选词填空
旅行　转告　转弯　事件　事实
履行　转播　转移　事务　事物

1. 他的承诺一句都没有( ),我怎么能再相信这样的人呢?
2. 秘书的工作主要都是些( )性工作。
3. 这是一个重要的历史( ),对中国的发展有着深远的影响。
4. 麻烦你,请( )一下小王,让他给我回个电话。
5. 对于我父亲来说,网络是个新鲜( ),他刚接触时,感觉网络真是太神奇了。
6. 专家说,车里尽量不要摆放玩具,因为这些东西在开车时会( )司机的注意力。
7. 从前方十字路口向右( ),邮局就在中国银行旁边。
8. 伤心只能是暂时的,只有接受( )、忘掉过去才能勇敢地生活下去。
9. 比赛的实况将通过卫星向全世界( )。
10. 心情不好时,我喜欢一个人去远方( )。

练习五、选择量词填空
顿　节　封　座　根
1. 我们每周都有二十( )课。
2. 好久没见面了,这个周末我们一起吃( )饭吧。
3. 前面是( )山,汽车不能前进了。
4. 我给你发了一( )电子邮件,请查收。
5. 妈妈过生日时,我特意买了五( )彩色的蜡烛。

练习六、写出下列词语的同义词
1. 征求( )　　2. 严禁( )
3. 转告( )　　4. 履行( )
5. 旅行( )

练习七、写出下列词语的反义词
1. 主观( )　　2. 迎接( )
3. 面前( )　　4. 压缩( )
5. 消失( )

 答案

练习一：
1.suō　2.chou　3.jiān　4.jìn　5.bō

练习二：
1. 形　2. 行　3. 付　4. 服　5. 辅

练习三：
1. 消灭　2. 消失　3. 艰巨　4. 艰苦　5. 看法
6. 意见　7. 形状　8. 形势　9. 信任　10. 相信

练习四：
1. 履行　2. 事务　3. 事件　4. 转告　5. 事物
6. 转移　7. 转弯　8. 事实　9. 转播　10. 旅行

练习五：
1. 节　2. 顿　3. 座　4. 封　5. 根

练习六：
1. 征询　2. 禁止　3. 转达　4. 执行　5. 旅游

练习七：
1. 客观　2. 送别　3. 背后　4. 扩充　5. 出现

附录
全书词义辨析包含词汇和页码

一月

第一周
第一天	安排、安置	2
第二天	躲、藏	5
第三天	觉得、感觉	7
第四天	继续、坚持	10
第五天	赶快、赶忙	12

第二周
第一天	考试、考	15
第二天	喜欢、爱好	17
第三天	感谢、感激	20
第四天	改正、纠正	22
第五天	好像、像	25

第三周
第一天	按、按照、依照	28
第二天	从前、以前	31
第三天	打算、计划	33
第四天	原来、本来	36
第五天	懂、明白	38

第四周
第一天	得、得到	41
第二天	而且、并且	44
第三天	性格、个性	46
第四天	参观、看	49
第五天	必须、必需	51

二月

第一周
第一天	好处、优点	54
第二天	学生、同学	57
第三天	忽然、突然	59
第四天	以后、今后	62
第五天	故意、有意	64

第二周
第一天	好看、美丽	67
第二天	似乎、仿佛	70
第三天	高兴、快乐	72
第四天	也许、可能	75
第五天	节省、节约	77

第三周
第一天	会、能	80
第二天	更、更加	83
第三天	增加、增长	85
第四天	有名、著名	88
第五天	原因、缘故	90

第四周
第一天	国、国家	93
第二天	创作、创造	96
第三天	因为、由于	98
第四天	或者、还是	101
第五天	真、真正	103

三月

第一周
第一天	对于、对	107
第二天	改变、转变	110
第三天	咱们、我们	112
第四天	家、家庭	115
第五天	意思、意义	117

第二周
第一天	位于、位置	120
第二天	据说、听说	123

第三天	了解、理解	125		第四周	
第四天	希望、盼望	128	第一天	消失、消灭	198
第五天	往往、常常	130	第二天	艰巨、艰苦	201
	第三周		第三天	看法、意见	203
第一天	互相、相互	133	第四天	形状、形式、形势	206
第二天	的确、确实	136	第五天	相信、信任	208
第三天	这么,那么	138			
第四天	认识、认得	141			
第五天	表示、表明	143			

	第四周	
第一天	缺乏、缺少	146
第二天	事、事情	149
第三天	时候、时间	151
第四天	开始、开头	154
第五天	运输、输送	156

四月

	第一周	
第一天	立刻、马上	159
第二天	陆续、连续	162
第三天	表演、演出	164
第四天	基本、根本	167
第五天	所以、因此、因而	169

	第二周	
第一天	帮助、援助	172
第二天	有时、时时	175
第三天	支持、支援	177
第四天	准、准确	180
第五天	控制、抑制	182

	第三周	
第一天	帮、帮忙、帮助	185
第二天	仔细、细心、细致	188
第三天	如果、假如、要是	190
第四天	除非、除了	193
第五天	虽然、固然	195

责任编辑：韩芙芸
封面设计：王 薇
印刷监制：佟汉冬

图书在版编目（CIP）数据

HSK 核心词汇天天学 . 上 / 刘东青编著 . —北京：华语教学出版社，2009
ISBN 978-7-80200-594-5

Ⅰ. H… Ⅱ. 刘… Ⅲ. 汉语—词汇—对外汉语教学—水平考试—自学参考资料
Ⅳ. H195.4

中国版本图书馆 CIP 数据核字（2009）第 089349 号

HSK 核心词汇天天学·上

刘东青 编著

*

© 华语教学出版社
华语教学出版社出版
（中国北京百万庄大街 24 号 邮政编码 100037）
电话：(86)10-68320585
传真：(86)10-68326333
网址：www.sinolingua.com.cn
电子信箱：hyjx@sinolingua.com.cn
北京外文印刷厂印刷
2009 年（16 开）第一版
2009 年第一次印刷
（汉英）
ISBN 978-7-80200-594-5
定价：49.00 元